49.95

CULTURE AND CUSTOMS OF
THE CENTRAL ASIAN REPUBLICS

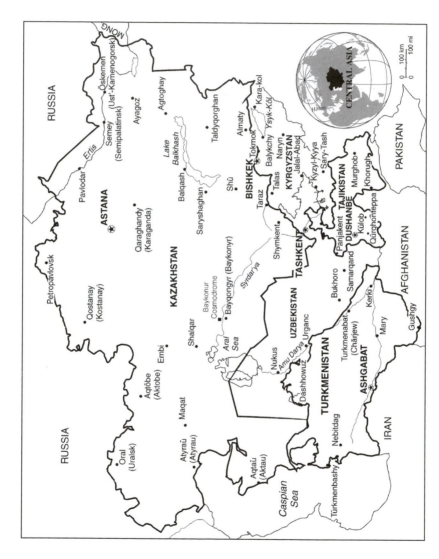

The Central Asian Republics. Cartography by Bookcomp, Inc.

Culture and Customs of the Central Asian Republics

❦

RAFIS ABAZOV

Culture and Customs of Asia
Hanchao Lu, Series Editor

GREENWOOD PRESS
Westport, Connecticut • London

Library of Congress Cataloging-in-Publication Data

Abazov, Rafis.
    Culture and customs of the Central Asian republics / Rafis Abazov.
        p. cm. — (Culture and customs of Asia, ISSN 1097–0738)
    Includes bibliographical references and index.
    ISBN 0–313–33656–3 (alk. paper)
1. Asia, Central—History.   2. Asia, Central—Social life and
customs.   I. Title.
    DK859.5.A18   2007
    958—dc22   2006029553

British Library Cataloguing in Publication Data is available.

Library of Congress Catalog Card Number: 2006029553
ISBN: 0–313–33656–3
ISSN: 1097–0738

First published in 2007

Greenwood Press, 88 Post Road West, Westport, CT 06881
An imprint of Greenwood Publishing Group, Inc.
www.greenwood.com

Printed in the United States of America

The paper used in this book complies with the
Permanent Paper Standard issued by the National
Information Standards Organization (Z39.48–1984).

10   9   8   7   6   5   4   3   2   1

Contents

Series Foreword

Geographically, Asia encompasses the vast area from Suez, the Bosporus, and the Ural Mountains eastward to the Bering Sea and from this line southward to the Indonesian archipelago, an expanse that covers about 30 percent of our earth. Conventionally, and especially insofar as culture and customs are concerned, Asia refers primarily to the region east of Iran and south of Russia. This area can be divided in turn into subregions, commonly known as South, Southeast, and East Asia, which are the main focus of this series.

The United States has vast interests in this region. In the twentieth century, the United States fought three major wars in Asia (namely the Pacific War of 1941–45, the Korean War of 1950–53, and the Vietnam War of 1965–75), and each had a profound impact on life and politics in America. Today, America's major trading partners are in Asia, and in the foreseeable future the weight of Asia in American life will inevitably increase, for in Asia lie our great allies as well as our toughest competitors in virtually all arenas of global interest. Domestically, the role of Asian immigrants is more visible than at any other time in our history. In spite of these connections with Asia, however, our knowledge about this crucial region is far from adequate. For various reasons, Asia remains for most of us a relatively unfamiliar, if not stereotypical or even mysterious, "Oriental" land.

There are compelling reasons for Americans to obtain some level of concrete knowledge about Asia. It is one of the world's richest reservoirs of culture and an ever-evolving museum of human heritage. Rhoads Murphy, a prominent Asianist, once pointed out that in the part of Asia east of Afghanistan and south of Russia alone lies half the world, "half of its people and far more that half of its historical experience, for these are the oldest living civilized traditions." Prior to the modern era, with limited interaction and mutual influence between the East and the West, Asian civilizations developed largely independent from the West. In modern times, however, Asia and the West have come not only into close contact but also into frequent conflict: The result has been one of the most solemn and stirring dramas in world history. Today, integration and compromise are the trend in coping with cultural differences. The West—with some notable exceptions—has started to see Asian traditions not as something to fear but as something to be understood, appreciated, and even cherished. After all, Asian traditions are an indispensable part of the human legacy, a matter of global "common wealth" that few of us can afford to ignore.

As a result of Asia's enormous economic development since World War II, we can no longer neglect the study of this vibrant region. Japan's "economic miracle" of postwar development is no longer unique, but in various degrees has been matched by the booming economy of many other Asian countries and regions. The rise of the four "mini dragons" (South Korea, Taiwan, Hong Kong, and Singapore) suggests that there may be a common Asian pattern of development. At the same time, each economy in Asia has followed its own particular trajectory. Clearly, China is the next giant on the scene. Sweeping changes in China in the last two decades have already dramatically altered the world's economic map. Furthermore, growth has also been dramatic in much of Southeast Asia. Today, war-devastated Vietnam shows great enthusiasm for joining the "club" of nations engaged in the world economy. And in South Asia, India, the world's largest democracy, is rediscovering its role as a champion of market capitalism. The economic development of Asia presents a challenge to Americans but also provides them with unprecedented opportunities. It is largely against this background that more and more people in the United States, in particular among the younger generation, have started to pursue careers dealing with Asia.

This series is designed to meet the need for knowledge of Asia among students and the general public. Each book is written in an accessible and lively style by an expert (or experts) in the field of Asian studies. Each book focuses on the culture and customs of a country or region. However, readers should be aware that culture is fluid, not always respecting national boundaries. While every nation seeks its own path to success and struggles to maintain its own identity, in the cultural domain mutual influence and integration among Asian nations are ubiquitous.

Each volume starts with an introduction to the land and the people of a nation or region and includes a brief history and an overview of the economy. This is followed by chapters dealing with a variety of topics that piece together a cultural panorama, such as thought, religion, ethics, literature and art, architecture and housing, cuisine, traditional dress, gender, courtship and marriage, festivals and leisure activities, music and dance, and social customs and lifestyle. In this series, we have chosen not to elaborate on elite life, ideology, or detailed questions of political structure and struggle, but instead to explore the world of common people, their sorrow and joy, their pattern of thinking, and their way of life. It is the culture and the customs of the majority of the people (rather than just the rich and powerful elite) that we seek to understand. Without such understanding, it will be difficult for all of us to live peacefully and fruitfully with each other in this increasingly interdependent world.

As the world shrinks, modern technologies have made all nations on earth "virtual" neighbors. The expression "global village" not only reveals the nature and the scope of the world in which we live but also, more importantly, highlights the serious need for mutual understanding of all peoples on our planet. If this series serves to help the reader obtain a better understanding of the "half of the world" that is Asia, the authors and I will be well rewarded.

Hanchao Lu
Georgia Institute of Technology

Preface

During the past two hundred years, Central Asia has been rediscovered by the West time and again. Restless travelers, adventurers, and spies romanticized the region's frontier culture and rough ways of life and its remoteness and climatic extremes. Some famous writers and poets of the past and present—Rudyard Kipling, Fitzroy MacLean, and Chingiz Aitmatov among them—have depicted the inner beauty of the simple ways of life of ordinary people and the uneasy relations between indigenous population and newcomers. Scholars, researchers, and cold war warriors have spilled rivers of ink debating the merits and secrets of the Great Game—the term introduced to describe the great powers' bitter rivalry over political control in the region. Art lovers have been fascinated by elegant oriental carpets, monumental architecture, and exquisite miniature paintings.

The Central Asian cultural heritage is indeed very rich and captivating. For centuries before the Great Game era, the Central Asians developed their cultural traditions within the Islamic domain, which further benefited from inflow of ideas, thoughts, and skills that traveled over the Great Silk Road. They were also greatly enriched by the interaction of two powerful traditions—Persian and Turkic; this interaction led to the crystallization of the unique Central Asian cultures and customs. The faultless lines of Registan Architectural Ensemble in Samarqand, the charming love lines of Omar Khayyam, and the twisted fantastic animals in Eurasian nomadic jewelry are only a few examples that illustrate the mastery and skills of Central Asian artisans. It is not surprising that Turkmenistan and Uzbekistan were named among the 1,000 most fascinating places in the world by the authors of the acclaimed book *1,000 Places You Have to Visit before You Die*.[1]

However, by the seventeenth and eighteenth centuries, the Great Silk Road was in decline, and the region was torn apart by endless wars and military campaigns that turned this prosperous region into a lawless land of feuding Khans and tribal leaders. On the eve of the nineteenth century, it had become one of the most isolated, inaccessible, and, in a sense, quite forgotten parts of the globe. The situation turned around again in the mid-nineteenth century when Central Asia catapulted into the world headlines as it became a bone of contention between the British and Russian Empires. Being weak and under-developed, the Central Asian states were unable to resist outside powers in the second half of the nineteenth century. The region was open to powerful forces of colonization and of cultural and political changes for nearly half a century, only to be closed to the outside world again by the descent of the iron curtain imposed by the Bolshevik regime after the October Revolution of 1917. The region remained virtually closed to Western influences in general and to the Islamic world in particular during most of the twentieth century. The Soviet government heavily pressured the people of Central Asia to accept a Soviet "national" identity and to create new "national" cultures at a time when their national ideologies were extremely weak. With this objective in mind, the Soviet authorities selectively combined the indigenous cultural achievements of the past generations with what was perceived to be a modern commu-nist culture in the region. The speed, magnitude, directions, and scope of the reforms changed the central Asian cultural landscape in unprecedented ways.

Only with the disintegration of the Soviet Union and the declaration of independence, in 1991, of five Central Asian republics—Kazakhstan, Kyr-gyzstan, Tajikistan, Turkmenistan, and Uzbekistan—did these nations find themselves unexpectedly free and alone in the world's arena.

Yet, not only did traditional Central Asian cultures preserve their creativity, imagination, and uniqueness through all calamities of the Soviet era, but they also prospered in many respects. The Central Asian cultures proved to be flex-ible, dynamic, and capable of adapting to many changes and incorporating many new features without losing their traditional flavors. Moreover, distinc-tive national cultures that began emerging between the seventeenth and the nineteenth centuries received a further boost with the division of the Central Asian region into five nation-states in the mid-1920s. Overall, the 70 years of persistent Soviet nationalist policy made an additional huge impact on the cultural development of the region.

Today, Central Asia represents a symbiosis of the traditional cultures and customs of the people of the Central Asian republics, of the legacy of the

Soviet-era cultural engineering, and of postindependence changes that have emerged through the powerful forces of globalization. It is a tremendously difficult task to identify common elements in the diverse cultures of Central Asia, which is larger than all the Western European countries combined. Central Asia is represented by an endless variety of local communities and cultures, with their own distinct language dialects, folklore, customs, cuisines, and costumes. Although, in the 1990s, the Central Asian republics began building post-Soviet nation-states at a very slow pace, this development gained particular momentum between 2001 and 2006 because of a number of factors, including increasing international assistance and the steep rise in oil prices.

This book was written with a single objective: to present the diverse, dynamic, and evolving cultures and customs of the Central Asian republics to the rest of the world. This proved to be an uneasy endeavor as I discovered that I had landed right in the middle of a minefield very soon after writing the first page of this book. The common elements that can be clearly defined as the shared Central Asian cultures and customs proved to be as elusive as mirages in the Karakum Desert. No single Central Asian colleague agreed with any other on the notion of the common Central Asian culture, as during the past 80 years they had increasingly begun to think of themselves as Kazakhs, Kyrgyzs, Tajiks, Turkmen, and Uzbeks. On many occasions I could hear contradictory and competing claims on historical personalities, traditions, myths, tales, poets, and artistic works—the list might continue without end. Thus, I had to make my very own decisions on how to portray them. On the top of this, I faced a challenging task in grasping the rapid changes that swept the region in the early twenty-first century.

There is a large body of literature written in native and Russian languages that endorses competing national claims. At the same time, there is a huge body of literature written in Western languages that depicts the Central Asian region as a single political, economic, geopolitical, and cultural entity and as a region held together by a unifying Muslim identity, thus downplaying the importance of national identities. Contemporary scholars both inside and outside the region cannot still agree on many issues and continue to engage in hot polemics about every aspect of the Central Asian culture.

I tried my best to passionately listen to the arguments of many individuals and groups. I wanted to introduce many publications on cultural development in the region and many arguments used by rival scholarly camps. However, being severely limited by space and time, I focused on surveying the most recognizable and distinctive elements of the Central Asian cultures and on the most meaningful and far-reaching recent changes, presenting in footnotes major scholarly arguments and scholarly discussion of various issues. For those readers who would like to enrich their knowledge even further, the bibliographic section will be of great help. Another part of the book's foundation is my personal experience based on the many years that I spent in the region and the many field study trips that I conducted across the various Central Asian republics during the past decade.

NOTE

1. Patricia Schultz, *1,000 Places You Have to Visit before You Die* (New York: Workman Publishing Company, 2003).

Acknowledgments

A comprehensive work and even a survey of the rich and diverse cultural heritage of Central Asia would require many volumes of academic studies. Thus, an attempt to bring the most important information into a single volume requires a careful selection and a certain degree of generalization. I tried my best in selecting the most important information and most important facts for this book through discussions and consultations with my colleagues and friends in and outside the region. I am fully aware that this is a concise survey of the cultures and customs of Central Asia that will review the rich cultural heritage of the Central Asian republics. I hope that, after finishing this book, readers will seek out more information, facts, names, events, and arguments to enrich their understanding of Central Asian cultures. It is also my intention that this publication will be a useful guide for scholars and members of the general public who wish to learn more about the subject.

This book emerged from several years of research on cultural and social development in Central Asia and became possible only with invaluable contributions and help from many people around me. My Central Asian colleagues generously shared their collections, archives, books, and thoughts during my travels to the Central Asian republics. I especially appreciate the help and assistance that I received from the librarians with whom I worked while I was writing this work. Their often-invisible work makes a huge difference to every researcher and student. Several colleagues and friends agreed to read and discuss chapters on various aspects of this study. Numerous conversations and debates with scholars, artists, and critics at various academic and nonacademic conventions enriched my knowledge about the peculiarities of cultural development and the too many nuances in political and social relations during the Soviet and post-Soviet eras.

A number of individuals from various parts of the world have read the early version of this book and contributed their constructive critical comments and corrections: Douglas Greenfield, Ian Boyle, Daniel Zaretski, Alia, and many other colleagues who chose to remain anonymous. I tried my best to incorporate all their suggestions and to correct all unfortunate inaccuracies in the course of the work on this book. However, any errors are the author's sole responsibility. I am also indebted to my students, who always provided me with their support and encouragement.

It is my pleasure to acknowledge the support of Dr. Catharine Nepomnyshchy, Alla Rachkov, and all my colleagues at the Harriman Institute at Columbia University for providing me with their trust and for creating the intellectual environment that supported my long journey of writing this book. I would also like to acknowledge the generous support from the Harriman Institute, which awarded me a book grant.

I would also like to thank my wife for all her support and understanding and for her interest in the numerous volumes of early and advanced drafts that I completed while I was working on this book. She was always my first and probably my most critical reader, and her remarks encouraged me to delve deeper into details and analyses.

I would like to thank Wendi Schnaufer, Senior Acquisitions Editor at Greenwood Publishing Group, and Kaitlin Ciarmiello, Editorial Assistant, for dealing patiently with my anarchic timetable and writing style. They carefully read my manuscript section by section and provided valuable comments.

Notes on Transliteration

Standardized transliteration of the Central Asian words, names, and geographical locations is a difficult task for many reasons. A single word might have three or even more variations of spelling in English: we can find the name of Turkmenistan's capital spelled in four different ways: Ashgabat, Ashgabad, Ashkhabad, and Ash'habat. Personal names can be found spelled three ways: Akaev, Akayev, and Akaiev, or Nazarbayev, Nazarbaev, and Nazarbaiev.

The inconsistencies in transliteration can be explained historically. First, during the twentieth century, the Central Asian languages underwent several significant changes: from Arabic script to Latin, in 1926–1929, and then from the Latin script to the Cyrillic (Russian) alphabet, in 1940. In the early 1990s, the governments of Turkmenistan and Uzbekistan decided to convert the alphabet from Cyrillic to Latin script, including several additional letters that do not exist in English to reflect the peculiarities of Central Asian sound systems. Meanwhile, the governments of Kazakhstan and Kyrgyzstan rejected the change, though they did not rule out such a move in future.

Second, transliteration of modern Central Asian languages into English has been problematic and inconsistent for many decades. One of the main reasons is that, in the past, many words, especially geographic and personal names, underwent double transliteration, first from national language into Russian and then from Russian into English. A good example is transliteration of words with a sound that was traditionally represented by "dzh" in Russian.

Let us take English name "John," which becomes "Dzhon" in Russian. Central Asian examples of "dzh" transliteration include such geographical names as the Kyrgyz city Dzhalal-Abad (now Jalalabad) and the Kazakh city Dzhambul (now Zhambyl). In the 1990s, the direct transliteration of geographic or personal names from Central Asian languages into English became widespread. For example, what used to be "Kirgiz" during the Soviet time became "Kyrgyz," "Karaganda" became "Qaragandy," "Issyk-Kul" became "Ysyk Kol," "Tashkent" became "Toshkent," and "Samarkand" became "Samarqand" reflecting pronunciation in the native languages. Also, many russified geographic names were written with a dash in the past—Dzhalal-Abad *oblast,* Kara-Balta, Alma-Ata. The current trend is to drop the dash in the spelling of geographic names—Jalalabad, Karabalta, Almaty.

The process of the transition from the russified version to the modern form has not been completed, and there are still some inconsistencies. The Soviet style "dzh" transliteration can still be found in the indexing of the Library of the Congress and in many publications on Central Asia, though the present trend of using "j" is making its way into modern publications. However, all spelling variations can also be found in the current literature. Some maps and geographical publications still hyphenate the geographic names; others do not use the dash; there are even publications that sometimes use all variations. In this book, most of the names of the cities and towns are given in accordance with the current language standards.

CENTRAL ASIAN PERSONAL NAMES AND TITLES

All Central Asian personal names in this book are given in a standard form—first name followed by the family name.

In the pre-Soviet past, the Central Asians traditionally referred to each other by their first names, followed by the father's name. For example, the Kyrgyzs traditionally used the following form—Usen Asan-uulu (son of Asan), Cholpon Razak-Kyzy (daughter of Razak). However, during the Soviet era, there was a change to a russified version, where the father's name, ending with the russified "-vich" for male and "-ovna" for female, became a person's patronymic. Examples are Usen Asanovich and Cholpon Razakovna. A russified family name (or surname) that ended in "-v" or "-ev" for male names and "-ova" or "-eva" for female names was added, as well. Examples are Usen Asanovich Asanov and Cholpon Razakovna Razakova. A hypothetical son of Usen Asanov would be Almaz Usenovich Asanov, a daughter Aida Usenovna Asanova. In the post-Soviet era, people increasingly turned to the traditional writing of their family names. One way to do this is to replace the suffix "-ov," "-ev," "-ova," or "-eva" with "-uulu" or "-kyzy": Aigerim Urstanbekova becomes Aigerim Urstanbek-kyzy. The other way is to drop the suffix "-ov", "-ev," or "-ova" and use a shorter version of the name. For example, "Sheradil Kasymjanov" becomes "Sheradil Kasymjan," and "Tologon Kasymbekov" becomes "Tologon Kasymbek." As this is an ongoing process, some people's names might be found in various publications in both russified and indigenous forms.

Chronology

2,000–1,000 B.C.	Bronze Age. The first irrigation systems were developed in Central Asia.
First millennium B.C.	The Sogd, Bactria, Khorasm (Khorazm), and Margiana (also Margush, Merv, or Mary) mentioned in ancient chronicles. Emergence and spread of the Zoroastrian religious teaching in Central Asia.
6th–5th centuries B.C.	Emergence and spread of Buddhism in Central Asia.
329 B.C.	Alexander the Great conquered Central Asia, including ancient Margiana.
3rd–2nd centuries B.C.	Greeco-Bactrian states in Central Asia were founded.
2nd century B.C.	The Great Silk Road started to function.
250 B.C.–224 A.D.	The ancient principality of Khorasan, on the territory of present-day southern Turkmenistan and northeastern Iran, flourished.
4th–5th centuries A.D.	The Kushan Empire in Central Asia flourished in Central Asia.
552–744	Turk Khanate.
568–571	War between western Turks and Iran.
582–593	Civil strife between western and eastern Turks.
7th century (1st half)	Establishment of ancient Turk alphabet.

622	Beginning of Muslim (Hijra) calendar.
654–683	First incursions of Arabs into Central Asia.
682–744	Second Khanate of Eastern Turks.
704–746	Turgesh Khanate.
711	Defeat of Turgesh Khanate by Eastern Turks Khanate.
7th–8th centuries	Arabs conquered Khorasan.
751	Battle between Chinese troops and combined troops of Arabs and Karluks on the Talas River.
766–940	Karluk Khanate.
10th century	Oghuz, a Turkmen tribe of Central Asia, converted to Islam.
900–999	The Samanid dynasty ruled in Khorasan.
999	Sultan Mahmud Gaznevi conquered Khorasan and established the Ghaznavids dynasty.
993?–1063	Life of Togrul Beg, founder of the Turkish Seljuk empire, which at the time of Togrul's death included all of modern Iran, Iraq, eastern Turkey, and Central Asia.
940	Balasagun conquered by the Karakhanids.
960	Islam proclaimed an official religion of the Karakhanids.
992–996	Karakhanids' armed incursions into Bukhara.
999	Karakhanids conquered Maveranahr region, the area between Syr Darya and Amu Darya Rivers.
1069/1070	Creation of Turk poem *Kutadgu Bilig* [Knowledge which brings happiness], by Yusuf Balasaguni.
1070	*De jure* formation of two Karakhanid states—Eastern and Western.
1035–1038	Seljuks defeated the Ghaznavids troops and conquered Merv.
1055	Togrul Beg defeated the Buwayhids in Baghdad and forced the declining Abbasid caliphate to accept the Seljuks as military protectors of the Caliphate.
1072–1074	Creation of *Divan Lugat at-Turk* [Dictionary of Turk dialects], by Makhmud Kashagari.
1219–1224	Genghis Khan (also spelled as Chingis Khan, first known as Temujin) turned his war campaign toward Central Asia.

1348	Establishment of Mogulistan.
1357	The Mongol ruler Janibak-Khan, of the Golden Horde, conquered Khorasan.
1370–1380	Invasion by troops of Tamerlane (Timur) into Mogulistan.
1384	Tamerlane (Timur) (1336–1405) invaded Khorasan.
1388	Tamerlane's troops stormed and destroyed Koneurgench, then one of the largest trading centers in Central Asia.
1391	Turkmen tribes rebelled against Tamerlane.
1398	Tamerlane's troops stormed and destroyed Delhi.
1419–1421	Turkmen tribes rebelled against Tamerlane's successors but were defeated and forced to migrate to Asia Minor.
1558	Antony Jenkinson, British traveler and agent for the British-Russian trade company, traveled to Bukhara and Khiva.
1593	Bukhara troops conquered Merv.
1641	Visit of Turkmen traders to Moscow mentioned in Russian chronicles.
1715–1717	The Khiva Khanate army defeated and wiped out Russian troops led by Alexander Bekovich-Cherkaskii (Devlet-Kizden-Murza).
1710	Kokand Khanate declared its independence from the Bukhara Khanate.
1731–1854	Russia acquired the Kazakh steppes (territory of present-day Kazakhstan), including Turkmen-populated Mangushlak.
1740	Nadir-Shah invaded Bukhara and Khiva Khanates.
1758–1759	Defeat of Jungar Khanate; Tsins conquered the Eastern Turkistan.
1758	Several representatives of the Kyrgyz tribes arrived in Beijing. Kyrgyz tribes recognized Chinese suzerainty.
1803	Russian Empire declared that the Turkmen tribes of Mangyshlak came under Russian protection.
1804–1813	Russian-Iranian war, which ended with the defeat of the Iranian army.

1812	Britain allied with Russia in the war against Napoleon Bonaparte of France. British Captain Cristie and Lieutenant Henry Lindsay, members of the Malcolm Mission to the Shah of Iran, were found fighting along with the Iranian troops against the Russian troops, the British ally in the war against Napoleon.
1813	Peace agreement between Russia and Iran signed in Gulistan. The Russian Empire officially acquired Georgia, Daghestan, and Azerbaijan.
1814	British-Iranian treaty directed against the increasing Russian influence in Central Asia.
1826–1828	Russian-Persian (Iranian) war and defeat of the Iranian troops. The war ended with signing of a peace agreement between Russia and Iran in Turkmanchai.
1828–1829	Russian-Turkey war and defeat of the Turkish armies in the Balkans and the Caucasus. The war ended with a peace agreement between Russia and Turkey, signed in Andrion.
1838–1842	First Anglo-Afghan war.
1839–1840	Russians undertook their first unsuccessful expedition to Khiva.
1842	Entire British garrison was slaughtered on the outskirts of Kabul. British retreated from Afghanistan. Two British officers, Colonel Charles Stuart and Captain Arthur Connolly, traveled through Turkistan but were captured and hanged in Bukhara.
1847–1851	Russian troops built a military fortress on the delta of Syr Darya River and established the Aral fleet on the Aral Sea.
1856–1857	British-Persian (Iranian) war for the control over Herat ended in the defeat of Persia. The Persian Shah recognized the independence of Herat.
1861	Turkmen tribes defeated Persian troops near to the city of Merv.
1865	Russian troops captured Tashkent, an important trade center and a strategic outpost of the Kokand Khanate. Russian authorities established the Turkistan *oblast,* which included the territory of present-day Turkmenistan.

1866–1868	The Russian advanced to the Bukhara Khanate.
1867	The Turkistan Governor-Generalship was established with its center in Tashkent. Russian ethnographic exhibition was opened in Moscow, along the Kyrgyz handicraft works were paintings by P. M. Kosharov.
1869	The Russian general H. G. Stoletov arrived on the eastern shore of the Caspian Sea and established the Russian city and port of Krasnovodsk.
1868–1871	Expedition of Alexei Fedchenko to the Kokand Khanate.
1869	Agreement was reached on acceptance by the Kokand Khanate of its vassal dependence on the Russian Empire.
1869–1870	The artist Vasilii Vereshchagin spent some time in Central Asia and brought back to Russia a number of paintings reflecting the lifestyle of local people.
1873	The Russian Empire defeated the Khiva Khanate and established control over its foreign policy, but a special treaty granted the Khan of the Khiva Khanate control over internal affairs. The Russians signed a peace treaty with the Bukhara Khanate. Russian troops faced a mutiny in Kokand, the center of the Kokand Khanate.
1876	The Kokand Khanate was abolished.
1878–1880	Second Anglo-Afghan War. The British established control over Afghanistan's foreign relations.
1879	Turkmens defeated the Russian expedition troops led by General Nikolai Lomakin under Geok-Tepe.
1880–1888	The Russian government built the Zacaspian railroad from Uzun Ada to Samarqand.
1881	Russian troops, led by General Mikhail Skobelev, defeated Turkmen tribes and stormed the fortress of Geok-Tepe (in the present-day Akhal *welayat* of Turkmenistan). The new borders with Persia (now Iran) were established.
1882	The Zacaspian military department was reorganized into Zacaspian *oblast*. It included Akhal, Krasnovodsk, and Mangyshlak districts.
1887	The border between Russia's possessions in Central Asia and Afghanistan were formally established.

1895	A convention was concluded between Great Britain and Russia that established spheres of influence in the Pamirs area.
1898	Popular uprising in Andijan against the Russians.
1914–1918	World War I.
1916	Largest uprising in the Central Asia against the Russians triggered by the Tsar's Decree to mobilize the Turkistanis for World War I.
1917	Russian Duma forced the abdication of Tsar Nicolas II, the last tsar of the Russian Empire.
March	Establishment of the *Sovets* (councils) of workers' and solders' deputies.
April	The Turkistan General-Governorship was abolished and the Turkistan Committee of the Provisional Government was established in Tashkent.
October 25	The Bolshevik Revolution in Saint Petersburg.
October 28–November 1	Bolsheviks came to power in Tashkent.
November 8	Vladimir Lenin's *Decree on Land* was published in the newspaper *Nasha Gazeta* [Our Newspaper].
November 29	Establishment of antirevolutionary government of Kokand Autonomy.
December 12	The Bolshevik authorities abolished the old (religious) judicial system across the region.
1918	
January	The first issue of the Bolshevik's newspaper *Izvestia* was published in Central Asia.
February	Decree on nationalization of all banks and bank branches in Central Asia.
April	Anti-Bolshevik riot of Semirechie Cossacks began.
April–May	The Turkistan Autonomous Soviet Socialist Republic (TASSR) was formed within the Russian Soviet Federative Socialist Republic (RSFSR).
April 21	Turkistan People's University was opened in Tashkent.
August	British occupation troops entered Zacaspian *oblast*.

September	British troops presided over execution of 26 commissars in Baku (Azerbaijan) by anti-Bolshevik troops.
October 5–15	The Constitution of Turkistan ASSR was adopted during the VI Extraordinary Session of Turkistan Soviets.

1919

January 19–21	Antirevolutionary riot in Tashkent led by K. Osipov.
March 19–31	Second Congress of the Turkistan Communist Party (TCP) and establishment of the Muslim Bureau of the TCP.
April 7	Establishment of the Revolutionary Military Council (government) of the Turkistan ASSR.
July	Mass riots in Bukhara, the capital of the Bukhara Khanate, and in several *begliks* (districts) populated by the Turkmens. Red Army captured Ashgabat.
December	Red Army entered the Khiva Khanate.

1920

February	Seid Abdulla Khan, the last khan of the Khiva Khanate, abdicated. Red Army forces captured Krasnovodsk.
April	First *Kurultai* (Congress) of People's Representatives declared the establishment of the Khoresm People's Soviet Republic (KPSR) and ratified the first Constitution of the KPSR.
September	Red Army supported by local rioters stormed Bukhara.
October	First *Kurultai* (Congress) of People's Representatives declared the establishment of the Bukhara People's Soviet Republic (BPSR).

1921

January	Second Congress of the *Sovets* (councils) of the Zacaspian *oblast*.
June	First *Kurultai* of the Turkmens of the Bukhara People's Soviet Republic (BPSR) was held.

1922

August 4	Enver Pasha, a Turkish military officer and one of the leaders of the *Basmachi* movement in Central Asia, was killed in a battle.

December 30   Union of Soviet Socialist Republics (USSR) was established, with the capital in Moscow.

1923

October   The Government of Turkistan issued a decree on the elimination of illiteracy in Central Asia.

1924

April   Resolution was issued on the necessity and timeliness of national state delimitation in Central Asia. Provisional territorial committees were formed—Uzbek, Turkmen, Kyrgyz, Kazakh, and Tajik.

June 12   Resolution was issued on the "nation-state delimitation in Central Asia."

November   First Kyrgyz newspaper *Erkin Too* [Free Mountains] was established. The Uzbek SSR and Turkmen SSR are formed.

1925

March   First Tajik newspaper, *Idi Tozhik,* was established in Dushanbe.

May   The Third Congress of the *Sovets* (councils) of the USSR officially incorporated the Turkmen SSR and the Uzbek SSR into the USSR. Soviet authorities in Central Asia abolished the private ownership of the land.

November   Establishment of the Kyrgyz Institute of Education. *Yosh Leninchi* newspaper was established in Uzbekistan.

1926   First film production center, *Turkmenfilm,* was established. First *kolkhoz* was established in Central Asia. Working Committee on converting Central Asian alphabets from Arabic script to Latin was established. First census was conducted in the region. *Kyrgyzstan Mamlekketik Basmasy,* the first publishing house, and the first radio center were established in Kyrgyzstan.

1927   About 20 *kolkhozes* were established in Turkmenistan.

March–April   The Second Congress of the *Sovets* (councils) of the Turkmen SSR adopted the First Constitution of the Turkmen SSR.

October   Russian Theater was opened in Ashgabat.

December   Radio station was opened in Ashgabat. Communist (Bolshevik) Party of Turkmenistan archive was established in Ashgabat.

March	Central Museum of Kyrgyzstan was opened.
1928	
January	Turkmen Institute of Culture (*Turkmenkult*) was established in Ashgabat.
November	The first *piatiletka* plans (five-year plan of economic development) of the Central Asian republics were adopted.
1929	The alphabets in Central Asian republics were officially converted from Arabic to Latin script; the Turkmen State Theater opened. Kyrgyz ASSR adopted its first constitution.
1929–1931	First wave of Stalin purges. Tribal leaders were deported to the so-called camps.
1930	Mass collectivization and settlement programs began in the regions with the pastoral-nomadic population. Primary education became compulsory. Peasants rioted in various areas of the region against mass collectivization campaign. Thousands of Central Asians escaped to Afghanistan, Iran, and China.
November	First season of Kyrgyz State Theater began.
1931	A new wave of repressions began against the traditional elite, as rich farmers, tribal leaders, and representatives of the indigenous intelligentsia were deported to Kazakhstan and other parts of the USSR.
1933	Red Army troops defeated the major remaining *Basmachi* groups. The iron curtain was established on the Central Asian borders with Afghanistan, China, and Iran. *Shark Yulduzi* literary journal was established in Uzbekistan.
1934	
May	First Congress of Writers of Turkmen SSR was held, in Ashgabat. First art exhibition of Kyrgyz painters was organized in Kyrgyzstan. First Congress of Uzbek writers took place.
1935	
October	First Kyrgyz Congress of female youth was held.
December	Union of Artists of Turkmenistan was established in Ashgabat. Russian Drama Theater was established in Frunze (now Bishkek).
1936	Extraordinary all-Turkmen Congress of *Sovets* (councils). The new constitution of the USSR was adopted.

1936–1938   Mass purges against the indigenous intelligentsia and political leadership were launched in the Central Asian republics. Thousands were sent to labor camps or executed, accused of opposing the political regime. The Kyrgyz State Philharmonic was established.

December   The Kyrgyz Autonomous Soviet Socialist Republic became the Kyrgyz Soviet Socialist Republic (Kyrgyz SSR).

1937

March   New constitutions were adopted in the Central Asian republics.

1938   Limited rehabilitation of repressed communist leaders. The Turkmen and Tajik State Philharmonic opened. The Union of Architects of Turkmenistan was established in Ashgabat.

1939   Census was conducted in the Central Asian republics.

1940   The Central Asian republics converted their alphabet from Latin to Cyrillic script.

1941

April   Turkmenistan Branch of the Academy of Sciences was opened in Ashgabat.

September   Soviet and British troops entered Iran to neutralize Nazis activities in the country. Central Asian governments announced that illiteracy had been eliminated among the majority of the adult population.

1941–1945   Soviet Union fought against the Nazis in World War II. First-ever mass mobilization of the Central Asians to the war.

1942   First cinema-producing center was established in Kyrgyzstan. Kyrgyz State Theater of Opera and Ballet was established.

1945   World War II ended.

1946   The Soviet troops left northern Iran.

1948   Tajik State University established in Dushanbe. Devastating earthquake in Ashgabat destroyed most of the city and killed between 30,000 and 40,000 people.

1950

September   Turkmen State University was established in Ashgabat.

1951

July   Turkmen Academy of Sciences was opened in Ashgabat. Kyrgyz State University was established in Frunze (now Bishkek).

1953   Josef Stalin died in Moscow. The Kremlin instituted political changes and began the rehabilitation of the Central Asian intelligentsia, political leaders, and other victims of Stalin's repressions.

1954   Kyrgyz Academy of Science was established.

1957   The Central Asian republics made seven-year education compulsory.

1959   Census of population conducted. Ashgabat TV center was opened.

1966   Devastating earthquake destroyed most of Tashkent city.

1978   Central Asian republics adapted new constitutions.

1979   Islamic Revolution in Iran took place. The Soviet army entered Afghanistan.

1985   Mikhail Gorbachev came to power. A campaign for changes in the region began. Several longstanding first secretaries of the Central Asian republics were accused of corruption.

1986   Dinmuhamed Kunayev, longstanding Kazakh leader, was dismissed and replaced by Genadii Kolbin. Students in Alma-Ata (now Almaty) organized unsanctioned meetings and demonstrations in protest at Kunayev's dismissal. Hundreds of high-ranking party and government officials facing corruption charges were dismissed across the Central Asian republics.

1989   Youth riots broke out in Ashgabat and Nebitdag, with deadly clashes in the Ferghana Valley of Uzbekistan.

1990   Central Asian republics declared their languages as the sole state languages.

June   The leaders of Central Asian Republics gathered in Bishkek (then Frunze) and agreed to establish the Central Asian Union. Interethnic conflicts occurred in the Osh region of southern Kyrgyzstan; Central Asian republics elected their first presidents.

1991

March 17	All-Union referendum on the future of the Soviet Union.
August 19	Anti-Gorbachev coup d'état in Moscow.
August 25	Communist Party of Kyrgyz SSR dissolved.
August 28	President Boris Yeltsin declared that the Russian Federation had established control over the key Soviet ministries.
August 29	Kyrgyzstan's Supreme Soviet adopted a resolution dissolving the Communist Party.
August 31	Kyrgyzstan's *Jogorku Kenesh* adopted the declaration on political independence of Kyrgyzstan.
October 12	Dr. Askar Akayev was elected Kyrgyzstan's president by popular vote.
October 27	The Turkmenistan Supreme *Sovet* (Parliament) declared the independence of Turkmenistan.
December 8	Belarus, the Russian Federation, and the Ukraine, founding members of the USSR, signed a treaty dissolving the Soviet Union.
December 17	Yeltsin and Gorbachev agreed that the Soviet Union would cease to exist on January 1, 1992.
December 21	All Central Asian republics signed the Alma-Ata Declaration and joined the Commonwealth of Independent States (CIS)
December 25	Gorbachev resigned the post of president.
1992–1997	Civil war in Tajikistan.
1992	The Central Asian republics became members of the UN, the International Monetary Fund (IMF), and the World Bank.
April	Central Asian republics signed an agreement recognizing existing borders.
May 18	Turkmenistan introduced its first post-Soviet constitution.
May	The Central Asian republics signed the CIS Security Treaty (Tashkent Declaration).
1993	
March	Turkic Orthographical Conference called for the change from Cyrillic to Latin script for all Central Asian Turkic languages.

April	Kyrgyzstan received the status of a "developing nation" from the United Nations.
May 5	Kyrgyz Parliament (*Jogorku Kenesh*) adopted new Kyrgyzstan constitution.
May 10	Kyrgyzstan introduced its currency, the *som.*
November	The national currency, the *manat,* was introduced in Turkmenistan. The Kazakh government announced introduction of the national currency, the *tenge.*
1994	Turkmenistan held a national referendum extending President Saparmurat Niyazov's presidential term until 2002. Presidential elections held in Tajikistan.
1995	
January	The first post-Soviet census was conducted in Turkmenistan.
February	Elections for the *Jogorku Kenesh* (Kyrgyz parliament) were held.
March	The Kazakh Parliament was dissolved.
September	Celebration of the 1000th anniversary of the Kyrgyz oral epic *Manas.*
December	The Central Asian Economic Union (CAEU) members declared their intention to establish the Central Asian Peacekeeping Battalion (Centrasbat).
1996	
March	The Russian language was granted the status of "official language" in Kyrgyzstan. Kazakhstan and Kyrgyzstan joined the CIS Custom Union.
April	President Akayev agreed to resolve border disputes with China within the Shanghai Forum (now the Shanghai Cooperation Organization).
1997	
November	Hillary Clinton visited Kyrgyzstan, Kazakstan, and Uzbekistan. Tajikistan's competing political parties signed the peace accord giving the Islamic Party a share of positions in the Tajik government and in the parliament, thereby ending the civil war.

1998

January 22   Space flight of first Kyrgyz cosmonaut, Salizhan Sharipov, with an American space expedition.

1999

August   Militants entered Batken *oblast* in Kyrgyztan and took Japanese geologists as hostages.

October   Japanese hostages were released, allegedly for US$4 million ransom.

November   Kyrgyz troops, with military assistance from Russia and Uzbekistan, expelled militants from Kyrgyzstan.

December   The People's Council (*Khalk Maslahaty*) of Turkmenistan extended indefinitely President Saparmurat Niyazov's term in office, making him president for life.

2000

Summer   Incursion of militants of the Islamic Movement of Uzbekistan into the territory of Kyrgyzstan and Uzbekistan.

October   Osh City (Kyrgyzstan) celebrated its 3,000th anniversary.

2001

September   Central Asian republics condemned terrorist attacks on the United States and declared their support for the fight against international terrorism led by the United Nations; they agreed to open their airspace for U.S. and international humanitarian flights for the duration of the war in Afghanistan.

November   U.S. military airbases were established at Kyrgyzstan and Uzbekistan.

December   First ever American military contingent arrived in Kyrgyzstan and Uzbekistan.

2002

August   Saparmurat Turkmenbashi renamed the months of the year after himself, his mother, and his spiritual guide, the *Ruhnama*.

June   U.S. extended the lease of Manas airport near Bishkek. Kyrgyzstan agreed to host a Russian military base and leased to Russia the facilities of the former Soviet airbase in the city of Kant.

August	Kyrgyz population passed the five-million mark.

2003

April	President Saparmurat Niyazov revoked the 1993 dual-citizenship agreement with Russia.
October	Seventh Congress of World Turkmens took place in Ashgabat, with Turkmens from 22 countries, including Afghanistan, Iran, Saudi Arabia, Pakistan, Syria, and Turkey.

2004

March	The United Nations and Turkmenistan signed the United Nations Development Assistance Framework (UNDAF), a strategic planning document for cooperation between the government and UN agencies for the next five years (2005–2009).
October	Kazakhstan hosted a Conference on Interaction and Confidence-Building Measures in Asia (CICA), where the representatives of 17 states discussed regional cooperation and security.

2005

March	Tulip Revolution in Kyrgyzstan; protesters stormed the presidential palace and forced President Akayev to flee the country.
May	Tajikistan's Interior Ministry and riot police conducted military exercises simulating large operations against terrorist and organized crime groups.
November	A U.S. air force base in Uzbekistan was formally closed.

2006

January	The Kazakh parliament approved a new Kazakh national anthem, entitled *Menin Kazakhstanym* (My Kazakhstan).
May	The International Monetary Fund's (IMF) officials reported strong economic growth in Kazakhstan, Kyrgyzstan, Tajikistan, and Uzbekistan that averaged about eight percent in 2005 and estimated at about seven to eight percent in 2006.
August	Tajik President Imomali Rakhmonov and Indian Prime Minister Manmohan Singh signed agreements on scientific, technological, and cultural exchanges.

September   The leaders of Kazakhstan, Kyrgyzstan, Tajikistan, and Uzbekistan discussed economic, security, and cultural cooperation. They established a consortium to settle disputes over the water resources and agreed to coordinate their efforts to save the shrinking Aral Sea and to improve the regional water management system.

1

Introduction: Land, People, and History

[At the time of the Great Game] the attention of the world was focused on Central Asia. Men risked their lives to get there. Not many succeeded and not all of them returned to tell the tale.
— Fitzroy MacLean, Scottish writer and diplomat[1]

The modern Central Asian republics (CARs)—Kazakhstan, Kyrgyzstan, Tajikistan, Turkmenistan, and Uzbekistan—are guardians of ancient and medieval civilizations that rose, flourished, and died in this land. Memories of innumerable caravans that for centuries moved people, goods, and ideas from the East to the West, and of fearless nomadic warriors who defeated the most powerful armies of their times, still live in local legends and epics. Past glories and achievements in science and art are reflected in numerous architectural monuments and found in archeological sites. The diversity of culture that was enriched by the interaction between the settled Iranian and the nomadic Turanian traditions proclaimed itself in the festivals and celebrations of local, familial, and communal events. The fact that these republics were created as the result of the nineteenth- and twentieth-century rivalry between the British and the Russian empires does not impinge on their aspirations to become developed nations. They look forward to investing the income from their riches—oil, gas, gold, cotton, silk, and other exports—into developing modern independent states that are increasingly open to the forces of globalization.

GEOGRAPHY AND ENVIRONMENT

On a geographical map, the Central Asian republics are represented by a large, bright, green-and-brown area—representing a combination of steppe and oases—in the middle of the Eurasian continent. They are bordered by the Russian Federation in the north, China in the east, Afghanistan and Iran in the south, and the Caspian Sea in the west. This landlocked region has a land area of approximately 1,542,200 square miles (around 3,994,000 square kilometers).[2] The region, which is shaped like an uneven pentagon, is about half the size of the continental United States (without Alaska), or twice the size of Mexico. From north to south, the Central Asian region measures about 1,500 miles (2,413 kilometers), and the distance between its eastern and western borders is estimated at about 2,000 miles (3,218 kilometers). The coastline of the landlocked Caspian Sea is about 1,000 miles (1,600 kilometers), and this body of water forms the region's natural western boundary. However, none of the countries in the region has direct access to any oceans, and, therefore, none has direct access to the most convenient modern maritime communication routes. All the Central Asian countries rely on the goodwill of their neighbors for access to the most convenient seaports on the Eurasian landmass.

Central Asia is a land of extremes and contrasts, and the region can be subdivided into five major geographical and climatic zones that do not necessarily coincide with national boundaries: the northern steppe and steppe-forest zone; the western dry desert zone; the southern and southeastern high-mountain zone; the fertile valleys and oases between the Amu Darya and the Syr Darya Rivers; and a series of moderately elevated valleys on the border between the high mountains and the central plain.

The large, flat steppe and forest-steppe of the northern zone covers nearly half of the Central Asian region and corresponds to the territory of Kazakhstan. The steppe is located at the same latitude and in the same climatic zone as the states of Montana, Minnesota, and North Dakota in the United States and is characterized by a continental climate, with extremely cold and snowy winters and hot, sunny summers. The temperatures range from -28°C (-18°F) to -14°C (7°F) in January and from +5°C (41°F) to +18°C (65°F) in July. Winter is usually dominated by extremely cold weather, with chilling winds and snowstorms. Summer is hot and dry, with little rain and an abundance of sunshine. Spring and autumn weather is relatively mild.

The dry and water-scarce desert zone of the southwestern areas of Central Asia extends into Turkmenistan and western Uzbekistan. There is little precipitation in both summer and winter, and the extremes of the continental climate—very cold and windy winters and unbearably hot summers—render the desert quite inhospitable. In the Karakum (Garagum)[3] and Kyzylkum

(Gyzulgum) deserts, the temperatures range from -18°C to +6°C (between -1°F and 43°F) in January and between +30°C and +35°C (between 86°F and 95°F) in July. During especially cold nights in winter, the temperature can drop as low as -28°C to -33°C (between -18°F and -27°F), and during sunny days in summer it can reach +45°C to +50°C (between 113°F and 122°F). There is a severe shortage of water in this zone, as rainfall ranges between 100 and 300 millimeters (between 4 and 12 inches).

The major highland mountain ranges stretch from southeastern Kazakhstan and Kyrgyzstan to Tajikistan and southern Uzbekistan. The highest of these are situated above 5,000 meters (about 16,400 feet) and form an uninhabitable chain of mountains often covered with ice glaciers and permafrost. The climate is more severe at high altitudes (3,000 meters (9,840 feet) and higher), ranging from -28°C (-18°F) to -14°C (7°F) in January and from +5°C (41°F) to +18°C (65°F) in July.

The fertile and densely populated valleys and oases between the Amu Darya and the Syr Darya Rivers encompass Uzbekistan, northern Tajikistan, and southwestern Kyrgyzstan. The Ferghana Valley, for example, is divided

The major highland mountain ranges stretch from southeastern Kazakhstan to Kyrgyzstan, Tajikistan, and southern Uzbekistan. Courtesy of the author, 2006.

among Kyrgyzstan, Tajikistan, and Uzbekistan; this is one of the most densely populated areas in Central Asia. The climate here is relatively mild and dry, with the temperature ranging from -14°C (7°F) to +7°C (45°F) in January and with an average daily temperature between +26°C (79°F) and +29°C (84°F) in July. In some parts, such as the southern part of the Ferghana Valley, the climate is subtropical, ranging from +5°C (41°F) to +18°C (65°F) in January and from +26°C (78°F) to +33°C (92°F) in July (sometimes the temperature may exceed 40°C or 100°F). Rainfall varies between 180 millimeters and 800 millimeters (between 7 and 32 inches), and most of the area depends on irrigation and drinking water from the major rivers that originate in the high mountains of the Tian Shan and Pamirs.

The series of moderately elevated valleys that begin in Kyrgyzstan, Tajikistan, and Uzbekistan and continue into southern Turkmenistan are the most livable areas in the region. They have plenty of drinking and irrigation water from numerous mountain creeks and rivers, as well as a mild climate and moderate rainfall. The weather there is also affected by the continental climate, but it is relatively mild and dry and is comparable to the climate in the midwestern United States. The temperatures range from -14°C (7°F) to +7°C (45°F) in January and between +26°C (78°F) and +29°C (84°F) in July.

SURVEY OF HISTORICAL, GEOGRAPHICAL, AND ADMINISTRATIVE DIVISION

The Central Asian region in the modern era presents as a geopolitical entity with clear political, economic, and cultural boundaries; historically, however, it is very difficult, to conceptualize Central Asia as a region in ancient and medieval times. In the past, there was never a single political entity that controlled the entire region in its present boundaries. Moreover, various parts of the Central Asian region were affiliated with different states, empires, or civilizations and at times had completely different cultural landscapes. In fact, the ancient and medieval maps of Central Asia were dotted with towns and cities that do not appear on modern maps. There are several core areas in the region that played an important role in various periods of history and that gradually glued the region together.

The first historical core of Central Asia is situated in the river basins of, and oases between, the two greatest waterways of the region. One is the Amu Darya (*Oxus* in Latin and *Jayhun* in Arabic sources), which begins in the Pamir Mountains in the far southeast corner of Central Asia and takes its precious water to the west for about 500–600 miles (750–900 kilometers), before turning to the north and ending in the Aral Sea. The area on the right bank of the river was traditionally called *Maveranahr* ("the area beyond the river" in Arabic), though the states and principalities of *Maveranahr* centered around Samarqand, Bukhara, and other cities often controlled the cities and towns on the opposite bank of the river, including Khorezm (Khwarezm), Urgench, and Kuniaurgench. The other river is the Syr Darya (*Iaxartes* in Greek and *Sayhun* in Arabic sources), which begins in the Tian Shan Mountains in the southeastern corner of Central Asia and flows to the northwest for about 500 miles (750 kilometers), then turns to the west and heads to the Aral Sea. Eventually, the name *Maveranahr* began to be used in reference to the area between these two rivers; in the words of the Russian orientalist Vasilii Bartold, the name referred to the "land under Islamic domain."[4]

The second historical core of Central Asian sedentary civilization was situated to the northeast of the Syr Darya River. It was called in Turkic *Jety-suu*—"the area of seven rivers." During the early medieval era, many cities flourished in this area flanked by the Tian Shan Mountains in the south and Balkhash Lake in the north, including Otrar, Balasagun, and Taraz. However, these sedentary centers were completely devastated during the Mongol invasion, and they never recovered.

The third area that played a significant role in Central Asian history is the Eurasian steppe. This land roughly corresponds to the vast territory from the Russian Altai Mountains in the east all the way to the Volga River in the west. For many centuries, numerous pastoral and pastoral-nomadic tribes raised horses, sheep, goats, and camels there, utilizing the steppe's practically endless supply of grass.

Three other areas that played no less a role in ancient Central Asian history have been cut off from the region in the modern era by political events. One is *Khorasan* ("the land of rising sun" in Persian). In the past, it was a large area to the south and southwest of the Amu Darya River in the eastern part of the Iranian Plateau and included such cities as Herat, Nishapur, and Merv. *Khorasan* was one of the centers of cultural and political development of the sedentary states in Central Asia and of the interaction between Persian and indigenous Central Asian cultures. The second area is Eastern Turkestan—the area of the Tarim River basin (also sometimes called Kashgar). It is situated to the east of the Tian Shan Mountains, and its oases are watered by the Tarim, Konche Darya, Kashgar, and many other rivers. The Eastern Turkistan area played a prominent role in the political and cultural development of Central Asia, especially during the first millennium A.D., as a center of Buddhist and Manichean civilizations. The third area is the steppe zone that stretches from the *Jetysuu* area to southern Siberia and Mongolia. This was the realm of many Turkic and Mongol tribal leaders for centuries, and it was often used as a base for military campaigns in Central Asia and in the Eurasian steppe.[5]

The modern external borders of the Central Asian region were established in the late nineteenth century, as the result of a formal arrangement between the British and the Russian Empires. This arrangement ended the bitter competition for political and military control in the region. The British expanded their influence over the territory of Afghanistan and Iran, and the Russian Empire established its influence over the land to the north of these two states, in the process confronting three political powers in the region—the Kokand and Khiva Khanates and the Bukhara Emirate. Eventually, the Kokand Khanate was dissolved due to political turbulence, but the Bukhara Emirate and the Khiva Khanate both preserved their semi-independent status well into the 1920s.

The internal administrative division of Central Asia after the Russian conquest was a very complex process completed in several steps. In the late nineteenth and early twentieth centuries, the territory of Central Asia was divided into several provinces (*gubernias* in Russian). The present administrative shape of Central Asia was established in the mid-1920s during the region's so-called national delimitation. The Kremlin introduced administrative delimitation in the Central Asian region and embraced the ideas of those Central Asian leaders who suggested dividing the region along vaguely ethnic lines. On October 27, 1924, the Central Executive Committee (a branch of the Soviet government) issued a decree on the delimitation of the Central Asian region and the establishment of the Soviet Socialist Republics.[6]

This step signified an important change in the political development of the region, as Central Asia was divided along still relatively vague and weak ethnic identities. The Soviet leaders believed that the borders would play purely symbolic roles for interstate relations because of the political and social integration and the intraregional cooperation within the Soviet Union, but they would be of the utmost importance for consolidating the national identities of each republic. There were several changes in the administrative structure, and some provinces and major cities were renamed several times during the Soviet era, but this administrative division has been preserved, with some minor changes, to the present time. Although this division was established primarily for administrative and planning purposes, it did reflect both the peculiarities of economic geography and, in some degree, the tribal and communal divisions in Central Asian society.

Initially the area was divided into two "sovereign republics": the Turkmen Soviet Socialist Republic (or Turkmen SSR) and the Uzbek SSR. Kazakhstan was established as an Autonomous Soviet Socialist Republic (Kazakh ASSR) within the Russian Federation. Kyrgyzstan was created as an autonomous province (*oblast* in Russian) within the Russian Federation. Tajikistan was initially established as an autonomous republic within the Uzbek SSR.

Karakalpakistan was established as an autonomous *oblast* initially within the Kazakh ASSR (1925–1930). In 1930, it came under the jurisdiction of the Russian Federation, and then, in 1936, was transferred to the jurisdiction of the Uzbek SSR.

The Soviet Constitution of 1936 finally established the Central Asian administrative borders and political status of these republics: Kazakhstan, Kyrgyzstan, and Tajikistan were elevated to the status of Union Republics, and this gave each of them the constitutional right to leave the USSR (they used this right in 1991). This contrasted sharply with autonomous republics within the Russian Federation, such as the Bashkir ASSR, the Checheno-Ingush ASSR, or the Buriat ASSR, which had the status of administrative units within the Russian Federation and hence had no constitutional rights to leave the Federation.

RESOURCES

The political importance and military might of the Central Asian states in the ancient and medieval eras were enhanced by their access to the three most indispensable resources of that time. First, they had access to a limitless supply of horses from the vast Eurasian steppe. These horses were vital for the warfare of that period, as they were used by light cavalry—the most effective and lethal military force until the industrial revolution. For centuries, Central Asian horse-mounted warriors proved their military superiority, as they could cover long distances within short periods of time and strike fatal blows from unexpected directions—very much like motorized divisions in modern warfare. They easily outmaneuvered the well-equipped but slow infantry armies of the major sedentary states and empires around Central Asia.

Second, the Central Asians had access to a practically endless supply of arable land—the most vital resource in any agricultural society. Not only did this fertile land combine with a favorable climate to produce food to support the local population, but it also sustained commercial crops for export to other countries. Significant areas of land were allocated for commercial agriculture and the production of valuable goods of that era, especially silk—an extremely precious and highly valued commodity in the Eurasian world for many centuries. These exports contributed to a healthy economy and relative prosperity.

Third, Central Asians had access to various metal deposits, including gold, silver, and iron ore. Until the twentieth century, they were never able to produce metals on a large industrial scale, but they made enough materials for their internal needs and for sustaining military campaigns. Local masters perfected their ability to create metalwork of such high quality that they successfully exported their products to many parts of the world.

With the beginning of the industrial revolution in the West, however, the importance of agriculture declined significantly. Worse, the major colonial powers grabbed land on different continents, thereby gaining access to a cheap and sustainable supply of all kinds of agricultural products and so establishing more productive large commercial farms and plantations in various parts of the world. Small, primitive family-run industrial outlets in Central Asia had no chance whatsoever of competing with the large-scale modern factories and plants. The technological revolution in warfare that began with the introduction of long-range gunpowder powered the weaponry and effectively canceled the advantage of the light cavalry. Thus, the Central Asian region entered a long era of economic and military decline and retreat. This culminated in the colonization of the region in the nineteenth century by the Russian Empire.

The economic development of the twentieth century, the rise of new technologies, and the restrictive nature of international trade during the cold-war era all elevated the importance of the Central Asian region for Russia. There was a growing demand in the Russian Soviet market for traditional resources—for example, cotton, animal products, and grain—that were produced at Soviet-style large collective farms: the *kolkhozes* and *sovkhozes*. Various metals—iron ore, gold, silver, copper, and especially newly discovered uranium ore—found markets in Russia and Eastern Europe. The discovery of huge reserves of two strategically important resources—oil and gas—in the early and mid-twentieth century had a deep effect on the economies of the republics. Some local experts claim that these reserves easily rival those of both Europe's North Sea and Mexico. For example, in 2005 Kazakhstan was in thirteenth place in the world in proven oil reserves, ahead of the United Kingdom, the United States, and Mexico.[7]

These natural reserves, however, are unevenly distributed among the Central Asian republics. Kazakhstan is the largest and richest country in the region, as its oil reserves range anywhere between 18 and 26 billion barrels (CIA est., 2005; second largest among the CIS members), with potential oil reserves ranging between 100 and 150 billion barrels. Gas reserves range between 1.8 and 2.5 trillion cubic meters. Kazakhstan also has large commercial deposits of coal, iron ore, chrome ore, cobalt, copper, molybdenum, gold, uranium, and other metals. Turkmenistan, too, has huge reserves of oil and gas (CIA est., 2005; the country was the world's ninth-largest gas exporter in 2005).[8] Its oil reserves range between 1.0 and 2.0 billion barrels (CIA est., 2005; the fourth largest among the CIS members), with potential oil reserves ranging between 10 and 25 billion barrels; and its proven gas reserves range between 3.0 and 5 trillion cubic meters, with potential gas reserves of between 20 and 30 trillion cubic meters.

Uzbekistan has significant oil and gas reserves, with proven oil reserves of between 0.6 and 2.0 billion barrels and potential oil reserves ranging between

2.0 and 3.0 billion barrels; its gas reserves range between 2.2 and 3.5 trillion cubic meters. Uzbekistan also has large commercial deposits of coal, copper, gold, molybdenum, silver, uranium, and other metals. The country is among the largest producers of cotton. Kyrgyzstan and Tajikistan have very small deposits of oil and gas that range between 10 and 50 million barrels of oil and 5.6 and 10 billon cubic meters of gas each. Yet, both states have significant deposits of antimony, gold, mercury, coal, uranium, and other minerals, though they need significant investment and new technologies to reach a commercially viable level of production.[9]

PEOPLE

The population of Central Asia is estimated at about 55 million (2006 est.), up from 7–9 million in 1905.[10] The population is comparable in size to that of France or of the states of California and New York combined. It is expected that this population figure will double within the next 35–40 years and so exceed 100 million by 2050, if the reproductive rates of the 1990s remain unchanged. If the current population were equally divided over the region, population density would be about 35 people per square mile (about 13 people per square kilometer). However, this picture is deceptive, as large areas in the steppe, deserts, and high mountains are very sparsely populated or not inhabited at all. As in many Third World countries, a significant number of people are concentrated in overcrowded metropolitan centers and in the region's fertile valleys (for instance, the Ferghana Valley, which is shared among Kyrgyzstan, Tajikistan, and Uzbekistan, or the Chui Valley, which is shared between Kyrgyzstan and Kazakhstan).

Most of the urban centers represent a colorful mix of many nationalities, who have lived together for generations sharing and enriching one another's cultures, customs, and traditions. It is not uncommon for people in the cities to speak two or even three languages, though there has been a significant decline in bilingualism since the 1990s, when all the states began exclusively promoting their state languages in all spheres of life. About half the population in the region live in villages *(ails)* and towns, and most of the rural settlements traditionally tend to be more monoethnic than the cities.

For centuries, Central Asia was a region where Mongol, Indo-Arian, and Middle Eastern races mixed in a giant melting pot. Many cultural elements vary from province to province and from state to state, but there are many elements that are similar among all people across the region. These include respect for the elder members of society *(aksakals)*, devotion to the large extended families that make up the fabric of Central Asian society, strong communal and tribal relations, and resilient oral historic and literary traditions.

Aksakal (Central Asian elder). Courtesy of the author, 2006.

The *Kazakhs* belong to an ethnic group of about 11 million people. They make up the majority of the population of Kazakhstan, though large groups of Kazakhs reside in China, Mongolia, Russia, Kyrgyzstan, and Uzbekistan. Most of the Kazakhs are Sunni Muslims whose ancestors turned to Islam between the twelfth and sixteenth centuries, though some beliefs of their pre-Islamic past have survived to the present, such as devotion to ancestors and spirits. The Kazakhs in rural areas have preserved a strong tribal identity; it is much weaker, though, among the urban populations. In the past, Kazakh society was divided into large tribal confederations—proto-states *(Zhuzes)*. There were three major tribal confederations, the Elder, Middle, and Younger Hordes (*Uluu, Orta,* and *Kichi Zhuzes* in Kazakh). Historically, they competed with one another for power and influence. These divisions still influence national politics. In the past, the Kazakhs were involved in pastoral nomadism, raising horses, sheep, and camels and supplementing this practice with hunting and trade. During the twentieth century, most of the people abandoned the pastoral nomadic lifestyle and settled in the towns and villages.

There are several competing theories about the origin of the Kazakhs, and about their links to the early Turkic khanates of the sixth to twelfth centuries and to the Mongols in the thirteenth and fourteenth centuries.

Central Asian girls in traditional Kazakh dress. Courtesy of the author, 2006.

Most historians agree that the Kazakhs lived in the territory between Mongolia and modern Kazakhstan for several centuries or longer. By the fifteenth and sixteenth centuries, the Kazakhs had become distinguished from their neighbors and had begun to develop their own identity, language, and political entities—the *Zhuzes*. Most of the Kazakh tribes became subjects of the Russian Empire between the eighteenth and late nineteenth centuries through diplomatic negotiations, though some tribes waged fierce resistance. In 1920, the Kazakh Autonomous Soviet Socialist Republic (KASSR) was established; it was renamed the Kazakh Soviet Socialist Republic (KSSR) in 1936.[11]

The *Kyrgyzs* (also Kirgizs, Kara-Kyrgyzs) make up the majority of the population of Kyrgyzstan and also live in compact groups in Afghanistan, China, Kazakhstan, Russia, Tajikistan, Turkey, and Uzbekistan. Their total number is close to 4.5–5.0 million people. Until 1926 they were also known as the *Kara-Kyrgyzs* (literally "black Kyrgyzs"). The overwhelming majority of the Kyrgyzs are Sunni Muslims whose ancestors turned to Islam between the eleventh and sixteenth centuries, though their beliefs incorporate significant influences of the pre-Islamic past (e.g., devotion to ancestors, belief in mountains spirits and the Universe). Since 1991 a very small number of

Kyrgyzs (probably fewer than 1 percent) have been converted to Evangelical Christianity. The Kyrgyz tribal identity is deeply embedded in the psychology of the people, and every man is expected to know his ancestors going back seven generations. Traditionally, Kyrgyz society is divided into two major tribal confederations—Right Wing and Left Wing (*Sol Kanat* and *Ong Kanat* in Kyrgyz)—and these two groups historically maintained significant autonomy and independence from each other. This division still affects the national politics and cultural development in the country. The Kyrgyzs' traditional lifestyle involved pastoral nomadism; they raised horses, sheep, goats, and yaks. During the twentieth century, their ways of life significantly changed, as the majority of them settled in urban areas.[12]

There are several competing theories about the origin of the Kyrgyzs and about their links to the legendary Yenisei Kyrgyzs of Siberia (some scholars reject the existence of any links). There are also academic disputes about the relationship of modern Kyrgyzs to the mysterious Kyrgyz Khanate and the Karakhanid nomadic empires (the latter controlled significant territories of present-day Kazakhstan, Russian Siberia, Mongolia, and Uzbekistan). Most historians agree that the Kyrgyzs have occupied the territory of modern Kyrgyzstan for several centuries and probably longer, though some Chinese and other historical chronicles and Kyrgyz legends indicate that the Kyrgyz ancestors probably lived in southern Siberia in the first centuries A.D.

During the period of the Turkic khanates (sixth to tenth centuries A.D.), various Turkic-speaking groups began forming the Kyrgyz ancestral tribes. They frequently moved among Altai, Xingjiang, and the eastern Tian Shan, because of the political turbulence and instability of the nomadic empires of that era. In the thirteenth century, the Mongols, who had invaded the region, recruited some Kyrgyz tribes through various agreements or by force. By the sixteenth and seventeenth centuries, the Kyrgyzs had become distinguished from their neighbors and had begun to develop the Kyrgyz identity and Kyrgyz language, which increasingly differed from the T⋯ languages of their neighbors. Most of the Kyrgyz tribes became subjects of the Russian Empire in the second half of the nineteenth century through diplomatic negotiations, though some tribes waged fierce resistance.

The *Tajiks* (also *Tojiki*) live mainly in Tajikistan. Additionally, significant numbers of Tajiks live in Afghanistan and Uzbekistan, and compact groups can be found in China, Kazakhstan, Kyrgyzstan, and Russia. According to various estimates, between seven and eight million Tajiks live in the region. The Tajiks are the only Persian-speaking people in Central Asia; they belong to the Persian-speaking world that includes a significant part of the population in Afghanistan, Iran, Iraq, and other countries. Their language, Tajiki, is close to the Persian spoken in Persia (modern Iran). Many Tajik families are bilingual, as they also speak various Turkic languages. The overwhelming majority of the Tajiks are Sunni Muslims, though there is an influential community of Ismailis (linked to the Shia teaching in Islam). Traditionally, the Tajiks were involved in commercial agriculture, producing grain, rice, cotton, silk, grapes, apricots, among others, for local and international markets. Agriculture was widely supplemented by various forms of crafts and the servicing of trade on the Great Silk Road. During the twentieth century, they significantly changed their economic activities as the majority joined collective farms *(kolkhozes)* or moved to cities to work at large industrial enterprises.

Scholars still dispute the origins of the Tajik people, the roots of their cultural heritage, and even the etymology of the word "Tajik." Some scholars translate the word as "crown"; others believe it was probably just the name of a medieval tribe. Nevertheless, there is some consensus within research communities about the origins of the Tajik people. Most Tajik scholars link modern Tajiks with ancient peoples who lived in the Central Asian city-states and kingdoms as long ago as 2,000–1,500 B.C. Modern Tajik culture may claim roots in the ancient cultures of Sogdiana and Bactria and the early Parthian states.

Old hunter proudly displays his trophy on the wall of his yurt. Courtesy of the author, 2006.

Since antiquity, three quite different groups of people have melted into the Tajik nation. The first of these was the rural population of the Pamirs and areas around it. The second was the highly sophisticated population of large and small cities and towns in the valleys of the Amu Darya, Zeravshan, Vakh, Panj, and other rivers. The third group was formed by the Turkic-speaking people that arrived in the region in several small and large waves and assimilated there. Most of the Tajiks became subjects of the Russian Empire in the late nineteenth centuries through diplomatic negotiations, though Russia had only symbolic and nominal control over many mountains areas.[13]

The *Turkmens* (also *Turkmenler,* Turkomans) belong to an ethnic group that makes up the majority of the population of Turkmenistan. A significant number of Turkmens live in Afghanistan, Iraq, and Iran. Until the 1920s they were also sometimes called the *Turkomans,* while some neighboring nations called them by the names of their tribes, such as *Yomuds, Teke,* etc. Traditionally, Turkmen society is divided into several tribes and tribal groups, which are historically significantly independent from one another. The tribal identity is still essential for the Turkmens, and it plays a significant role in national politics. The Turkmens speak the Turkmen language, one of the languages of the Oguz linguistic group of the Turkic language family. The overwhelming majority of the Turkmens are Sunni Muslims whose ancestors turned to Islam between the ninth and fifteenth centuries, although, like their neighbors, they have preserved some elements of their pre-Islamic past (devotion to ancestors and other beliefs), as well as some traditions of Sufism. In the past, the Turkmens were involved in pastoral nomadism, raising horses, sheep (especially the highly valued karakul sheep), and camels. During the twentieth century, a significant number of people abandoned the pastoral nomadic lifestyle and settled in the towns and villages.

Many scholars trace the origin of the Turkmens to the legendary Oguz nomadic empires that controlled significant territories of present-day Afghanistan, China, Iran, Kazakhstan, Mongolia, and Uzbekistan. At present, official Turkmen historians claim that the Turkmens have strong links to the ancient civilizations of Central Asia. Other scholars trace their origin to the Turkic khanates (sixth to tenth centuries A.D.). During that era, various Turkic-speaking groups began to form the tribal confederations of Turkmen ancestors and moved within greater Central Asia because of the political turbulence and instability of the nomadic empires of that era. Yet a third school argues that the Turkmens consolidated their identity between the fourteen and seventeenth centuries, as they became distinct from their neighbors and began to develop their own culture and language.[14] Many Turkmen tribes vigorously resisted the Russian Empire's advance in the nineteenth century, but after several defeats they accepted the imperial domination of their lands. With the Soviet nation-state delimitation in the region in the 1920s, the majority of Turkmens found themselves in a newly established republic—Turkmenistan—yet large communities of Turkmens remained in Afghanistan, Iran, and Iraq.

The *Uzbeks* are the largest ethnic group in the region, comprising approximately 25 million people. Most Uzbeks live within the territory of Uzbekistan, though large Uzbek communities—each exceeding a million—live in neighboring Central Asian countries and in Afghanistan. The overwhelming majority of the Uzbeks are Sunni Muslims. Historically, the Uzbeks were involved in commercial agriculture, producing grain, rice, cotton, silk, grapes, apricots, and other products for local and international markets. In the cities, they were actively engaged in various forms of crafts and the servicing of trade on the Great Silk Road.

The Uzbek nation was formed by two quite different groups of people. The first group was the Persian-speaking settled population of Bukhara, Samarqand, and other large and small cities and towns in the valleys of the Syr Darya, the Amu Darya, and other rivers. The second group was the Tur-kic-speaking pastoral-nomadic population that lived largely to the north of the settled oases but, like all other Turks, traced their ancestry to the major Turkic tribal confederations. The Uzbeks probably began forming their distinct language and culture between the fourteenth and sixteenth centuries, as Turkic-speaking groups began increasingly to settle in the cities and towns.[15] The Uzbek tribal leaders led several wars defending their land against the aggression of the *Shahs* of Persia (Iran) and succeeded in maintaining the independence of their states.

In the second half of the nineteenth century, the Russian Empire established its control over the major centers populated by the Uzbeks. Yet many Uzbek communities remained outside the Russian domain in the semi-independent Bukhara Emirate and in Afghanistan. The Soviet nation-state delimitation in the 1920s placed the majority of Uzbeks into a newly established republic—Uzbekistan.

The *Karakalpaks* (or Qaraqalpaqs) are an ethnic group of about 650,000 people (2006 est.). They mainly live in the Karakalpakstan, which occupies the northwestern part of Uzbekistan. Small Karakalpak communities also live in various regions in Afghanistan, Kazakhstan, Kyrgyzstan, and Russia. The overwhelming majority are Sunni Muslims. Most Karakalpaks live in predominantly rural areas and preserve major features of their traditional life. Large families with more than four children are quite common; in 1999, the average size of a Karakalpak rural family was 6.7 people, down from 7.1 in 1989. Several generations often live in the same household or in close neighborhoods. Groups of extended families form a subclan unit called the *koshe*; several *koshe*s make up the *uru*. People are still expected to trace their ancestors back as much as seven generations and to know their tribal affiliation. Historically, the Karakalpaks were engaged in subsistence animal herding, especially sheep, camel and horses, but, in the twentieth century, they were settled and brought to the Soviet *kolkhozes*.

In the sixteenth and seventeenth centuries, the Karakalpak tribes controlled the territory of the lower delta of the Syr Darya, though they frequently moved to the north and south of this area due to pressure from neighbors and to ecological changes, such as droughts and desertification. Throughout the sixteenth and seventeenth centuries, the Karakalpaks were subjects of different powerful neighbors, such as the Bukhara Emirate, the *Kichi Zhuz* (one of the three Kazakh tribal confederations), and the Khiva Khanate. In the eighteenth century, most of the Karakalpak tribes moved to the lower delta of Amu Darya (this territory corresponds to the present Karakalpakistan). Most of the Karakalpaks became subjects of the Russian Empire in the mid-nineteenth century through diplomatic negotiations. In the mid-1920s, Karakalpak Autonomous Oblast was created as a part of Kazakh ASSR, but it ended up as an administrative unit within Uzbekistan.

The *Russians* constitute the largest ethnic minority group in the Central Asian region, though their numbers have been steadily declining since 1991. According to various estimates, there were between 4.5 and 6 million Russians total (2006 est.) in all the five Central Asian republics, including about 4 million in Kazakhstan, 700,000 in Uzbekistan, 330,000 in Kyrgyzstan, 120,000 in Turkmenistan, and 50,000 in Tajikistan. An overwhelming majority of the Russians are Orthodox Christians. Central Asian Russians live mainly in major metropolitan regions and large cities and are often employed in the industrial and service sectors, though large communities of Russians in Kazakhstan and Kyrgyzstan are also engaged in intensive commercial farming.

The Russian migration to and from the region reflects the economic and political growth and decline of the Russian Empire and the Soviet Union. The Russians first arrived in the region in large numbers in the second half of the nineteenth century. Initially, most of them were military personnel of the Russian imperial troops stationed in the strategic cities and towns of the region or peasants and industrial workers who worked in newly established factories and plants. In the early twentieth century, in an effort to escape poverty and economic hardship in Russia proper, large waves of peasant families arrived in Central Asia, especially in the Orenburg, Turkestan, and Western Siberian provinces. After 1924, the Soviet authorities initiated large inflows of Russians to the region; some of them came voluntarily in search of better jobs and economic opportunities, while many others were forcibly relocated to the region during the era of Stalin's purges and major Soviet economic campaigns.

Many of them were skilled workers, engineers, administrators, and managers, who got jobs in the newly established industrials enterprises, mines, factories, and educational institutions. However, after the dissolution of the Soviet Union, in 1991, a significant number of the Russians left the region as a result of the steep economic recession and the political uncertainties of the 1990s, which led to the closure of many industrial enterprises and to escalations of interethnic tensions. In the early 2000s, there were reports that Russians continued to leave the region for Russia, albeit in smaller numbers.

There are many other large and small ethnic groups in Central Asia. Some of the groups, such as the Uigurs, Turks, Arabs, and Kurds, arrived in the region many centuries ago, settling in large and small towns and cities and becoming an inseparable part of the Central Asian nations. Others, such as the Germans, Ukrainians, Koreans, and Poles, moved in mainly during the twentieth century; they still maintain their distinctive cultures and speak own languages at home. Since 1991, some of the ethnic groups, such as the Uigurs, Chinese, and Turks, have been growing relatively fast. At the same time others, such as the Koreans, Germans, Poles, Ukrainians, Byelorussians, Tatars, and Bashkirs, have been declining. Recently, new groups, such as Afghans, Indians, Iranians, and Pakistanis, have all begun moving into the region, though their numbers are still small.

There are also several very small indigenous groups, such as the Yaghnabis, that trace their history to ancient and medieval times and that have preserved their unique cultures and languages in the extremely isolated mountain areas of Tajikistan and Uzbekistan.[16]

CENTRAL ASIAN LANGUAGES

Central Asians love to compare their region to a melting pot where about 100 nationalities and ethnic groups can live together and can speak their own languages. The most widely spoken languages belong to three language groups: Turkic, Iranian, and Slavic.

The language situation in the CARs has been very dynamic and has shifted from one extreme to another during the past 100 years. Until the 1920s, most Central Asians wrote in the Arabic script and used Persian and Turkic languages in folklore and literature, in local administration, and in education. Very few people spoke Russian, probably no more than between 2 and 6 percent of the region's population in the region. The Soviet government initiated a switch from the Arabic script to the Latin alphabet in the 1920s. In the 1940, however, all Central languages switched again, abandoning the Latin for the Cyrillic alphabet. The literary languages were codified, and mass education in national languages was introduced.

Between the 1960s and the mid-1980s the Central Soviet government heavily promoted the Russian language as the lingua franca in all Central Asian republics. It urged that education at all levels be increasingly conducted in Russian; and it also required all administrative, technical, military, and other documentation to be chiefly in Russian. This was often done at the expense of local languages. In the late 1980s and early 1990s, the Central Asian governments demanded greater use of their native languages. All republics in the region passed new language laws that made their local languages the only state languages in their respective countries and initiated a gradual switch from the Russian language to the local tongue in all areas of life, including state administration and education. Some countries, such as Turkmenistan and Uzbekistan, went even further by abandoning the Cyrillic alphabet and re-embracing the Latin. In the newest trend, in the early 2000s, many locals, especially in large cities and metropolitan areas, began learning English. Moreover, youth slang in clubs, discothèques, elite schools, and Internet cafés has been increasingly absorbing many English words to create a colorful body of jargon.[17]

Kazakh Language

The Kazakh language is mainly spoken in Kazakhstan and in some parts of Kyrgyzstan and Uzbekistan, as well as in the Xingjiag Uygur autonomous region in China and in Mongolia. The language belongs to the Kypchak linguistic subgroup of the Turkic group of the Altaic language family. The Kazakh people were among those that used the Arabic alphabet before changing to Latin script in the late 1920s and then to Cyrillic in 1940. The Kazakh language was declared the state language of Kazakhstan in 1991. The contemporary Kazakh language is based on the Cyrillic script, but with a total of 42 letters; 9 letters have been added to the Cyrillic alphabet to reflect certain specifically Kazakh sounds. Distinctive features of the language include correspondence of the Kazakh initial Zh to the initial Y (in Uzbek) or Dz (in Kyrgyz). For example, *zhol* (in Kazakh) corresponds to *yol* (in Uzbek) and *dzhol* (in Kyrgyz) (road). The language is agglutinative, so grammatical functions are indicated by adding various suffixes to fixed stems. Sentence subjects precede predicatives, and the Kazakh language uses postpositions rather than prepositions.

Kyrgyz Language

The Kyrgyz language is the state language of Kyrgyzstan and is also spoken in Kazakhstan, Uzbekistan, Tajikistan, the Xingjiang Uygur autonomous region in China, and some other areas. The language belongs to the linguistic subgroup of the Turkic group of the Altaic language family. Kyrgyz used the Arabic alphabet until the late 1920s; the alphabet was changed to Latin at that time and then to Cyrillic, in 1940. Kyrgyz was declared the state language of Kyrgyzstan in 1990. The contemporary Kyrgyz language is based on the Cyrillic script. Several letters have been added to the Cyrillic alphabet to reflect some specific Kyrgyz language sounds, giving a total of 36 letters. The language is agglutinative, so grammatical functions are indicated by adding various suffixes to fixed stems (e.g., *mekteb* [school], *mektebte* [at school], *mektebim* [my school]). Verbs agree with their subjects in case and number.

Tajiki Language

The official language of Tajikistan is Tajiki. It is very close to Iranian, the official language of Iran, and is also spoken in Afghanistan, Pakistan, and many other countries. The Tajiks are the only Iranian-speaking people in Central Asia. In the 1920s, Tajiki underwent its first major transformation as the government switched from the Arabic to the Latin script in the late 1920s and then to the Cyrillic script in 1940. During this era the Tajiki language absorbed many words from Russian. In the early 1990s, there were debates about switching from the Cyrillic script back to Arabic, but the government decided to retain the Cyrillic alphabet for the time being. As of 2006, Tajiki is based on the Cyrillic alphabet and has 39 letters—33 letters taken from the Russian alphabet and 6 letters created to reflect specific Tajiki sounds.

Turkmen Language

The Turkmen language is spoken in Turkmenistan and in some parts of Kazakhstan, Uzbekistan, Afghanistan, Iran, and Iraq. The language belongs to the Oghuz, also known as the Southern or Southwestern Turkic linguistic subgroup of the Turkic group of the Altaic language family. Like the other languages of the region, Turkmen used the Arabic script before the Bolshevik Revolution, and this was changed first to the Latin, in 1929, and then to the Cyrillic, in 1940. The new alphabet *(Täze Elipbiýi),* based on the Latin script, was introduced in 1995. It consists of 30 letters: 8 vowels and 22 consonants. The Turkmen language is agglutinative, with grammatical functions indicated by adding various suffixes to fixed stems, and there are no irregular verbs.

Uzbek Language

The Uzbek language is spoken in Uzbekistan and in some parts of Kazakhstan, Tajikistan, Turkmenistan, Afghanistan, and China. The language belongs to the Eastern Turkic (Karluk) linguistic subgroup of the Turkic group of the Altaic language family. There are many dialects spoken in the country, but the modern Uzbek language was codified on the basis of the Tashkent and Ferghana dialects. The Arabic script used for Uzbek was changed first to Latin in 1927 and to Cyrillic in 1940. In 1994, the Uzbek government decided to switch the Uzbek alphabet from Cyrillic back to Latin, but it was agreed that there was a need for a grace period of about 10 years. The modern Uzbek alphabet based on the Latin script has 26 letters: 8 vowels and 16 consonants, with three letter-combinations.

Russian Language

Russian is widely spoken in Central Asia, though since 1991 its use has been in continuous decline. Literary Russian is based on the Moscow (central) dialect and is written in Cyrillic. Of the many Russian dialects that can be found in Russia proper, the Russian spoken in Central Asia is mostly the southern dialects of the language. But, also, Central Asian Russian speakers tend to use classical Russian, which has fewer borrowings from foreign languages, while in present-day Russia proper, the language of the streets and the mass media tends to contain more borrowed words, especially from English. The Russian language is still widely used in educational institutions across the Central Asian republics, especially at university level (with the exception of Turkmenistan).

Other Languages

Ethnic minorities in Central Asian republics often use their own languages at home and in everyday life; for example, Germans speak various dialects of German languages, Tatars use Tatar language, and so on. Foreign languages such as English, German, and French were always popular among young people and were taught at schools and universities. In a recent trend, there has been a sharp increase in the use of the Turkish language, as many students have received their education in the Turkish Republic and Turkey opened or supported many schools, colleges, and universities. Several private and semiprivate organizations launched newspapers in Turkish to target the Central Asian audience, with mixed results. Turkey also agreed to transmit its television and radio programs to the region, and their audience has been slowly but steadily growing. The Arabic language is also steadily gaining popularity as it is taught at all *madrasas* (religious Islamic schools), and many universities introduced Arabic studies in the 1990s.

Old *berkutchi* (bird hunter) with his hunting bird. Courtesy of the author, 2006.

THE GREAT SILK ROAD

Many Central Asian scholars love to highlight the richness of the Central Asian civilizations, which absorbed the best traditions of ancient Greek, Persian, Chinese, and Indian cultures. They strongly believe that the ancient trade route—called the Great Silk Road—significantly contributed to these interchanges.[18]

The Silk Road connected China with western Europe, with few interruptions, for nearly two millennia. The road, which is about 5,000 miles long (more than 7,500 kilometers), started somewhere in what is now central and northern China. One of the routes passed through China's western provinces, crossed the Tian Shan and Pamir mountains, and continued through Khotan, Yarkent, Balkh, Zemm, and Merv (the territories of present-day Uzbekistan, Turkmenistan, and Afghanistan). The other route went through Turfan, Kashgar, Samarkand, Bukhara, Amul, and Merv. Then it continued to the eastern Mediterranean Sea and to Byzantium or Rome.[19] From time to time, the route would change due to political turbulence, military campaigns, or climatic changes. In the late medieval era, the major cities on the road also served the trade between India and Persia and the rising eastern European states, including Russia. Merchants carried wool, karakul (astrakhan fur), gold, silver, and weaponry to the East and brought carpets, silk, opium, spices, and luxury goods to the West.

The first recorded references to the Great Silk Road can be dated to between the second and first centuries B.C. The road had its peaks, when there was peace in the vast steppe of Eurasia, and its nadirs at times of war in the region. The first Western description of the road is attributed to the Venetian Marco Polo (1254–1324).[20] He traveled along the road and reached the court of Kublai Khan (1215–1294), the Mongol emperor and the grandson of Genghis Khan.

The importance of the Great Silk Road is difficult to overstate. It contributed to cultural and scholarly exchanges between people of the East and the West, and many people received their education and enriched their knowledge of geography, algebra, astronomy, medicine, and many other subjects by studying at the numerous centers of academic learning in the ancient and medieval cities on the Great Silk Road. The road also contributed immensely to the wealth of Central Asian cities on the trade route, including Bukhara, Khiva, Merv, and Samarkand. However, it had practically disappeared by the seventeenth and eighteenth centuries with the rise of cheaper maritime routes from Europe to India and China, and due to political instability in Central Asia. Central Asians benefited from the Great Silk Road by collecting custom duties or providing military convoys to the trade caravans. Numerous remains of local medieval inns *(karavan-sarais)* can still be found in the territories of the region. Some contemporary scholars claim that the entire history of the Central Asian region is simply inseparable from the history of the Silk Road.

HISTORY

The history of Central Asia is intriguing, enriched as it was by interactions with the ancient civilizations of Greece, Persia, East Asia, and the Middle East. Numerous ruins and remains of ancient cities may be found in the lands of the region, making it one of the most fascinating destinations in the region for historians, archeologists, and curious tourists. Many cities, such as ancient Merv, Samarqand, and Bukhara, were destroyed many times and reemerged literally from the ashes, while others could never recover their past glories and left empty mausoleums, walls, ruins of palaces, and magnificent monuments buried in sand.

A number of powerful forces significantly affected the history of the region, and we have to take these into account if we are to conceptualize Central Asian history. Some scholars claim that the region's main cultural characteristics were formed by the centuries-long interaction between nomads and settlers and between nomadic cultures and the cultures of the oases. Others emphasize that Central Asia was a region where the vigorous and energetic culture of numerous Turkic-speaking tribes came face to face with the refined culture of the Persian-speaking communities. Yet others note that Central Asia has historically been a frontier region where the three greatest civilizations—Chinese, Christian, and Islamic—met one another, and so it has had to accommodate all interests through interactions and interchanges.

At first look the history of Central Asia looks like a chaotic calendar of wars, military campaigns, and numberless attempts to build mighty empires. Numerous khans, warriors, sultans, and generals fought each other and took over the thrones. Many chronologists and historians have tried to meet the challenge in explaining the cycles of war and peace throughout Central Asian history but have failed. The most difficult part in an attempt to conceptualize that history is in the interpretation of the nomadic history and nomadic circles of political life.[21]

Ancient Empires

It was probably in the ninth and eighth centuries B.C. that people of the region developed agriculture and industries, gradually became involved with international trade, and acquired military and administrative skills. The mountainous and desert terrain and remoteness from the major centers of Chinese, Indian, and Persian civilizations helped local rulers to preserve a significant degree of autonomy and made it very difficult for foreign invaders to establish political and military control over the region. At the same time, geography and the physical terrain made it very difficult for ambitious local leaders to build large, centralized states. Historians still debate the history and mysteries of the ancient states and empires in Central Asia; thousands of artifacts, jewelry, fragments of statues, and terracotta shards have been discovered, but historians have little written information on the political history and everyday life in those empires. And yet, the scholarly community has reached some consensus about the history of several large ancient empires that emerged in the region, including Bactria, the Parthian Empire, Sogdiana, and the Kushan Empire.

Ancient Bactria emerged in the eighth and seventh centuries B.C. It was home to a Persian-speaking people and is thought to be the birthplace of Zoroaster, the prophet of ancient Persia. Bactria is situated between the Hindu Kush and the Amu Darya River, in today's Afghanistan, Tajikistan, and Uzbekistan. Its capital city, Bactra, was located in northern Afghanistan. Bactria was located on the strategic route linking Europe and China via western

Asia. To control this area and to try to subdue the troublesome nomads who inhabited the Bactrian territory, the Persian king Cyrus the Great (585–529 B.C.) incorporated Bactria and the nomadic Bactrians into the vast Persian Empire that once stretched from Egypt to India. The Bactrians nevertheless retained some autonomy. Alexander the Great (356–323 B.C.) defeated Bactria in 328 B.C. and installed a Greek governor before continuing to India on his campaign. For the next half-century, Bactria was ruled by Alexander's Macedonian Greek successors, but during the reign of the satrap Diodotus I Soter (reigned c. 256–235 B.C.), Bactria revolted and became independent. Bactria remained an island of Greek culture in Central Asia and at its zenith controlled a significant part of what is now Afghanistan, Tajikistan, and Uzbekistan. Around the mid-second century B.C., however, an invading force of Saka nomads from the steppes overran the country.

Sogdiana was an ancient state situated to the north of Bactria, in the fertile valleys on the Zeravshan River (modern western Tajikistan and southern Uzbekistan), though at the zenith of its power it expanded its political control over a significantly larger territory. It existed between the eighth and seventh centuries B.C. and the second century B.C. Ancient chronicles report that Alexander the Great defeated the Sogdian ruler and included Sogdia in the Bactrian Greek kingdom. The state collapsed under the constant attacks of various nomadic tribes in the mid-second century B.C., but its cities, which were under the control of various rulers, remained prosperous and played important roles on the Great Silk Road.

The Parthian Empire existed between the mid-third century B.C. and the second century A.D. At an early stage, it had its center in Nisa city (later moved to the southwest) and controlled territory in what is now southern Turkmenistan, Uzbekistan, and northern Iran. Through a successful series of wars, it expanded its possessions, first in the Persian Gulf and then all the way to Palestine. This empire was most famous for successfully campaigning against the most powerful force of that era—the Roman Empire—and for its tolerance toward various religious practices, including Zoroastrianism. At its height, the Parthian Empire was among the largest in the world of its time, though we know little about political and cultural life in this state. In the second century A.D., the state was weakened and began crumbling, and in the end it was captured by Persia's Sasanid dynasty.

The Kushan Empire emerged in the first century A.D. and lasted probably until the fourth century A.D. During its early stages, it had its center somewhere in southern Uzbekistan, but eventually it moved its capital to the south, to what is now the Peshawar province of Pakistan. The Kushans successfully campaigned in the south, establishing control over a vast territory of what is now Afghanistan, Pakistan, and northwestern India.[22] The Kushan

Empire was famous for embracing and spreading Buddhism in greater Central Asia, as during this era numerous temples and monasteries were built in various parts of the region. In fact, the Buddhist monuments carved during the reign of the Kushans in Bamyan province remained the largest in the world until they were destroyed by Taliban troops in 2001. Like its Roman counterpart in the west, the Kushan Empire experienced decay and crumbled under attacks from various seminomadic tribes in the third and fourth centuries A.D.

Between the second and fourth centuries A.D., all Central Asian sedentary states and empires experienced crisis. Despite their cultural, economic, and even technological superiority, the ancient states proved to be helpless when facing the waves of seminomadic barbarian tribes from the Great Eurasian steppe who invaded the sedentary oases and overran their fortresses and citadels.

Nomadic Empires

Nomadic armies had an enormous comparative advantage in military warfare.[23] They utilized the maneuverability of their light cavalry equipped with highly effective composite curved bows, the speed of their strategic movements, and an endless supply of both horses and trained cavalry. These armies were extremely cheap to maintain since they were based on a combination of compulsory enlistment and a small, core professional army. It was possible to quickly enlist commoners with their own equipment for a military operation, and it was easy to dismantle the whole army upon completing a campaign.

Nomadic tribes, especially Turkic-speaking groups, contributed greatly to the history of the region, though the early history of Turkic peoples began in a different place.[24] Most Turkic-speaking Central Asians trace their ancestors' homeland to the territory that is now northern Mongolia, Russian Altai, and southern Siberia, close to the basin of the Orkhon and the Yenisey Rivers. The history of the ancient Turks and their mysterious nomadic khanates is still hotly debated as it is very difficult to trace; the nomads did not leave substantial written records and did not build big cities, towns, or castles. For various unexplained reasons that might have included changes in their social structure and social organization, demographic factors, and improvements in military technologies and tactics, nomads and pastoral nomads from eastern Asia—the area of modern Mongolia, northern China, and Russia's southern Siberia—began overcoming their tribal divisions and started organizing large and mobile forces to launch military campaigns against the close and distant sedentary states in China, the Eurasian steppe, the Persian world, the edges of the Fertile Crescent, and even Europe.

These large population movements in the area populated by the nomads began in the first and second centuries A.D. or even earlier, but especially large campaigns began in the third and fourth centuries A.D. and continued for nearly a millennium. Numerous Turkic-speaking tribes were brought together by ambitious and capable khans who established control over the territory of what is now southern Siberia, western China, and, gradually, Central Asia. Between the fourth and thirteenth centuries A.D., more than a dozen large and small khanates and nomadic empires emerged and established their control over the whole or parts of Central Asia from their bases on the Eurasian steppe. These Turkic khanates waged frequent campaigns against the Chinese Empire and Central Asian city states, establishing many successive Turkic khanates, including, most notably, the Turkic Khanate (552–745), the Uigurs' Khanate (745–840), the Karakhanid Khanate (eighth and ninth centuries), and the Seljuks' Khanate (eleventh through thirteenth centuries).

The Huns were among the first and probably the most famous steppe warriors from Central Asia. They emerged in the fourth century from the Eurasian steppe, defeating their enemies on the Volga River and steadily moving west until they reached Central Europe, in the fifth century. The Huns defeated the Ostrogoths and the Visigoths and successfully fought the Eastern Roman Empire and threatened its capital, Constantinople. They reached the zenith of their power in the mid-fifth century under the rule of King Attila (?–453). Under his leadership, the Huns devastated southern Europe by crushing every power in central and southern Europe. Only in the late 450s, after the death of Attila and the division of his powerful empire between his sons, were the Huns weakened and ultimately defeated.

Another nomadic empire was the Turkic Khanate (*Gokturk*—"Blue Turk" in Turkic) (552–744). A capable Turkic leader, Bumin Khaghan (also called Tuman Khan), united numerous tribes in his native Altai area and by 552 A.D. had established control over the territory from Mongolia and China to the Aral Sea area. After the death of Bumin Khaghan, his sons quarreled and began a civil war that continued on and off for nearly 70 years. By the mid-seventh century, the empire was split into two parts—the Eastern and the Western Khanates. The Western Turkic Khanate established and maintained control over the *Jetysuu* and *Maveranahr* areas. The *Gokturk* Khanate was among the first Turkic empires to manifest the dawning Turkic domination of the Greater Eurasian steppe. The *Gokturks* were also the power that directly collided with the expanding Muslim Arabs, halting their advance to the east.

The Arabs who established their control over the Khorasan in the 630s and 650s campaigned in *Maveranahr* for nearly 60 years, until the death of their general, Qutayba ibn Muslim, in 715, in Ferghana. Yet, the *Gokturks* who settled in the *Jetysuu* and *Maveranahr* were evidently among the first Turks to embrace Islam. This was in sharp contrast to the eastern Turks, who predominantly followed shamanism. In the mid-eighth century, the empire began crumbling due to various factors, including internal instability, pressure from the Chinese Empire and the rebellion of several tribal groups led by the Uigurs.

The Uigurs' Khanate (745–840) replaced the *Gokturks* and took control of most of the territories controlled by the *Gokturks* but maintained their power base in the area to the east of Central Asia, with the capital in Ordu Balig (Qarbalghasun). At the peak of their power, the Uigurs extended their dominions from western China to the Caspian Sea shores. In an important development during the Uigur reign, Manichaeism and Buddhism flourished in the Tarim basin and expanded their influence well into the *Jetysuu* area. Moreover, in the late eighth century, the Uigurs declared Manichaeism the state religion. The Uigur Khanate fell to pieces between the 820s and the 840s, due to internal strife and famine.

The Karakhanid Khanate (840s–1040s) became another important nomadic state that established its control over Central Asia. The Karakhanid tribal confederation emerged as a formidable power that united tribes in the *Jetysuu* area, western Kashgar, and eastern *Maveranahr* and left important footprints in the history of Central Asia. First, the Karakhanid elite were converted to Islam, although their conversion was to its popular form, introduced to them by members of wandering mystic Islamic brotherhoods—the Sufis. Second, the Turkic-speaking Karakhanids began settling in the core of Central Asia, in the area around the Syr Darya River and in the eastern parts of *Maveranahr,* gradually Turkicizing the latter areas.

The Seljuks' Empire (eleventh through mid-thirteenth centuries) was established in a very different place and had a much greater impact on Persia, the Fertile Crescent, and Europe than its predecessors. This Turkic dynasty was founded by Seljuk, the leader of a relatively large tribal group that belonged to a powerful Oguz tribal confederation with a power base around the Syr Darya River basin. For various reasons, tribes led by Seljuk left their homeland and campaigned in the southwestern outskirts of Central Asia and in Khorasan. The Seljuks first established their control over the jewels of the Central Asian civilizations—Khorezm (Khwarezm), Merv, Herat, Balh, and other cities on the lucrative trade road between China and the West, the Great Silk Road. They used intrigues, skillful diplomacy, and military power to acquire vast territories in Central Asia, Persia, and Mesopotamia, including what is now northern Afghanistan, Iran, Iraq, and other areas.

Between 1040 and 1055, Togrul Beg, a ruler of Seljuk tribes, captured Baghdad, then the capital of the Islamic world, and, in a very important move to legitimize his political authority in the Muslim world, he pronounced himself a protector of the Caliph, the spiritual leader of the Sunni Muslims. His successors, Alp Arslan and Malik Shah, campaigned in Syria, Palestine, and even Asia Minor (Anatolia), which they took from the Byzantines. In 1071, the Seljuks defeated the Byzantines in the decisive battle of Manzikert. However, soon after, in the early twelfth century, the Seljuks Empire experienced a rapid decline, due to internal strife and a series of diplomatic missteps, and collapsed. Its small remnants in Anatolia survived until the mid-thirteenth century but were defeated and subdued by the Mongols.

The Seljuks Empire was very different from other Turkic states. Its leaders adapted sedentary Persian culture and used the Persian language and Persian administrators to a much greater degree than had other Turkic Khans. They also attempted to gain legitimacy in the Muslim world not only by crude power but also by presenting themselves as pious and devoted Muslims. By capturing and settling on the outskirts of the Byzantine Empire in Asia Minor, they paved the way for the emergence of one of the most important players in European politics for nearly 500 years—the Ottoman Empire.

Settled Centers

Relations between the nomads and the sedentary populations of Central Asia were uneasy and complicated. The nomads regularly invaded cities and towns, taking large booties and demanding subordination and regular tributes. Otherwise, they had little interest in becoming involved in the complex administrative, political, and economic developments of the sedentary centers. They were often satisfied with these arrangements and left administration and governance in the hands of sedentary bureaucrats and aristocrats. Over time, local aristocrats learned to use nomadic forces to their own advantage, regularly hiring nomadic armies to fight in their frequent campaigns against their opponents, to settle scores with their enemies, to fight off various contenders for power, or to acquire power for themselves. Thus, there was established a kind of fragile balance and coexistence between the "wild steppe" and the "civilized centers."

Several sedentary centers played an exceptionally important role in the cultural and political development of the Central Asian region.

Bukhara (also Bukhoro) was one of the largest cities on an oasis on the lower stream of the Zeravshan River's basin. Ancient Bukhara emerged as a center of the important agricultural region in *Maveranahr* and by the fifth century A.D. it had became an important entrepôt on the Great Silk Road. In the seventh and eighth centuries A.D., Muslim Arabs established their control over the city, making it an important administrative, political, and economic center in the area. In the ninth and tenth centuries, Bukhara was included in the powerful Sasanid Empire, becoming also an important centre of Islamic learning. In the thirteenth century, the city was destroyed several times by various Mongol armies, and, according to the Russian orientalist Vasilei Bartold, it was deserted for nearly a decade. It took several centuries before Bukhara was restored to its past glory. It became the capital of the Bukhara Emirate in the sixteenth century.

Merv (also Margiana) was one of the ancient trading and industrial centers of Khorasan, the largest city in the Merv oasis and, probably, in the whole region before the Mongol invasion. It was situated in what is now Mary *welayat* of Turkmenistan, about 19 miles (30 kilometers) east of the contemporary city of Mary. Ancient Merv became an important entrepôt on the Great Silk Road and was a large trading center in ancient times. A small town was probably founded on the site in the seventh and sixth centuries B.C. and gradually became an important center of the Merv oasis. In the fourth century B.C., it was conquered by Alexander the Great and renamed Alexandria. It was embroiled in several wars and in the third century was included into the ancient Bactrian state.

The Bactrian state, however, did not last long, and Margiana experienced turbulent times. In the seventh century A.D., it was taken over by the Arabs and became politically important in the Abbasid Caliphate. Caliph Al-Mamun spent several years in Merv in the early ninth century, making the city a major political center of his caliphate. At its zenith, between the tenth and eleventh centuries, it was part of the Seljuk Empire and was the site of numerous monumental mosques, *madrasas*, magnificent palaces, *karavan-sarais*, and administrative buildings. In the thirteenth century, the city was destroyed by the Mongols, who not only stormed the city and slaughtered most of its people but also destroyed vital water dams and the irrigation system of the oasis. After the Mongol invasion, Merv never recovered its past glory and remained a relatively small city.

Khorezm (also Kwarezm) was an agricultural, trading, and industrial center and one of the oldest centers of settled civilization in Central Asia. It is mentioned in *Avesta* and in ancient Persian writings. The city is situated on the fertile delta of Amu Darya River and close to the Aral Sea. It became an important agricultural center and a large regional trading hub probably in the sixth and fifth centuries B.C. In the fourth century B.C., its rulers attempted to build an alliance with Alexander the Great, but Alexander chose not to venture into the hostile tribal areas around the Aral Sea. Khorezm was embroiled in several wars and in the first and second centuries A.D. was included into the Kushan Empire, but it became independent in the third century A.D. In the early eighth century, it was taken over by the Arabs and became one of the important political centers in the region. At its zenith, between the eleventh and the thirteenth centuries, it was a center of the empire ruled by the Khorezmshah dynasty, whose rulers controlled vast areas from the Caspian Sea to the Syr Darya River and the *Jetysuu* region. Khorezm was destroyed by the Mongols in 1220; they stormed the city and killed most of its people. Gradually, it recovered, but it was later devastated by Timur (Tamerlane). It continued to be a regional political and trade center until the seventeenth century, when the rulers moved their capital to Khiva city.

Samarqand is considered the oldest center of settled civilization in Central Asia and has been an important agricultural, trading, and industrial center since ancient times. It is situated at the fertile oasis and close the midstream of the Zeravshan River's basin. The city was an important agricultural center and a large regional trading hub by the seventh and sixth centuries B.C. In the fourth century B.C., Alexander the Great conquered the city. Samarqand rose to particular prominence as one of the most international trading entrepôts on the Great Silk Road. In the early eighth century, it was taken over by the Arabs, who made it an important political center in the region and one of the most prominent centers of Islamic art and learning. Destroyed by the Mongols in the thirteenth century, the city was restored a few decades later. At its zenith, in the fourteenth century, Samarqand became a capital of the Timurid (Tamerlane) Empire, becoming the largest urban center in Central Asia. However, it was devastated by campaigning warlords in the sixteenth and seventeenth centuries. It continued to be an agricultural and trade center in the area in the eighteenth and nineteenth centuries, though it lost its status as political capital of the area to Bukhara city.

Mongol and Timurid Empires

The next page in Central Asian history is probably one of the darkest for many countries and peoples in the vast areas of the Eurasian continent. The Mongols, a pastoral people now found predominantly in East Asia, rose to prominence in the early thirteenth century under the leadership of the Mongol conqueror Genghis Khan. Under his leadership and that of his successor, the Mongols established the most powerful army of that time and ruled the world's largest empire.

As a first step, the Mongols subdued rival groups, including Tatars (Western Europeans used this name in the reference to the Mongols) and Turkic-speaking tribes. Many of these tribes joined the Mongol army through negotiations or were forcibly pressed to do so. The Mongol army therefore consisted not only of Mongols but also of numerous Turkic-speaking people, and those tribes would play an important role in later stages of the Mongol Empire.

The large, well-disciplined Mongol army launched a major campaign against the Central Asian states between 1219 and 1221. The army of Khwaresm-Shah (Khoresm-Shah) was too corrupted and too disorganized to offer any formidable resistance. In many cases, the military units simply deserted the cities they were assigned to defend. Within a short period of time, Otrar, Samarqand, Bukhara, and many other urban centers had fallen. In 1221, Mongol troops destroyed Khwarezm, Khwarezm-Shah's capital. The Mongols employed superior tactics in besieging these fortresses and, despite heroic resistance, the cities were taken and sacked. As a next step, the Mongols captured and destroyed the ancient city of Merv, one of the most populous cities in the world at that time. The destruction included Merv's ancient library—believed to hold one of the largest collections of ancient Central Asian, Iranian, and Middle Eastern manuscripts. The conquest of Central Asia was complete, and the area was incorporated into the Jagatai Khanate, which existed for nearly 150 years.

The Mongol invasion was particularly devastating for Central Asian civilization, as the Mongols not only destroyed the cities and towns but also damaged the irrigation systems, burned forests and gardens, and killed entire populations of many districts and provinces. The ecological damage done by this conquest was so great that many oases and valleys were turned into deserts and did not recover sufficiently for habitation and cultivation until the modern era. Yet, for all that, the Mongols were not beyond being significantly influenced by those they had subjugated. Before long, the Turkic elements and Turkic language grew in dominance, and the conquerors were gradually converted to Islam, the dominant religion of the region's major urban centers.

Like many other nomadic conquerors, the Mongols built a vast but unstable empire. Very soon, numerous successors of the Empire's founders began to compete with each other, plunging the whole region into a series of wars and bitter rivalries. This chaotic environment of uncertainty, political instability, and unrestrained rivalry provided an excellent breeding ground for the rise of a new leadership strong enough to challenge the status quo. In the mid-fourteenth century, just such a leader emerged in the region.

Tamerlane, the leader of a very small group of tribal fighters, grew to prominence in the 1360s by gathering around him a formidable force of several hundred men. Gradually he attracted the attention of local rulers. He beat all other contenders and established his control first over Samarqand city and then over the rest of the region. But his ambitions did not stop there, for he now declared that he wanted nothing less than the restoration of the Mongol Empire of Genghis Khan. Tamerlane organized several successful campaigns into surrounding territories, erasing all competing principalities and trade centers and taking all valuable assets. He established Samarqand as his capital. But, in sharp contrast to the Mongol rulers, he invested in building glorious palaces, public houses, mosques, and *madrasas*. He organized one of the best armies of his era, consisting of heavy and light cavalry, infantry, and military engineers.[25]

With minimal delay once he has consolidated his local rule, Tamerlane launched campaigns into more distant territories. In the 1380s, he conquered a significant part of Persia. This was followed by military campaigns in the Caucasus, in 1392, and in India, between 1398 and 1399. He also defeated Khan Tokhtamısh, of the powerful Golden Horde, in several decisive campaigns between 1394 and 1395. Although he never fought in the Mediterranean or Europe, his actions greatly affected the development of the Western world. One of the most significant and important events for Eurasian history was the defeat of Bayazid I (Yilderim—"lightning"—in Turkic), Sultan of the Ottoman Turks (ruled 1389–1402). This constrained the Ottomans' ability to launch major offensives in Europe for many years to come and significantly redrew the political map of the Middle East. In 1405, Tamerlane decided to mount another far-afield expedition, this time to China. However, his army suffered a winter of unprecedented cold, and the king himself died during this ill-fated expedition, allegedly due to pneumonia.

Tamerlane left a controversial legacy in the region. On the one hand, he was a patron of the arts, architecture, and the sciences, making Samarqand a center of learning and crafts. During his reign, architects from all over the world built many spectacular palaces, public buildings, *madrasas,* and mosques in his empire, the most celebrated of which were in Samarqand. Because of the centralization of political and economic power, trade flourished during the Tamerlane era. On the other hand, he became notorious for cruelty and atrocities in his never-ending wars and military campaigns. He ordered the destruction of many architectural wonders in the region, such as the grand mosques in Kune-Urgench and in other Central Asian cities, to make sure that no one would rival the glory and magnificence of his capital. On several occasions, he ordered atrocities that appalled even his contemporaries, who were used to the bloodshed and cruelties of their era. For example, in 1387, he ordered the massacre of all the citizens of Esfahan (Iran)—about 70,000 people—and commanded his troops to construct towers of their skulls.

The Tamerlane Empire that stretched from India and China to the Mediterranean Sea was revealed as essentially unstable without the centralizing force of his personality; many parts began breaking away immediately after his death. However, his dynasty, the Timurids, ruled Transoxiana and Khorasan for nearly 100 years. One of his descendants, Babur, who was forced to flee his domain, founded the powerful Mogul Empire of India, in 1526.

Era of Decline

As the Tamerlane Empire disintegrated, the whole region was plunged into a cycle of never-ending rivalries and wars. As in the past, nomadic khans often played an important role in the dynastic competitions and conflicts. Once in power, they regularly launched campaigns into neighboring territories or turned their weapons against yesterday's allies for loot and in order to provide a source of income for their nomadic armies. In this environment, rulers relied on military campaigns, as dwindling budgets and local taxes on impoverished peasants, traders, and craftsmen could not cover the rising appetites of the army commanders and officers. In turn, this led to the further militarization of Central Asian society, with numerous feudal semi-independent principalities and states diverting significant resources from economic development to expensive military adventures. This also harmed intraregional and international trade—an important source of revenue for state budgets, of new technologies for the economy, and of new ideas for society. Military action also led to ecological damage, as warlords often neglected investment into the irrigation infrastructure and in some cases ordered their armies to destroy the irrigation systems of their competitors.

This perpetual cycle of wars led not only to economic decline and falling standards of living but also to the perpetuation of economic, military, and intellectual backwardness for several centuries. By the seventeenth and eighteenth centuries, three states had emerged in Central Asia that constantly weakened one another in never-ending quarrels.

The Bukhara Emirate *(Bukhoro Amirligi)* emerged as a feudal state with its center in Bukhara (present-day Uzbekistan). It was established in 1557 by a khan from the Sheybani family, after the collapse and disintegration of the Timurid state. At its zenith, the state controlled the territory of *Maveranahr,* parts of Khorasan, and northern Afghanistan. In 1753, a khan from the Uzbek tribal dynasty Mangyt captured Bukhara and established a new dynasty. His successors, however, exhausted the emirate's army in a series of wars with Afghanistan, Iran, and the neighboring Central Asian states. Bukhara's rulers portrayed themselves as successors of Timur and copied him by sponsoring restoration and some construction works—mainly mosques and *madrasas*—in an attempt revive the glory of the Timurid era.

The Khiva Khanate emerged in the sixteenth century in the territory of present-day Turkmenistan and northwestern Uzbekistan. The Khanate was established when a local ruler asserted his power after the disintegration of the Timurid state. At its height, the state controlled vast territories of contemporary eastern Turkmenistan and western Uzbekistan, and its merchants maintained trade relations with close and distant partners, including India, Persia, and Russia. In the early eighteenth century, khans from the Kungrat tribal dynasty seized political power. Khiva's rulers had fiercely competed with Iran and the neighboring Bukhara Emirate, exhausting the Khanate's army in a series of wars.

The Kokand (Qokand) Khanate emerged in the eighteenth century. It was a small breakaway principality in the eastern part of the Bukhara Emirate centered in the fertile Ferghana Valley. In 1710, Shoukrukh Beg, of the Uzbek tribal dynasty Ming, seceded from Bukhara and established the city of Kokand as the capital of the Khanate. The Kokand rulers gradually expanded their territory, over time capturing Khojent, Osh, Tashkent, and other cities. Between the second half of the eighteenth century and the beginning of the nineteenth century, Kokand colonized almost all the territories of what is now Kyrgyzstan, parts of Tajikistan, and eastern Uzbekistan.

All these khanates were engaged in selfish and never-ending campaigns against one another. They devastated one another's economies and failed to modernize their own armies, political systems, or economies, remaining weak oriental despotic states well into the modern era.

European Contacts and the Russian Empire

By the seventeenth and eighteenth centuries, Central Asia had gradually become terra incognita for Europeans, isolated as it was from growing international trade and outside the major commercial communication lines because of the collapse of the Great Silk Road. Its relative remoteness and political instability made any travel to the region extremely dangerous and added to the region's isolation. Although the Central Asians had continued to maintain their cultural, trade, intellectual, and military relations with some countries in South Asia, and to some degree with the Chinese, Persian, and Ottoman Empires, Europeans knew little about political developments in Central Asia.

Numerous wars and conflicts ruined the land and economies of the Central Asian tribal confederations and of the Bukhara, Khiva, and Kokand Khanates. Some tribes accepted political and military control by the Central Asian khanates. Others began seeking allies outside the region. For example, throughout the eighteenth century, several Kazakh tribes and tribal groups negotiated peaceful deals with the Russian Empire. In the eighteenth and early nineteenth centuries, some Turkmen tribes on the shore of the Caspian Sea established well-developed trade and political contacts with the Russian Empire. There were reports that leaders of some Kyrgyz tribes sent several delegations to the British, Chinese, and Russian emperors asking for their help or protection. But the Russian and British were slow to move into the region, as they were busy with their own internal issues or with expanding their empires into other territories.

The situation changed, however, in the middle of the nineteenth century. The Russians became increasingly interested in reaching the Central Asian market for their goods, securing the land trade routes with Persia and India, and halting the British advance from their bases in northern India toward Afghanistan and Central Asia. This race for influence in Central Asia and the associated bitter British-Russian rivalry became known as the Great Game. British strategists argued that the Russians might advance to Afghanistan and Persia, thereby threatening the maritime trade routes in the Middle East, and that they might stir up mutinies in the Indian colonies in order to weaken the British Empire. Russian strategists, in turn, saw great economic and military benefits in advancing into Central Asia and further to the south and considered that from this base they could project their military power into the British colonies and dependencies in case Russian-British relations turned sour.[26]

After Russia's defeat in the Crimean War (1853–1856) and especially after abolishing serfdom (1861), Tsar Alexander II (ruled 1855–1881) and his ministers opted for an advance into Turkistan through the Kazakh steppe. In 1868, Russian troops subjugated the Bukhara Emirate and took over Samarqand. In 1873, they defeated the Khiva Khanate. Then, in an important battle at Geok Tepe fortress, in January 1881, the independent-minded Turkmen tribes were also defeated, but it would take several years before all major Turkmen groups finally accepted Russian rule.

Between 1855 and 1864, the Kyrgyz tribes in the Ysyk-Kol valley, Chatkal, and other areas came under Russian protection, a step directly counter to the interests of the Kokand Khanate. Imperial Russian troops soon collided with the Khanate, which had already been weakened considerably in military power by mass uprisings among the Kyrgyz tribes, its own internal conflicts, and the cruelty of Kokand's ruler, Khudoyar Khan. Kokand was consequently unable to offer significant resistance to the Russian troops led by Generals Mikhail Cherniaev, Konstantin Von Kaufman, and Mikhail Skobelev, and they conquered Tashkent in 1865, followed by Kokand, Osh, and Andijan, in 1875. But it took more years before the Russians overcame the residual popular resistance, in the form of a "holy war" supported by some of the Ferghana Valley's Kyrgyz tribes. Finally, they negotiated a settlement with Kurmanjan Datkha (the "Kyrgyz queen," as she was often called by the Russians), the leader of the Kyrgyz tribes in Alai. The influential Kyrgyz tribes under her leadership accepted the status of a Russian protectorate.

By the end of the nineteenth century, the Russians and the British had negotiated spheres of influence in the Central Asian region and in Persia, with the British government recognizing Russian "interests" in western Turkistan and the Russians reciprocating with regard to British interests in Persia and

Afghanistan. Around the same time, Saint Petersburg forced the Chinese imperial government to recognize Russian control over Central Asia, thus establishing the official border between the two empires.

The European colonization of the Central Asian region brought significant changes to Central Asia between the 1890s and 1917. One set of changes arose out of the arrival of capitalism and the beginning of the colonial exploitation of the region's natural resources. Capitalism created powerful market forces and economic initiatives for rapid economic growth and technological changes. Within a few decades, the local economies experienced major transformations, as numerous new and old cities and towns began flourishing in place of the *karavan-sarais* and fortresses. There also was a significant increase in and diversification of trade within the region and with Russia, Iran, and China.

In the early 1800s, it could take weeks of dangerous travel with trade caravans, fighting off marauders and greedy local warlords, to reach bazaars in neighboring cities, let alone in neighboring countries. This situation radically changed with the establishment of Russian military control and especially with the completion of the Transcaspian railway (1888) and the Orenburg-Tashkent line (1905). The new mode of transportation made trade between Russia and Central Asia easier and faster. Steel, glassware, and other industrial goods, as well as grain, were brought to the local markets in exchange for primary products such as cotton, leather, and silk. Hundreds of small workshops and plants were opened in major towns and cities all over the region, producing or repairing agricultural equipment and processing agricultural products (leather, wool, and so on) for export to Russia. New technologies in land cultivation and a better standard of agricultural equipment led to significant increases in productivity. New commercial crops were introduced to local farmers, as many people gradually began to cultivate tobacco and cotton. By 1917, a number of small mines (lead, copper, coal) had opened.

Economic changes and growing trade contributed to changes in the social structure. More families abandoned subsistence agriculture and switched to commercial crop cultivation or animal husbandry. Some of the poorest members of society left agriculture altogether in search of new sources of income. They accepted wage labor in various workshops or plants, accumulating industrial and managerial skills. Others were trapped in misery, hunger, and hardship. The new economic realities also began to erode the tribal and regional isolation and affected the nucleus of traditional Central Asian society—the extended family—as people began to engage in various economic activities outside their families, communities, and tribes. Market relations also undermined traditional lifestyles and values among native people, who had long subsisted on the produce of their farms and in limited barter (exchange) trade with their neighbors. Local landlords increasingly concentrated wealth in their hands, while Russian settlers seized land from pastoral nomads and local farmers.

The early twentieth century's capitalism also dramatically increased the polarization of society. New political groups emerged in the region over time, as grievances and tensions grew among the local populations. Peasants and farmers were increasingly frustrated by the consolidation of land in the hands of a few and by the regular land expropriations by the Russian administration. The tribal and communal elite were inflamed by the new administrative and legal arrangements and reforms, seeing them as eroding their grip on power. In the meantime, the growing class of educated merchants and native intelligentsia learned about the anticolonial movements in other countries and began organizing small political groups with an anticolonial agenda. All these tensions grew into sporadic riots and rebellions that led to major uprisings in 1898, 1905, and 1916.

Bolshevik Revolution and Civil War

The February Revolution of 1917, resulting as it did in the abdication of Tsar Nicolas II and the establishment of the Russian Republic, did not bring stability, order, or any improvement in the everyday life of ordinary people. Moreover, the new republican government did not end Russia's involvement in the war against Germany, and it conducted very limited political and economic reforms that had barely any effect on the ground. Against this background, the Bolsheviks rose to prominence on a promise to bring radical political and economic changes, including reforms of the Russian colonial administration. In the fall of 1917, they seized power in the Russian capital, Saint Petersburg, and made moves to assert their power in all provinces, including Central Asia. These events profoundly affected Turkistan and deeply polarized its population, as the confrontation between the political forces within the former Russian Empire quickly escalated into civil war and political anarchy. A rifle or revolver became one of the most frequently used means of settling arguments, and various political factions, and sometimes simply gangs of criminals, began fighting each other and brutalizing civilians in the merciless state of war that had developed.

However, in Central Asia, the Bolsheviks faced fierce resistance from, in their words, "bourgeois, landlords and other exploiters." The resistance forces were diverse, including monarchist White Guards, anarchist groups, and local Islamic, nationalist, and tribal leaders. Not all of this support for the anti-Bolshevism position was necessarily politically motivated; often it was based on a desire simply to preserve the preexisting order and way of life or an attempt to bargain for more concessions from previously powerful masters.

Still, in a number of ways, the Revolution also provided great impetus to the further growth of anticolonial and pro-independence sentiment and to the rise of nationalism in Central Asian society. Some intellectuals became involved in regionwide debates about the future of Central Asia, discussing a range of ideas, from the nationalism of *Alash Orda* in Kazakh land to pan-Turkism and the pan-Islamic ideas of *Shuro-Islami* in Kokand and Tashkent. Very small groups representing the native population, and especially intellectuals, supported various political parties, including pro-independence nationalist organizations, social democrats, and the Bolsheviks. The revolutionary groups were organized in major urban areas in an attempt to establish political and military control at the local level. Meanwhile, similar groups in Russia were energetically engaged in taking over the old administrative structures and creating new political institutions. Initially, ordinary Central Asians, especially the natives, remained undecided about the ideology and motives of the various political forces, though they were inclined to remain loyal to their tribal and community leaders.

In a step designed to establish themselves firmly in Central Asia, the Soviet authorities promised to support the national drive and to break with tsardom's practice of suppressing cultural and political developments on the outskirts of the Empire. On April 30, 1918, the All-Turkistan Congress of Soviets declared the establishment of the Turkistan Autonomous Soviet Socialist Republic (TASSR) with its center in Tashkent, giving a significant decree of political and cultural autonomy to the Central Asians.

By mid-1918, the situation had become extremely complicated, with monarchists and British and local militia all involved in the civil war. In the summer of that year, a British expeditionary regiment, led by General W. Malleson, entered and occupied the Zacaspian *oblast* (what is now Turkmenistan). The British also provided military and financial assistance to all major anti-Bolshevik forces. With the escalation of the civil war and the intensity of the fighting, neither Bolshevik nor anti-Bolshevik groups showed any mercy to their adversaries, prisoners of war, or those in the local population who provided support to rival groups; there was wholesale killing of political leaders, commanders, and ordinary soldiers and their families. The White Guards regularly executed members of the Bolshevik Party in the areas under their control, while Red Army soldiers systematically executed pro-monarchist Russian officers and confiscated and/or vandalized the property of wealthy individuals. As the atrocities of the civil war increased, most of the people in the region had no choice but to take sides. Native populations often set up their own militia, frequently led by ambitious commanders, tribal leaders, or sometimes simply adventurers. These militia groups were known as the *basmachi* fighters. The *basmachi* (from Turkic *basma*—"assault") fought against either the Bolsheviks or the representatives of the pro-tsarist White Army or both, resisting the imposition of any outside control over their towns and villages.

Initially, the Red Army troops were not successful, and, in 1918 and 1919, they were repelled from most of the territory of Turkistan. Gradually, however, the Bolsheviks and their army re-emerged from defeat and gathered strength on their promise to end the civil war, conduct wide-ranging economic and social reforms, including redistribution of land and water, and provide greater freedoms and opportunities for the local population. In fact, the Bolsheviks did begin to involve the native population in the local legislature (*Sovety* in Russian) and local governments (*Ispolkomy* in Russian) and to form representative provincial governments, recruiting the native intelligentsia. They also introduced a nationality program, promising greater cultural and political autonomy to the native population.

By 1920, the situation in Central Asia had changed significantly. The Red Army gradually restored its control over the region's most important strategic centers and drove the White Guards and the British troops out of the TASSR and defeated the most significant *basmachi* fighters' groups. In 1920, the Red Army also intervened in major uprisings of the people in Bukhara against Sayyid Alim Khan, the last ruler of the Bukhara Emirate, and in Khiva against Sayyid Abdulla, the last ruler of the Khiva Khanate. With the direct assistance of the Soviet authorities, People's Republics were established in both places.

Central Asian Republics and Political Reforms

The Bolsheviks came to power with a promise to establish a new political system that would eliminate social injustice, exploitation, and inequality. They claimed that only their ideology was capable of providing a model for sustainable and just development. In the name of achieving these goals, the Communist Party established total control over all aspects of people's life—cultural, political, social, and economic. The party tolerated no competing views and, in the name of political stability and a "bright communist future," disapproved of creative thinking and innovations. In time, the Soviet leaders went so far as demanding the subordination of all cultural life to the ideological norms and dogmas of the political system of the Union of the Soviet Socialist Republics (USSR).

The Soviet authorities established a new political system that completely altered the political landscape in Central Asia. Its major features included one-party (communist) domination, a paternalistic state, total state control over all aspects of public and, to a large degree, private life, and the use of state institutions, especially law enforcement agencies, for enforcing Party ideology. The Communist Party introduced a series of political changes to consolidate political power and to alter political identities that had tradition- ally been formed along tribal, social, and ethnic lines. The newly established national communist parties in all Soviet republics controlled local parlia- ments (Supreme Soviets), the councils of ministers, and the administrative apparatuses of the republics at all levels. It should be noted, however, that from the very beginning of the Soviet state there were significant variations in the approaches of communist leaders to the changes and reforms.

During Josef Stalin's reign (1922–1953), many policies and reforms were introduced that radically reshaped the essence of the Soviet system. Stalin used all the forces to hand in the most brutal ways, crushing everything that stood—or that he believed stood—in the way of his agenda.[27] From the beginning, his government banned all political parties, while some native political groups were amalgamated into the ruling Bolshevik (Com- munist) Party. As a next step, former members of opposition parties were purged, and public debates on political issues were banned. The Soviet authorities attempted to win the native population's political loyalty by involving them in administration and governance; this was done through a policy of "indigenization" *(korenizatsia)* of state administration, by which certain positions at all levels—local, provincial, and state—were reserved for personnel from the native population. The Kremlin tried to enforce social equality, promoting the most talented youth to the highest politi- cal and administrative positions, regardless of tribal affiliation or social background, and giving free access to education, social, and other benefits to all people. The policy of *korenizatsia* also included mass enrollment of natives in the Communist Party and the creation of a new class of national "Soviet" intelligentsia.

Throughout the 1920s and 1930s, there were a number of large campaigns of purges, deportations, and executions of the most influential khans and *bais* (wealthy individuals). In the 1930s, Stalin's purges embraced the ruling party itself. In addition, between 50,000 and 200,000 ordinary citizens of the Central Asian Republics disappeared in Stalin's concentration camps or were executed as "enemies of the people," and between 100,000 and 800,000 died of starvation during the collectivization campaign.

Stalin's successor, Nikita Khrushchev (ruled 1956–1964), earned for him- self a special place in Soviet history as the first Soviet leader to denounce the practices of the Stalin era, especially the mass purges. Khrushchev attempted to reform the political system established by Stalin, introducing a wide range of changes and condemning the terror, though in a very inconsistent manner. He also significantly liberalized the intellectual and cultural environ- ment in the Soviet Union by relaxing censorship and allowing some degree of intellectual freedom, but he also personally banned the works of certain artists and artistic groups simply because he disliked them.

Khrushchev-led political and economic changes, while inconsistent, significantly liberalized the previously rigid economic planning. Khrushchev is also known as the first Soviet leader to invest significantly in improved living standards of the population by initiating mass public-housing projects. He also attempted to promote a rapid and large increase in agricultural production, but his plans failed spectacularly, leading to food shortages in some provinces of the USSR. His government allowed relatively free movement of rural populations to cities for the first time since the 1930s, but he maintained the iron curtain and did not allow overseas travel. In 1964, Nikita Khrushchev was quietly removed from office in a peaceful "palace coup," having become, in the words of the historian William Tompson, too "unmanageable."[28]

The next premier—Secretary-General Leonid Brezhnev, who would lead the USSR from 1966 to 1982—became successful by largely maintaining the status quo, but his leadership style was still very controversial.[29] He rejected Khrushchev's political and social liberalization and economic experiments but stopped short of returning to the purges of Stalin's years. He completely abandoned the Khrushchev style of erratic campaigns but gave relative freedom to the national party bureaucracy in terms of cadre policy and redistribution of the national budget, and he displayed indifference to growing corruption.

The regime launched an industrialization program and massive construction projects and extracted natural resources on a large scale. This initially led to a significant rise in living standards, including the development of more or less comprehensive welfare and health-care systems. However, during Brezhnev's reign, intellectual debate and free thinking were still not allowed, and state censorship became even harsher; by the late 1970s, economic growth had significantly slowed. Many people called this era the time of "stagnation."

The Communist Party's public relations image relied on a glowing picture of internal party unity and comprehensive welfare-system prosperity; the reality, however, was very different. Economic development failed to keep up with the population growth and changes in world markets and was significantly undermined by rapidly growing military expenses. Moreover, the political system became extremely corrupt. Many party leaders amassed fortunes through bribes, embezzlement of public funds, or accounting manipulations. In the case of Central Asia, the most lucrative and prestigious positions began to be taken by well-connected individuals or members of the patronage networks (*blat* in Russian slang). Many appointments and promotions were determined not by the talent of individuals but by bribes, personal connections, or support from (often tribal-based) patronage networks.

The Kremlin, the fortress that served as the seat of the Soviet government, intended to eliminate tribal and regional rivalries in Central Asia, but old identities that had survived the harsh Stalin-era transformation now flourished under Leonid Brezhnev's indecisive leadership. A new, large bureaucratic machine was created that consisted of carefully selected Communist Party members and that was called the *nomenklatura;* its personnel gained unlimited control over public resources, the legislature, and government actions, with little accountability or scrutiny from the public. Spreading nepotism and political corruption undermined the whole system, as the *nomenklatura* began establishing exclusive control over all resources in the country.

Economic Changes in the Soviet Era

In their economic policies, the Soviet authorities always emphasized state-led development in which the centralized command economy mobilized all the resources of the state for rapid economic transformation. An important part of this policy was the focus on speedy industrialization, especially in the heavy industries, and the development of state-controlled large-scale agriculture. The cornerstone of this system was centralized economic planning. The five-year plan was ideally intended to produce accelerated and balanced development. In reality, though, these plans often emphasized large and prestigious projects, ignoring cost-effectiveness and especially the rapid technological changes of the second half of the twentieth century. In addition, because Soviet policies prohibited private entrepreneurship, the labor force and people's creativity were used inefficiently. The economic policies were designed to create full employment, but this politically motivated concept, combined with the centralized command planning, undermined private incentives and consequently retarded economic development and growth.

In the first stage of Soviet economic development, during the 1920s, the main objective was to rebuild an economy destroyed by civil war. Rival groups on all sides in the civil war era had randomly robbed the civilian population and destroyed properties, especially industrial enterprises and transportation infrastructure, thereby driving large segments of the population into subsistence economic activities. One of the most important reforms of the post-civil-war era was introduced in agriculture.

Large agricultural farms did not survive the civil war. Most of the people were engaged in traditional subsistence farming and livestock breeding, and often they were barely able to cover personal or family needs in food production and unable to produce anything to sell in the market. To strengthen agriculture, the Soviet government invested significant resources from the central budget into Central Asia, especially into production of such highly valued cash crops as cotton and silk. As a next step, in May 1925, the government abolished private ownership of land. In 1926–1927, the land and water reforms were taken even further as the land was expropriated from large and rich farms, and religious endowments and distributed among the poor farmers. Yet, subsistence farming still dominated the agricultural sector.

As the small subsistence farms could not achieve the desired productivity growth or meet their agricultural produce quotas, the Soviet government took the first steps toward creating cooperatives and then imposed mass collectivization, forcing all individual farmers to join Soviet collective farms—*kolkhozes*. Many Central Asian farmers resisted the expropriation of their land and cattle into the *kolkhozes,* and many families chose to flee to neighboring Afghanistan, China, or Iran in order to escape the brutal excesses of collectivization and sedentarization.

In the 1930s and 1940s, the Soviet authorities directed large investments from the central Soviet budget into the development of heavy industry and petrochemicals and into machinery, textiles, light manufacturing, and mining enterprises. Hundreds of new industrial plants were built in Central Asia during the first stage of industrialization (1928–1940), including textile and silk-processing factories, electric power stations, and many others. During the 1930s, the region also began to emerge as a prominent oil-producing center. Industrial production grew at an average annual rate of around 12–14 percent during the first three *piatiletkas* (five-year plans). With this remarkable economic growth, people began migrating into the Central Asian republics, mainly from Russia, Byelorussia, and Ukraine. Some of them came voluntarily; others were deported or forced to make the move.

In the late 1930s, the collectivization campaign was largely completed in the region. It had long-lasting consequences. First, large-scale farming and the mechanization of the agricultural sector made it easy to control and direct the choice of agricultural crops and to specialize in certain products, such as cotton. This dramatically increased the output of agricultural produce and elevated most of the farmers out of utter poverty and social despair. Second, the new agricultural structure allowed the imposition of changes in social and political behavior and the enforcement of the so-called cultural revolution (see the next section). Throughout the Soviet era, Kyrgyzstan, Tajikistan, Turkmenistan, and Uzbekistan specialized in the production of cotton, as well as wool, silk, fruits, and vegetables. By 1989, such agricultural collective farms accounted for between 40 and 50 percent of the republics' gross domestic product (GDP).

World War II had a negative affect on economic development in the USSR. However, Central Asia remained outside the main theaters of war and thus avoided the economic catastrophe that was experienced in the western parts of the USSR, such as Ukraine and Byelorussia. In fact, in 1941–1942, many enterprises were evacuated from the western provinces of Ukraine and the Russian Federation and relocated to the Central Asian region, in some cases along with their workers, engineers, and technical staff. A number of these factories and plants remained in the republics after the war, and they became the backbone of local heavy industry.

In the postwar period, the central Soviet government allocated significant resources to developing Central Asia's oil- and gas-producing sectors and to building large pipelines to deliver these products to central Russia, the Caucasus, and Ukraine. The Soviet authorities often ignored the service sector, however, and it remained relatively underdeveloped and inefficient throughout the Soviet era. The retail and hospitality sectors became notorious for their "Soviet"-style low-quality service. By the 1980s, serious imbalances in retail-sector resourcing had led to chronic deficiencies of consumer goods and other products. Even health care and educational services, in which the Soviet authorities had invested massively throughout the 1940s, 1950s and 1960s, were in decay in the 1980s. In this environment, the black market burgeoned. In the 1980s, the so-called shadow economy flourished, providing access to retail goods, health care, and other services that were supposedly free, and freely available, in the Soviet system for cash.

Overall, the results of nearly 70 years of Soviet state-led development were quite mixed. On the one hand, Soviet economic policy and centralized allocation of resources accelerated industrial development and economic growth to unprecedented rates. Central Asian GDP was doubling every 14 to 17 years. The state provided most of the population with free training and lifetime employment opportunities and elevated significant sectors of the population out of absolute poverty. Famine and mass diseases became practically unknown after World War II. The government invested further in the development of free secondary, specialized, vocational, and higher education and social welfare systems.

On the other hand, Soviet policies were implemented brutally and often at very high human, environmental, and economic costs. In the late 1970s and 1980s, along with the rest of the USSR, Central Asia entered a decade of stagnation, due to accumulated distortions in the economy, unsustainable military spending, and the inability of the Soviet system to catch up with the latest wave of technological progress. Many government projects became dangerously underfunded, including housing, communication, and transportation infrastructures. Also, by the 1970s, the region's economic development increasingly relied on unsustainable exploitation of natural resources and on the ecologically damaging monoculture of cotton.

The Soviet development strategy stimulated a very high level of economic growth in the early stages of industrialization because it managed to mobilize all human and financial resources into achieving certain economic objectives through investing into building new assets. However, in the longer term, this system proved to be extremely inflexible, as it did not promote innovation and initiative and maintained obsolete technologies year after year. It also overcentralized control over research and development (R&D) into a few large industrial centers in the Russian Federation; this made the Central Asian economies highly dependent on the Soviet central government for technological transfers and technical knowledge. By 1989, the Central Asian republics still produced only one-third of their GDP in the industrial sector, specializing in the processing of raw materials (e.g., oil, gas) and the manufacturing of agricultural machinery, electric motors, textiles, garments, and consumer goods.

The Gorbachev-Ryzhkov administration's economic mismanagement and mistakes in implementing reforms led to the collapse of economic relations between the republics in 1990–1991. The Central Asian governments, along with the governments of other Soviet republics, began to question the wisdom of centralized control over the economy. Gradually they demanded greater autonomy in economic decision making and in the use of revenues from the export of natural resources; they even raised the question of nationalizing property and enterprises controlled by the large Moscow-based ministries and agencies.

The Soviet Cultural Revolution

At the center of Soviet policies was the dismantling of traditional cultures and the creation of a new Soviet culture and a new Soviet identity. The cultural and social changes introduced by the Sovietization policy had two dimensions that were intended to further strengthen the Soviet identity and gradually make it an inseparable part of the Soviet nation. First, throughout the seven decades of their rule, the Soviet authorities carefully crafted the education system, the new cultural setting (including written "scientific" histories and new forms of modern art), and the "new" social organization of society to reflect their aim of a totally Sovietized society. Second, the Sovietization policy addressed a perceived obstacle to consolidating the Soviet identity by attempting to reduce the social differences between indigenous populations and Russians.

The development of literacy was part of the Soviet Cultural Revolution policy among the masses, and a campaign to raise the literacy rate was launched in the 1920s. At the same time, the Soviet authorities attempted to

limit the cultural influences of the past. Between 1924 and 1933, the first ter-
tiary education institutions were opened in all major cities, maintaining the
national languages as the primary languages of instruction. The government
also invested substantial resources in establishing a comprehensive network
of schools and colleges, which by the late 1940s covered all cities and towns
in the region. In the 1960s and 1970s, the Kremlin leaders took the Sovietization policy even further by more vigorously implementing a Russification
policy. In 1990, for example, almost 86 percent of students in Kazakhstan
and 76 percent of students in Kyrgyzstan and Turkmenistan received their
higher education in Russian.[30]

The establishment of a cultural infrastructure was, in the Kremlin's eyes,
one of the ways to strengthen national and Soviet identity. During the 1920s
and 1930s, the first groups of talented young natives were sent to study modern art and the sciences. With their return to the Central Asian republics, the
government opened public libraries, theaters, art exhibitions, academies of
science, and museums.

The newly established publishing houses produced hundreds of books,
newspapers, and magazines, initially mainly in the local language, though
after World War II an increasing number of publications in the republics
were produced in Russian. For example, between 1925 and 1971, in Kyrgyzstan, 20,000 books and brochures were published in print runs totaling 128
million copies. By comparison, in the whole Kyrgyz land before the Revolution, there was only one publishing house, and that had only a few dozen
titles listed. Similar trends can be seen in all the other Central Asian republics.
In the early 1920s, the first national newspapers were published and sold a
few hundred copies; by the end of 1980, there were several hundred newspapers in the region with total daily sales reaching several million copies.[31]
In 1940, the first film-production centers were established, producing first
documentaries and later first motion pictures. At the same time, the Soviet
leaders attempted to create a national intelligentsia and a new elite in every
Central Asian republic by promoting the most gifted and ambitious young
people from the lower social strata.

All these cultural changes and the Soviet social experiments nevertheless had
a dark side. During the 1920s and 1930s, Stalin's regime eliminated the old
national intelligentsia, as well as the religious, political, and tribal elite, first by
sending them into exile in Siberia or other parts of the Soviet Union and then
by executing them in labor camps and prisons. In Central Asia, it was Islamic
leaders who were particularly targeted in this campaign, as from the 1930s the
Soviet government persistently and brutally implemented a policy of atheism,
closing mosques and *madrasas* and prohibiting all religious practice.

Postwar development helped to advance social changes further. Yet, the region's indigenous societies preserved some important characteristics of their traditional lifestyles that became curiously mixed with certain elements of modernity. Traditionalism in Central Asia showed itself able to oppose the innovations and social transformations that were imposed by the Soviet system. Despite all the social changes, Central Asian societies maintained some of the features of patriarchal societies and strong tribal and kinship traditions. Certain particularities of the Soviet modernization in fact contributed to the preservation of these aspects. For example, collectivization placed tightly bound extended families, tribal units, or neighborhood communities into *kolkhozes,* keeping old ties intact. Traditionally, the extended family and social networks provided support to all members of villages *(ails)* and developed a kind of economic welfare net. "Patron-client" relationships gave rise to strong regionalism in all Central Asian republics.

Over time, however, the shortcomings of Sovietization and the nationality policy and, especially, the increasing pressure of Russification sparked a growing unease among the local populations and even among the Russified intelligentsia. The situation was worsened by a growing gap between propaganda and reality and by the failure of the state to improve standards of living significantly and halt rising underemployment and unemployment, especially in the cities. The intelligentsia began to use a term introduced by the contemporary Kyrgyz writer Chyngyz Aitmatov to talk about society's *Mankourtization*—"forgetting of roots"—as people increasingly lost their sense of cultural heritage and faced the destruction of the traditional fabric of society. The first sign of resistance to the Russification policy appeared in the 1970s, when various literary works written by local writers, such as Olzas Suleimenov and others, began championing national cultures and national identities.

At the same time, the significant social and cultural achievements in the republics under the Soviet system cannot be entirely dismissed, and some groups in Central Asian society today acknowledge the positive aspects of the Soviet legacy. The Soviet authorities succeeded in their state-building project, in establishing cohesive political and territorial entities, and in developing national identities. The so-called cultural revolution brought about the elimination of mass illiteracy, helping to build modern national cultures, literatures, and standardized literary languages; it introduced many art forms previously unknown. The Soviet state also created the national intelligentsia, including large groups of administrators, educators, and scientists, and attempted to eradicate social inequality by creating opportunities for some social groups that had long been deprived by society.

During the twentieth century, an advanced education system, programs in science, technology, and public health and a welfare system were established with significant contributions and help from other Soviet republics. Thus, despite economic stagnation and relatively low personal incomes in the region, the United Nations Development Program (UNDP) felt that the Human Development Indicators (HDI) in the republics in the 1980s were well ahead of those for many developing states, such as Afghanistan, Pakistan, India, Turkey, and Iraq. If measured by the HDIs, which take into account the level of education, access to social and health-care benefits, and so on, the republics were in thirty-first place in the 1991 HDI global rankings.

Gorbachev's Revolution and the Collapse of the Soviet Union

By the mid-1980s the Central Asian republics, like all other Soviet republics, faced a serious economic, social, and political crisis. The overcentralized, state-controlled Soviet economy entered a period of severe recession triggered by several major factors, including a steep decline in world prices for major Soviet export commodities, such as oil, gas, and metals; a series of mistakes and miscalculations in strategic economic planning; excessive military spending, including the cost of the war in Afghanistan; and the failure of the Soviet leaders to reform and restructure the USSR's national economy.[32] The situation was further worsened by the large-scale corruption of inept and inefficient, but politically well-connected, managers. They misappropriated significant financial resources, misreported revenues, and often simply cooked the account books, while suppressing initiatives and innovations in their enterprises.

Economic difficulties, along with extensive corruption, led to a rise in social tensions, as the governments in all Soviet republics, especially in Central Asia, were increasingly unable to fully fund health-care and welfare programs and to raise salaries in the public sector. They were also incapable of creating new and better-paid jobs for young people, especially in rural Central Asia, as the labor market was distorted by the lifetime employment practices at many enterprises. On the back of rising poverty and widespread underemployment and social tensions, a small group of corrupt party bureaucrats, government officials, and managers (the so-called *nomenklatura*) maintained lavish and scandal-prone lifestyles. Some members of the *nomenklatura* took advantage of their privileged positions to continuously enrich themselves, covering up their corrupt practices and incompetence; others blindly followed the party propaganda and slogans, suppressing any attempts at creative thinking.

Mikhail Gorbachev (who led the USSR from 1985 to 1991) launched his policy of changes *(perestroika)* in the mid-1980s as an attempt to address what he called a "crisis" in the political development in the Soviet Union. At the same time, he launched his policy of openness (glasnost) in an attempt to rally various sections of the society behind a small group of Gorbachev-led reformers, to expose the corrupt practices, and to expose corrupt politicians to public scrutiny. He also wanted to encourage public debate about the future development of the Soviet republics. Both supporters and fierce critics of the Gorbachev-led government dubbed this policy "revolutionary," because of the scale of the changes and their impact on domestic and international development.

Among the major steps Gorbachev undertook between 1986 and 1990 was an attempt to reduce military spending in order to significantly increase spending on health care, welfare systems, and cultural projects. The government also tried to liberalize central planning and to partially decentralize the Soviet economy, giving more autonomy and initiative to the national governments in all Union republics, including those of Central Asia. In addition, he reduced state censorship of media, art, and culture; abandoned state control over intellectual development, including literature and journalism; and embarked on partial political and economic liberalizations. He forced a whole generation of elderly Communist Party leaders to retire en masse, replacing them with younger people.

Almaty (Central Square). Courtesy of the author, 2006.

Yet, many of these reforms were implemented very slowly, inconsistently, and frequently without public consultations, leading to large-scale protests, such as those in Almaty, in December 1986, and Tashkent, in 1990. Very often, the same groups of *nomenklatura* received the fruits of the reforms and changes. Eventually, Gorbachev initiated a policy of "acceleration" *(uskorenie)* in order to speed up the reforms, but in reality it created chaos. New waves of reforms, adjustments, and legal changes were introduced in a rush, without creating proper implementation mechanisms, at times without completing the previous reforms, and often driven by conflicting interest groups. Altogether this produced an environment of uncertainty and anxiety.

The most worrying development was the collapse of law and order, as reforms failed to create clearly defined property rights, commercial and private entrepreneurial activities. In addition, although the rigid Soviet laws and restrictions had been removed, new legal frameworks and practices were not established, leaving law-enforcement agencies incapable of working in the new environment.

Although the people cheered positive changes, inconsistencies in implementing reforms and growing political and economic uncertainty and lawlessness alienated many sectors of society, which became increasingly critical of Gorbachev's reform agenda and his ineffectiveness. The intelligentsia and urbanites in the major cities demanded more effective reforms, more freedoms, and democratization of the political process. Meanwhile, the working class and the trade unions demanded sharp increases in their salaries, pensions, and various social benefits. Local communities in native republics began demanding that schools be opened that taught in their native languages; that teaching in major colleges and universities be switched from Russian to native languages; that the number of publications and television and radio broadcasts in their languages be increased; and that the native languages become the state language in their republics.

By 1990–1991, the reformers and conservatives were deadlocked in heated debates about the future of the Soviet political system, though the degree of politicization of society was different in various parts of the Soviet Union. The Central Asian republics experienced a rise in social and interethnic tensions between 1989 and 1991 that inflamed a series of deadly interethnic and intercommunal conflicts in Kyrgyzstan, Tajikistan, Turkmenistan, and Uzbekistan and the appearance of radical nationalist Islamic groups and organizations. As a result, the Central Asian *nomenklatura* moved toward the reintroduction of tight controls over political and social development and public discourse in the republics. The Central Asian leaders also began demanding more sovereignty in implementing domestic political and economic policies related to such issues as taxation, the social welfare system, language, and cadre and nationality policies, along with other changes.

The debates and confrontations over the nature of these changes culminated, in 1990 and 1991, in a bitter political struggle between the Kremlin and the Union republics, and between conservatives and reformers. This confrontation diminished further both the Kremlin's ability to control political developments and the Communist Party's exclusive grip on power and led to numerous constitutional changes at both Union and republic levels.[33] Gradually there emerged a powerful political block led by Boris Yeltsin, formerly Gorbachev's protégé but now his political archrival and the head of the government of the Russian Federation. Yeltsin's faction insisted that Gorbachev and his government resign. In this environment, some leaders both in Moscow and in the Union republics raised the question of revising the Soviet Constitution and the Soviet Union Treaty of 1922.

The conservative members of the Communist Party perceived that these reforms and demands were undermining the stability of their familiar way of life, including their exclusive access to resources, lifetime employment opportunities, power distribution, and total personal autonomy. In order to resolve the political deadlock, the conservative members of the Soviet Politburo, the highest decision-making body in the USSR, launched a coup d'état in August 1991. The coup failed, and the Russian leadership, under Boris Yeltsin, declared its intention to dissolve the USSR. The peaceful disintegration of the Soviet Union gave the Central Asian republics the opportunity to declare their independence, and that is exactly what they did, in 1991, ending 70 years of the Soviet system.

Trial of Independence

The Central Asian republics attained their independence though peaceful agreements and in a relatively orderly manner. They accomplished this through legal procedures in December 1991 and by mid-1992 had taken over most of the former Soviet institutions, including industrial enterprises, financial and banking entities, and the military. However, the whole process of adapting to the new environment, new situation, and new policy objectives—called "transition" in the postcommunist studies literature—proved to be very complex and difficult. In addition to political changes, this included, according to the International Monetary Fund, "macrostabilization, price and market liberalization (including international trade), restructuring and privatization state enterprises, and the redefining of the role of the state."[34]

When the Central Asian republics declared their independence after the dissolution of the Soviet Union, in 1991, many experts—including those from the IMF and the World Bank—anticipated that these republics would rapidly undergo a transition similar to that of western European countries under the Marshall Plan or the rapid economic growth and restructuring that were seen in the newly industrialized countries (NIC) of Southeast Asia in the 1980s. Both regions had successfully restructured their economies within a decade. The Central Asian republics had all the major factors in place to succeed—human capital, educational institutions, a relatively well-developed infrastructure, and a technocratically oriented elite.

In 1990, the Central Asian republics, with an HDI ranking of 31, were ahead of many Asian countries, and they enjoyed a per-capita GDP between US$2,000 and 4,600, which was similar to that of the rapidly growing NIC members in the late 1980s. The economic structure of the Central Asian republics was in fact quite close to the economies of the rapidly transforming Eastern Europe countries, as they had well-established industrial manufacturing sectors, agricultural sectors dominated by large farms, and sizable energy sectors. The region's literacy rate, which was close to 99 percent among both men and women, was among the highest in Asia. The well-educated population was backed by a well-established and free tertiary-education system.

Declarations of sovereignty by the Central Asian states suddenly opened a world of opportunities and challenges for these newly independent states. But many issues had to be addressed immediately, such as economic anarchy, interethnic tensions, the collapse of the centralized supply-and-distribution chain, the breakdown of interrepublic trade, and social discontent. The leaders of these states chose different approaches in addressing the transitional issues. The governments of Turkmenistan and Uzbekistan decided to follow a gradual reforms approach, privatizing only small and medium enterprises, continuing some elements of central planning, and controlling major sectors of their national economies, particularly gas, oil, and cotton production. The government of Kyrgyzstan, on the other hand, adopted the most radical approach to economic reform, in line with IMF recommendations; it embraced speedy mass privatization, full economic and trade liberalization, and a total rejection of centralized state planning. Kazakhstan was somewhere in between these two approaches, rejecting central planning and introducing gradual privatization but retaining some state control over the most important sectors of the economy. The government of Tajikistan lost control of economic development, as the country spent most of the 1990s engaged in a civil war (1992–1997), becoming one of the poorest countries in the world (with GDP per capita income that is about half that in Sudan, Zimbabwe, or Haiti).[35]

For five consecutive years, from 1991 through 1996, the economies of most of the Central Asian republics experienced steep recessions, with the partial exception of Uzbekistan. The republics went through a moderate economic recovery in 1996 and 1997 at an average annual rate of 4–5 percent, but they were hurt by the Asian and Russian financial downturns in 1997 and 1998. According to IMF estimates, in 1999 their real GDP was 29 percent of the 1989 level in Tajikistan, 61 percent of the 1989 level in Kazakhstan, Kyrgyzstan, and Turkmenistan, and 97 percent of that level in Uzbekistan.[36] The post-Soviet-era reforms in these republics helped to restructure the national economies but failed to achieve the two major economic objectives of the transition as defined by the IMF—"to raise economic efficiency and to promote [economic] growth."[37] Because of their dismal economic performances in the 1990s, all Central Asian governments sharply decreased spending on all social welfare and educational programs and eliminated large-scale Soviet-era-style funding and subsidies for many cultural projects.

The economic restructuring imposed a heavy social cost on most of the population, creating sharp regional and social disparities. In these republics, as in many developing countries, business activities and investments were increasingly concentrated in the major metropolitan centers such as Almaty, Bishkek, and Tashkent. In the meantime, small towns and villages experienced a steep economic decline. Throughout the 1990s, privatization created a large class of private owners as small retail, catering, and service shops emerged in all cities and even in remote villages. However, many industrial enterprises were closed because they could not compete with cheap foreign imports and because they lacked the managerial expertise and capital for technological upgrading.

Poverty became widespread, affecting between 40 and 80 percent of the population. There were indicators that women and children were especially vulnerable to the economic and social changes, despite all the paternalistic actions of the government. The official statistics claimed that unemployment remained at around 3–9 percent throughout the 1990s, though independent experts argued that these figures did not reflect the reality and that unemployment was actually between 20 and 25 percent of the labor force, with the rate in remote rural areas running at between 30 and 35 percent. Many small enterprises chose to operate in the "shadow economy" outside the legal environment, due to mass corruption and imperfect regulations. There were no reliable local studies on this phenomenon; however, in 2001, the *Economist Intelligence Unit* estimated that the "shadow economy" might account for up to 30–40 percent of GDP. In 2004, the average PPP (Purchasing Power Parity) per capita stood at around US$2,900 (US$980 in Tajikistan, US$1,600 in both Kyrgyzstan and Uzbekistan, and US$5,870 in Kazakhstan)—that is, about one-twelfth that in the United States.[38]

Citing economic difficulties and political instability, especially as Afghanistan and, for a short time, Tajikistan slid into civil wars, the Central Asian republics introduced a tougher approach to dealing with domestic issues, including stricter policies towards nongovernmental organizations (NGOs), opposition groups, and the independent media. Gradually, authoritarian or semiauthoritarian regimes emerged in all countries of the region, varying from a Stalin-style regime in Turkmenistan to "soft," semidemocratic regimes in Kazakhstan and Kyrgyzstan. All Central Asian leaders promoted themselves as capable of governing and maintaining law and order and sdelivering prosperity and stability. These leaders have been engaged in a systematic process of consolidating and strengthening formerly weak national identities. This process has included the dismantling of Soviet identity *(sovetskii narod)* and Soviet institutions. The governments have sponsored the development and strengthening of national and nationalist symbols, including the renaming of all major cities, towns, and streets, and have moved toward establishing native languages as the sole languages of education, administration, and media.

RECENT TRENDS

By 2000–2001, the Central Asian republics had completed the first stage of transition and had entered a new era in their economic, social, political, and cultural development. This era was largely shaped by several internal and external factors. First, the U.S.-led war in Afghanistan against international terrorism that started in 2001 suddenly put the Central Asian republics on the front pages of the major news outlets and on the radars of the major great powers. With the arrival of the U.S. military bases and NATO troops onto Central Asian soil for the first time ever, Western governments significantly increased various forms of assistance to Kyrgyzstan, Tajikistan, and Uzbekistan. Second, the Central Asian governments finally strengthened their grip on power, establishing strong presidential regimes with some elements of paternalistic states, in the process becoming more and more restrictive of independent media and opposition organizations. After a decade-long, painful, and often chaotic transition, the political situation has largely stabilized, and the republics have revamped their political and administrative institutions and capacities.

Third, economic development in all these republics improved as the rapid rise in world prices for major Central Asian export commodities—oil, gas, gold, iron ore, cotton, and silk—helped their economic recovery. The national governments were thus able to increase salaries for public-sector workers and to spend more on various educational, social, and welfare programs, on cultural projects, and on fighting poverty. Fourth, a young generation that had experienced little of the Soviet way of life, and whose outlook was therefore free of Soviet-style state control and censorship and ideological and intellectual restraints, entered productive life, increasingly replacing the old guard. Fifth, artists and members of creative communities finally overcame the distressing shock of transitional changes, began searching for new forms of expression, and started actively creating new works. Importantly, the Central Asian intellectuals withstood the period of chaos and uncertainty and began working more actively in reevaluating their intellectual and cultural past and reassessing their national identities. They also abandoned the old concepts and began accepting the realities of the market-oriented world and globalization.

New cultural trends sprang to life, as the artists started synthesizing old (i.e., premodern), Soviet- and post-Soviet-era traditions. This process further ignited debate about cultural development in every national republic and in the region in general. For some, this development helped to preserve the uniqueness of national traditions and to show them to the world. For others, it facilitated the building of bridges with an increasingly globalizing world. In the meantime, some groups claimed that it was a manifestation of the commercialization of art and artistic work and that it undermined the true nature of the national culture. By and large, these cultural questions and these debates continue to shape cultural development in the Central Asian republics in the early twenty-first century.

NOTES

1. Fitzroy MacLean, *A Person from England* (New York: Harper and Brothers, 1958), p. 16.

2. Some numbers in this chapter are rounded.

3. Since 1991, a significant number of geographic names have been changed in Central Asia in order to reflect the new political and cultural environment. This also reflects an attempt to replace the Russian or Russified names, which were widely introduced during the twentieth century, with traditional local names and traditional local spelling. The author provides both spellings—old and new—in all of the most important cases.

4. V. V. Bartold, *Raboty po istoricheskoi geografii* [Works on historical geography] (Moscow: RAN, 2002), p. 477.

5. Ibid., pp. 210–233, 495–502.

6. The essence of the delimitation process is still hotly debated by scholars. For evaluation of the latest views on the process in the USSR, see Francine Hirsch, *Empire of Nations: Ethnographic Knowledge and the Making of the Soviet Union* (Ithaca: Cornell University Press, 2005).

7. http://www.photius.com/rankings/economy/oil_proved_reserves_2005_0.html (accessed April 3, 2006).

8. http://www.cia.gov/cia/publications/factbook/rankorder/2183rank.html (accessed April 3, 2006).

9. For an assessment of mineral potentials in Kyrgyzstan, see World Bank, *Kyrgyzstan. The Transition to a Market Economy. Country Report* (Washington, DC: World Bank, 1993).

10. In 1979, the last Soviet population census was conducted simultaneously in all Central Asian republics. For assessments of the population in the early twentieth century, see Ian Matley, "The Population and the Land," in *Central Asia: 130 Years of Russian Dominance. A Historical Overview,* ed. Edward Allworth, 3rd ed. (Durham and London: Duke University Press, 1994), pp. 92–130.

11. Until the 1920s, the Kazakhs were often called Kyrgyz or Kaisak-Kyrgyzs (not to be confused with "Kara-Kyrgyzs," attributed to modern Kyrgyzs).

12. For a detailed anthropological survey, see Saul Abramzon, *Kyrgyzy i ikh etnogeneticheskie i istoriko-kulturnye sviazi* [The Kyrgyzs and their ethnological and historical-cultural relations] (Frunze: Kyrgyzstan, 1990).

13. For a detailed historical and anthropological survey, see Bobozhan Gafurov, *Tajiki. Drevneishaia, Drevniaia i srednevekovaia istoria* (Dushanbe: Irfon, 1989).

14. For additional information, see Rafis Abazov, *Historical Dictionary of Turkmenistan* (Lanham, MD, and London: Scarecrow Press, 2005).

15. For a detailed review, see Edward Allworth, *The Modern Uzbeks: From the Fourteenth Century to the Present* (Stanford: Stanford University Press, 1990).

16. John Schoeberlein, "Shifting Ground: How the Soviet Regime Used Resettlement to Transform Central Asian Society and Consequences of This Policy Today," in *Migration in Central Asia: Its History and Current Problems,* ed. Komatsu Hisao et al. (Osaka: JCAS, 2000), pp. 41–63.

17. Rafis Abazov, *Historical Dictionary of Kyrgyzstan* (Lanham, MD, and London: Scarecrow Press, 2004), pp. ix–xi.

18. See Susan Whitfield and Ursala Sims-Williams, eds., *The Silk Road: Trade, Travel, War and Faith* (London: British Library, 2004).

19. See Frances Wood, *The Silk Road: Two Thousand Years in the Heart of Asia* (Berkeley: University of California Press, 2002).

20. See his memoirs: Marco Polo, *The Travels of Marco Polo,* revised from Marsen's translation; edited with an introduction by Manuel Komroff; illustrations by Witold Gordon (New York: Liveright, 2002).

21. For such an attempt, see Ibn Khaldun, *The Muqaddimah: An Introduction to History,* trans. and introduced by Franz Rosenthal; abridged and edited by N. J. Dawood (Princeton: Princeton University Press, 2005).

22. The history of the Kushan Empire is still widely debated among scholars. For a history of the empire, see Bobozhan Gafurov, ed., *Central Asia in the Kushan Period* (Moscow: Nauka, 1975).

23. Erik Hildinger, *The Warriors of the Steppe: A Military History of Central Asia, 500 B.C. to 1700 A.D.* (Cambridge, MA: Da Capo Press, 1997).

24. David Roxburgh, ed., *Turks: A Journey of a Thousand Years, 600–1600* (London: Royal Academy of Art, 2005).

25. Beatrice Forbes Manz, *The Rise and Rule of Tamerlane* (Reprint, Cambridge: Cambridge University Press, 1999).

26. Peter Hopkirk, *The Great Game: The Struggle for Empire in Central Asia* (New York: Kodansha International, 1992).

27. Martin McCauley, *Stalin and Stalinism,* 3rd ed. (Harlow, Essex, UK: Pearson Longman, 2003).

28. William Tompson, *The Soviet Union under Brezhnev* (Harlow, Essex, UK: Pearson Longman, 2003), p. 15.

29. Ibid., p. 17.

30. Anatoly Khazanov, *After USSR. Ethnicity, Nationalism and Politics in the Commonwealth of Independent States* (Madison: University of Wisconsin Press, 1995), pp. 249–251.

31. Abazov, *Historical Dictionary of Kyrgyzstan,* p. 29.

32. For a detailed discussion, see David Marples, *The Collapse of the Soviet Union, 1985–1991* (Harlow, Essex, UK: Pearson Longman, 2004).

33. For details, see John Anderson, *International Politics of Central Asia* (Manchester: Manchester University Press, 1997).

34. International Monetary Fund, *World Economic Outlook: Focus on Transition Economies* (Washington, DC: International Monetary Fund, 2000), p. 91. A good overview of transition can be found in Marie Lavagne, *Economies in Transition,* 2nd ed. (New York: Palgrave, 1999).

35. United Nations Development Program (UNDP), *Human Development Report 2004* (New York: UNDP, 2004), pp. 141–142.

36. International Monetary Fund, *World Economic Outlook,* p. 89.

37. Ibid., p. 90.

38. UNDP, *Human Development Report 2004,* pp. 140–142.

2

Thought and Religion

Hoja Nasreddin was asked why he ran away from rain, which was God's mercy. "I am not running away from it. I just don't want to step on it!" replied Nasreddin.

—Central Asian anecdote

Religious practices in Central Asia represent a complex interaction of two extremes. One is a highly sophisticated body of spiritual and doctrinal thought developed by intellectuals living and working in major urban centers in the region. The other is a combination of popular local traditions, communal rituals, and superstitions that have been shaped largely by tribal and community elders *(aksakals)*, chiefs, and local spiritual "authorities"—hillers, saints, and dervishes.[1]

Modern Central Asians are very proud of their intellectual contribution to the development of Muslim philosophy and "high" culture. Wherever possible, they highlight the centrality of their region in the Golden Age of the Islamic world. Ordinary people, politicians, and highly affluent intellectuals often discuss Central Asia as one of the cradles of the Islamic civilization. Indeed, for many centuries, religious discourse and interchange were of great importance for the spiritual development of Central Asian societies. They shaped multifaceted cultures and traditions, affected the legal and political systems, promoted intellectual debates, and had a profound impact on many other aspects of people's lives. Many religious thinkers of the ancient and medieval worlds found in Central Asia—crossroad of world civilizations and major communication hub of the Great Silk Road—both refuge and an inspirational environment for developing and refining their thinking. Central Asians played an important part in the development of Zoroastrian, Buddhist, Manichean, Eastern Christian, and Islamic theological and legal thought, philosophy, and culture. For example, the Zoroastrian concepts of a benevolent creator, judgment day, divinity, paradise and hell, and good and evil attracted the interest of Plato and Aristotle, Saint Augustine and Saint Cyril of Alexandria, and influenced Judeo-Christian discourse on the manifestation of the Divine, eschatology, angelology, and demonology, to name a few. Such philosophers and theologians as Al-Bukhari, Al-Farabi, Al-Khoresmi, Al-Beruni, Abu-Khamid Al-Ghazali, Nakhshbandi, and Omar Khayyam have been widely recognized in the Muslim world, and their ideas shaped much intellectual discourse throughout the medieval era.

At the same time, other observers highlight the influence of popular or "low" religious traditions (or "low Islam," as Ernest Gellner defines it).[2] After all, it is argued, peasants and nomads of Central Asia had little access to the great works of the thinkers, and nomadic people who wandered for thousands of miles across inhospitable steppe, deserts, and mountains had little opportunity for exposure to formal religious education and rarely had access to skilled clergy. Largely illiterate and much of the time struggling simply to survive, they could not access the works of the Central Asian Islamic theologians, philosophers, and writers of the distant past. Even in modern times, very few of those books have been translated into contemporary Central Asian languages or gained wide readership among the public or contemporary scholars. The skeptics remind us that the Central Asian republics lived under the atheistic Soviet system for nearly 70 years. During those years, the national governments more or less consistently implemented the policy of atheism, at certain periods brutally and rigorously, and thus radically changed the everyday behavior of the people and affected the customs of many communities. For instance, practically all the Islamic universities were closed; all property held by Islamic charitable endowments (Waqf) were nationalized by the state. Many mosques, along with churches and monasteries, were closed or destroyed at the height of the state-sponsored attack on all religion, in the 1920s and 1930s.

Several generations of Central Asians lived in the secular Soviet state, but nevertheless they were able to preserve their religious identity and many religious traditions. Religious traditions are deeply incorporated into Central Asian culture and in many ways are inseparable from the various national cultures and traditions. Even hardcore communists would traditionally take their newborn children to a local Islamic authority (mullah) for a blessing prayer.[3] Most parents would call local aksakals to gather for a joint prayer and blessing at various stages of their children's lives. Even at the peak of the Soviet atheistic campaigns, parents would call a mullah to confirm a marriage according to the Islamic teaching, since a man and a woman could become husband and wife in the eyes of the local communities only after the special wedding prayer—*niqah*. Likewise, at times of grief, Central Asians, including secular government officials, would perform burial rituals according to Islamic tradition.

At present, both "high" and "low" religious traditions can be found across the religious spectrum in the Central Asian republics. During the Soviet era, people of different religious backgrounds—Orthodox Christianity, Catholicism, Protestantism, Judaism, and others—moved into the region, and they continue to live and work together, especially in the large cities. Indeed, Central Asia is quite diverse culturally: between 75 and 79 percent of people in the region are Muslims, about 15–20 percent are Christians (Orthodox, Catholics, Protestants), and between 1 and 3 percent profess other religions (as of 2006). Additionally, there are very small groups that call themselves atheists or agnostics.[4] The distribution of religious communities differs significantly among the republics and even among provinces within the republics. For example, in Tajikistan and Turkmenistan, Muslims make up about 95 percent of the population, but in the capitals these numbers stand at about 75–85 percent. Meanwhile, in Kazakhstan, Muslims constitute between 65 and 70 percent of the population but only about 60 percent of the population in the capital.

Many polls and surveys conducted in Central Asia indicate that religion still shapes people's identities and significantly affects intellectual debates in the region, but they also suggest that people are very liberal in their attitudes toward religion. For example, according to the World Values Survey conducted in 2003, 85.1 percent of respondents in Kyrgyzstan declared that they "belong to a religious denomination," but only 13.6 percent declared that they attend religious services more than once a week. In the United States, by comparison, 19.5 percent of respondents said that they attend religious services more than once a week.[5]

PRE-ISLAMIC TRADITIONS AND BELIEFS

The spiritual and religious landscape of the region is historically diverse. Zoroastrians, Manicheans, and various others claim Central Asia as a cradle of their civilizations and see the region as centrally important in the development of their belief systems. A millennia-long tradition of shamanism, animism, witchcraft, and paganism brought together numerous local superstitions and folklore. Some of these religious systems and beliefs disappeared long ago, leaving few visible traces in the modern culture and customs of the people. Others still affect their lives, perception, and behavior in significant ways. A closer look at the history of various religions in the region provides insights into the specific ways in which the role of the religion is perceived in the region today.

The popular beliefs that survived the thousands of years to the present have their main roots in the pre-Islamic religious practices of the Turkic-speaking nomadic people. The Turkic pantheon included the main god, who controlled the heavenly universe, and his rival, who controlled the underworld. Both were served by numerous lesser gods. These gods had some human characteristics and protected and patronized specific human activities, sometimes even visiting the world of humans to intervene in certain events. This system distantly resembles the ancient Greek pantheon; for example, *Tengri* is a far-off equivalent of Zeus, *Erglig* is an equivalent of Hades, *Su Iesi* is an equivalent of Naiad.[6] Also like their Greek counterparts, the Turkic gods lived in the mountains—in Altai (southern Siberia) and in Khan Tengri (Tian Shan). The Turkic polytheistic belief system had strong elements of shamanism and incorporated many shamanistic rituals. Its mythology can be traced to the early Turkic traditions of Siberia around Orkhon and the upper basin of the Yenisey River. Some elements of those ancient beliefs have been preserved for many centuries, though noticeable differences among various Turkic people gradually emerged as a result of exposure to the proselytizing activities of numerous missionaries and the specific cultural influences of neighbors.

The pantheon of the early Turkic belief system was multilayered. In the center of this belief system was the god of blue sky—*Tengri (Tenri).*[7] He was the most powerful and mighty—creator of the universe and master of the powerful forces of nature. He could protect or punish humans at his will, but he could be cajoled by various sacrifices. Sometimes the nomads sacrificed to *Tengri* the most valuable possession they had—their horses—asking the almighty for favors. Even today, in some extremely remote areas, one can occasionally see the skull and skin of a sacrificed horse hanging on a tree or shrub.

Next to *Tengri* there was a goddess that symbolized the earth and motherhood: *Umai (Umay).* She was the supremely powerful sovereign of fertility of earth, animals, and humans. People asked her to send good harvests and fertility for domestic animals. Women asked her to send them children; those who had difficulty conceiving tried to soften the goddess with various gifts and through magic rituals. Families also asked *Umai* to protect their children from bad eyes or bad luck. In some early reports, *Tengri* and *Umai* were sometimes depicted as a couple who together ruled the universe.[8]

Tengri and *Umai* did not rule alone; some Turkic tribes, for example, believed in a god-commander of land and water called *Zher-Suu (Yer-Su).* This god was also depicted as a protector of the homeland of some specific tribes and as the one who created water and land—mountains, in particular. To the pantheon was also added the god of the underworld—*Erglig*—who guarded the world of dead and traveled up to the earth's surface to hunt for people's souls. He also represented absolute evil.

Many Turkic tribes also believed in totems—sacred animals that played a role in the tribe's earliest beginnings or protected tribal ancestors from various disasters. The wolf, for example, was regarded by many as a totem-protector of all Turkic tribes. According to legend, after a terrible war and a disastrous series of battles, foreign invaders massacred a whole tribe, including women and children. Only one little boy survived. He was protected, fed, and brought up by a wolf. When the boy grew up, this wolf gave birth to 10 boys, who later founded 10 powerful tribes. All of them remembered their protector and placed the image of the wolf on their banners. Variations on this legendary theme are found here and there in Central Asia; some Kyrgyzs, for example, believe that their ancestors were saved by a deer *(buru)*, while some Kazakhs say it was a golden eagle *(berkut)*.

In addition, people worshiped numerous local spirits, saints, and patrons. For instance, both the Kyrgyz and the Uzbeks in the Ferghana Valley thought that several saints—*olyas*—found a resting place on the Suleiman-Mountain in the city of Osh, one of the most sacred places in Central Asia, and that those saints provided the best protection in family and business matters for those who visited and prayed on the mountain. The Turkmens believed in numerous patron saints—*baba*—who could provide protection in various cases. Thus, *Zengibaba* was perceived as a saint-protector of cattle, *Musababa* a saint-protector of sheep, and so on. There were special rituals developed to cajole the *babas,* to be performed at places believed to be related to specific saint-protectors.

In everyday life, the ancestors of the Turks asked shamans to communicate with the gods or spirits and to help them to protect communities from disasters, diseases, and bad luck. In the distant past, tribal and state leaders, as well as ordinary people, consulted widely with shamans. Although the influence of the shamans had diminished significantly by the advent of modernity, it has still not disappeared altogether.

In the meantime, the settled populations of the major oases to the south of the nomadic belt introduced and developed highly sophisticated bodies of knowledge and spiritual inspiration. These ideas reached out to areas far beyond Central Asia and in one way or other influenced all the major world religions. In ancient times, numerous Central Asian cities hosted many belief systems—Zoroastrianism, Buddhism, Hellenism, early Christianity, and Islam.

Sometime in the first millennium B.C., perhaps as late as the seventh or sixth centuries B.C., Zoroaster (known in ancient Persian as Zarathustra) began preaching the revelation he claimed to have received from "the Lord Wisdom" *(Ahura-Mazda)*.[9] His teaching came to be systematically presented the sacred scripture known as the *Avesta*.[10] Zoroaster preached the oneness of God, who is served by a retinue of assistants whose form and role distantly resemble the archangels in Christianity and who is challenged by Evil (*Ahriman* in Persian). Humans have freedom to choose between right (Truth) and wrong (Lies), between good and evil. Upon each person's death, his or her soul is taken to the Bridge of Discrimination, where a judgment is rendered on whether it is fit to enter paradise or hell. In Zoroastrianism, fire symbolizes *Aura Mazda*'s power, presence, and purity, and therefore sacred fires had to be maintained in every Zoroastrian temple (in the past Zoroastrians were often wrongly called fire worshippers). This belief in the never-ending struggle between good and evil influenced many thinkers. Persian priests in major urban and political centers of the Persian Empire resisted the teaching of Zoroaster, and he was forced to find refuge in the Kingdom of Khoresm, in *Maveranahr* (now Uzbekistan). Despite his persecution, his teaching found numerous followers among the people of Central Asia, and its influence gradually expanded to the Iranian world. There the religion received greater recognition, and the Persian king Darius I and his son, Xerxes I, formally acknowledged the acceptance of its teachings. Under the Sasanid dynasty (third century A.D.–seventh century A.D.), Zoroastrianism was declared the state religion of Persia.

In the sixth century B.C., another body of teachings arrived in Central Asia—Buddhism. This system was established by Siddhartha Gautama (563?-483 B.C.), also called Buddha (translated as "awakened" or "enlightened"). He lived and taught in what are now northern India, Pakistan, and Afghanistan—in fact, there is a legend that Buddha himself met two merchants from Central Asia and informed them of his teachings. Buddha's followers systematized his teaching in a sacred writing called the "Three Baskets" *(Tipitaka)* that covers the three main dimensions of his teaching. The first part introduces the practice of Buddhism at its highest level. The second part presents lessons and sayings of the Buddha. The third deals with his cosmology and theology. The Buddha's teachings place human nature into never-ending cycles of birth, life, and death, in which individual human actions affect their lives after another rebirth. He also preached five principles of morality, exhorting his followers not to kill, steal, be untruthful, be unchaste, or take intoxicating substances. Unlike the Abrahamic religious traditions (Judaism, Christianity, and Islam), Buddhism does not conceptualize God in any traditional sense and does not recognize a teleological judgment day.

Numerous followers of Buddha came to what is now Central Asia, Afghanistan, and Western China, spreading his doctrine and establishing

Buddhist communities, which peacefully coexisted with other religious communities. Ruins of Buddhist monasteries and remains of picturesque frescos depicting the life of the Buddha can still be found in places in Tajikistan such as Kalai-Kafirnigan and Adzhiina-Tepe, as well as in Afghanistan and elsewhere. Two Buddhist temples dating from between the seventh and tenth centuries were also discovered in Akbeshim, in the Chui Valley of Kyrgyzstan.

In the fourth century B.C., Alexander the Great brought the polytheistic religion of the Greeks to Central Asia. The Greek culture flourished for a century or two, significantly influencing the cultural development of the region. However, its religious influence seems to have been mainly limited to the ruling elite. It is not clear to what extent this system affected the religious beliefs of ordinary people in urban centers, nor whether it affected at all the vast population of the rural settlements. Gradually, Zoroastrians regained their influence among the Central Asians.

In the fifth and sixth centuries A.D., the region experienced an inflow of eastern Christian missionaries, also known as Nestorians. Nestorius (386?–451 A.D.), who was the patriarch of Constantinople (now Istanbul), came into conflict with the Catholic Church in the mid-fifth century A.D. over doctrinal differences on several key theological issues. Among others, these differences included Nestorius's insistence on the distinctiveness of divinity and humanity in Jesus Christ; this conflicted with the mainstream affirmation of "hypostasis"—the doctrine that the divine and the human are synthesized in the person of Jesus. The Council of Ephesus condemned Nestorius and his supporters and exiled them from Constantinople. To escape persecution, the Nestorians settled in Persia, India, Central Asia, and as far afield as Mongolia and China. They established large churches and monasteries in Samarqand, Kashgar, Chang'an (modern Xi'an), and a number of other places. The remains of some of these churches, built between the fourth and the eighth centuries A.D., were excavated in the territories of Kyrgyzstan, Tajikistan, and Uzbekistan.

All these religions left significant marks in Central Asia's cultural history. Unfortunately, at present, many pieces of art, architecture, and literature that provide some insights into the role of those religions in the life of Central Asian communities can be found only in the region's historical sites and in various museum collections scattered around the region and the world.

HISTORY OF ISLAM IN CENTRAL ASIA

Islam emphasizes five fundamental principals that all devoted Muslims must follow throughout their life. These principles are called the Five Pillars of Islam.

Creed. All devoted Muslims must declare and accept without reservation the fundamental principle that "There is no God, but Allah, and Muhammad is the Messenger of Allah."

Prayer. Devoted Muslims must pray five times a day. In their prayer they face Kaa'ba, the holy place in the city of Mecca in Saudi Arabia. It is strongly encouraged that people go for their prayers to mosques or gather for the prayer in any other suitable house or place. However, people also can pray at any other place, including their homes, offices, and fields. In Islam, Friday is a holy day, and this day is reserved for a special prayer at noon. In many Muslim countries of the Middle East and in some other regions, people rest on Fridays, rather than on Sundays, though Central Asian Republics, like some other Muslim countries, have chosen to have the weekend on Sundays.

Charity. Regular charity, called *Zakat,* is also an obligation of devoted Muslims. All Muslims are strongly encouraged to give money or other forms of support to poor members of their communities, especially at the end of the fasting month, called *Ramadan.* It is believed that this will keep selfishness and greed at bay.

Fasting. During one month each year, Muslims are expected to fast, abstaining from food, drink, sex, and any activities that might harm others for the duration of the day, from sunrise to sunset. It is expected that this will help people to understand the life of the poor and hungry and teaches discipline and compassion. Traditionally, young children, the elderly, sick people, some women and people in other categories are exempt from fasting.

Pilgrimage. Devoted Muslims are expected to make a pilgrimage, called the Hajj, to the holy city of Mecca, in Saudi Arabia, at least once in their lifetime. It is believed that the pilgrimage will purify people and cleanse them of their sins.

Islam arrived at Central Asia more than 1,200 years ago and deeply affected the local cultural, social, and political development in the region. The history of Islam in Central Asia has been full of dramatic and unexpected turns and productive cultural exchanges and has presented followers of other religious systems with a complex labyrinth of relationships. Just as in medieval Europe, there were devastating religious wars and conflicts in Central Asia in which the populations of whole cities and towns were massacred merely for following different sets of beliefs. During times when many communities lived in isolation due to hostilities and broken communications, independent-minded and intellectually curious nomads often filled the spiritual vacuum by incorporating Islamic moral and spiritual concepts into their folklore, while Muslim *sheikhs* borrowed folkloric forms in order to explain the major Islamic tenets to locals. In the modern era, both Russian colonization and the Soviet secular political experiment left distinctive marks on the lives and practices of Islamic communities in the region.

Islam was first brought into the Central Asian region in the early eighth century A.D. by Arab warriors and missionaries. The first Arab warriors and missionaries were successful in defeating local rulers in a long series of military campaigns. Following these victories, relations between locals and the new-comers were very uneasy, as the Arabs often took harsh action against certain religious groups, especially the followers of Zoroastrianism and Shamanism, destroying their temples and sacred places and persecuting their religious leaders. These practices provoked strong resistance from local populations and led to a series of uprisings and longstanding mutual antipathy. On many occasions, both sides fought in the name of their respective religions. For example, in 720–722, 728, and again in 776–778, local populations mounted major insurgencies against the Arab occupiers and their local supporters, defeating several Arab garrisons. It took several decades before the major cities in the region fell firmly under the control of the Caliphate and local rulers became uniformly loyal to the Arabs. It was probably during these turbulent times that followers of various local pre-Islamic beliefs and traditions developed a sophisticated secret system of signs, codes, and symbols in order to hide the true meaning of their mystic knowledge in various artistic and cultural artifacts. These signs and mysteries could be found all over the region, and they still survive in the tales and legends about hidden secret libraries and monasteries, forbidden treasures and vanished cities.

By the late eighth to the early ninth centuries, major uprisings in the region had been subdued, and all sides had largely learned to live with one another; with this toleration came a mutual appreciation of cultural and religious diversity. For about 400 years Central Asia became known for great cultural and political interchanges that significantly enriched and empowered the Islamic Caliphates. This era would become known as the classical Islamic era, and it gave rise to achievements in many respects equivalent to the achievements of the European Renaissance several centuries later. During this era, in Central Asia, the Arabic script was adopted for state administrative purposes, and local rulers ordered the construction of new and magnificent public buildings throughout the region. Muslim scholars translated ancient Greek, Persian, and other texts that had survived in the region probably since classical Hellenic times, and they spread their learning to the major intellectual and cultural centers of the world—Baghdad, Damascus, Cairo, Samarqand, Merv, Herat, and many others. Central Asian scholars were among the first to establish new major centers of learning—*madrasas*. Many scholars from Central Asia contributed greatly to the most celebrated achievements of Islamic civilization.

The nomads of the Great Eurasian steppe were quite a different matter. They were slow to accept Islam, and the process of their conversion continued well into the twelfth and thirteenth centuries, in some areas well into the fifteenth century.[11] And yet, the representatives of the Turkic and Mongol tribes also made their own contributions to the region's cultural development.

Even when the fully Islamic rulers of Central Asian fiefdoms regarded the nomadic Turks as less than pious Muslims, they retained much respect for them as fierce soldiers who, for instance, contributed greatly to the Seljuk Turks' defeat of the Eastern Roman Empire.

However, at about the same time that the Inquisition began to target religious alternative thinking in thirteenth-century Western European countries, conservative Islamic scholars (*Ulemah* in Arabic) began waging campaigns against their liberal and independent-thinking colleagues. While in medieval Europe conservative clergy waged their crusades against the heresies of Albigensianism in southern France and elsewhere and began putting books and people to the fire, their counterparts in the Muslim world were following a similar pattern of behavior, targeting the literary works of their opponents and the temples and businesses of religious minorities. As in many other parts of the world, this was an outcome of intellectual debate between two groups of religious intellectuals. One group—the conservatives—wanted to keep teaching in accordance with the original principles, rejecting any free interpretations or reinterpretations of existing rules, traditions, and customs. They claimed that religious thought achieved its perfection under the guidance of the great thinkers of the past and that there was no need for rethinking or changes. "The Doors of *Ijtihad* (free interpretation) were closed!" an influential group of *Ulemah* claimed. The opposite group—very small but outspoken—claimed that there was a need to adjust the religious interpretation of many things in accordance to the realities of a changing world. "The doors of *Ijtihad* must be kept open!" was their counterclaim.

It is important to understand that arguments based in logic and reasoning were not necessarily the most important in these debates. The political power of the conservative *Ulemah* in premodern society is hard to overestimate. They controlled thousands of Islamic schools *(madrasa)* and many universities. They were the largest landowners in the region, as they controlled *Waqf* (Islamic endowments)—lands and properties accumulated though donations to mosques and *madrasas* by wealthy individuals and even khans themselves over hundreds of years.

These debates became particularly intense in Central Asia in the nineteenth and early twentieth centuries. The pride of the *Ulemah,* who congregated mainly around the leading *madrasas* and mosques in and around Bukhara, was hit by harsh realities. For years they had seen themselves as the center of Islamic thinking, the last true guardians of pure and unrevised Islamic thought—even more pure than in the then-capital of the Islamic world, the Ottoman's Istanbul. Yet, they had to face colonization by foreign powers. By the end of the nineteenth century, all the Central Asian Khanates—Bukhara, Khiva, and Kokand—had been defeated by a relatively small expeditionary army of the Russian Empire. Despite all calls for a holy war *(jihad)* against the invaders, the bravery of local troops could not match the technological advances of Western weaponry. Nor did it help when the *Ulemahs* fiercely rejected the idea of modern schooling systems in favor of spiritually pure religious education. Their views were increasingly at odds with reality. Some *Ulemahs,* for example, referred to trains and cars as "devils carts" *(Shaitan-araba)* and forbade their use by devoted Muslims—but no horse- or bullock-powered cart could match the power and speed of even the early trains and engines.

Responding to these new challenges, many groups of Central Asian intellectual reformers *(Jadids),* including some Islamic scholars, declared that the Muslim communities must learn from the West. Yet, the conservative *Ulemahs* condemned their reformist opponents and stubbornly exhorted the faithful to stick to the letter of the old interpretations. This confrontation grew even more intense and reached a climax after the Bolshevik revolution of 1917, during the civil war (1918–1922). The conservative Islamic clergy declared a Holy War against the Bolshevik nonbelievers and their supporters. On many occasions, they even led assaults on and gave their blessing to atrocities against political opponents. In retaliation, the Bolshevik commissars ordered Red Army troops to destroy not only the Muslim resistance movement but also the very symbols of this resistance—the mosques and *madrasas.* Very soon after the end of the civil war, the Soviet government abolished all *Waqf* holdings, confiscating all land and properties and closing numerous *madrasas* and mosques. During the peak of the atheistic campaigns, in the late 1920s and early 1930s, hundreds of mosques and *madrasas* were converted into public buildings such as libraries, secular schools or cinemas; others were destroyed.

However, the Stalin-led government revised its policies toward all religious communities, including the Islamic, during World War II (1939–1945). The Soviet authorities liberalized their policy toward Islamic practices, lifting some restrictions and allowing a limited number of mosques and Islamic universities. The changes of that era established a cornerstone for government policies for many years: people were allowed to practice Islam as long as their practice was kept a private matter and as long as practicing Muslims did not criticize the existing regime, did not participate in politics, and did not organize any groups, movements, or parties based on religious values.

Stalin also initiated the establishment of a special institutional structure to control the Muslim communities in Central Asia. The Spiritual Board of Muslims of Central Asia (also known by its Russian abbreviation, SADUM) was founded in 1943, and it worked from headquarters in Tashkent. The SADUM was in charge of religious education and all appointments of Imams and religious authorities in all neighboring Central Asian republics. In addition, it controlled overseas educational exchange programs, pilgrimages to Mecca *(Hajj),* the issuing of all *fatwas,* and the dissemination of propagandistic material about Soviet policies.

This silent acceptance of religious development in Central Asia and control of its expression existed without major changes until the mid-1980s. Muslims in the region had to weather periodic atheistic campaigns and public condemnations of "remnants of religious beliefs" in Central Asia; however, the Soviet state failed to achieve its major objective—the establishment of an atheistic state, free of religious influences, where the newly created Soviet rituals would replace all religious traditions. As Shahram Akbarzadeh, a scholar of Islam in Central Asia, puts it: "Soviet authorities could exercise control over the number of clerics trained to read (and interpret) the Koran but could hardly destroy traditional [Islamic-related] practices and festivals."[12] Thus, behind the customary rosy Soviet reports about the success of atheism and de-Islamization, Islam preserved its strong position at family level. Practically all family traditions—for example, childbirth, naming, boys' circumcisions, weddings, funerals—were performed according to Islamic traditions and with Islamic authorities such as Imams or *Ishans* present. As Islamic public education was outlawed, many Muslim scholars organized private classes and passed their devotion and their knowledge on to their children and relatives. In some cases, such classes were taught systematically to considerable numbers of pupils and over considerable periods of time. Some of those private classes grew up into full-scale unregistered underground *madrasas,* with very diverse curricula and discussions focusing on anything from purely spiritual issues to radical political ideas preached by various Islamic groups in the Middle East.

For all that, the Soviets did make significant advances in the secularization of many aspects of life. By the mid-1980s, the Islamic educational network had been fully dismantled, only two very small Islamic universities were open, and many Islamic traditions had been driven out of public life and especially away from politics. Several generations of people grew up with very limited knowledge of Islam and Islamic creed.

It was, however, Mikhail Gorbachev's program of reforms—glasnost and perestroika—that brought major changes in the relationship between the state and religious communities in the late 1980s. Within a short period of time, all major religious restrictions were formally or tacitly lifted, and all Muslim communities were allowed to open new or to legalize existing underground mosques, freely perform *Hajj,* attend religious schools, and in other ways practice their faith.[13]

ISLAM IN EVERYDAY LIFE IN CONTEMPORARY CENTRAL ASIA

Religious practices in everyday life in Central Asia are largely shaped by popular Islamic customs (or "low Islam," according to Ernest Gellner's definition). To a great degree, they reflect local traditions, communal rituals, numerous superstitions, and popular perceptions; to a much lesser degree, they reflect the letter of the divine law—the *Sharia*. In the post-Soviet era, Islam has regained some of its position in the everyday life of the Central Asian states; yet the religious landscape in Central Asia still differs a lot from that of the Middle East. In general, most people still prefer liberal Western dress and are open-minded as to forms of socialization and behavior. Many of them go to local fortunetellers and bring sacrifices to local saints, and if, for example, a family finds itself on the verge of breaking up, it may very well rush to witchcraft experts in the belief that its relationships have been affected by an ill-wisher's spell.

A number of prominent politicians, scholars, and intellectuals in the region have been involved in debates on the meaning of the changes in the region's religious life and the interaction between doctrinal Islam and popular Islamic practices. Conservative Islamic activists have attempted to take their personal beliefs and religious views into the public domain, stirring heated public debates about the role of the religion in political life and the relationship between the religion and the state.

The official Islamic clergy, especially the elder generation, tend to continue the Soviet-era practice of nonintervention in the politics of the state, though they work actively among the general population. For example, since independence in 1991, they have mobilized local communal, foreign, and some public funds for building and restoring mosques and *madrasas*. New mosques have been built or reopened in practically every town and city throughout the region, at an average rate of about three mosques a day. That rate was maintained throughout the 1990s, and the number of mosques skyrocketed from about 300 in 1990 to more than 10,000 in 2000. New Islamic schools were opened in almost all districts of the region. The number of people performing the *Hajj* grew from a privileged 100 or so a year in the 1970s and 1980s to several thousand a year in the 1990s and early 2000s. However, there are small but rapidly growing groups of Islamic activists, usually religiously trained young people, who demand stricter observance of Islamic traditions and greater involvement of religion in political life.

The government response to these debates and new demands was quite uniform in all five Central Asian republics. When the Central Asian governments introduced new constitutions in the early 1990s, they all initiated the inclusion of articles stating that "Religions and all cults shall be separated from the state"; that "formation of political parties on religious ... grounds" should not be permitted; and that "No religious organizations shall pursue political goals and objectives."[14]

Despite this unanimous governmental approach to the issue of relations between state and religion, many experts believe that the response from the region's respective societies will be to "follow different paths of religious development."[15] This expectation reflects differences in both the pre-Soviet and Soviet-era developments and differences in political, social, and cultural environments.

Islamic resurgence has been relatively moderate in Kazakhstan and Kyrgyzstan. Although a number of new mosques and *madrasas* were opened in both countries, their societies have remained highly secular.[16] Only about 1 percent of schoolchildren have been enrolled in the various *madrasas,* and a few hundred students have enrolled in various Islamic universities at home and overseas. In the early 1990s, several activists attempted to create political groups that demanded a greater role for Islam in political and public life in both republics, but they did not get significant support among the population and could not establish a visible presence or win seats in the national parliament.

Completely the opposite development has taken place in Tajikistan. In the early 1990s, Islamic activists established the Islamic Party of Renaissance of Tajikistan (IPRT) and united with some democratic groups to challenge the political domination of the Communist Party of Tajikistan (CPT). The IPRT attempted to mobilize its supporters to defeat the CPT candidate in the presidential elections in 1991. After losing the election, the IPRT and its supporters declared that the elections were fraudulent and attempted to topple the Communist Party–led government. The political confrontation, complicated by regional clan-based rivalries, escalated into a devastating full-scale civil war that continued for five years. During this conflict, several small religious groups were forced to flee to Afghanistan, where they found refuge among the radical Islamic groups there. Only in 1997 did the rivals agree to establish a government of national reconciliation, in which the Islamic parties and groups were granted up to 30 percent of seats. This established a precedent, being the first time an Islamic party in the territory of the former Soviet Union had became a member of a ruling parliamentary coalition.

Uzbekistan has also experienced an Islamic resurgence in the post-Soviet era, although the government has kept very tight control over all religious communities and banned political participation by any Islamic groups. In fact, it harshly persecuted any attempts at public participation by or criticism from religious groups. In this environment, a radical militant organization, the Islamic Movement of Uzbekistan (IMU), emerged in the eastern provinces of the country. This movement grew into one of the most radical political organizations not only in Uzbekistan but in Central Asia generally, coming up with demands for the establishment of theocratic Islamic states throughout the region. The Uzbekistani security forces drove the IMU out of its base in Uzbekistan's part of the Ferghana Valley between 1999 and 2001.

The IMU activists first found refuge in neighboring Tajikistan and then escaped to Afghanistan, where they received support among the Taliban-led government. The Uzbekistani government blamed the IMU for organizing bombings in Tashkent in 2004 and for political unrest in Andijan in 2005.

In Turkmenistan, the government has also implemented controversial policies toward Islamic activists. On the one hand, it uses Islamic symbols as an integral part of the national ideology and national identity, sponsoring new and grander mosques and restoring old ones and funding pilgrimages to Mecca. On the other hand, it has kept tight control over religious development and actively persecuted nonconformist representatives of the Islamic community.

By and large, the religious environment remains very dynamic and very diverse. New, radical religious organizations, such as *Hizb-Ut-Tahrir* and various others, have become more active, while influential official Islamic clergy have consistently preferred not to be involved in political life. In most of the large cities, religious belief and level of commitment remain a private matter. In this environment, highly devoted women in *hijabs* may be seen walking calmly next to girls wearing the most extravagant Western-style miniskirts.

CHRISTIANITY

Orthodox Christianity

Orthodox Christians represent the second-largest religious community in Central Asia, maintain a relatively high profile in all the republics, and work closely with the head of the Moscow Patriarchate. The Orthodox Christian Church can claim more than 1,500 years of presence in Central Asia. In fact, medieval chroniclers and travelers mentioned the existence of Christian churches and monasteries in Samarqand, Balasagun, and many other parts of the region throughout the medieval era. But practically all of them disappeared during the so-called dark ages in Central Asia between the thirteenth and sixteenth centuries, as all the local Christian communities disappeared, to be represented only by slaves captured at various bazaars and on trade routes on the Eurasian steppe or by the Caspian Sea.

Russian colonization brought in significant changes in the nineteenth and early twentieth centuries, as Russian, Ukrainian, and Belarusian settlers established their Orthodox Christian communities on the newly colonized land and opened dozens of churches and Christian schools in all the major cities in the region. However, Orthodox priests traditionally preached exclusively among fellow Christians and rarely conducted any large-scale campaigns to convert local populations to Christianity.

During the Soviet era, the Christian communities in Central Asia experienced the same fate as the Muslims. The Bolsheviks punished the Orthodox clergy for their support of the pro-monarchist movement and consequently either executed or exiled them to Siberia. Many priests chose to escape to other countries, including China, Turkey, and Australia. Many churches and monasteries were closed or destroyed or vanished due to neglect or lack of funding. During World War II, the Orthodox Church was again allowed to practice under strict state control. The Orthodox communities gained a new and powerful impetus in the mid-1980s. Most restrictions were removed, and many people turned to their religious practices as the Soviet communist ideology collapsed.

The independence of the Central Asian republics has affected the region's Christian churches in contradictory ways. On the one hand, the Orthodox Church has been freed from strict state control and interference and people have become free to practice their beliefs. On the other hand, the Orthodox communities have began facing a new and increasingly serious problem— outmigration of the Slavic population to Russia, Ukraine, and other countries. Between 1991 and 2007, nearly three-quarters of the Slavic population left Tajikistan and Turkmenistan, and almost half left Kyrgyzstan and Uzbekistan; Slavs also, and to a lesser degree, left Kazakhstan. If these emigration trends remain unchanged, many churches in the region will probably close their doors within the next 20 to 30 years.

Other Christian Communities

Protestant and Catholic Christian communities appeared in Central Asia in the late nineteenth and early twentieth centuries with the immigration of Germans, Poles, and some others to the newly colonized areas. Their numbers increased rapidly during World War II as the so-called Volga Germans from Russia, as well as German prisoners of war, Poles, and other ethnic groups, were deported to Central Asia. In the post–World War II era, their contribution to the local population reached about 2.5 percent, with the total number exceeding between 1.1 and 1.2 million people by the mid-1980s. Like their fellows in other parts of the USSR, they were allowed to open their churches and practice under very strict state control. Since 1991, many of the so-called Central Asian Germans have decided to migrate to Germany. According to various estimates, about 1 million Germans left Central Asia in the 1990s, but those who have remained try to keep their ministries active.

Throughout the twentieth century, other groups—Baptists, Adventists, and others—were active in the region, although they faced severe restrictions and persecution from the Soviet authorities. In the 1990s, many legal restrictions were lifted, and these groups began expanding their work in local Central Asian communities. There were reports that small groups of Kyrgyzs, Kazakhs, and Uzbeks were baptized. However, there is not enough information and no clear picture about the trend, as local native communities and community leaders actively resist and condemn such missionary activities among their groups.

JEWS

Some ancient Jewish texts claim that during the reign of King David, in the tenth century B.C., Jews were already traveling to Central Asia as traders. Four centuries later, the Persian King Cyrus liberated the Jews from Babylonian captivity and encouraged them to settle within his empire, including his Central Asian dependencies. Since then, Jews have lived in the region to escape persecution in their homeland or traveling for trade. There is, in fact, evidence that they have been a continuous presence in the territory of Central Asia for nearly 2,000 years, in that time largely preserving their culture and religion but experiencing their ups and downs during various stages of their history.

In the Middle Ages, Jewish communities were spread throughout several cities of the region, but the most prominent one was in Bukhara. By the mid-nineteenth century, this community, known as the Bukharian Jews, had shrunk to a few thousand. During the Russian colonial era, however, there was a significant inflow of Jews from many Russian provinces. The Soviet decades saw further inflows of Jews to the region, especially in the 1940s and 1950s, as many were sent into exile or voluntarily moved to Central Asia from other parts of the Soviet Union. Their religious activities were also restricted. In the 1970s and 1980s, the Soviet government selectively permitted some Jews to leave the USSR for Israel and the United States.

The 1990s brought major changes in the life of the Jewish communities, as all restrictions on their religious practices were lifted. This new freedom was offset, however, by growing uncertainties about the political and economic stability of the Central Asian republics. In the first post-Soviet decade, a significant number of Jews chose to migrate to Israel and other Western countries. By the early twenty-first century, a greatly reduced population of between 30,000 and 70,000 remained in the region, maintaining synagogues in Almaty, Astana, Bishkek, Samarqand, Tashkent, and some other cities and successfully running various businesses.

ISLAM IN CENTRAL ASIA AFTER 9/11

The events of 9/11 caught Central Asians by surprise, as they found themselves on the frontline of the international war on terrorism and the immediate attack on the Taliban-led forces in neighboring Afghanistan. Both the Central Asian governments and ordinary people of the region strongly condemned the terrorist attacks on the World Trade Center, in New York, and on the Pentagon, just outside Washington, DC; a fourth plane was brought down by passengers in Pennsylvania before it could hit its target. The Central Asian republics unanimously joined the U.S.-led coalition, playing a critical role in the decisive stages of the war against the Taliban-led government in 2002–2003 by granting overflight permission to the coalition air forces for various operations and humanitarian relief efforts and providing infrastructure for logistic support of the U.S. forces.[17] From the beginning. Kyrgyzstan, Tajikistan. and Uzbekistan even granted access to their territories for U.S. and NATO-operated military bases, although as of 2006 the United States maintains only one large military airbase in the region, in Kyrgyzstan.

The war in Iraq, in 2003–2007, however, was quite a different matter. Most Central Asian officials and the ordinary people were reluctant to support the U.S.-led "Coalition of the Willing," though they refrained from public actions or statements. In 2003, only Kazakhstan joined the U.S.-led allies in the war against Saddam Hussein's regime and sent troops to Iraq.

Since the beginning of the U.S.-led war against international terrorism, the Central Asian governments have toughened their positions toward the participation of Islamic organizations in political life. They have reinforced their secular policies and reconfirmed bans on the participation by any religious organizations in political activities. The governments' stances have hardened even further against supporters of the IMU, and they have also began to persecute the underground political movement *Hizb-Ut-Tahrir*. This organization claims that its sole purpose is peaceful education and social programs, but government officials have accused it of preparing the ground for political change, including the establishment of an Islamic state in the region. The *Hizb-Ut-Tahrir* has always vigorously denied such allegations.

There has been little open debate about the role of religion in public life, as the governments have strictly controlled all major media outlets. In general, people are also quite reluctant to discuss religious issues and personal attitudes toward religions in public (in conversations with foreigners, they often prefer to stick to the weather or the quality of lamb). By and large, the Central Asian societies remain deeply divided on the role of religion in social life. Evidences from various studies indicate that older believers who grew up and formed their views during the Soviet era largely support the existing status quo; they believe that religion should remain a private matter and that religious organizations should not participate in political life. In the meantime, the younger generation is divided between those who strongly support the secular nature of their countries and those who call for a return to Islamic roots and who demand a greater role for the religion in public and political life. In between there is a large segment of the young generation that is busy searching for jobs and that is more concerned about everyday life than about political debates on the role of the religions.

NOTES

1. The acclaimed Western scholar Ernest Gellner divides religious traditions into "high" (intellectual) and "low" (popular) forms. Ernest Gellner, *Postmodernism: Reason and Religion* (London: Routledge, 1992).

2. Ibid., pp. 3–12.

3. Communist Party regulations forbade party members to take part in any religious ceremonies; penalties included expulsion from the party, demotion from any official position or military rank held, or even loss of a public-sector job. Ordinary citizens were allowed to organize or participate in religious ceremonies, but they were strongly encouraged to choose civil equivalents. For elaboration on this, see Sergei Poliakov, *Everyday Islam: Religion and Tradition in Rural Central Asia* (Armonk, NY: M. E. Sharpe, 1992).

4. All figures were calculated by the author using published demographic trends and data and recent censuses conducted in the Central Asian republics, as of 2005. The figures given are regional averages and may vary slightly from republic to republic.

5. http://www.worldvaluessurvey.org (accessed June 12, 2006).

6. For a detailed description of the gods in Turkic myths, see Serikbol Kondybai, *Kazakhskaia mifologia: kratkii slovar* [Kazakh mythology: a concise dictionary] (Almaty: Nurly Alem, 2005).

7. M. S. Orynbekov, *Genezis religioznosti v Kazakhstane* [Genesis of religiosity in Kazakhstan] (Almaty: Daik-Press, 2005), pp. 5–24.

8. The Turkic pantheon is described in detail in Kondybai, *Kazakhskaia mifologia.*

9. Scholars still debate about the exact time when Zoroaster lived. Most agree that he was a real person, but he may have lived at any time from the eleventh to the sixth century B.C. For a discussion on this, see Manly Hall, *Twelve World Teachers: A Summary of Their Lives and Teachings* (Los Angeles: Philosophical Research Society, 1996).

10. Mary Boyce, *Textual Sources for the Study of Zoroastrianism* (Chicago: University of Chicago Press, 1984).

11. For research on the interaction between Islam and native religions, see Devin Deweese, *Islamization and Native Religion in the Golden Horde: Baba Tukles and Conversion to Islam in Historical and Epic Tradition* (Philadelphia: Pennsylvania State University Press, 1994).

12. Shahram Akbarzadeh, "Political Islam in Kyrgyzstan and Turkmenistan," *Central Asian Survey* 20, no. 4 (2001): 453.

13. The Gorbachev reforms also ended the Soviet engagement in Afghanistan that was so unpopular among Central Asians.

14. Article 8, sections 3 and 4 in the Constitution of the Kyrgyz Republic. For the text of the Constitution, see Rafis Abazov, *Historical Dictionary of Kyrgyzstan* (Lanham, MD, and London: Scarecrow Press, 2004), p. 266.

15. Shirin Akiner, "Islam, the State and Ethnicity in Central Asia in Historical Perspective," *Religion, State and Society* 24, no. 2/3 (1996): 122. For the most recent comprehensive scholarly discussion of this issue, see Vitaly Naumkin, *Radical Islam in Central Asia: Between Pen and Rifle* (Lanham, MD: Rowman and Littlefield, 2005).

16. For a detailed evaluation, see U.S. Department of State reports on international religious freedom in Kazakhstan and Kyrgyzstan, http://www.state.gov/g/drl/rls/irf/2004/c12783.htm.

17. For a scholarly analysis, see Shahram Akbarzadeh, *Uzbekistan and the United States: Authoritarianism, Islamism and Washington's New Security Agenda* (New York: Zed Books, 2005).

3

Folklore and Literature

Hear what they have to say to you!
Tell your experience, what you've seen,
Tell your people where you've been!
　　　　　　　　　　—From the Kyrgyz epic *Manas*[1]

Entry into the fascinating world of Central Asian folklore and literature, unlike the magic world of Narnia, requires no mysterious rings but only quite earthly objects. Extraordinarily, these objects are music CDs or DVDs, in which the nomadic bards of Central Asia have reflected their lifelong experiences on the never-ending steppe in musical form. Music was also a favorite form by which the wandering Sufis encrypted their secret messages; likewise poets, scholars, and statesmen of the medieval era expressed their thoughts musically. Even some modern poets and writers may find their works recited by an enthusiastic bard to the accompaniment of a musical instrument. The rich folklore and literary heritage of Central Asia—which include numerous epics, tales, and legends—were created by brilliant poets and writers of the past. Many of them have not been translated into Western languages and still await discovery by Western audiences.

Central Asian bards, poets, and writers have had a prominent place in public life throughout the region's turbulent history. Ordinary people have always shown great respect for the enchantment of creative writing and have always strongly believed in the special role of men of letters as messengers of the people of the streets and bazaars, messengers who presented their thoughts and wisdom to the ears of mighty rulers. They also strongly believed in the special mission of bards—called *akyns,* among Kazakhs and Kyrgyzs, and *bagshys,* among Turkmens, who were expected to safeguard the wise words of the nation's ancestors and to pass on high moral values from one generation to another. Even in times of hardship or economic recession, libraries have always been popular places and bookstores have thrived, for the people always knew the value of books and loved reading. Today, library buildings in the region are often encircled by numerous small but vibrant private bookshops and rows of individual booksellers. The latter usually arrive in hordes on weekends to offer the latest bestsellers or the shabby remnants of their old personal libraries on little sidewalk tables.

However, a first glance at the bookshelves of the region might surprise a newcomer: among the books of the most distinguished Central Asian writers and poets of the precolonial era there would be works by Firdowsi, Ibn Sina (Avicenna), al Farabi, Omar Khayyam, Jalal ad-Din Rumi, Nizami, and many others—names one would naturally expect to see in the libraries of Tehran, Kabul, Damask, Baghdad, or Herat.[2] These authors and their like represent the golden age of Persian, Middle Eastern, and South Asian literature. We must remember, however, that at that time Central Asia was an inseparable part of the greater Muslim civilization of the Middle East and of the Persian-speaking world. Premodern Central Asian literature is the common heritage of many nations that appeared on the political map only in the nineteenth or twentieth century. Since the Central Asian nations gained their independence in the early 1990s, most of their scholars, especially historians, have made constant efforts to legitimize their newly independent states within the current borders and to lay claim to the cultural heritage of the past. They do so by attempting to reconceptualize and rewrite the historical textbooks and to "nationalize" the regional cultural heritage.

A further look through the stacks of Central Asian national libraries would reveal a fundamental change in the nature of literature. Twentieth-century prose and poetry were clearly developed under a strong Russian influence. The literary world became highly fragmented, as most of the books in the Central Asian republics were published in the five Central Asian languages: Kazakh, Kyrgyz, Tajik, Turkmen, and Uzbek.[3] Although most of these works dealt with similar issues and were created within a single familiar cultural framework and often with similar approaches and techniques, they were still significantly different from the literary works created in other parts of the Soviet Union. They developed a unique national flavor and instituted a genuinely national literary heritage. There is also a unique universe of modern Central Asian prose and poetry written in or translated into Russian, the lingua franca of the Soviet state. Many of these books were written by local Russian-speaking writers, and their plots were based on local themes and issues. They were also written for a specific group of readers—the Russified native population and those who arrived in the region from different parts of the Soviet Union during the Soviet era.

FOLKLORE AND ORAL TRADITIONS

Over many centuries, the nomadic and settled peoples of Central Asia have created an exceptionally rich body of folklore. It preserves their cultural and moral traditions, values, and historical memory of great events on the Eurasian steppe and features legendary and real heroes. Oral tradition was especially important, as many written works vanished in times of war and political calamities. In addition, a significant proportion of the population was illiterate, and there was no way for nomads to carry personal libraries or keep written records of their lives.

The most popular folklore forms included epics, love stories, legends, fairy tales, short stories and comical anecdotes *(tamasha, latifa),* ritual songs, and proverbs. Many works originated in the very distant past. The oral history was carefully preserved by generations of professional storytellers and bards. Only in the nineteenth and twentieth centuries have enthusiasts and scholars collected, recorded, and published the most significant examples of folklore.

Central Asian heroic epics display various similarities to, and differences from, Western epics and legends; for example, characters similar to *Romeo and Juliet, Cinderella,* the protagonists of the *Odyssey,* and *Dracula* may be found in Central Asian stories. However, they act and behave very differently from their Western counterparts: after losing her loved one, a Central Asian Juliet would most likely take a sword and cut all her enemies into pieces; a Central Asian Cinderella would most probably meet her future prince not at a royal ball but when she fought him until the first blood; a Central Asian Odysseus would probably have a couple of wives, who would wisely rule their people while waiting for their hero's return from his long campaigns; and the Central Asian Dracula is almost always a woman, though she possesses all the traditional dark, supernatural powers and qualities of a true bloodthirsty vampire.

Central Asian heroic epics are often sung by bards *(akyns, baghshys),* traditionally to instrumental accompaniment. The *akyns* incorporate new themes into their story lines or address contemporary historical issues in order to give them new relevance, making these epics a kind of oral historical and ethical encyclopedia of their nations. There are hundreds of heroic epics in Central Asia, some of them published and well studied but a great number of them remaining hidden from a wider audience in archives and libraries. Many of these epics have a number of versions that reflect local histories and significant cultural, tribal, and historical traditions.[4]

Alpamys (also Alpamysh, Alpamsha)

This is the story of the life of Alpamys, a Turkic *batyr* (knight) who achieved wide recognition through his personal qualities and extraordinary strength.[5] The story consists of two parts. The first part introduces Alpamys, who is betrothed to Barchyn from birth but is separated from her due to quarrels between their parents; he returns and has to demonstrate his virtues in a contest for the hand of "the magnificent lady" by winning a horse race, an archery competition, and a wrestling tournament. The second part tells about the obstacles he faces leading a tribal army to defend the motherland from the cruel Kalmyk khans. Alpamys decided to travel to foreign land, but he has been captured by his enemies and has been imprisoned for seven years. Yet, his spiritual and moral strength and true friendship have helped him overcome all difficulties and escape. However, upon his return home, he faces a supreme challenge; his wife has been asked to remarry, and he must prove his identity in a song contest and his skills in an archery competition.

Geroglu (also Goroglu, Gor-Ugli)[6]

This is the story of the life of Geroglu, which means "son of the grave" (he was born after his mother died in an accident).[7] He grows up, and, when the time comes, he has to win his bride—Unus-*Peri* (fairy)—in series of adventures (in an Uzbek version he also wins two more wives—Miskol-*Peri* and Gulnor-*Peri*). With 40 knights *(yigits)*, Geroglu founds Chambel, an ideal city-kingdom and becomes an ideal ruler, showing unfailing generosity to his people and leading numerous campaigns for justice and the freedom of his nation. He defends the ordinary people and the motherland from cruel foreign khans and sorcerers with supernatural powers. His life is filled with numerous adventures and travels.

Korkut (also Korkut-Ata, Gorkut, Dede Korkut)

This is a collection of stories about the life of Dede Korkut, an old and wise oracle. Unlike many other Central Asian heroes, Korkut is presented not as a brave knight or general but as a person blessed by the saints who helps many leaders and ordinary people with his prophetic words. He lives for many years (in some versions several hundred) and travels to many places, but ultimately he returns to his homeland. He does not die, but neither is he alive. His soul travels endlessly about his fatherland, protecting the souls of the people. There are 12 major stories about Korkut; they were created over several centuries and collected in the sixteenth century in a book titled *Kitebi Dede Korkut* (The book of my grandfather Korkut).

Manas

The most acclaimed Kyrgyz heroic epic is named for Manas, a legendary Kyrgyz hero *(batyr)*,[8] who united the Kyrgyz tribes and led them to defend the Kyrgyz land from foreign aggression, thus establishing the first Kyrgyz state in the days before history. The *Manas* consists of three parts. The first part—*Manas*—revolves around the life of Manas himself and narrates his numerous campaigns against enemies. The second part—*Semetey*—recounts the life and deeds of Semetey, son of Manas. The third part—*Seitek*—tells about the life and actions of Seitek, son of Semetey and grandson of Manas. The plot is believed to be set between the ninth and eleventh centuries. The *Manas* is the world's most extensive epic; it contains about 500,000 poetic lines (recorded version of Sayakbay Karalayev),[9] which makes it some 30 times longer than the Greek epic the *Iliad* and two-and-a-half times longer than the ancient Indian *Mahabharata*. The epic reflects the history and spirit of the Kyrgyz people and their long struggle against numerous aggressors and foes:

Thought to themselves: "The Final blow!"
Yes, they had doubts that they'd pull through,

Manaschi (a singer who devotes his life to memorizing and reciting the Kyrgyz national epic *Manas*) performs before a public audience. Courtesy of the author, 2006.

Being besieged on all sides too!
Even women took daggers and knives,
Ready to save their honour and lives.[10]

Oguznama (also Oguz-nama, Literally "Epic about Oguz")

This is one of the most acclaimed epics among the peoples of Central Asia. *Oguznama* tells the story of Oguz Khan and his sons and of the establishment of the early Turkic states in the western parts of Central Asia and Asia Minor. Most scholars trace the epic's origin to the medieval period, dating it between the eleventh and thirteen centuries.[11]

Legends are another popular genre in Central Asia. Traditionally, they are significantly shorter than the heroic epics. They are devoted to the adventures and deeds of local heroes, often real historical personalities, who were honored for defending people, tribal pride, or land against foreign invaders, forces of nature, or cruel khans. Some legends also narrate the extraordinary adventures of the heroes in their search for their beloved "ladies." Legends about Jamshid, Rustem, Siavush, and many others have been well known around the region for centuries. Some legends were devoted to the lives of real historical personalities; in others, it is nearly impossible to separate fantasy from fact. Interestingly, there are many legends about the extraordinary lives and adventures of women, such as Aysulu, Gylduzsun, Kyz-Zhibek, Kulshe-Kyz, Makpal-Kyz, Shyryn-Kyz, and Tomaris (Tomiris). For example, Kyz-Zhibek presents the story of the tragic love of a beautiful young woman, Kyz-Zhybek, for a knight, Tolegen, and the trials they had to face.

Numerous Central Asian fairy tales encompass local themes, as well as popular themes from the Middle East, South Asia, and Mongolia. Many fairy tales are still popular among audiences of all ages for their thrilling plots and meaningful lessons. Many fairy tales present lives of ordinary herdsmen, *batyrs,* and wise khans who bravely fight against numerous and powerful enemies, defeating them in battles and long campaigns. Other themes include allegories featuring animals—beers, wolves, camels, foxes—who are given magical powers to help good people, families, or tribes; there is a large body of children's allegoric tales in which animals are used to ridicule human deficiencies such as greed and arrogance. There are also numerous tales about magic, witchcraft, and spirits, including djinns, *divs,* and *peris,* as well as humorous stories about poor but wise tricksters such as Aldar Kose, Kozhanasyr, and Khoja Nasreddin.

Short humorous stories *(latifa, tamasha)* have been extremely popular among Central Asians since the Middle Ages. People traditionally begin celebrations, family and public events, and even formal business meetings by telling comic stories about the adventures of traditional heroes like Aldar Kose or Khoja Nasreddin or about local comic personalities. One old story about Khoja Nasreddin goes as follows:

A wealthy neighbor invited Nasreddin to a party. Nasreddin was working at his farm and came in a hurry without changing from his old workclothes. At the party everyone ignored him, did not invite him to sit, and did not offer him any food. Angered, Nasreddin left the house silently, changed into new and expensive clothes, and came back to the party. This time everyone noticed him, welcomed him at the entrance, and offered him the best seat at the table and the best food.

Nasreddin, noticing the changed attitude, sat down at the table and began dipping his sleeves into the plates saying loudly:

"Eat, my beautiful clothes, eat! People are honoring you, not me!"

Other favorite stories feature local clowns or the comic habits of well-known public figures. The people also enjoy teasing—in a gentle way—each other or people from neighboring towns, provinces, or states. It is expected that a teased person will not be offended but will instead reply with his or her own joke or tease. For example, a popular joke that people from place "A" tell about people from place "B" goes: A man from "B" visits his wife, who has just given birth. He asks, "Do I have a boy?" "No," she replies, "it's not a boy." "Then what is it?"

LITERATURE OF CLASSICAL AND PRECOLONIAL ERAS

Lyric, heroic, court, and religious poetry constitutes the main body of the Central Asian literary heritage of the classical period from the ninth century to the fifteenth century. Important features of this poetry were the incorporation of allegoric symbolism, elegant wording, and melodious rhythm. Every prominent minister and counselor at the royal court of a Central Asian ruler was expected to create poetic verses or to sponsor poets who wrote praise poetry. In fact, Avicenna, an encyclopedist and one of the founders of contemporary medicine, wrote half of his medical works in verse.

The classical literature of that era followed strict conventions of form, style, and genre. For example, the *dastan* is a grand epic poem. The *dastan*s honored real historical personalities of the past or legendary and popular folk heroes in fantastic, romantic, or heroic forms. The *ghazel* is a short lyrical poem that consists of several verses devoted to a single topic, usually centered on love and passion. The *qasyda* is a collection of verses that elegantly explores various topics and ends with a panegyric to a ruler, a patron, or a saint. A *rubai* (from Arabic—"four") is a four-line verse (quatrain) that rhymes the first, second, and fourth lines (e.g., aaca, bbxb); these individual *rubai* are beautifully knitted, extended (usually romantic) poems. The *qitah* is a short poem that features popular themes, jokes, word-puzzles, or symbols; it is recited at public events or gatherings. The *maqamah* is a poem devoted to a single theme and written in a very high style. The *masnavi* (translated "two by two") is a poem written in rhymed pairs (e.g., aa, bb) that might bring together many verses.

Central Asian literature of the medieval and premodern eras developed along two distinct, though closely related, lines. One group was written primarily in Persian, and the other was written in the Turkic language, though Arabic was also used, primarily in theological writings.[12] Persian traditionally predominated in the major settled areas of the region, such as Samarqand, Bukhara, Merv, Herat, and Urhench, from the early medieval era. Meanwhile, the Turkic language predominated among nomadic tribes in the northern, northwestern, and eastern parts of the region. However, with every new wave of Turkic-speaking groups into the oases and large cities, the influence of their language came to be felt in the literature. Although the first major literary works in Turkic were written in the tenth and eleventh centuries in the eastern parts of Central Asia—the *Jetisuu* area—Turkic literature really did not begin to flourish until a few centuries later.

The classical era gave Central Asia many talented and prolific poets. As in Renaissance Europe, many works of that era were created by people with an encyclopedic knowledge who wrote universal works. The canon of Central Asian literature lists, among others, Firdowsi, Kashgari, Dekhlevi, Nizami, Sa'adi, Jami, Unsuri, and Alisher Navai as representatives of the classic heritage.

Abu Al-Qasem Mansur Firdowsi (935?–1020)

Central Asians, especially Tajiks, consider Firdowsi to be one of the greatest early writers, poets, and historians. He was born into a family of poor *dehqan* (petty gentry) and devoted nearly his entire adult life to the completion of a single work—the monumental epic poem *Shahnama* (also *Shahnameh*) (*Book of Kings,* c. 1010). Firdowsi incorporated both prose and poetry into the work to beautifully depict historical deeds of real and imagined personalities, thus creating an encyclopedia and a universal history of his land. The *Shahnama* describes Persian history under 50 *padishahs* (kings), from the mythical rulers of ancient times, such as Kiyoomars, Hooshang, and Tahmoores, to historical figures such as Azarnidokht, Farokhzad, and Yazdeg III. Firdowsi's depiction of history as a never-ending struggle between good and evil reflects a Central Asian worldview that goes well back into the Zoroastrian philosophy and cosmology. For Firdowsi, evil forces and evil thoughts originate in foreign lands or in the dark facets of human psychology; only through devotion to one's ancestral land and traditions can one overcome them. The *Shahnama* is a celebration of justice and humanism that inspires in people a belief that individuals can overcome even the greatest obstacles in their lives. In the Persian-speaking world, this grand epic, which consists of 55,000 *bayts* (couplets), is considered to be one of the greatest achievements of Persian literature. Plot lines and heroes from the *Shahnama* find their way into popular songs, legends, and fairy tales and even into medieval scholarly studies of history and philosophy.

Mahmud ibn Husayn ibn Muhammad Kashgari (c. 1029–c. 1101)

Many Central Asians consider Mahmud Kashgari one of the greatest writers and philosophers. He was among the first to develop literary criticism and to study the Turkic language and early medieval Central Asian literature systematically. His *Dewani lughat at Turk* (Dictionary of the language of the Turks) is a study of the folklore, legends, and idioms of the Turkic language of his era. In the tradition of his era, his work was written in the form of a universal encyclopedia, created to celebrate the achievements of the Turkic world in comparison to the Persian- and Arab-speaking world. It also highlighted rivalries and differences between these cultures.

It is important to remember that Central Asian literature of the classical era was developed under the strong influence of the Islamic mystical movement—Sufism. The Sufis introduced symbolism, secret signs, and clandestine meanings into many pieces of poetry and prose. Many celebrated members of mystical orders were also influential men of letters: for example, Omar Khayyam, Ahmed Yassavi, Suleiman Bakirgani, and Jalal ad-Din Muhammad Rumi.

Omar Khayyam (c. 1048?–c. 1122?)

Omar Khayyam is one the best-known and celebrated representatives of Sufi poetry. Omar Khayyam, like many writers and poets of his time, was a person of universal education and knowledge. Medieval authors attributed significant works on philosophy, law, history, and science to him. However, it was spiritual travel with Sufi teachers and his picturesque *rubai* (quatrains) about passion, love, and praise of women's beauty that brought him wide recognition. His poetry and his life captivated many generations in the East and in the West; in 1957, Hollywood moviemakers even produced a movie, *Omar Khayyam,* about his life and creative work. Unfortunately, very few of his poems survived the dark ages of Central Asian history, but even those few that survive inspired many authors, bards, and ordinary people. His poetry is full of emotions and the search for inspiration and for personal affection and contains Sufi allegoric symbols: The loved one's brow against my lip,/ Her beauty fresher than the rose.[13]

Nizam Al-Din Mir Alisher Navai (also Nawai) (1441–1501)

Alisher Navai is considered one of the founders of Uzbek literature, as he wrote in the Turkic *(Turki)* language.[14] His areas of interest also included painting, calligraphy, architecture, music, and mysticism. In fact, he was known as a devoted member of the Naqshbandi Sufi order and as a student of the great mystic of his time, Jami. Navai left a very rich literary legacy that includes poems, prose, and academic works on different disciplines. His most acclaimed collection of poems is the *Hazoi Ul-Maonii* (Treasury of thoughts), which includes about 3,000 *ghazels.* Navai's *Hamsa* (Quintuplet), which was inspired by the famous poet Nizami, continues the Middle Eastern and Persian poetic traditions. It consists of five poems written in different styles and devoted to different aspects of human life. Two poems—*Leila and Mejnun* and *Farhod and Shirin*—reflect traditional Arabic and Persian themes about lovers who battle for happiness. It is a mystical allegory about the struggle between justice and injustice and the search for inner strength in fighting against universal evil. Some scholars also attribute his poem *Lisot ut-Tair* (Language of birds) and various others to his Sufi scholarship and reflections. His work *Muhakamat al-Lughatayn* (Judgment about the two languages) played a far-reaching and extremely important role in propagating the development of the Central Asian literature in Turkic languages, as it defended the usage of the Turkic language in literature and poetry. Previously, this role had been reserved exclusively for Persian language, and Turkic language was viewed as the language of the streets and of commoners.

Alisher Navai and his contemporaries started new trends in the literary world of Central Asia: they began departing from classical "high" Persian and Turkic and increasingly incorporated the language of the streets and bazaars into their works. This trend coincided with the formation of early national identities and national languages in the fifteenth century.

Magtymguly (Pen Name Pyragy or Fragi) (1733?–1782?)

Magtymguly is one of the best examples of the trend toward an increasing usage of the Turkic language in literature and poetry. Turkmen authors often compare Magtymguly to Shakespeare; in contemporary Turkmenistan, he is considered the founder of modern Turkmen poetry, literature, and language. He probably began writing his first poems at the age of 20. Many of them are devoted to his people and to humanistic ideals. He also describes the devastating effects of tragic social and political events, such as wars and tribal skirmishes, on the lives of ordinary people. He courageously experimented with new forms of poetry and made wide use of the simple language of ordinary Turkmens. Magtymguly's writing significantly affected the development of the Turkmen language and the literature of his time. Many of his poems became popular songs and were widely known among Turkmens and other Turkic-speaking people. Much of his work was written in the best Sufi tradition and is devoted to Love: love of woman, of the Creator, and of his country.

> A war would never catch a Turkmen unaware;
> Its past hardship the country would put behind;
> The roses would never wither here—among them none
> Would whine about being parted with gleemen of Turkmenistan.
> The brotherhood here—tradition; and friendship—the law
> Of the glorious clans and powerful tribes,
> And if a battle called the people to take arms,
> The enemies would tremble before sons of Turkmenistan.
>
> —Makhtumkuli, *Stikhotvorenia* (Verses),
> (Ashkhabad: Turkmenistan, 1989), p. 15. Translated by the author.

Magtymguly's poems circulated widely in their day in what used to be the Bukhara Emirate, in the Khiva Khanate, in Afghanistan and Persia, and elsewhere and became well known in Afghanistan, Iran, Turkey, and other parts of Central and South Asia. Much of his personal collection of manuscripts was lost during his travels. In fact, many of his verses were preserved only by Turkmen *baghshys*.

MODERN LITERATURE

Nineteenth- and Early-Twentieth-Century Literature

The literature of the nineteenth and early twentieth centuries reflected complex changes in Central Asian societies.[15] It bridged the gap between the classical poetry and literature of the palaces and royal courts, which was usually written in "high" language and strict styles, and new literature, which experimented with European models—"new" forms, especially in prose. The literary heritage of this era is an intricate reflection of these changes. Some works remained in the Procrustean bed of classical forms and genres, though the lyrics of this era often degenerated into endless repetition of clichés and truisms. Others explored earthy topics and issues from the everyday life of ordinary people— moral decadence, corruption, polarization of societies, social ills, and coloniza- tion—and are written in the vernacular of the bazaars and streets.

The evaluation and formation of a personal artistic position in relation to the collapse of the "old" and the rise of the "new" became a very divisive issue in the artistic community. In the past, the whole world had been divided into two simple parts. One was the universal evil that in the eyes of writers and bards was epitomized by the world outside Central Asia: the world of danger, militarism, threats and frequent barbarism, inferior cultural achievements, and uncivilized attitudes toward such notions as honor, love, and passion. The other was the world of the universal good— the highly civilized world of Central Asia that had its roots in the true religion and magnificent civilizations of the past, whose high moral values and cultural and technological achievements were a source of inspiration and eternal power. Now, however, European colonialism brought a kind of chaos to the traditional perceptions: the colonizers hardly possessed high moral values, they were infidels and they came from barbaric lands, yet they had easily defeated Central Asia's rulers and established their colonial domination.

In this situation, the main question was: should Central Asians learn from the colonizers, or should they turn back to the "true" roots and values? Many intellectuals rejected all foreign values, seeing the colonial powers' lifestyle, education, and political systems—everything without exception—as extremely corrupt and alien. They called for a return to "true" old values. These writers and poets tried to escape into a utopian world of the "golden past" or into lyri- cal nonpolitical literature. Another group of intellectuals, however, focused on rethinking Central Asians' relations with the Western world (including Russia) and Western thinking that had relatively suddenly arrived at their doorsteps. This group opposed the view of the traditionalists, seeing in the achievements of modernized nations an example to follow. They admired the railroads, industries, planned cities, printing technologies, and high education standards of Russia and the Western world.

These two groups evinced highly disparate propensities. The conservatives (qadimiy) came to demonstrate strong anticolonial and anti-Russian feelings. The others—the reformers (jadids)—tacitly accepted the colonial system.[16] The literary world was even more complex, since it comprised not only members of both camps but also many groups and individuals who had to make painful decisions as to which camp to support.

These views and debates are reflected in the Central Asian literature of the era. For example, Davlat Batabay-Uly (Batabayev) (1802–1874), Sholtan-bai Kanay-Uly (Kanayev) (1818–1881), Mahambet Otemis-Uly (Utemisov) (1804–1846), and others rejected the changes brought by the Russian colonial administration to the Kazakh steppe and called for resistance to colonial rule. They were among the first writers to incorporate political polemics into their poetry. In the meantime, poets and writers such as Ybyrai Altynsarin (1841–1889) and Abai (Abai Kunanbai-Uly [Kananbayev]) (1845–1904) called for change and for enlightenment and learning—including learning from the Russians. It was not surprising, then, that Abai was among the first transla-tors of the Russian poets Aleksandr Pushkin and Mikhail Lermontov, among others, into the Kazakh language.[17] Abai's poems *Masgud* (1887) and *Azim turaly anyz* (Story about Azim) (1887?) continue the indigenous Kazakh folk-lore traditions; yet, his *Kulembyu* (1888) and *Men akyry bolys boldym* (Finally I became an officer) (1889) criticize the admirers of the Russian bureaucratic system. Mohammad Mukimi (1850–1903), Furkat Zakirzhani (1858–1909), Avaz Otar (1884–1919), and others turned to the everyday realities and lives of ordinary people, writing about their problems, thoughts, and hopes; in satirical poetry they ridiculed the rich and powerful for their greed and short-sighted actions. Satirical lines are also to be found in the works of the Turk-men poet Mamedveli Kemine (1770–1840), who devoted many of his poems to philosophical thoughts about the roots of social injustice, poverty, and corruption in the Turkmen land.

Central Asian literature of the colonial era developed as result of the strug-gle between the new and the old, enlighteners and conservatives. The most radical and irreversible changes, however, arrived after the Bolshevik revolu-tion of 1917. The changes were so fundamental that they totally transformed the national literatures, introducing new styles, forms, and structures at an unprecedented rate.

SOVIET LITERATURE

In general, Central Asian Soviet-era literature revolved around three major themes—the revolt against old traditions and prejudices; the search for and the establishment of social justice; and an awakening of a new hero and a rebel spirit in the ordinary person. These themes were developed against a background of dramatic polarization wrought by the Bolshevik revolution in Central Asian society and the extraordinary social, cultural, and politi-cal changes instigated by the Soviet system, which radically altered the lives of every person in the region. The Schwarzenegger of Central Asian Soviet literature, however, was not of a kind readily adaptable to today's Hollywood "action-hero." His main mission was to change himself and people around him. His rebellion was against social injustice, traditional ways of life, rich and oppressive lords *(bais),* and restrictive ancient rituals. Also he challenged the age-old conception of family and personal honor and their associated codes of revenge and forgiveness.

The social changes in the literary and intellectual world of Central Asia made a huge impact on the development of the literature and criticism in the region. The Bolsheviks removed the old social barriers and encouraged every talented individual from every kind of background—working class people, peasants, ethnic and religious minorities, descendants of slaves, Muslim reformers—to write from their personal experience and the experience of the people around them (as long as they accepted Bolshevik values). In the literary world, the Bolshevik revolution also created enormous opportunities for young Central Asian intellectuals. The Soviet authorities also opened doors for experimentation in new genres, styles, and themes by exposing locals to classic Western and Russian literature and poetry as great numbers of works were translated en masse into local languages. All these changes significantly undermined the influence of the classical Central Asian literary heritage and helped to build a completely new literary universe.

Central Asian literature of the 1920s, for example, reflected the bloody confrontation between old and new. The political struggle between various social groups was strikingly depicted by the Turkmen poet Durdy Glych in his poems *Baylar* (The rich) (1928) and *Garyplar* (The poor) (1928). The Turkmen writer Ata Kaushutov, in his play *Krovavyi les* (Bloody forest) (1929), and the poet Ata Salikh, in his poem *Zhertva adata* (Victim of adat) (1928), examined the struggle for women's emancipation within the deeply traditional Turkmen society. The Tajik writer Sadriddin Aini's novels *Odina* (1924), *Dokhunda* (1930), and *Kullar* (Slaves) dealt with pre-Revolutionary oppressions and the Bolsheviks' inspired social changes in Tajik society. Fitrat's *Shaitan* (Satan) and *Zahroning emoni* (Day of last judgment), in true Faustian style, depict various religious issues and the thoughts of an ordinary peasant concerned about certain doctrinal aspects of Islam. Abdulhamid Chulpan (1898–1937) depicted the destruction and devastation that civil war had brought to his country in *Urtok Karshibov* (Comrad Karshibov) and *V moikh glazakh ostalis' poslednie slezy* (Last tears of my eyes). The Kazakh writer Saken Seifullin (1894–1938), in his lyrical poem *Kokshetau* (1938), turned to the history of the Kazakhs' struggle for a better life. And, in his novel *Tar zhol, taighak keshu* (Thorny road) (1926), he wrote about the patriotic inspiration of those who participated in the revolution and civil war. While Russian literature about the civil war often revolved around class struggle, Central Asian literature usually centered on the conflict between the individual and the family, tribe, or community, between old traditional values and newly discovered ideological devotion. The ideologically progressive main characters often faced betrayal, hidden resistance, or rejection from the people they trusted.

The first flush of revolution-inspired creativity was short-lived. By the 1930s, the Soviet regime no longer tolerated any criticism or deviation from the ruling party line and had initiated mass purges among the creative intelligentsia. Those who disagreed with or challenged the ideological pressure paid a very high price—a whole generation of young artists was jailed, exiled, or executed. In a contradictory revision of its initial policy encouraging innovation and experiment, from the 1930s onward the government imposed a straitjacket of rules in the form of the "socialist realism approach in literature."[18] Socialist realism stipulated "truthful, historically concrete reflection of reality in its revolutionary development."[19] In practice, the Communist Party tightly controlled all literary content and demanded that writers present Soviet life in unremittingly optimistic terms, soliciting work on such topics as the "construction of communism" and the "brotherhood of the people." Such writings were often little more than propaganda.

The ideological restrictions were powerfully enforced through professional organizations, the Unions of Writers that were established in all Central Asian republics. The Union of Writers controlled the whole literary process from manuscript soliciting to publishing. And the writers had good reasons to comply with these regulations. Union membership provided significant benefits, including privileged accommodation, access to consumer goods, free domestic and international travel, and priority in publishing new works in Union-controlled literary journals. Gradually, many writers turned into bureaucrats who tightly protected their privileges and blocked talented nonconformist young authors from membership. Exclusion from the Unions often meant the end of a writer's career.[20]

The writers in each of the Central Asian republics were also under direct pressure from the Kremlin and local governments to create a new Soviet culture that would be "national in its substance." Thus, many Central Asian intellectuals turned into nation-builders working on the introduction of distinct "national" (e.g., Kazakh, Kyrgyz, Tajik) symbols, characters, and cultures. To do so, they often "nationalized" local folklore, myth, legends, and epics, portraying them as components of the "true" people's culture. They not only reinvented the rich cultural heritage of the past as a national heritage but also reintroduced them in new, modern, European forms, such as short stories, novels, plays, and social dramas.

The leading theme of the 1930s was social change and the struggle to achieve the goals of the collectivization and industrialization campaigns. The social changes reshaping Turkmen society are explored in Durdyev's poem *Klassovaia bor'ba* (Bloody struggle) (1930), Alty Karaliev's *Aina* (1937), Esenova's *Shemshat* (1938), and many others. The Tajik writer Ikrami, in his novels *Zmeia* (Snake) (1934) and *Shodi* (1940), and the writer Dzhalil, in his novel *Gulru* (1940), expressed similar themes. The Uzbek poet and writer Manzura Sabirova (penname Aydyn) (1906–1953) focused, in her numerous short stories, on the difficulties that women in Uzbek society faced before and after the Bolshevik revolution. The Kazakh poet Ilias Zhansugirov (1894–1938), in his poems *Dala* (Steppe) (1930), *Kuishi* (Bard), and *Kulager* (both 1935), reinterpreted the traditional Kazakh historic epics by linking the past to the present through his historical and philosophical thoughts about changes in the fatherland.

Like many Soviet writers of that era, Central Asian authors wrote about building the "new Soviet life" through the *kolkhozes* and industrial enterprises. But what distinguished the Central Asian writers was that they dramatized and complicated these stock themes by adding new local flavor and unusual nuances and by representing the culturally distinctive patriarchal ways of Central Asian life and religious backwardness as qualities in need of Bolshevik redemption. A typical cliché in the writing of this period was the depiction of newcomers (Russian Bolsheviks, agitators, or commissars) as people of superior moral and spiritual power who helped the influential local characters to abandon the old (and "wrong") ways of life and to "discover" the irresistible power of the Soviet ideology and "culture."

From the 1940s to the 1960s, the major literary themes were Soviet patriotism and the Great Patriotic War (1941–1945). Reflections on the difficulties of the war and patriotic sentiment in Turkmenistan may be found in Beki Seitakov's novel *Devushka v pogonakh* (A girl with shoulder-straps [A girl in the military]) (1942) and in his monumental four-volume novel, *Dogandar* (Brothers) (1958–1972) and in Berdy Kerbabayev's *Gurban-Durdy* and *Ailar* (1942). The Tajik poets Tursun-Zade, in his *Syny Rodiny* (Sons of the Motherland) (1942), and Mirshakara, in *Ludi s kryshi mira* (People from the roof of the world) (1943), also wrote on patriotic issues. In the postwar decades, the Tajik poet Gaffor Mirzo, in his poem *Asror* (1957), and the poet Ansari, in his *Gulshan* (1957), wrote about the life of the Soviet people. Kamil Nugmanov (penname Iashen) (1909–) turned to different pages of Uzbek history in his plays *Ravshan va Zulkhumar* (1957) and *Yulchi Yulduz* (Guiding star) (1957); he wrote about people's struggle for their freedoms and for a better life. Novels by the Uzbek writer Sharaf Rashidov (1917–1983) were probably most typical of this era: in his *Kudratli tulkun* (The great wave) (1964), he wrote about young people and the issue of moral and personal degradation in Soviet society among those consumed by personal egoism and self-indulgence. Many Kazakh writers also turned to historical issues; I. Esemberlin's *Koshpendiler* (Nomads), A. Nurpeisov's *Kan men ter* (Blood and sweat), S. Zhunisov's *Akhan Sere,* and A. Alimzhanov's *Makhambettin zhebesi* (The arrow of Makhambet) all covered various dramatic and decisive events in Kazakh history. The Kyrgyz writer Chingiz Aitmatov's *Pervyi uchi'tel* (The first teacher) (1962) depicted the impact an individual had on a small traditional village in the mountains as he taught new values and new ideals. The best works of that era focused on changing relationships in small, close-knit communities in remote areas, as difficulties and sufferings helped people to overcome family, tribal, and communal differences. Importantly, during this era, a new common character emerged in Central Asian literature—this time, a local hero returns home, bringing a whole new universe with him or her after experiencing a "new" life in a completely different, "real Soviet" environment.

In the 1970s and 1980s, mainstream writers continued to explore the crucial social issues surrounding the development of Soviet society. During this time, Central Asian literature was more in line with popular Soviet themes, as many writers depicted the life of large collectives, where innovators and enthusiasts struggled against opportunists and conservatives. Yet, some Central Asian writers ventured away from propaganda and the socialist realism theme and began exploring such forbidden issues as the rise of nationalism or anticolonial struggles, or they simply revised and even challenged state-imposed dogmas and ideas, especially official Russia-centric interpretations of history and cultural development. For example, the Kyrgyz writer Tologon Kasymbekov (1931–), in his books *Syngan klych* (Broken sword) (1978),[21] *Kel-Kel*, and others, turned to the traditional issues—difficult eras in Kyrgyz history—but radically departed from the ruling party-approved interpretation of the conflicts of those periods and paved the way for the creation of historical accounts with a strong nationalistic flavor.

The quality of Soviet-era literature was very uneven. Even Soviet literary critics recognized the existence of works they deemed "primitive with no artistic merit," having "clichéd characters … with stereotype heroes" and "vaguely defined" conflicts.[22] The Schwarzenegger of Central Asian literature, like his American action-hero counterpart, was predictably a good-looking, politically correct person who inevitably challenged bad guys and always won the battle (and often the heart of an attractive woman), despite numerous tricks by his enemies. Yet, there were many literary works that reflected upon genuine conflicts between the old and the new or critically examined the emancipation of women and men from the stultifying restrictions of old tribal, communal, or religious customs. And these, by and large, were the works that the ordinary people were reading. Some extraordinarily talented writers and poets created works that captivated many people in Central Asia and beyond. It is also important to remember that the Soviet authorities were investing heavily in the development of the national identity of the newly created nation-states, and, to this end, they sponsored national literature, poetry, art, and education. In addition, it must be kept in mind that the Central Asian languages were standardized only in the 1920s and 1930s. Therefore, the national writers and poets of that era were often pioneers who revolutionized national culture by writing not in classical Persian or Turkic but in the languages understandable to ordinary peasants and workers.

Chingis Aitmatov (1928–)

Aitmatov's early writings combined fine psychological portraits of ordinary people with the magical culture, landscape, and pastoral lifestyle of traditional Kyrgyz society in such works as *Povesti gor i stepey* (Tales of mountains and steppes) (1962), *Proshchai, Gulsary!* (Farewell, Gulsary!) (1966), and *Belyi parokhod* (The white steamship) (1970).[23] His stories *Dzhamilia* (1958) and *Pervyi uchitel'* (1962) were adapted for the screen and became classics of Kyrgyz cinema. Aitmatov was the first Kyrgyz author to raise the analysis of traditional Kyrgyz folklore to the level of philosophical inquiry. In his later writings, he remained faithful to his early themes but added fresh nuances. His writing gravitated toward mystical imagery and philosophical parable. He combined traditional folklore images with motifs of classical world literature in his *I dol'she veka dlitsia den'* (The day lasts more than a hundred years) (1980), *Plakha* (Execution block) (1986), and *Tavro kasandry* (Kasandra's brand) (1997). Most of his novels, which were adapted for the screen by the Kyrgyz film studio, have had a powerful impact on the formation of the Kyrgyz worldview. Aitmatov's literary works won him the reputation of "one of the most distinguished non-Russian authors writing in Russian."

Berdy Kerbabayev (1894–1974)

Turkmen writer, translator, and commentator. Between 1924 and 1926, he edited several poetry collections of the Turkmen poet Magtymguly. In 1931, he published his first collection of short stories. In the 1930s, he translated several important novels of Leo Tolstoy, Mikhail Sholokhov, and Maxim Gorkii from Russian into Turkmen. Between 1940 and 1955, he published his own monumental three-volume novel, *Aýgytly Ädim* (Decisive step), which was also published in Russian under the title *Reshaushchii Shag*. In 1947, he published his novel *Aysoltan iz strany belogo zolota* (Aysoltan from the country of white gold), and, in 1957, he published the novel *Nebitdag*. Kerbabayev played an important role in the development of the literature of Turkmenistan in the twentieth century.

Mukhtar Auezov (1897–1961)

Kazakh writer, translator, and dramatist. In 1917, he wrote his first play, *Enlik-Kebek*. In the 1920s, he published several short stories and plays. His first serious short stories and novels, such as *Shatkal* (Gorge) (1935), *Izder* (Footprints) (1935), *Burkut'shi* (Hunter with a golden eagle) (1937), and *Kobylandy* (1945), brought him nationwide recognition. Between 1942 and 1956, he published his monumental four-volume novel *Abai* (1942–1947) and *Abai zholy* (The path of Abai) (1952–1956), which are among the most acclaimed works of twentieth-century Kazakh literature. These books were translated into Russian and other languages of the Soviet Union. He was among the first Kazakhs to translate the works of major Russian and Western writers (from Russian) into the Kazakh language, including Nikolai Gogol's play *Revizor* (Inspector-General), and Shakespeare's *Othello* and *The Taming of the Shrew*. Auezov's literary heritage includes more than 100 plays, short stories, and novels that made him one of the most prominent Kazakh writers in Kazakhstan.

Aibek, also Oibek (penname; real name, Musso Tashmuhamedugli) (1904–1968)

Uzbek poet, writer, translator, and commentator. His early collections of poems, *Tuifular* (Feelings) (1926) and *Kungilnailari* (Flutes of the heart) (1929), reflect his search for his own personal style and themes. His poetry underwent significant changes in the 1930s, and he penned the poems *Mest'* (Revenge) (1932) and *Bakhtygul va Sagyndyk* (Bakhtygul and Sagyndyk) (1933), which reflected the confrontation between old and new in postrevolutionary Uzbekistan. He then turned to historical issues in the poem *Navai* (1937), depicting the universal theme of contradiction between an intellectual and a ruler. He next published his first novel, *Kutlugkon* (Sacred blood) (1943). In the 1944 novel *Navai,* he attempted a sweeping portrait of a great historical personality and thinker whose life and actions were interlinked with the lives of both ordinary people and ruthless intellectuals; a key theme was the responsibilities of the intellectual in promoting universal good and containing absolute evil. In the 1950s, he wrote the poems *Zafar va Zukhro* (Zafar and Zukhra) (1950) and *Khakguilar* (Truth lovers) (1952). He translated several Russian and

Russian-language Western works into Uzbek, including Alexander Push-kin's *Eugene Onegin* and Goethe's *Faust*.

Olzhas Suleimenov (1936–)

Kazakh writer and politician. While a student at Kazakh State University he began to write poetry. In 1958–1959, he attended the Gorky Literary Institute (Moscow). In 1959, he published his first collection of poems in Moscow. From 1961 to 1975, he worked variously as a journalist, an editor of the literary journal *Prostor,* and an editor at the studios of *Kazakh-film* and in administration for the Kazakh Union of Writers. His poem *Zemlia poklonis' cheloveku* (The Earth—bow to a man!) (1961) brought him wide recognition. In 1975, Suleimenov published his book *Az i ia,*[24] a historical-philosophical essay on Turkic historical destiny.[25] In it he explored the history of the interaction between nomads (Turks) and settlers (Slavs) and the place of the Kazakhs in the historical development of Eurasia. The publication was condemned by Moscow's policymakers as "nationalistic," and it was confiscated and banned until 1989. Suleimenov became one of the most prominent Kazakhi dissidents of the 1970s, and only the personal intervention of the Kazakh first secretary Dinmuhammed Kunaev saved him from imprisonment. *Az i ia* won him nationwide recognition in Kazakhstan and a reputation as the "opener of difficult issues in the national history. After political rehabilitation, he worked in various positions with the Union of Writers. He became one of the most influential writers in Kazakhstan in the 1980s. His active public life in the 1980s won him a reputation as the "voice of the Kazakh intelligentsia":

> A word—[is] a leisurely reflection of a human deed.
> The height, depth, and colors are begot by the tongue.
> Reflected in the words are a sip,
> And a strike of a blow,
> And a smile,
> A sound of hooves through the aeon,
> And incline of a weighed-down vine.[26]

Russian and Russian-speaking writers left a significant body of literature on Central Asia written from the insider's point of view. Their works are rich in vivid depictions of traditional local cultures and customs and of the attitudes of various communities and groups to changes brought by outsiders. These insights are combined with a deep knowledge of the everyday life and dispositions of ordinary people. Such works as *Dzhunaid-khan,* by Boris Cheprunov, *Chelovek meniaiet kozhu* (Man sheds his skin) (1933), by Bruno Yasenski, *Zvezdy nad Samarkandom* (The stars over Samarqand), by

Sergey Borodin, and many others paid special attention to the civil war and *Basmachi* (native resistance movement) of the 1920s. Emblematic is the creative writing of Michael Sheverdin (1909–1984). His western-style adventure novels, such as *Po volch'emu sledu* (In the wolf's footsteps) (1951), *Teni pustyni* (Shadows of the desert) (1963), and *Pereshagni bezdnu* (Step over the chasm) (1972), comprehensively portrayed the bloody confrontations of the civil and postwar eras in Turkistan and depicted the intricate relationships between the Bolsheviks and the native population.

POST-SOVIET LITERATURE

Like the Bolshevik Revolution in 1917, the breakdown of the Soviet Union and the breakaway of the Central Asian Republics in 1991 marked an important milestone in the development of the literature of the region. Suddenly, many restrictions that had been imposed by the Communist Party *apparatchiks* disappeared. Many topics previously considered politically incorrect became open for public discussion. Also, the national intelligentsia, especially the writers and poets, discovered that they could discuss the development of national culture, national identity, and national history (even its darkest pages) without the approval of Moscow. Interest in national culture and national symbols skyrocketed, and there began a wide public search for hidden symbols and coded anticolonial sentiments in past and present literature and in the works of the banned writers. In addition, there was a powerful call to abandon the Russian language and even the Cyrillic script and to return to the national languages in all aspects of life, such as education, administration, and mainstream culture. (Turkmenistan and Uzbekistan in fact chose to shift their written languages from Cyrillic script to Latin in the early 1990s.) There was no longer any need to maintain the politically correct balance of national and Russian-language publications.

There was also much heated debate about the national literatures of the Soviet and pre-Soviet eras. Many argued that much of Soviet-era literature was so ideologically infested and so superficial in depicting communist-era topics that it did not present any value in the post-Soviet and postcolonial era. At the same time, the Central Asian intelligentsia argued that many authors of the prerevolutionary and postrevolutionary eras who were banned for their anticolonial and anticommunist or politically incorrect views should be rehabilitated and given a place in the national cultural heritage. Yet another group argued that the wholesale rejection of Soviet-era literature could not be justified; after all, those works had laid the foundation for the national literatures of the Central Asian republics. Those writers also reflected the realities of everyday life, the depth of the political and social divides in the societies, and the confrontation between representatives of different generations and different social groups. These debates hit the pages of national newspapers, magazines, and literary journals and sparked lively polemics about the historical development of art, literature, and poetry.

While intellectuals were busy reevaluating the achievements and faults of their national literature and the ways in which to respond to the changing world, the world itself arrived at their doorsteps in the form of crises that struck the literary circles on many fronts. Practically all of the Central Asian governments withdrew or significantly cut their generous subsidies to publishing houses, writers unions, book clubs, and individual authors. It was now up to the market or to rich philanthropists to decide which authors could publish and survive in this very unstable environment. At the same time, the reading audience was shrinking at catastrophic rates, with recession, poverty, and unemployment affecting more than three-quarters of the population. Many people, even professionals—teachers, researchers, doctors, lawyers—could no longer afford to buy books. And, most important, many writers themselves, especially of the younger generation, failed to pen significant pieces worthy of wide public attention, locked as they were in a perpetual struggle to survive, or embroiled in never-ending polemics between each other, or simply unable to adapt to the new reality.

All of these factors engendered pessimistic themes and an emphasis on crisis at the personal, communal, or societal level. The verses of the Kazakh poet Konysbai Ebil to some degree reflect this trend:

I don't care
If it is bazaar or market:
If you have knowledge—show it;
I can't define anyone as the "enemy of the nation" [anymore]
And there is also no one who has concerns about the people.[27]

Yet, despite these problems, some authors managed to continue to write, producing some interesting works. Paradoxically, the call to return to national roots was not realized in a grand revival of premodern genres and styles, although there was increasing public interest in traditional heroic epics, legends, and *tamasha* (humor and satiric stories). Many old works were republished with new and extensive commentaries. Most contemporary authors continue the modern Western traditions in writing novels, short stories, poems, and polemical essays on various social, cultural, and political issues.

It would not be an exaggeration to say that Central Asia literature has been at a crossroads ever since independence in 1991. Many factors account for the slow and painful transition. The most noticeable trend is that the reading audience is much smaller than in the past and is continuing to shrink at a slow pace. Although living standards have been gradually improving, about 50 percent of the population still lives below the poverty line, according to the World Bank (2005), and many social groups have been struggling to adapt to the new economic reality.

The second important trend is the fragmentation and polarization of society in all the republics in the region. They are stratified not only in terms of income. There can be seen the emergence of significant differences in living standards between urban and rural areas, with growing differences and even rivalries between representatives of different provinces that begin in politics and extend to all other aspects of life. There is also a growing gap between the secular intelligentsia and the religiously oriented intelligentsia, and significant differences and values and lifestyles between people who grew up and were educated during the Soviet era and those who came of age during the post-Soviet period.

Third, the process of de-Russification has divided society further as the younger generation switches to its national languages and makes English the second language of choice. There are significantly fewer Russian-language writers and journalists both among the Russian diaspora and among Russian-speaking locals, especially in Tajikistan, Turkmenistan, and Uzbekistan. In addition, the independence of the Central Asian republics was achieved peacefully and without major conflict, unlike that of many Third World countries in the postcolonial era. Very often, the Central Asian governments cool down debate and marginalize the most radical and critical voices in the name of social and interethnic stability, thereby creating new limitations on the freedom of literature and the media. Independence coincided with a rapid acceleration of the pace of globalization and an explosive influx of Western mass culture.

As a general trend, all the Central Asian governments simultaneously reduced censorship, abandoned restrictions on the importation of Western products, and abandoned preferential treatment of and subsidies to local publishers and writers. The regional literary world was transformed into a Western-style literary market because of a combination of two factors: the flood of Western literature and media, especially television, and the scarcity of local cultural products. For example, publishers find it much cheaper and commercially more viable to publish translations of already established Western bestsellers, such as the *Harry Potter* books or *The Da Vinci Code,* than to nurture local talent. In addition, it is more profitable to publish popular fiction—adventures and detective stories—than to deal with writers of high literature, who reach a very small audience.

NOTES

1. *Manas,* vol. 1 (Moscow and Bishkek: Door, 1995), p. 201.

2. Very few actual works by the writers of that era have survived to the modern era; their masterpieces were preserved in oral traditions by numerous bards and poets and by calligraphers in neighboring regions. Some survived in *Tazkira* (anthology) form. A number of manuscripts are scattered in various libraries and museums or private collections and are as yet to be studied.

3. In addition, some literature has been published in Karakalpak, Uigur, Korean, German, Tatar, and a few other languages of smaller ethnic groups of Central Asia.

4. For a scholarly study of Turkic oral epic poetry, see Karl Reichl, *Turkic Oral Epic Poetry: Traditions, Forms, Poetic Structure* (New York and London: Garland, 1992); also see Viktor Zhirmunskii, *Turkskii geroicheskii epos* [Turkic heroic epics] (Leningrad: Nauka, 1974).

5. Viktor Zhirmunskii and Kh. Zaripov, *Uzbekskii narodnyi geroicheskii epos* [Uzbek national heroic epics] (Moscow: OGIZ, 1947), pp. 60–110.

6. There are several versions of this epic, which varied among the Kazakhs, Uzbeks, Tajiks, and Turkmens. For an example of the Turkmen version, see N. Ashirov, ed., *Geroglu, Tartibe salan Ata Govshud Geroglu* (Ashgabat: n.p., 1958).

7. Here I use a Central Asian version of the epic, which differs in some details from other versions; see Zhirmunskii and Zaripov, *Uzbekskii narodnyi geroicheskii epos,* pp. 184–210.

8. *The Manas Reader,* by the editors of *Manas* (New York: Grossman, 1971).

9. At present there are more than 60 versions of the epic, each recorded from a different prominent *manaschis.* All copies are kept and studied in the National Academy of Sciences of Kyrgyzstan. Many of the versions have never been published.

10. *Manas,* p. 130.

11. Reichl, *Turkic Oral Epic Poetry,* pp. 33–39.

12. Arabic, to some degree, played a role similar to that of Latin in medieval Western Europe. It was the language of major theological works and debates, of jurisprudence (*Shariah*), philosophy, and science, and of Islamic religious ceremonies. Traditionally, those works have been studied within the body of Middle Eastern literature and theology, and there are numerous works on this heritage available to public. The author has chosen to leave those works to experts on the Middle East and classical Islam.

13. Omar Khayyam, *A New Version Based upon Recent Discoveries* (ed. by Arthur J. Arberry) (New Haven: Yale University Press, 1952), p. 65.

14. Alisher Navai also wrote in fluent Persian and penned several widely acclaimed poems in the Persian language.

15. There is no precisely defined date for the transition between the precolonial and colonial eras in Central Asian cultural history, as the region was conquered by the Russian Empire step by step over several decades.

16. For discussion of the heated debate between the conservatives and reformers, see Allworth Edward, *The Modern Uzbeks: From the Fourteenth Century to the Present. A Cultural History* (Stanford, CA: Hoover Institution Press, 1990), pp. 122–130.

17. In contemporary Kazakhstan, Abai is also considered among the founders of contemporary Kazakh literary language. *Kazakhskaia SSR: Entsyklopedia* [Kazakh SSR: an encyclopedia] (Almaty: Kazakh Encyclopedia, 1984), pp. 514–515.

18. For a comprehensive review of the development of Central Asian literature during the Imperial Russian and Soviet eras, see Edward Allworth, "The Changing Intellectual and Literary Community" and "The Focus on Literature," in Edward Allworth, ed., *Central Asia: 130 Years of Russian Dominance: A Historical Overview,* 3rd ed. (Durham and London: Duke University Press, 1994), pp. 349–433.

19. Union of Soviet Writers of the USSR. Ustav Soiuza sovetskikh pisatelei SSSR [The Statute of the Union of Soviet Writers of the USSR] (Moskva: OGIZ Gos. izd-vo Sov. Zakonodatel'stvo. 1935).

20. Nor, however, was membership a guarantee of safety. In the 1930s, the Unions of Writers all over the Soviet Union experienced a wave of purges as their members were accused of nationalism and of counterrevolutionary and anti-Soviet activities. This Stalin-initiated campaign brought mass arrests, imprisonments and executions.

21. For a translation into English, see Tolegen Kasymbekov, *The Broken Sword* (Moscow: Progress, 1980).

22. Khalyk Kor-Ogly, *Uzbekskaia literatura* [Uzbek literature] (Moscow: Vys'shaia shkola, 1968), pp. 146–147, 161–162.

23. Most of Aitmatov's works have been translated into English. See Chingiz Aitmatov, *Piebald Dog Running along the Shore and Other Stories* (Moscow: Raduga, 1989).

24. "Az i la" author plays with words (1) "Az and la" - Slavonic names of the first and last letters of Russian alphabet, and (2) "Azia" in Russian means "Asia."

25. For detailed discussion, see Harsha Ram, "Imagining Eurasia: Olzhas Suleimenov's AZ i IA," *Slavic Review* 60, no. 2 (Summer 2001).

26. Trans. by author. Olzhas Suleimenov, *Izbrannoie* [Selected works] (Moscow: Khudozhestvenaia Literatura, 1986), p. 88.

27. Konysbai Ebil, "Kekberi kirdi tusume," *Zhas Alash* 60–61 (Mamyr 22, 2004), p. 11.

4

Media and Cinema

I think that a common characteristic of Central Asian cinema of the last decade is the attempt to communicate big, grand ideas through simple stories.

—Gulnara Abikeyeva, film critic from Kazakhstan[1]

MEDIA

As in many other former communist countries, the mass media in Central Asia remain one of the most influential forces in public life. The downfall of several powerful ministers in Kazakhstan, Kyrgyzstan, and Uzbekistan in the early 1990s was caused by publications by investigative journalists. In parts of Central Asia, some people still fear the news, as television and newspapers often bring unwelcome reports of the latest laws or presidential decrees that may negatively affect everyone's daily lives or of the dismissal of key ministers or local government officials. The Central Asian media possess a level of public trust rarely seen in the Western world. Government officials never underestimate that power; moreover, they—like their counterparts in Russia and some other countries—have tried to establish tough controls and censorship, so much so that the Freedom House annual report for 2002 on the mass media in Central Asia claimed that "[the attitude of governments] chills the free expression of views and opinions and limits access to information."[2]

However, the situation with the media is not rigid and has been constantly changing since 1991. Independent-minded journalists and Central Asian government officials have been locked in a fierce struggle ever since Mikhail

Gorbachev, leader of the Soviet Union from 1985 to 1991, declared the era of glasnost (openness) and perestroika (changes) in the mid-1980s. On one side of this struggle are the independent media advocates who would like to overcome the direct control and censorship and to transform the boring officialdom of the progovernment propaganda of Soviet-style newspapers, radio, and TV channels into a free and dynamic Western-style media with appeal to a wider audience. On the other side are government officials who have been continuously cutting state subsidies to media outlets and film studios and who would still like to retain their control over media content, to silence criticism, and to keep the media outlets as part of the state propaganda machine.[3]

THE PRESS

In large cities like Almaty, Bishkek, and Tashkent, colorful newsstands and ostentatious news kiosks present a contrasting assortment of the latest local and imported newspapers and magazines. A casual observer sees no sign of the struggle between independent-minded journalists and government officials of Central Asia on the shelves of the newsstands. Conservative official newspapers sit contentedly next to attractive and trendy youth newspapers; popular magazines for women and adult publications with scantily clad girls and boys are displayed next to horoscopes and dour political magazines or esoteric financial newspapers.[4] A distinctly different situation prevails in the news markets in small provincial *(welayat, oblast)* and district *(raion)* centers across the region, where the newsstands and kiosks are often shockingly empty and display a very limited and dusty assortment. Local readers may well not care that some newspapers are weeks old and that some magazines were published a year or two ago, as they very likely do not read them, anyway. Yet a few devoted readers can be found both in the large cities and in the provinces. They come to get their favorites every morning, while most people pass by without even noticing the existence of the newsstands. Periodical retail is a very tough and competitive business in Central Asia, and nobody knows if it is profitable at all.

While it can be said that the production and the distribution of modern Central Asian periodicals are not without faults and shortcomings, the current system represents a huge improvement over the one that prevailed during the Soviet era. Until 1991, Communist Party officials and Soviet government *nomenklatura* controlled most of the news gathering, media production, and distribution processes. In fact, the establishment and development of the modern press in Central Asia was largely associated with the Soviet state. The Bolsheviks, who fought a bloody civil war to establish the Soviet system in Central Asia between 1918 and 1922, ultimately defeated their opponents but found themselves in a very hostile environment. As soon as the major battles were over, they discovered that most of the ordinary people were quite ignorant about communism and the Bolsheviks themselves; the people's interests were locked into local, community, and tribal affairs. They received their news from local commentators *(uzun-kulaks)* in bazaars or mosques and were not at all builders of the "bright new communist future." The Soviet authorities realized they had to reach out to every family and every village *(ail)* if they wanted to propagate their ideas to the local citizens and to divert Central Asians from the old ways of life. It was obvious that the mass media would become one of the propaganda instruments in their hands.

There were virtually no mass media, in the modern understanding of the term, in the region before the Soviet era, with the exception of a few colonial newspapers. Though some Central Asian reformers *(jadids)* attempted to launch periodicals in the 1900s and 1910s, they rarely succeeded beyond a few hundred copies distributed over a few years.[5] In the 1920s, the Bolsheviks pioneered the establishment of true mass publication and effectively developed the very first newspapers and magazines into powerful Communist Party mouthpieces. Unlike the Western media, the Central Asian periodicals of that era were never intended as entertainment resources. Almost all of them, including magazines for children and youth, artistic journals, and even comics and satirical publications, were politicized to propagate socialist ideas and communist ideology. There was practically no commercial advertising during the Soviet era, as private and semiprivate periodicals, and private entrepreneurship, did not exist at that time. All periodicals were controlled by the Communist Party or government agencies at different levels or by large state-run enterprises. All media outlets were heavily subsidized, and their publications were distributed through equally heavily subsidized delivery channels. The combination of state subsidies, government initiatives, and extremely affordable prices for newspapers and magazines (in many cases they were simply free of charge) created a completely new universe of Soviet media with its own culture, clichés, lies, and ideals. The case of Kyrgyzstan is an excellent example. The first and, at that time, only mass newspaper—*Erkin Too* (Free Mountains)—was established in 1924, with a circulation of a few hundred copies. By the mid-1980s, there were about 90 newspapers in the republic, with a total annual circulation of about 184.4 million copies in a country of about four million people.[6] That amounted to 46 copies per person per year, a figure that could easily land Kyrgyzstan ahead of many developing countries. Family subscription to three to five and even to six to eight periodicals was quite common by the 1970s and 1980s, as many people subscribed to professional and general newspapers and magazines.

The situation changed radically with independence in 1991.[7] Most media enterprises were privatized and lost state support and subsidies. Throughout the 1990s, many newspapers and other publications closed or were significantly downsized as state subsidies evaporated. Communist Party newspapers and many local publications changed their titles or contents entirely or simply disappeared. The situation worsened even further when people stopped subscribing or buying newspapers and magazines due to economic hardship and exorbitant prices.

Since the 1990s the media market in the Central Asian republics has stabilized, and the countries have begun moving in different directions. In Kazakhstan and Kyrgyzstan, the independent media have been doing relatively well. As the media market matured and competition increased, editors and journalists learned to work in the new environment and to deal with government authorities that tried to impose various forms of control, restriction, and censorship.[8] In Turkmenistan and Uzbekistan, most media enterprises have remained under state control, though many of them have lost a considerable portion of their subsidies. In fact, the 2003 Freedom House report declared Turkmenistan's mass media "among the most tightly controlled in the world."[9] The press in Tajikistan also suffered because of the despair associated with the civil war and its aftermath of political and economic turmoil; thus, according to the 2005 *Freedom in the World* report, most journalists still "avoid reporting on sensitive political issues, including corruption, and directly criticizing the president and other senior officials."[10]

Were twenty-first-century readers to compare the Central Asian press with the press of the Soviet era, they would find substantial differences. At present, newspapers in the region publish neither the lengthy reports of the Communist Party nor statistics on the growth rates of cows, sheep, and camels on collective farms—popular themes in the Soviet era. Although the major newspapers added financial and economic sections and preserved and even expanded their cultural, entertainment, sport, and cartoon sections, they still do not publish the alternative views of the political opposition or permit open debates on their pages.

Yet readers would find a variety of mass media choices in the post-Soviet Central Asian republics. Old-fashioned, well-established periodicals are easily available, as are many "young" newspapers and magazines and newly established media outlets that promote their very first issues. Most of the new media are free of direct government control (except in Turkmenistan and Uzbekistan) and were established to make profits, though self-censorship is very common, as journalists are afraid of losing their jobs or jeopardizing their friendly relations with government agencies. As a sign of the new era, many of the new periodicals target specific groups of the society—businessmen, youth, women, artists, the intelligentsia, and politicians. Like many Western periodicals, they are full of commercial advertising.

A major point to remember is that periodicals in Central Asia are published in five state languages—Kazakh, Kyrgyz, Tajik, Turkmen, and Uzbek, plus Russian (the region's lingua franca). The press communities of every republic are isolated from one another not only by language but also by numerous other barriers, including political and economic; yet, they do share some common features. Local observers distinguish several major segments in the modern media market in the region, though a meticulous researcher would almost certainly find many smaller subsegments. The first group is often the so-called *nomenklatura* periodicals, for their close links to the government and the ruling political elites. This segment of the market is represented mainly by the old Soviet-style officialdom periodicals that are still in place in all Central Asian republics. These newspapers are typically progovernment and are often controlled directly or indirectly by various government agencies or receive some form of state subsidies. They usually run to between 6 and 8 pages in their weekday editions and somewhat longer—12–40 pages—in their weekend editions, and they have two editions—one in the national language and the other in Russian.

The second group is represented by a wide range of so-called national cultural newspapers that are published exclusively in the national languages. They discuss various issues related to the resurgence of the national languages, cultures, and national literature and poetry or to the renewed writing of national histories.

The third group might be classed, broadly, as entertainment periodicals, and they target various groups within society. The most popular and widely circulated newspapers, such as *Karavan* (Kazakhstan), *Vechernii Bishkek* (Kyrgyzstan), and *Darakchai* (Uzbekistan),[11] look like a cross between Western tabloid newspapers and liberal official newspapers, in some degree resembling, say, New York's *Daily News* or the British *Sun*. They are full of national news, commentaries about trends in politics, culture, and business, and various events, but at times they devote space to lengthy and generally dry interviews with or comments by government officials or influential politicians.

The fourth segment of the Central Asian press consists of periodicals run by the political opposition. These devote most of their space to exposing corruption among government officials or individual politicians, criticizing the shortcomings of government actions, and discussing new agendas for reform and change.[12]

A separate though declining segment of the media market comprises major publications produced jointly with or exclusively in Russia. National (Kazakhstan or Kyrgyzstan) editions of such popular newspapers as

Komsomolskaia Pravda, Moskovskii Komsomolets, SPID Info, and a few others carry either national supplements or represent a mixture of lead stories developed by Russian and Central Asian investigative journalists on national news and related articles.

There are also many newspapers dedicated to various issues and interests, especially to family, auto, and sports. Humorous and satirical newspapers are also much loved by Central Asian audiences, and many kiosks carry periodicals with the latest collections of jokes, cartoons, and anecdotes. Anecdotes about incumbent politicians or government officials can rarely be found in these periodicals, but there is an abundant supply of them on the Internet.

There are many glossy magazines on the Central Asian newsstands, though in this category the region's periodicals are in their infancy. Because of a combination of factors—difficulties in obtaining new technology, the high costs of running color print, and the small size of the national markets—the overwhelming majority of "glossies" are imported from Russia or the West and are often published exclusively in Russian. Many regularly carry articles related to national news and trends. The largest group of glossy weekly and monthly magazines are the women's magazines, such as *Cosmopolitan, Elle, Burda,* in the Russian and national languages, and *Liza, Vot-Tak, 7ia, Bumerang, Rovesnik,* and *Detskii Mir* in Russian. Like their Western counterparts, these publications are filled with a combination of gossip about international and national stars, the latest fashion trends, recipes, diets, travel stories, and personal stories from national writers and journalists, as well as recommendations for everyday life, crosswords, and so on. In the early 2000s, there were several new successful local projects. For example, a group of young journalists began publishing the glossy *Time Out Almaty* in Kazakhstan and *Time Out Tashkent* in Uzbekistan.[13]

"Adult" newspapers and magazines have also made inroads into the Central Asian media market, but, after public protests and numerous and furious complains from local conservative and religious activists, the Central Asian governments quickly passed a series of decrees and laws designed to restrict the circulation and display of those publications.

Developments in the media market led to substantial changes in journalism as a profession. Gone were the days when membership in the Communist Party and political loyalty to the government were the main requirements for launching a career in the mass media and, with it, membership of that exclusive professional association, the Union of Journalists. The younger generation—especially those whose education and entry to the field occurred after 1991—are usually dynamic and articulate journalists. Many Central Asian journalists are women, especially in youth, cultural, women's, and entertainment publications, while men tend to dominate the fields of investigative journalism, political commentary, and analysis. One indicator of women's growing success in the journalistic field in Kazakhstan is that, in 2004, female reporters won two out of eight of the national Union of Journalists' prestigious awards.[14] Many mass-media workers in Central Asia, especially women, supplement their incomes working as stringers for major international news agencies and for newspapers that report on political events and cover corruption and the harsh treatment of opposition leaders—even in the most oppressive countries in the region. Still, the state-controlled official periodicals employ predominantly well-connected and loyal-to-government journalists, who are often represented by the older, conservative generation of the second oldest profession.

One of the factors that has shaped the development of the press in Central Asia is the changing ownership structure. During the chaotic transition from socialism to capitalism, many previously state-owned and state-run newspapers became independent, and the associated journalistic collectives often became owners of their periodicals. Some journalists decided to break away from their old publications and establish new ones. For many of them, however, weathering the difficult times of transition and untamed market changes proved too difficult, especially when state subsidies dried up or journalists failed to adapt to the transforming environment. The periodicals market experienced a first wave of consolidation, closures, and acquisitions in the mid-1990s, when hundreds of small newspapers simply closed their doors or were bought out by local investors. Very soon, larger newspapers began to experience a similar fate. But, this time, there were a number of large companies, political groups, and powerful oligarchs on hand to rescue some of the major newspapers.

In the early twenty-first century, the print market in the region more or less stabilized, though the process of stabilization took a different direction in each republic. In Turkmenistan, for example, the state and state-controlled agencies are probably the only owners of major periodicals. The government's extremely heavy-handed control of the press brought the country a ranking of second-worst in the world with regard to press freedoms. In its 2005 *Annual Survey of Press Freedoms*, Freedom House ranked Turkmenistan 193rd out of 194, with only the Democratic People's Republic of Korea ranked lower.[15] In Tajikistan and Uzbekistan, most of the press outlets are under state control, though there are a few independent and semi-independent news agencies and newspapers. The government of Uzbekistan tries to keep tight control over information inflow; hence, in 2005, Freedom House placed Uzbekistan 184th out of 194 in the same scale of press freedoms.[16] The situation is different in Kazakhstan and Kyrgyzstan, where a number of independent and privately owned newspapers and magazines mushroomed in the 1990s.[17] A few periodicals in these two countries have preserved a significant degree of independence by fighting off the attempts of government officials to impose draconian restrictions and various forms of censorship. Critical works and numerous investigative publications by several independent newspapers in Kyrgyzstan, such as *Res Publica* and *MSN,* were crucial in organizing public dissent against the long-time president Askar Akayev and in mobilizing people for a peaceful so-called Tulip Revolution, in March 2005. These events ultimately led to the ousting of the president and his government and to many political changes in the republic.

Technological advances have also contributed to a reshaping of the Central Asian mass media. Computer technology, which arrived in the region much later than in many other parts of the world, affected the workflow of the newsrooms and changed the production and printing processes entirely. Although it is still quite possible to see old-fashioned typewriters on the desks of many journalists and editors, especially outside the major metropolitan areas, personal computers are ultimately winning the battle. Some newspapers are still published in black and white, on the cheapest possible paper, using equipment that saw better days during the Soviet system. Financially more successful periodicals in Turkmenistan, Kazakhstan, and Kyrgyzstan, on the other hand, are printed in color, utilizing modern information technology. The new technologies have also made it possible to move from the old Soviet-era format of 4–6 pages to a new format of 12–24 pages, though the mere size of the weekend editions of the *New York Times* or the *Daily Telegraph* would send many Central Asian editors into a fainting fit.

During recent years, foreign language newspapers, mainly in English and Turkish, have found their way into the regional media market, a development that would have been practically impossible in the Soviet era. As a reflection of wide cultural transformations in the region, the circulation of newspapers in Russian experienced a steep downsizing in the early 1990s, as their audience continued to shrink in all republics, with the lone exception of Kazakhstan. In the meantime, the circulation of newspapers in the national languages experienced steady growth between the mid-1990s and the early 2000s. Paradoxically, the only panregional newspaper in the early 2000s—the *Times of Central Asia*—was foreign-owned and was published not in any Central Asian language or in Russian but in English.

In the early 2000s, fewer people than two decades earlier could afford to buy newspapers because of the sharp decline in living standards in the 1990s. Private subscriptions have practically disappeared today, and even the most devoted readers buy newspapers from the newsstands, and not often. The situation has improved in the first decade of the twenty-first century as, between 2002 and 2006, economic growth contributed to rising incomes and a better quality of life in most of the Central Asian republics. For example, according to the UNESCO Institute of Statistics (2003), Kyrgyzstan was in 35th place out of 51 countries surveyed regarding per capita circulation of newspapers, behind Brazil, Pakistan, Lithuania, Portugal, and Egypt; Turkmenistan was in 44th place, behind Indonesia, Burma, and Armenia.[18]

RADIO

Radio is the most accessible and the most democratic sector of the mass media in Central Asia. In some remote mountainous and desert areas of the region, people lack TV reception, while in some villages (ails), people do not see newspapers for months. This leaves radio as the only link with the outside world. In spite of restrictions imposed by the governments over coverage of some events and the inaccessibility of other media outlets, the click of a radio switch gives even an illiterate person a chance to learn about the latest news in the region or in the outside world. The affordability and popularity of radio are reflected in statistics. According to the CIA World Factbook (2003), there were about 428 radios per 1,000 people in Kazakhstan and 402 radios per 1,000 in Uzbekistan, putting these countries in 94th and 97th places respectively in the world—just behind Malaysia, Jamaica, and Russia.[19]

For decades, the people's devotion to radio was fueled by a combination of curiosity, an educational environment that emphasized the importance of the sciences, and military considerations. Throughout the Soviet era, children were encouraged to join free radio clubs in schools or science centers to learn the foundations of science, practice elements of engineering, and engage in innovations by building their own radio sets. Many thousands of children, for example, listened to the radio signals from the first spaceship, Sputnik,—using home- or school-made devices. Radio sets existed in practically every house, even during the years of notorious deficit of consumer goods in the Soviet market.

Quite unexpectedly for the Soviet government, though, in the course of time many people tuned their receivers to Western radio programs, as all the radio stations during the communist era were state-controlled and quite often transmitted ideological programs and propaganda talk shows. Western radio stations were the first to introduce famous Western and Middle Eastern music groups to the Soviet Central Asian audience; for many years, such groups as the Beatles and the Rolling Stones were banned from Soviet radio broadcasts. In addition to music programs, listeners were tuning their transistor radios to such radio stations as the Voice of America (VOA), the BBC, and Radio Liberty/Radio Free Europe (RL/RFE) for alternative views on world news. Not only was Western music banned during the Soviet era; the cold war extended from the political battlefields to the air waves, as well. Soviet authorities regularly jammed foreign radio stations as part of their extensive censorship of the news coverage of many international and domestic events.

The liberalization of the media market after 1991 did not leave radio unchanged. Numerous entertainment-oriented private radio stations burgeoned throughout the 1990s. Most of the young radio stations were quick to abandon Soviet-era officialdom and to learn from their Western colleagues. They introduced talk shows, an assortment of contests, direct telephone lines, and music programs for all kind of tastes. The popular Kyrgyz radio station *Piramida,* for example, presents a daily mix of pop music, news, and talk shows that target young urban audiences in Kyrgyzstan. In Kazakhstan, the government-operated Kazakh-Radio KR1 and KR2 combine entertainment programs with official news reports and commentaries. In the meantime, an independent Western-style entertainment/music radio station, *EuropaPlus,*[20] which produces a mixture of rock and pop, quizzes, news, and gossip, became one of the most popular radio stations in the country. Another example comes from the city of Hujant, in Tajikistan, where local DJs regularly quiz their audience with an array of questions, giving the winner a chance to chose a song for a friend or colleague. *Radio Grande* of Uzbekistan established a hit-parade ranking of the top 20 most popular bands on its play list and regularly posts the results on its Web site.[21] Since the early 2000s, practically every radio station in the Central Asian republics has established its own Web site (sometimes with an English-language mirror site) with its own chat-rooms, exchange and survey boards, news, and gossip pages and, often, its own hit list of top songs, albums, groups, and/or singers.

With so many stations broadcasting, the national governments in Central Asia use various tools to keep control of program content, especially when it is related to domestic politics and policymaking issues. For example, during the February–March 2005 elections in Kyrgyzstan, political rallies in the cities of Bishkek, Jalalabad, and Osh were not covered on the local airwaves until almost the last days of the rebellion. Many listeners in Kyrgyzstan learned about the political turmoil only from the VOA, RL/RFE, and other stations. In another case, demonstrations and consequent clashes with Uzbek police and army troops in the city of Andijan, in Uzbekistan, in May 2005, were comprehensively covered by all major international radio stations broadcasting to the region but were barely mentioned on local radio.

Remarkably, the radio programs in the region are broadcast in about a dozen languages, targeting all major ethnic groups living in Central Asia. In a new trend, an increasing number of hours are devoted to various programs in English, including educational programs for young people studying the language.

There has also been a gradual growth in the number of religious programs. In contrast to the Soviet era, when only atheistic radio programs were allowed, various religious leaders now use radio to reach a wider audience. Although there are no radio stations exclusively owned by any religious groups or churches in the region, their representatives have begun appearing regularly on private and public stations, discussing social, ethical, and theological issues.

TELEVISION

Contemporary television programs in Central Asia probably represent a delicate balance between national traditions and the powerful forces of globalization. Foreign visitors might well be charmed by the colorful traditional folk dances, music, and plays that occupy significant blocks of local TV programming. They might also be surprised that a large number of Western TV shows, especially drama, cartoons, and sitcoms from the United States, Mexico, and Italy and local variations of those shows, have made big inroads into the national TV channels. Almost all foreign movies are dubbed into local languages or Russian. Such series as *The Sopranos, The Simpsons, The Beverly Hillbillies, Dallas, Star Trek,* and *El Clon* (produced by Telemundo) from the United States, *Rich and Famous,* from Argentina, and *Marielena,* from Spain, have shown their appeal to a large crowd of devoted followers. Some commercial TV channels include a large number of Russian-made movies and shows for their local Russian-speaking population. Increasingly, large blocks of news and shows come from Turkey and various other countries. All of these programs are particularly popular on the commercial channels and are often transmitted in their original languages. The national television channels have changed immensely since the Soviet era, offering their viewers more entertainment choices, as well as the annoyance of frequent commercial breaks.

Indeed, there have been a lot of changes since the opening of the first regular TV transmissions, in the mid-1950s. Throughout the 1960s and 1970s, TV sets were luxury, as whole neighborhoods or villages visited the few lucky residents who had sets. Gradually, as in the West, people got used to TV entertainment, and, by the 1990s, practically every family had a TV receiver at home. At present, Central Asians are far ahead of such countries as Afghanistan (3 TV sets per 1,000 people) and Pakistan (19 TV sets per 1,000 people) in terms of TV-set ownership per capita. For example, there are 253 TV sets per 1,000 in Kazakhstan and 238 TV sets per 1,000 in Uzbekistan—which puts these countries in 77th and 84th place in the world, respectively, just behind Israel, Hong Kong, Qatar, and Puerto Rico.[22]

It took about two decades to establish regular TV coverage in the major towns and cities in the region. By the mid-1970s, national TV stations functioned in all five Central Asian capitals, and there were only about three or four state-controlled channels broadcasting for about 10–14 hours a day. During the Soviet era, generous state subsidies allowed national TV stations to have large studios, with their own facilities for producing music, educational programs, and movies and broadcasting. Tight state control and censorship over TV broadcasting was a major characteristic of national TV channels. The Soviet government used television as its main propaganda tool, with access to every family or household in the region. Not surprisingly, TV broadcasting was filled with a combination of lackluster news, official interviews, and lengthy reports on Communist Party events, sometimes interspersed with music programs, Soviet movies, and popular sporting events such as soccer, ice hockey, gymnastics, figure skating, and boxing. Foreign movies and music shows were severely restricted during that time. For example, some veterans of broadcasting report that only after several secret meetings of officials were the first Beatles songs allowed on Soviet TV. And then they were performed by an approved Soviet opera singer.[23]

However, the gradual liberalization of the Soviet system in the late 1970s and 1980s brought more entertainment programs to TV stations. A number of new music, children's, folk, sport. and other programs became popular staples on national TV. Yet. a significant chunk of the programs was still devoted to events at the *kolkhozes* (collective farms) and factories and to communist propaganda. Only Gorbachev's policy of glasnost, in the second half of the 1980s, changed Soviet television significantly, although in Central Asia the transformation was very limited, slow, and cautious, as the national leaders never fully abandoned some level of state control and censorship. Nonetheless, little by little, the national television channels were freed from the ideological restraints of the past and became commercially and entertainment oriented in the late 1980s, turning to national, cultural, historical, and art issues.

An avalanche of changes took place in 1991–1992. In some areas, TV broadcasting in Central Asia moved in directions similar to those it was taking in Russia, while in other areas it moved in different ways. Television broadcasters began switching most of the locally produced programs from Russian to national languages and began devoting more time to national themes. In the meantime, the Central Asian governments maintained various levels of indirect state intervention and state control over the contents of the programs.

In the late 1990s and early 2000s, a wave of consolidations and acquisitions significantly changed the ownership structure in the regional TV markets, and the TV stations became more professional and commercially oriented by adopting new business models and introducing new programs. For example, Tajikistan and Kazakhstan were ranked 80th and 81st in the world in their number of television broadcasting stations, behind Peru, Oman, and Kuwait.[24] As of 2005, most of the TV stations in Kazakhstan and Kyrgyzstan were controlled by a very few powerful family businesses with strong links to the ruling elite. In Tajikistan, Turkmenistan, and Uzbekistan, the state-run agencies controlled a significant portion of public television and directly influenced broadcasting policies.

In Kazakhstan, national TV producers managed to introduce a number of new programs that are probably among the most entertaining, dynamic, and Westernized in the whole region, although almost 60 percent of the programming consisted of foreign products.[25] Among the most popular nationally produced shows and programs are the notable news talk shows *Zhana Kyn, Bugun, Kazakhstan* (Kazakhstan TV channel), *Zharkyrauyk dostar!, Khabar Zher* (Khabar TV channel), *Zhansarai, Tangy auenderi, Eltanym, Keshe, Bugin, Erten,* and *Taulyk Tynysy* (Rakhat TV channel).[26] The Hit-TV channel is devoted to Kazakh, Russian, and international music hits and show business news and devotes several hours a day to the best Kazakh rock, folk-rock, and pop groups and singers.

In Kyrgyzstan, the state-controlled national television stations, including KTP and KOORT, have the largest audiences and are accessible all over the republic. There are also 14 independent or privately owned television stations and eleven radio stations, including *Piramida Television and Radio, Independent Bishkek Television, Asman Television,* and *Almaz Radio.* In Kyrgyzstan, about 60–70 percent of the broadcast time on national and private TV is given to foreign programs, but national programs such as *Ala Too, Erkin Too, Apta, Yr Deste, Rabayat, Tagdyr,* and *Zhetigen* have gained wide interest among the people.[27]

In Tajikistan, the national producers increased the hours of Tajik-language broadcasting. In addition to imported shows, sitcoms, and foreign-made movies, Tajikistani television began producing its own popular programs, such as *Akhbor, Iztizob, Nabzi Ruz, Khamadon, Robita, Inson va Konun, Tafsir,* and *Suoli Ruz.* Anchor personalities on the *Akhbor* news program, such as Iormuhammad Samadov, Nasiba Guliamova, Saodat Toirova, Samariddin Ainuddin, and Irina Al'kova, are among the most popular journalists in the country, competing with leading pop stars in popularity.

In Turkmenistan, most television stations remain under state control and censorship. They are still the most important sources of public information for the local people, as the Turkmenistani government does not allow foreign broadcasting companies to operate in the country. One of the most frequently screened programs on Turkmen TV is a reading from Saparmurat Nyazov's *Rukhnama* book, with a small portrait of him always shown in the corner of the screen.

Probably one of the most important signs of liberalization of television broadcasting in the region is the rapidly increasing number of satellite dishes and cable TV, which receive local, regional, and international programs, including programs from Russia, Western Europe, the Middle East, and East Asia. In fact, one of the symbols of social and business success in many places in the region is the ownership of a satellite dish, as almost every wealthy household, even in small towns and villages, feels obliged to mount a dish antenna on its property. Since the early 2000s, satellite dishes have become more affordable for the slowly growing middle class of Central Asia.

CINEMA

Central Asian cinema has a long history and significant traditions; in the twentieth century, between 600 and 800 full-length movies were produced by the five national studios. At the industry's zenith, those studios turned out between 20 and 25 full-length movies annually,[28] along with 40 to 60 short films and about 100 documentaries. Admittedly, the quality of this prolific output was uneven. Western audiences might well have struggled to understand and appreciate the typical Central Asian motion picture, given its very different cultural, artistic, and screenwriting parameters. In addition, these films could hardly compete with Hollywood for production values, special effects, and action, as the Central Asian industry has traditionally been based on low-budget films. The lack of state-of-the-art special effects, however, is fully compensated for by the opening up of an entirely new universe. These movies depicted the lives and psychological intrigues of very different societies in simple, sometimes naturalistic ways, mirroring the best traditions of European experimental cinema of the 1950s and 1960s. Occasionally, Central Asian filmmakers produced real gems, truthfully illustrating the emotional dramas of individuals in extreme situations and providing a fresh look at traditional human values, the dramatic effect of the Soviet transformation upon the lives of individuals, and the challenges presented by the social and class struggle during critical periods in the particular nation's history.[29]

As in many developing countries, the cinema had very humble beginnings in the region. The first movie theaters in the Turkistan Governor-Generalship were opened in Tashkent, then Vernyi, and other urban centers in the early twentieth century. Well into the 1920s, screens were dominated by Russian- and Western-made movies. The silent pictures of that time, ranging from melodramas to horror and action movies and accompanied by live music, were widely popular and had a powerful cultural impact on local populations. The cinema became, in the words of the celebrated Uzbek producer Shukhrat Abbasov, "the art of the young [generation],"[30] as many young people relentlessly tried to master new forms of artistic expression. It took several decades, however, before the first full-length motion and documentary films were produced locally. The national film industry in the Central Asian republics began in the mid-1920s, as the Soviet authorities approved the establishment of national studios and provided allocations for the necessary equipment for Tashkent, Ashgabat, and Alma-Ata.

Central Asian cinema first began in Uzbekistan in the 1920s with the establishment of several large studios. Most of the early movies were produced jointly with various Russian studios and were under the leadership of Russian directors. In 1925, for example, Uzbek studios produced their first experiments: *Minaret smerti* (Minaret of death), *Musul' manka* (A Muslim woman), and *Pakhta-Aral.* These were followed by *Vtoraia zhena* (Second wife), *Shakaly Ravata* (Jackals of Ravat), *Chadra* (Hijab) (all in 1927), *Doch' sviatogo* (Daughter of a Saint) (1931), and *Ramazan* (Ramadan) (1933). The first movies focused on the most critical social and economic issues in Central Asia, class struggle and the emancipation of women. The early filmmakers in Uzbekistan also used typical Soviet topics of industrialization in such movies as *Pod'iom* (Rise) (1931) and portrayed historical issues in such movies as *Tong oldydan* (Before the sunrise) (1933). The first filmmakers in Turkmenistan moved in a similar direction, producing motion pictures about radical social changes in Turkmen *ails* and collectivization, such as *Beloye zoloto* (White gold) (1929), *Zabyt' nelzia* (Never forget) (1931), and *Umbar* (1937). The movie *Dursun* (1940) is typical; it demonstrates the social and personal conflicts faced by Turkmen women in their struggle for emancipation and against religious and cultural stereotypes.

At the same time, in Kazakhstan, Kyrgyzstan, and Tajikistan, producers focused mainly on documentary pictures. Most documentaries of that era were propagandistic in nature. Yet, they realistically and dramatically captured the difficulties and dramas associated with land and water reforms, collectivization and industrialization, construction of new roads and schools, and elimination of the so-called wreckages of feudalism. Among other popular topics were the changes brought by the "Soviet cultural revolution," including the attempts to reduce the role and ultimately to eliminate the influence of Islam in public life and, of course, the emancipation of indigenous women. Kazakh filmmakers, for example, worked on many chronicles, such as *Na Jailau* (At the Jailau) (1929), *Shkoly likbeza* (Literacy schools) (1929), *Kooperatsia v aulakh* (Cooperation in Ails) (1929), and *Kyzyl asker* (Red soldier) (1929). One of the most powerful documentaries of that era was *Turksib*

(1931), which depicted the collision between the old ways of life and modernization and celebrated the "victory" of socialism over "backward feudal traditions." Turkmen filmmakers exploited similar topics set in their national context with such documentaries as *Vokrug Turkmenii i Bukhary s kinokameroi* (Around Turkmenistan and Bukhara with a camera) (1929), *Sholk* (Silk) (1929), and *Khlopok* (Cotton) (1929).

Between the late 1930s and the early 1950s, the national cinema studios became more professional and began producing movies using the new technologies of color and sound. The improvements were due to three simple factors. By this time, those local talents who had been sent to study filmmaking at the major Russian studios and educational institutions had come back as producers, actors, and screenwriters. The second factor was the effect of World War II, as studios from Byelorussia, the Ukraine, and some parts of Russia were relocated, with their entire personnel, from the war zones to major Central Asian centers. The third was the increasing pressure from government authorities to produce patriotic motion and documentary movies.

The next period—from the 1960s to the 1980s—became the golden age of national cinematography in the Central Asian republics. The national studios became individually identifiable, with their own styles and idioms and their emphasis on their national cultural peculiarities, although low-budget, generic romance, revolutionary and so-called industrial films (movies about workers and Communist Party activists) were also quite common. This era, too, marked an important transformation in the role of the motion picture in society. The function of cinema shifted from serving purely propaganda purposes to becoming a major form of entertainment, as, for the first time in the twentieth century, many people in the region were finally elevated out of absolute poverty. Cinemas were opened in practically every town and village throughout the region. The local governments even subsidized mobile film projectors that screened movies in open-air cinemas in the most remote areas. The number of movie theaters (including open-air facilities) mushroomed and reached about 20,000 in 1972.[31] During this era, the Central Asian cinema market was also opened to films imported from other countries, primarily from Eastern Europe and from the developing world, especially India. Very few Western movies made their way to Central Asian audiences, as the Soviet authorities extended the iron curtain to the cinema. However, people in the filmmaking industry usually faced no such limitations, as many major Western productions and prize-winning works were screened secretly for high-ranking Communist Party officials, joined by filmmakers.

During this era, the national studios produced many motion pictures that are still considered the best achievements of their respective national cinemas. Kazakh moviemakers, for instance, had the opportunity to study the greatest traditions of Soviet cinematography by working with Sergey Eisenstein, Vsevolod Pudovkin, and Ivan Pyr'ev.[32] Gradually, a number of directors in the national Kazakhstan filmmaking industry achieved prominence, not only at the national level but also at the all-Soviet level; these included Sh. Beisembayev, S. Raimbayev, K. Abuseitov, and Zh. Baitenov. Some examples of the works that emerged during this period afford us a glimpse of the major themes in Kazakhstani cinematography. The historical-revolutionary film *Jambul* (1953) explored the life of a prominent Kazakh poet and bard; the social drama *Botagoz* (1958) was about the transformation of the rigid social customs of Kazakh society and the emancipation of a Kazakh woman during the Sovietization process; the historical *Ego vremia pridet* (His time will come) (1958) was devoted to the conflict between Chokan Valikhanov, a Russian educated Kazakh officer in the Russian Imperial service, and the zealous guardians of traditionalism in the Kazakh steppe communities; the patriotic *Pesn' o Manshuk* (Song about Manshuk) (1970) explored the personal drama of a simple Kazakh woman's life during the Great Patriotic War; and *Kyz-Zhybek* (1972) retells a popular Kazakh epic about the tragic love of a medieval female warrior who had to go through many sacrifices for her love, her fiancé, and her country.

Along with the serious major films, Kazakh directors produced some lighter works, including melodramas, Western-style action thrillers, and musicals. The hilarious *Aldar-Kose* (1963) explored the life of a famous Central Asian trickster and his lone war against social injustice; *Konets atamana* (The end of ataman [chieftain], 1971) was an action thriller about the work of the Bolshevik intelligence service against the White Guard Cossack bands; the lyrical *Alpamysh idet v shkolu* (Alpamysh goes to school) (1978) tells of the adventures of a little boy who goes to school and discovers a completely new world; the musical *Gurmangazy* (1972) dramatizes the artistic life of a famous Kazakh composer and improviser.

Kyrgyzfilm studio productions have long distinguished themselves for their skillful representation of a combination of emblematic Kyrgyz national, cultural, and social motifs. The studio regularly filmed the most acclaimed literary works by major Kyrgyz authors. Several directors achieved considerable recognition for their works in the national cinema, including Bolotbek Shamshyev, Bekesh Abdulayev, Tynay Ibragimov, and Tolomush Okeyev, whom one modern critic has called "one of the most remarkable filmmakers of the region and of Soviet history."[33]

Social dramas such as *Saltanat* (1955), *Daleko v gorakh* (Far in the mountains) (1958), and *Urkuia* (1972), which depicts the conflicts within small Kyrgyz village communities in the early days of the Soviet system, are the most representative products of Kyrgyz cinema; the historical-revolutionary

Toktogul (1958) depicts the artistic life and lifelong struggle for social justice of one of the most acclaimed Kyrgyz poets and bards; and the lyrical dramas *Znoi* (Heat) (1963), *Pervyi uchitel* (First teacher) (1965), *Jamilya* (1969), *Belyi parokhod* (White steamship) (1976), and *Zolotaia osen* (Golden autumn) (1980) are cinematic interpretations of works by the celebrated Kyrgyz writer Chingiz Aitmatov.

Action movies and dramas were popular among wide audiences. The historical-revolutionary films *Vystrel na perevale Karash* (A Gunshot on the Karash Pass) (1969) and *Alyie maki Issyk-Kulia* (The red poppies of Issyk Kol) (1972) powerfully depict the devastating effect of the civil war on ordinary people; and the lyrical melodramas *Ulybka na kamne* (Smile of a stone) (1975), *Pole Aisulu* (The field of Aisulu) (1977), *Kak pishetsia slovo "solntse"* (How to spell the word "sun") (1979), and *Ranniie zhuravli* (Early cranes) (1980) depict the everyday lives of traditional Kyrgyz society, dramatizing Kyrgyz customs and personal relations in a traditional society.

Tajik film producers tried to blend classical Persian artistic traditions with new themes of Soviet cinema. Tajik directors such as Margarita Kasymova, M. Aripov, S. Khamidov, A. Turayev, and Davlyat Khudonazarov succeeded in creating many significant works that were widely popular among Tajik and, more general, Central Asian audiences.

The revolutionary drama *Dokhunda* (1957), adapted from the Tajik writer Sadriddin Aini's acclaimed novel, is one of many distinguished works worth mentioning. The social drama *Znamia kuznetsa* (The banner of a blacksmith) (1961) was inspired by a poem, *Shahnama*, by Firdowsi; the epic *Chelovek meniaiet kozhu* (The man sheds his skin) (1960) shows a dramatic confrontation between builders and opponents of the Soviet system, played out against a background of the romance between an American engineer and a simple Russian girl; the social drama *Zumrad* (1962) focuses on the emancipation of Tajik women; the epic *Skazaniie o Rustame* (The tale of Rustam) (1971), *Rustam i Sukhrab* (Rustam and Sukhrab) (1972) and *Skazaniie o Siavushe* (The tale of Siavush) (1977) are adaptations of classical Persian poems that illustrate the endless confrontation between love and hatred and the psychological traumas of war; the philosophical drama *Pervaia lubov' Nasreddina* (The first love of Nasreddin) (1978) tells about the early life and the tragedy of this beloved Central Asian trickster.

Among the "entertainment" movies that have received wide recognition are the comedies *Ia vstretil devushku* (I met a girl) (1957), *Synu pora zhenitsia* (Time for our son to wed) (1960), *Nasreddin v Khojente ili ocharovanyi prints* (Nasreddin in Khojent, or charmed prince) (1960), and the musical comedy *Belyi roial'* (White grand piano) (1969), which in humorous ways displays traditional and modern ways of life in Tajik society; the melodrama *Unosti pervoie utro* (First morning of youth) (1979) examines the lives of young people in modern society.

Turkmenfilm worked along lines similar to those of other Central Asian studios, though it naturally put more emphasis on Turkmen cultural themes and on glorifying the moral and ethical values of Turkmen society and Soviet social and economic changes. However, the development of the national moviemaking industry was negatively affected by two factors, one natural and the other political. First, the devastating 1948 earthquake destroyed the entire studio and most of its equipment. Second, the artistic works of national filmmakers became subject to political witch-hunting, and they were eventually condemned by the Central Committee of the Communist Party in 1961 for not being sufficiently "socialist realist." Yet several national directors managed to navigate all of these difficulties and create works that achieved wide recognition not only at the national but also at the regional level. These included such directors as A. Karliyev, U. Mutanov, Kh. Agahanov, B. Mansurov and Kh. Narliyev, who became renowned for their motion pictures.

Among the most notable Turkmen movies are *Syn pastukha* (Shepherd's son) (1955); *Khitrost' starogo Ashira* (The cunning of old Ashir) (1956); *Chest' sem'i* (Family honor) (1957); *Pervyi ekzamen* (First exam) (1959); and *Aina* (1959). These movies attempt to use historical and contemporary issues to address philosophical and ethical problems in a changing Turkmen society. Throughout the 1950s, Turkmen producers tried to develop their own forms of expression and took the first steps in creating a national cinema, though they experienced difficult times, facing day-to-day interference by Communist Party officials. As a result, many directors turned to politically correct revolutionary themes and produced pictures, such as *Utolenie zhazhdy* (Quenching one's thirst) (1967), *Rabynia* (Slave) (1970), and *Reshaiushchii shag* (Decisive step) (1966), that in one way or another addressed the issues of class conflict and revolutionary change in Turkmenistan. The historical *Makhtymkuli* (1968) presents the tragic life of the greatest Turkmen philosopher, poet, and bard; the social drama *Tainy Mukama* (Secrets of Mukam) (1974) illustrates the oppressive feudal traditions of nineteenth-century Turkmen society that ruined the life of a talented female singer; the drama *Nevestka* (The daughter in law) (1972) truthfully depicts the personal tragedy and destructive effect of war by presenting the life of an ordinary Turkmen woman whose loved one is killed in battle; the social drama *Umei skazat' "net"* (Be able to say "no") (1977) depicts power and the humiliating effect of certain rigid social traditions in Turkmen society. The melodrama *Derevo Jamal* (The tree of Jamal) (1981) beautifully describes the tragic life of a young woman who becomes a shepherd in a small and extremely isolated Turkmen community.

In contrast to the politically motivated films, Turkmen children's films such as *Prikluchenia Aldar-Kose* (The adventures of Aldar Kose) (1970), *Mal da udal* (Small but brave) (1974), *Volshebnaia kniga Murada* (The magic book of Murad) (1975), and *Starik i devochka* (An old man and a girl) (1981) are charming in their depiction of the lives and thoughts of Central Asian children. Most of these films are based on fairy tales or on local themes.

The Uzbek film studio was one of the largest and most productive studios in Central Asia. It distinguished itself by producing acclaimed historical, revolutionary, and adventure action movies. The names of some Uzbek directors, such as K. Iarmatov, Shukhrat Abbasov, Ali Khamraev, A. Akbarkhodjaev, Khatam Faiziev, Usup Razykov, and E. Ishmukhammedov, became well-known throughout Uzbekistan and beyond in Central Asia.

The historical dramas *Krushenie emirata* (The downfall of the Emirate) (1955), *Avitsenna* (1957), *Sviashchenaia krov'* (Sacred blood) (1956), and *Fukrat* (1959), which depict various pages of Uzbek history, are among the movies that best represent the major themes and approaches in Uzbek cinema that warrant mention. And the revolutionary *Tashkent—gorod khlebnyi* (Tashkent—the City of Bread) (1968), brilliant in its simplicity, exposes the terrible consequences of the civil war through a touching story presented through the eyes of a little boy who escapes from famine and war in his village in Russia by fleeing to Tashkent with a dream of finding work and making enough money to buy a few bags of grain; through his adventures in Tashkent, the film depicts the life of Central Asia society, rich and poor, good and evil, and shows social traditions and culture. The film became an unexpected hit and was popular among many generations of viewers throughout the region. Historical themes were continued in *Bez strakha* (Without fear) (1972), which tells a brutal story of the emancipation of Uzbek women, epitomized in a young heroine's rejection of the *Hudjum* (the veil that covers women's faces, in accordance with Islamic tradition); *Odna sredi ludei* (Alone among the people) (1974), which portrays the social and cultural challenges in the life of the poetess Nadira; *Abu Raikhan Beruni* (1975), which depict the lifelong quest for knowledge of the medieval scholar and poet Beruni; and *Iunosts genia* (Youth of a genius) (1983), which illustrates the early career of the medieval scholar and enlightener Avicenna. The revolutionary *Khamza* (1961), *Buria nad Aziei* (The storm over Asia) (1965), and *Vsadniki revolutsii* (Horsemen of the revolution) (1968) were the films with similar themes that glorified the powerful call of the Bolshevik revolution and revolutionary changes in Central Asia.

It was, however, entertaining action movies that represent the revolution and civil war in Central Asia as semi-exotic ventures into the mystic Orient that made the studio famous among Central Asian and Russian viewers, as well as among viewers in many developing countries. Revolutionary western-style adventure films such as *Chrezvychainyi komissar* (Commissar extraordinary) (1970), *Gibel' chernogo konsula* (Death of the black consul) (1970), and, especially, *Sed'maia pulia* (The seventh bullet) (1973) dramatize confrontations of the revolutionary years through the eyes and experiences of individual heroes against a background of the Gordian knot of personal, communal, and cultural relations.

Uzbekfilm also produced several joint films with various foreign partners, mainly from the socialist and developing countries. The drama *Lubov' i iarost'* (Love and rage) (1979; with Yugoslavia) presents a love story developed against the background of the civil war in Central Asia. *Prikluchenia Ali Baby i soroka razboinikov* (Adventures of Ali Baba and the forty thieves) (1980; with India) retells the classic fairy tale from *The Arabian Nights*.

In the 1980s, as the iron curtain and the iron hand of censorship began to fade away, Central Asian moviemakers attempted to turn their attention to new themes and to address the social and psychological traumas of the Stalinist era, the conflict between individuals and collectives, and the people's dissatisfaction with the realities of Soviet life. Young and ambitious directors made many interesting movies in an effort to bring new depth to the national cinema via highly emotional and intellectual pictures that emulated those of the European masters of the 1950s. For example, Serik Aprimov's *Konechnaia ostanovka* (The last stop) (1989) "transmits locus genii in a manner similar to Jia Zhanke's analytical long-take style"[34] as it follows the travels of a young man from military service in the Red Army to his home village in the middle of nowhere and exposing the bleak realities of Soviet life, with rampant drinking and violence graphically depicted in an epical style of photography. The *Voskhozhdenie na Fudziamu* (The ascent of Fujiama) (1988) is about the brutal and senseless realities of that period in Kyrgyz society. The *Kairat* (1991), in a "dreamlike and surgically precise"[35] way, shows the never-ending travels of a young student through his life and along numerous roads in his country.

The 1990s have totally transformed Central Asian cinema, bringing new realities that continue to shape the region's industry. Initially, there was a surge of public optimism as governments relaxed or abandoned censorship and producers experienced new-found freedom of artistic expression. This sense of freedom spurred the so-called new wave of motion pictures, as very young directors and artists came together to produce films free of the tight restrictions inherent in Soviet officialdom. However, the changes proved to be too far-reaching, and the whole industry found itself near collapse. Kazakhstan was forced to reduce production to such an extent it is currently ranked 84th in the world in per capita movie production, behind Senegal,

Egypt, Sri Lanka, and Honduras.[36] In Kyrgyzstan, Tajikistan, and Turkmenistan, movie production was stopped all together for several years.

Several factors contributed to the collapse of the national cinema industry in the region in the 1990s. First was the fact that the old Soviet model of movie production did not work in the new environment; the generous subsidies to national film-producing studios were removed, and most movie theaters were privatized. All national studios have been hit hard and have became pale shadows of their past selves not only because of the absence of funding but also because of a lack of knowledge of sophisticated marketing practices and management expertise. The second factor was that with the abolition of the iron curtain, the cinema market became fully open to foreign films. All the TV channels and movie theaters were immediately conquered and remain dominated by Western, mainly Hollywood, products. This domination has prevailed to such a degree that some movie theatres do not show nationally produced products for months on end. Third, Central Asian populations began abandoning their habit of spending time in movie theaters as economic downturns, mass poverty, and unemployment, combined with high crime rates on the streets of many cities and towns, forced people, including youth, to quit spending free time going out.[37] Fourth, the newly "discovered" satellites and cable, as well as video rentals, became dangerous competitors to national TV and cinematography as they captured a significant portion of the entertainment market. Related to this factor is that, with little or no copyright enforcement in the region, people can buy pirated copies of many of the latest blockbusters from Hollywood or Bollywood,[38] or any internationally acclaimed movie, within days of their first release for as little as $5 to $8 per DVD.

In the first decade of the twenty-first century, the situation in the Central Asian cinema industry has begun to stabilize. Though nearly half the movie theaters closed their doors,[39] especially in rural areas, the surviving ones have moved beyond the Soviet-era barebones style by diversifying into true Western-style entertainment centers featuring multiscreen complexes and numerous cafeterias and shops. Documentary moviemakers have even experienced a little boom, with a rise in the production of short films for tourism companies, for government-controlled TV stations, and for various public companies and individual philanthropists. The filmmakers have learned to produce low-budget movies for wider audiences, often exclusively for screening on national television. Some film directors have found small niches in the market by making movies for high-end intellectual audiences, especially overseas.

In this environment, the Central Asian film studios are engaged in an ongoing struggle for survival by any and all possible means. Two basic models have emerged in the region. One is a return to state subsidies to assist in new film ventures; thus, government officials have regained an important role in commissioning new screenplays and final products. Movie producers continue to lobby the national governments and, in a recent development, large companies to acquire funding for individual projects, large and small. In the early 2000s, for example, Kazakhstan funded such expensive movies as *Kochevnik* (The nomad) (2005), with plans at this writing to fund several more, including *Mongol—molodost' Chinghiskhana* (Mongol—the youth of Genghis Khan)[40] and *Mustafa Shokai*.[41] In the 1990s, Uzbekistan's government funded at least 6 movies a year,[42] and in the early 2000s the number was increased to 15.[43] The second model is to produce low-budget movies aimed at "highbrow" audiences and international movie festivals. Central Asian directors regularly receive foreign support from such international sponsors as the financier George Soros and others. In addition, there have been many attempts to develop co-production arrangements with foreign studios. Some success stories have emerged, such as *Beshkempir: The Adopted Son* (1998), which the *New York Times* called "a realistic, subtly erotic coming-of-age tale and the first independent film to come from Kyrgyzstan."[44] It shows the everyday life of a boy and his friends in a traditional Kyrgyz village, highlighting remarkable details of Kyrgyz traditions. In Uzbekistan, filmmakers have produced a number of charming movies that tell the stories of ordinary people against a background of major historical events, intrigues, or social change. For example, *Voiz* (Speaker) (2000) shows how the extraordinary events in family life brought about by the Bolshevik revolution in his country bring an ordinary cart-driver three wives, a high-ranking position in the new Soviet government, and the tragic love of a woman whom he can never marry.

By and large, moviemaking has been kept alive in Central Asia through the difficult years of transition by the endless efforts of enthusiasts who believe, as the Kazakh producer Shapiga Musina says, "It is very important sometimes to let pictures speak. They can often say more than words."[45] They nourish the hope that the national cinemas might revive themselves one day. Cheaper technology, including computer animation, editing, and the computerization of special effects, in combination with a slowly growing interest in national cinema and the rise of the middle class and local philanthropy, might channel both financial resources and public interest to national cinema. Some, though, such as the Tajik producer Bakhtiyr Khudonazarov, are very pessimistic and "don't see any [future]" in the national cinema in the region.[46]

THE INTERNET

The Internet arrived in Central Asia relatively late; in the mid-1990s, it was practically unavailable to the general public. In the late 1990s, international organizations, philanthropists, Western governments, and NGOs helped to introduce the wider population in the region to the world of the Internet. International aid organizations, the U.S. government, and foundations (such as the Soros Foundation), for example, funded the establishment of Internet hubs in all major universities and libraries across the region. While the thought of Central Asia does not exactly bring to mind flashy Web sites, e-governance, and e-commerce, by the early 2000s Central Asian cyberspace had become quite sophisticated and developed.

All major government agencies and all large businesses in the region have established well-designed Web sites, making documents and significant information available online. Some government officials, however, still understand e-governance in terms of state control over the Internet, and some business people limit their understanding of e-commerce to actively promoting Central Asian brides on the international dating and marrying portals.

The younger generation have very different ideas about the Internet. To many of them, it provides a unique window of opportunity for free expressions, chat, the search for friends, exchanges about music or personal life, politics, playing games, and networking—very similar, in other words, to its use in any Western country. Together with the radio stations, dating, chat, and hobby portals have facilitated the shaping of a kind of youth subculture group in every major metropolitan area in the region, each with its own values, interests, customs, and lifestyles.

The Internet has become a popular source of public information, as practically every newspaper has its searchable Web site, usually providing free access to everyone. Almost every media outlet runs its own comprehensive and user-friendly Web site, often with searchable archives containing a wealth of information on cultural, political, social, and economic issues; these Web sites can easily compete, in the quality of their presentation of news and reports, with those of many established media outlets in the West. However, the cost of access and the rudimentary infrastructure hinder the Internet's spread and availability in the region. While it is relatively easy to access the Internet in all the capital cities and major urban centers, most of the rural population is still excluded from the cyberworld. Even for the urban dwellers, the Internet is accessible only in the major cities and to only a relatively small number, as the cost of an annual Internet subscriptions often equals the average monthly salary. This is probably one of the main reasons that the region lags well behind many countries in terms of the number of Internet users per 1,000 citizens. Out of 167 countries surveyed regarding Internet use, Kyrgyzstan, for example, ranks 105th (29.53 per 1,000 people) and Kazakhstan 121st (16.46 per 1,000).[47] By comparison, in the United States there are 556 Internet users per 1,000 people, and 336 in France.[48] Some Central Asian governments have even tried to impose additional restrictions on the cyberworld: in the early 2000s, the governments of Uzbekistan and Turkmenistan experimented with imposing direct control and monitoring of Internet usage and sometimes blocked certain Web portals.

NOTES

1. Gulnara Abikeyeva, "The Space of My Dream," *Transition on Line,* November 26, 2003, www.tol.cz.

2. Adrian Karatnycky et al., *Nations in Transit 2002* (New York: Freedom House, 2002), p. 422.

3. For an examination of issues and problems in this area, see Andrew Wilson, ed., *Virtual Politics: Faking Democracy in the Post-Soviet World* (New Haven: Yale University Press, 2005).

4. The situation is quite different in Ashgabat, the capital of Turkmenistan, where the government still maintained total control over mass media distribution in the 1990s and early 2000s.

5. On attempts to establish independent media in Turkistan before the Bolshevik revolution, see Edward Allworth, *The Modern Uzbeks: From the Fourteenth Century to the Present: A Cultural History* (Stanford: Hoover Institution Press, 1990).

6. For data, see *Narodnoie Khoziaistvo SSSR* [National Economy of the USSR] (Moscow: Finansy i statistika, 1989).

7. There were enormous changes in the Soviet media during Gorbachev's perestroika era; yet, the conservative officials in the Communist Party in the Central Asian republics used every method imaginable to keep tight control over the media in their respective republics. For details of the transition, see Elena Androunas, *Soviet Media in Transition: Structural and Economic Alternatives* (Westport, CT: Praeger, 1993).

8. An analysis of the development in Kazakhstan may be found in Oleg Katsiev, "Prospects for Development of an Independent Media in Kazakhstan," in *Civil Society in Central Asia,* ed. Holt Ruffin and Daniel Waugh (Seattle and London: University of Washington Press, 1999), pp. 122–134.

9. Karatnycky et al., *Nations in Transit,* p. 597.

10. Aili Piano and Arch Puddington, eds., *Freedom in the World 2005: The Annual Survey of Political Rights and Civil Liberties* (Lanham, MD; New York; Toronto; and Oxford: Rowman and Littlefield, 2005), p. 624.

11. http://www.worldpress.org/Asia/102.cfm.

12. Turkmenistan and Uzbekistan have banned all major opposition newspapers since the mid-1990s.

13. See http://www.timeout.orexca.com/index.shtml (accessed September 14, 2005).

14. http://www.internews.kz/index.php?itemid=99.

15. http://www.freedomhouse.org/research/pressurvey/allscore2005.pdf.

16. http://www.freedomhouse.org/research/pressurvey/allscore2005.pdf.

17. Kyrgyzstan is an excellent example. In 2002, there were about 50 independent, semi-independent, and privately owned newspapers and magazines there, including the popular *Vechernii Bishkek, Delo No, Asaba, Res Publica,* and *AKI-press.* Many newspapers had circulations of between 20,000 and 50,000 copies, while *oblast* newspapers often had circulations below 5,000 copies.

18. The figure was 26 to 28 newspapers per 1,000 people; UNESCO Institute for Statistics, March 11, 2003, http://www.nationmaster.com/graph-T/med_new_cir_cap (accessed June 20, 2006).

19. By comparison, according to the CIA World Factbook for December 2003, there are 1,944 radios per 1,000 people in the United States. A total of 221 countries were surveyed; Data are available at http://www.nationmaster.com/graph-T/med_rad_cap (accessed June 20, 2006).

20. See http://www.europaplus.kz/ (accessed June 20, 2006).

21. See the station's weekly Hit Parade of top 20 songs on the Web site http://www.grand.uz/ (accessed June 20, 2006).

22. By comparison, according to the CIA World Factbook for December 2003, there are 740.53 TV sets per 1,000 people in the United States and 655.388 per 1,000 people in Canada. Two hundred and fifteen countries were surveyed in this study; see http://www.nationmaster.com/graph-T/med_tel_cap.

23. This claim was made in a documentary about the "Russian Sinatra," the Muslim Magomayev (1942–).

24. A total of 227 countries were surveyed for the CIA World Factbook for March 2005. See http://www.nationmaster.com/graph-T/med_tel_bro_sta.

25. Quoted at http://www.eurasianet.org/resource/kazakhstan/hypermail/200104/0021.html (accessed August 29, 2005).

26. For this review I used the TV guides published in *Kazakhstanskaia Pravda* and *Karavan* in May 2006.

27. For this review I used the TV guides published in *Slovo Kyrgyzstan—TV nedelia.*

28. The national studios, as of 1989, included Kazakhfilm, Kyrgyzfilm, Tajikfilm, Turkmenfilm, and Uzbekfilm.

29. A fairly good list of Soviet movies can be found on the Web site http://www.ssees.ac.uk/videos/russdate.htm.

30. Sh. Abbasov, "A teper' mne khochetsia pokhuliganit' ... ," *Kinoman,* no. 10 (December 2005): 8.

31. Author's calculations (approximate).

32. During World War II, several Russian studios were evacuated from Russia to Alma-Ata.

33. Alla Verlotsky, "Filming the Silk Road," *Transition-on-Line,* May 3, 2003, at www.tol.cz.

34. Nathan Lee, "Undiscovered Country," *New York Sun,* May 2, 2003.

35. Ibid.

36. Other Central Asian republics did not even make it into the ranking at all. There were 104 countries surveyed in 2003. See http://www.nationmaster.com/graph-T/med_fil_pro_cap (accessed June 20, 2006).

37. For example, Kazakhstan and Kyrgyzstan are in 70th (66.14 films per 1,000 people a year attended) and 71st place (62.35 per 1,000 people), respectively, in the world in per capita cinema attendance, behind Russia, Ukraine, China, Zimbabwe, and Oman. The United States, by comparison, is in second place (4804.99 per 1,000 people). See http://www.nationmaster.com/graph-T/med_cin_att_cap.

38. Collective name for movies produced at Indian film studios in Bombay (Mumbai).

39. For example, in Uzbekistan, only 161 out of 317 remained open as of 2005. *Kinoman,* no. 10 (December 2005): 7.

40. *Time Out Almaty,* May 18–31, 2006, p. 48.

41. *Kinoman,* no. 1 (January 2006): 23.

42. *Sanat,* no. 3 (2002); see http://www.sanat.orexca.com/rus/archive/3–02/cinema.shtml (accessed June 20, 2006).

43. T. Nadyrov, "Tainy Uzbekskogo Kino…," *Kinoman,* no. 10 (December 2005): 4–7.

44. Judy Stone, "Talent Finds a Career in an Asian Hinterland," *New York Times,* February 21, 1999, p. 37.

45. Beverly Andrews, "Cinema: Out of Kazakhstan, a Hunter's Family," *Inter Press Service,* December 20, 1996.

46. Abikeyeva, "The Space of my Dream."

47. See http://www.nationmaster.com/graph-T/int_use_cap (accessed on August 19, 2005).

48. United Nations Development Program, *Human Development Report 2005: International Cooperation at a Crossroad* (New York: United Nations Development Program, 2005), pp. 262–263.

5

Performing Arts

Dombyranyn kulagyn Kazakh kana burai alady. Only a Kazakh can understand the *dombra*.

—Aldabergen Myrzabekov, Kazakh poet[1]

A concert presenting the contemporary Central Asian performing arts would entertain listeners by a contrasting combination of two major musical traditions. Sharpened to perfection, sophisticated and meditative rhythms of old urban centers display the influences of the millennia-old Persian musical legacy, Islamic traditions, and inspiration from the *dervishes* (members) of various Sufi orders. Sounds of nature and nomadic circles of life—from drawn-out and howling winter winds to the cheerful awakening and hopping of young foals—are voiced by bards *(baksy)* and by their simple instruments reflecting the ancient traditions of the nomads of the Eurasian steppe, deserts, and mountains and the shamanistic legacy of the pre-Islamic past. Numerous traders, scholars, professional musicians, and conquerors who traveled along the Great Silk Road added Arab, Mediterranean, and Chinese flavors in some areas in the region but in other places left the performing arts traditions intact.[2]

The performing arts of Central Asia were safeguarded from Western cultural influences until the late nineteenth and early twentieth centuries by the countries' geographic remoteness. The situation changed only in the mid-1920s as the Soviet authorities initiated the so-called Soviet Cultural Revolution. Soviet policy included "cultural modernization" through nurturing and fiercely promoting contemporary European genres of the performing arts; through an ideologically directed "cleansing" of the pre-Soviet cultural legacy by dividing it into backward "feudal-religious" and progressive "people's" elements; and through a national "demarcation" of artistic traditions and the development of artistic expressions of the "new" Soviet national identity, along with bold experimentation with syntheses of traditional Central Asian artistic forms and classic European genres. In addition, the national governments imposed strict state controls over the creative work. These controls would remain, like a sword of Damocles hanging over the heads of all artists, throughout the Soviet era.

The Soviet authorities approached the performing arts as devoted gardeners approach a lawn: they generously fed and tenderly looked after the object of their affection but mercilessly attacked any independent and uncontrolled, and thus dangerous, "weed." Indeed, the Soviets both directly and indirectly encouraged the mass involvement of young people in the performing arts. For example, performing art studios were created in practically every city in the region. The so-called Houses of Culture (*Madaniyat Uyi* in Uzbek) and clubs of amateur artists were opened in every city and town across the region. Dance classes became an integral part of extracurricular activities in every middle school and high school. Hundreds of semiprofessional dance groups were established in the Central Asian republics; they recruited the strongest talents through numerous amateur contests, competitions, and concerts. Nonetheless, at the same time, hundreds of performers, directors, and screenwriters were purged for their independent thoughts and actions.

As in many other areas of Central Asian cultural development, this Gordian knot of interactions between traditional and modern, Asian and European, religious and secular, ultimately produced interesting and unique results. On the eve of the twenty-first century, the performing arts in Central Asia took new and clearly distinguishable national forms recognizable as Kazakh, Kyrgyz, Tajik, Turkmen, or Uzbek, very different from Afghan, Iranian, Uigur (western China), or Turkish traditions. In addition, the Soviet-imposed iron curtain protected the Central Asian performing arts from the influences of the outside world and especially from Western pop culture. But, at the same time, this prevented Western audiences from learning about Central Asian art and severely restricted the opportunities available to Central Asians to demonstrate their achievements to international audiences. Because of this history of restrictions, the performing arts of Central Asia are still awaiting discovery by the Western world.

FOLK INSTRUMENTS

The Museum of Folk Musical Instruments in Almaty probably presents the most complete representation of the variety of the region's musical traditions anywhere; its collection contains hundreds of instruments. The diversity of musical instruments of Central Asia has traditionally been limited only by the artistic creativity and memory of the region's instrument makers. In a time when most of those artisans were self-taught masters working from no precise recorded design—their method was often no more than to try to remember the approximate shape of the instrument—they would make it first and then do their best to connect that instrument with the sounds they thought appropriate. Eventually, in the Middle Ages, in the region's older, settled centers, a limited number of professional instrument-making schools emerged, where the masters developed and followed a canon to reproduce classic instruments, paying meticulous attention to detail. Some of these instruments resemble their cousins in the Middle East, the Caucasus, western China, and Mongolia—anywhere, in fact, linked to the region by the Great Silk Road.[3] Other instruments were unique to certain oases or geographic areas, as the remoteness and rudimentary transportation isolated many areas of Central Asia from the rest of the world.

The instrumental traditions of the region evolved around its major social divide, between the nomads and the settlers. The nomadic bard or musician usually preferred to play a single, light, and simple stringed instrument, because of its convenience and practicality.[4] Such instruments were much easier to carry, along with one's belongings, on the back of a horse, camel, or donkey. The settlers, on the other hand, had more choices and could afford a greater variety of instruments. Moreover, thanks to the well-developed trade along the Great Silk Road, they could import musical instruments from other countries.

By the eighteenth and nineteenth centuries, with the formation of national identities, national languages, and elements of national culture, some musical instruments became associated with certain ethnic groups. People began differentiate to Kazakhs, Kyrgyzs, Turkmens, Uigurs, and others by their distinguishing songs and musical motifs, as well as by the musical instruments used to accompany them.

The "nationalization" of musical instruments accelerated in the twentieth century with the creation of the national republics in the mid-1920s. For the first time in Central Asian history, folk musical instruments were systematically studied and categorized as specifically "national" instruments. Folk music instruments were introduced into orchestral music, and national folk instrumental orchestras were created in every Central Asian republic. After decades of improvisation and attempts to standardize the instruments and playing techniques, the modern folk orchestras emerged with the capacity to express their rich musical heritage and to play complex and sophisticated music compositions created by both local and Western composers.

Soviet scholars organized many folk musicological and ethnographic expeditions in the region, recording hundreds of traditional folk instruments (see Table 5.1). Many of the instruments are still widely used, but some can now be seen only in museums or private collections.

The stringed instruments were usually made of wood, with pear-shaped bodies and long necks, and with two or sometimes four strings. The *dombra*— a typical two-stringed instrument—resembles a lute. There are also three-stringed *dombras,* which can mainly be found today in the Semipalatinsk region of Kazakhstan. The body of the instrument is about 100–130 cm in

Table 5.1
National Musical Instruments

Country Type	Kazakhstan	Kyrgyzstan	Tajikistan	Turkmenistan	Uzbekistan
String	Qobuz	Kiyak	Ghijjak	Gijak	Qobuz
	Dombra	Komuz	Dumbura	Dutar	Ghijjak
			Dutar		Violin
			Rubab		Dombira
			Tandur		Dutar
			Chang		Rabab
					Tanbur
					Chartar
					Panjtar
					Shashtar
					Setar
					Qanun
					Cang
Wind	Duduk	Choor	Nay	Tuyduk	Nay
	Sabizgi	Temir	Tutiq	Dilli	Tutuq
	Shan	komuz	Qushnay	tiiyduk	Quray
	qobuz	Sunray	Juftnay	Gopuz	Nay
	Surnai	Karnay	Sunray		Sibizgha
	Karnai		Karnay		Balaban
					Qoshnay
					Karnay
Percussion	Daulpaz	Doolbash	Naghara		Naghara
		Dool	Tavlak		Dol
			Daira		Daira
			Qayraq		Qayraq
			Safail		Safail
			Zang		Zang

Source: Johanna Spector, "Musical Traditions and Innovations," in *Central Asia: 130 Years of Russian Dominance, a Historical Overview,* ed. Edward Allworth (Durham and London: Duke University Press, 1994), pp. 450–451.

length. The strings were traditionally made of sinew, though modern, mass-produced *dombras* are supplied with nylon strings. The *dombra* is used mainly to play a traditional musical piece called a *kui,* the unique character of which lies in its constant change of musical meter. The instrument is popular among Kazakhs, who differentiate two types of *dombras,* eastern and western. The two types vary in the width of the neck. Fast, virtuoso *kui*-playing requires smooth and unobstructed movement of left hand on the instrument; hence the long and narrow fingerboard of western *dombras.* The eastern *dombra* has a shortened and widened fingerboard. The instrument's size affects the sound it produces. The bigger the instrument, the deeper and more distinctive the timbre. *Dombra* players employ different techniques of playing, such as strumming with strong movements of the right hand when both strings are played and gentle plucking individual strings.[5]

The *kobyz* is a two- or four-stringed wooden instrument played with a bow and is traditionally made from a single piece of wood. The lower half of the upper soundboard is made of leather. In the past, the strings for the instrument were made of horsehair, though now metal strings are also used. When played, the *kobyz* is held vertically, placed on a knee. The *kobyz* used to be the instrument of storytellers, singers, and shamans. A modernized *kobyz* is played like a cello and might be used to reproduce tones closer to a violin. A Kazakh legend tells about Korkyt, the creator of the *kobyz* and the protector of all shamans.[6] According to the legend, Korkyt could not accept the prospect of aging and death. He began wandering, thinking of nothing but his dream of eternal life. What he saw around him, however, was death. The fallen and decaying tree in the forest, the grass in the steppe burned under the sun, even the crumbling mountains—everything was talking about the briefness of life and the eventual death of Korkyt himself. Finally understanding and accepting death, Korkyt took a piece of wood, shaped it, and hollowed it out, making the very first *kobyz.* He attached strings to it and started playing, giving to it all of his thoughts, unfulfilled dreams, and feelings. The majestic sound of the music filled the air and spread around the world, reaching and capturing the hearts of the people and ultimately making Korkyt truly eternal.

The *surnay (syrnai, zurna)* is a traditional long-bore instrument that starts as a straight pipe and widens into a conical end; it is a distant cousin of the Turkish *zurna* or the Arabic *mizmar.* The instrument, which can be several feet long, is traditionally made of wood or cane. It can produce a sustained, loud, and deep tone. It was often used to call for public gatherings during various community events, such as wedding, or military actions.

The *komuz* (also *chertmek*) is a traditional long-necked, three-stringed instrument with a wooden, pear-shaped body. It also resembles a lute and is considered a close cousin of the *dombra.* The body of the instrument is made of a single piece of wood, usually from the apricot or walnut tree. The strings are traditionally made of sheep-gut, though in the modern era synthetic materials are widely used. The Kyrgyzs believe the *komuz* was the first Kyrgyz musical instrument and that it was introduced by the fearless hunter Kambar, who created it to inspire his children and grandchildren, through music and songs, to be brave and strong. The *komuz* has long been an inseparable part of traditional Kyrgyz culture.

The *nay (ney, nye)* is a straight, end-blown flute that comes in different lengths. It is a close cuisine of the Arab *nay*. In the distant past it was often made of wood, though modern *nays* are usually made of metal (brass), and it usually has five or six finger holes. From medieval times, the instrument was popular among dervishes and the settled population of what are now Tajikistan and Uzbekistan.

The *dutar* (also *saz*) is a two-stringed instrument with a neck about two feet long and a small, pear-shaped body; though Herati *dutar* have more strings. It is a close cousin of the *dombra* and the *komuz*. The strings are usually plucked

Young girl plays Kyrgyz national instrument the *komuz*. Courtesy of the author, 2006.

by a player to produce a warm, vibrating tone. In the past, the strings were made of silk, though metal strings have been widely used since the beginning of the twentieth century. This instrument is especially popular among the Turkmens.

The *gidjak (gidzjak)* is a two-, three-, or four-stringed instrument played with a bow. The three-stringed *gidjak* is often used as a solo instrument to play traditional folk music, while the four-stringed *gidjak* is used in folk orchestras. Since the twentieth century, it has been made with metal strings.

The *doyra* is a traditional instrument that resembles a tambourine. It is traditionally made of wood covered on one side with a thin piece of leather. The player usually flicks his or her fingers against the skin membrane to produce a rapid and very sharp sound. The *doyra* is widely used in the settled areas of Tajikistan and Uzbekistan during public events such as weddings.

The *temir-komuz* (also *o'oz komuz*) is a small steel (*temir* in Kyrgyz) instrument somewhat like an elongated Jew's harp and played in a similar way, using the mouth as a resonator. It has a semicircular body of about two inches (six to seven centimeters) that is stretched in the middle and narrowed at the end. A thin, flexible steel tongue *(til)* is soldered at one end to the lower part of the instrument, while the other end is bent at a right angle. The player places the instrument on the lips and plucks the tongue of the *temir-komuz* with the right hand to produce a deep tone of variable duration. The instrument may also be made of brass, bronze, or copper.

The *rubab (rabab, rubob,* also *Kashgari rubab)*[7] is a long-necked instrument with two double strings and one single string and a small, round or pear-shaped body. The body is traditionally made of wood and one side of it is covered with leather; strings are made of metal.

TRADITIONAL MUSIC

In traditional Central Asian society before the industrial revolution, music and song accompanied every step of a person's life—from weddings to carpet making, from horseback riding to planning war.[8] There is a Central Asian folk story about singing. One day, *Shaitan* (Satan) came to take away the soul of a herder. The herder agreed to go, under one condition—that he be allowed to sing his last song while riding the *Shaitan*. The *Shaitan* agreed. The herder climbed on his back and began his song, which went on and on and never ended. After seven days, the *Shaitan* gave up, saying that he was ready to leave the herder alone; before he left, he asked, "Tell me—when will your song end?" The herder replied, "My song will never end, for I sing and praise all that I see—from a lone tree or rock on the steppe to the clouds and moon in the sky, from the girl I love to the lamb that I cook!"

Animal herders on the vast Eurasian steppe, in the Karakum desert, and in the many mountain valleys spent long nights guarding their sheep and horses against wolves, robbers, and marauders. They often kept themselves awake and entertained by singing and listening to solo recitative-style songs, romantic or heroic epics, and ballads of *zhyrshy, akyns,* or *bakh'shy.* Women who took care of lambs, calf, or foals in mountains, steppe, or deserts cheered each other with long night songs such as *bekbekei-yrlar* or lyrical songs such as *kuigen, seketbai,* or *seket,* periodically interrupting the recitals with loud laughter, shouts, or cries in order to scare away wolves and other predators. They also sang to their little ones, songs such as *Baldar-yrlar* (children's songs) or *alla* and *lalaik.* In difficult days, they expressed their sorrow and pain by singing *arman-yrlar* (sorrow songs). The women's performances were quite different from the men's. As the nomads tended to be less rigorous in following restrictive Islamic traditions, there were numerous occasions when men and women attended mixed parties and celebrations and even held improvised competitions between amateur all-female and all-male groups or singers.

The settlers in a multitude of small villages and towns along the major rivers, such as the Amu Darya, Syr Darya, and Zeravshan, often ended their long days with a meal in a *chaikhana* listening to folk songs, *maquma, gazels,* or epics by professional or semiprofessional bards, accompanied by various musical instruments—a *dombra* or *rubab.* A number of important features characterized the popular performing arts in premodern Central Asia. In the first place, such events were all-male gatherings, since by long custom the sexes did not mix in public places. The performances were usually solo; the singers sang alone and often accompanied themselves. Just as in pre-industrial Europe, some professional musicians and singers lived at the courts of wealthy patrons, while others wandered from town to town performing at community and family events.

Central Asian women in settled areas were largely excluded from public life due to restrictions imposed by *Shariah*; however, they, too, developed musical traditions. Extensive hours spent making woven carpets or woolen felt rugs were cheered by long, rhythmic songs, often sung in a group. The women usually sang songs in chorus or joined a lead singer. And, of course, traditionally these were exclusively female events—although there were few professional women singers to hire for such events.

There were numerous public events related to the agricultural seasons or various family occasions. Here, too, the people of Central Asia created numerous folk songs specifically devoted to these events. In this regard, there was a sea of difference between the musical traditions of settled populations on the one hand and those of nomads and pastoral nomads on the other. This dissimilarity emerged because of the disparity between the agricultural calendars of settlers and those of nomads, as well as regional differences; many communities were isolated because of the underdeveloped transportation infrastructure. In addition, there were significant variations between the Turkic and the Persian musical traditions. The former dominated in the northern areas of Central Asia, while the latter were stronger in the southern and southwestern parts of the region. Modern musicologists highlight the fact that settlers around Bukhara, Herat, Khojent, Merv, Samarqand, and other cities were strongly influenced by Persian culture, while the nomads and pastoral nomads elsewhere retained many elements of their ancient Turkic traditions.

Also, there were sophisticated musical traditions in the major urban centers, where Persian traditions were especially strong. Urban musical traditions, especially among professional musicians, were also enriched by elements from the Middle East and South Asia. Despite the impact of such borrowings, however, the musical traditions in Central Asia retained their distinctively different musical structures and particular musical scales.

Table 5.2 represents experts' assessments of the national instrumental traditions in Central Asia. Yet, one has to treat this with caution, bearing in mind that in many geographical border areas the musical traditions have no rigid boundaries and that this picture reflects the development in the first half of the twentieth century.

Central Asian urban centers also became centers of classical compositions called *shashmaqam* (close cousin of the Middle-Eastern *maqam*). The *shashmaqam* is translated as "six *maqam*" and contains six sections in different musical modes. As the Central Asians did not have a notation system, the

Table 5.2
Structure and Range of the National Musical Traditions

	Kazakhs	Kyrgyzs	Turkmens	Tajiks and Uzbeks
Melody structure	Descending Ascending-descending	Ascending Descending	Recitative	Descending Ascending-descending
Range	Recitative, small; song, large	Mostly sixth	Recitative, fourth to sixth	Up to 2 1/2 octaves in art music
Modal structure	Majorlike Minorlike Pentatonic (much less) Chromaticized	Majorlike Minorlike Pentatonic Chromaticized	Pentachordal Majorlike Minorlike Phrygian	Majorlike Minorlike Chromaticized Augmented seconds

Source: Adopted from Henry Farmer, "Turkestani Music," in *Grove's Dictionary of Music and Musicians*, vol. 8 (New York: Macmillan, 1954), pp. 610–612.

shashmaqams were transmitted from generation to generation through practice. Beautiful *shashmaqams* were performed by musicians whose claim to fame rested on their virtuoso skills and their performances at major public gatherings.

Both popular folk music and more sophisticated urban music were performed at the courts of Central Asian royalty, rich landlords, and merchants. Every wealthy individual in the region, as in neighboring countries, felt it an obligation or a matter of personal pride and prestige to patronize famous artists. In return, the artists entertained their sponsors and guests and created songs and musical pieces dedicated to them. Usually they were professional, well-educated artists of high caliber, pupils of the most established and famous teachers and singers. In addition, they were well traveled in different parts of the Muslim world and were thus well aware of the latest musical trends in Hindustan, Persia, and the Arab and Ottoman worlds.

The Russian Empire's colonization of Turkistan in some degree disrupted the old cultural relations between the Central Asian region and its southern neighbors—Afghanistan, India, and Iran. At the same time, the colonization exposed Central Asians to European cultures, including Russian. Some groups of Central Asian society, however, strongly resisted any innovation

Folk songs remain popular in Central Asian republics. Courtesy of the author, 2006.

or influence from the Western world. Others embraced the new ideas and boldly experimented with new forms and genres. It is important also to note that the rise of capitalism, improved education, and the standardization of languages furthered the rise of new trends. A gradually emerging sense of a national identity, a national language, and a national culture began replacing old identities based on religious, tribal, or communal characteristics. Thus, musical traditions also began taking on a stronger national flavor. This process was greatly encouraged, if not enforced, by the Soviet authorities with the establishment of the national republics in the mid-1920s.

As folk music began taking on a national flavor, its development was greatly encouraged and funded by the Soviet state. Numerous amateur and semiprofessional groups and orchestras began to emerge all over the region. This process of development of national folk traditions matured with the establishment, in the early 1930s, of professional folk orchestras. For example, the first National Orchestra of Kazakh People's Instruments was established in 1934, using exclusively Kazakh national instruments adopted and modernized for performing both folk and classic compositions. The Kyrgyz orchestra of *komuz* players *(komuzchi)* was established in 1938. It adopted a single Kyrgyz musical instrument—the *komuz*— to play folk and classical Kyrgyz, Russian, and Western music.

WESTERN MUSICAL TRADITIONS

The Central Asian elite first came in contact with classical Western musical traditions in the nineteenth and early twentieth centuries, when touring Russian professional and semiprofessional orchestras and groups performed in major Central Asian cities. Very soon, the younger generation of native musicians and composers began looking for new avenues of expression, working on a large scale in the Western style.[9] Hundreds of the most gifted youths were sent for training to the best music schools in Moscow, Saint Petersburg, and Kiev in the 1920s and 1930s. Here, again, numerous amateur and semiprofessional musical groups, orchestras, and music clubs were established in the 1920s and 1930s, creating a large pool of talent and enthusiasts. The native musicians—most of them very young people—studied the best European traditions with feverish intensity and began experimenting with classical Western music, creating their first works by the late 1930s and early 1940s.

In general, these experiments involved three developmental stages. First, the musicians learned Western musical notation and musical instruments in order to play exclusively Western music. Second, they made numerous attempts to play traditional Central Asian music with Western-style orchestras and choruses. Third, they experimented with performing Western symphonies and melodies with local musical instruments, adapting the instruments for this purpose.[10]

Numerous attempts at creating new musical pieces to symbolize the "national" music and musical traditions have been made since the mid-1920s. This process was greatly accelerated with the rise of national professional musicians and composers who received their musical education in various parts of the USSR and then established their own music schools in their native republics. The Soviet authorities encouraged and sponsored the introduction of new musical paradigms, especially among the younger generation of Central Asians. This included the establishment of numerous music clubs, amateur music ensembles, groups, and choirs, where musicians could sing and play Western and native musical instruments and practice patriotic songs in both the Russian and native languages.

At the same time, however, the Soviet authorities severely restricted artistic freedom and often dictated what form national opera and symphonic music should take. Practically all plays, symphonies, and operas were commissioned by state-appointed boards that brought together government bureaucrats, party officials, politicians, and very few music critics. These bodies could censor anything—topics, plots, style, even the way the main characters were portrayed. And yet, Central Asian composers, together with their Russian counterparts, produced great national symphonies, operas, and various compositions.

By the mid-1930s, local composers were creating their first mature musical dramas, operas, and symphonies, usually turning for inspiration and story line to local themes, epics, legends, and fairy tales. For example, the first Kazakh opera, *Kyz-Zhibek* (by E. G. Brussilovskii), which adapted the plot of a traditional Kazakh epic, was presented to an audience in Almaty in 1934. This opera was followed by *Zhalbyr* (by E. G. Brussilovskii) (1935), *Er Targyn* (Brave Targyn; by E. G. Brussilovskii) (1937), *Abai* (by A. K. Zhubanov and L. A. Khamidi) (1944), *Sary arka* (Yellow steppe; by E. G. Brussilovskii) (1944), *Amangeldy* (by E. G. Brussilovskii and M. T. Tulebayev) (1945), *Birzhan zhene Sara* (Birzhan and Sara; by M. T. Tulebayev) (1946), and *Telegen Tokhtarov* (by A. K. Zhubanov and L. A. Khalmidi) (1947) and by the first Kazakh operettas, *Aisulu* (by S. M. Mukhamedjanov) (1964) and *Kamar Suluu* (Beautiful Kamar; by E. R. Rakhmadiev) (1963).

The other Central Asian republics experienced similar trends. For example, the first Kyrgyz musical dramas, *Altyn kyz* (Golden girl; by V. A. Vlasov and V. G. Fere) and *Adjal orduna* (Life instead of death; by V. A. Vlasov, A. Maldybayev, and V. G. Fere), were created in 1937 and 1938, respectively. This was followed by the first Kyrgyz opera, *Aichurek* (by V. A. Vlasov,

A. Maldybayev, and V. G. Fere) (1939), in which the authors turned to the classical epic *Manas* for the main plot and told the story of a beautiful woman, Aichurek. These early experiments were followed by the operas *Patrioty* (Patriots; by V. A. Vlasov, A. Maldybayev, and V. G. Fere) (1941), *Manas* (by V. A. Vlasov, A. Maldybayev, and V. G. Fere) (1946), *Aidar zhana Aisha* (Aidar and Aisha; by A. Amanbayev) (1952), and *Ak shumkar* (White falcon; by S. N. Ryazanov) (1957). In 1943, M. Abdrayev, A. Maldybayev, A. Amanbayev, and A. Tuleev presented the first Kyrgyz operetta, *Kim kantti* (Who has done it?).

Tajik musicians and composers created their first musical drama, *Lola* (by S. A. Balasanian and S. U. Urbakh), in 1939. The first Tajik opera, *Shurishi Vose* (The Vose Uprising; by S. A. Balasanian), was performed in 1939. As in other Central Asian republics in the 1940s, Tajik composers turned to patriotic themes in their works, creating the musical dramas *Pesnia gneva* (The song of rage; by S. A. Balasanian) (1942), *Zolotoi kishlak* (The golden village; by I. O. Roganskii) (1944), and *Tohir va Zukhra* (Takhir and Zukhra; by A. S. Lenski) (1944). Balasanian also wrote the first Tajik operetta, *Rozia,* in 1942.

Turkmen composers also began experimenting with traditional Turkmen melodies and Western music during the same period and soon came up with their first musical compositions and dramas. *Zukhre ve Takhir* (Zukhre and Takhir; by A. G. Shaposhnikov) (1941), the first Turkmen opera, was based on a classic Middle Eastern epic about two lovers. It was followed by the operas *Sudba bakhshi* (The fate of bakh'shi; G. Kakhiani) (1941), *Iusup ve Akhmet* (Iusup and Akhmet; by B. S. Shekhter and A. Kuliyev) (1942), *Shasenem ve Garib* (Shasenem and Garib; by A. G. Shaposhnikov and D. Ovezov) (1944), and *Leili ve Medjnun* (Leili and Medjnun; by U. S. Meitis and D. Ovezov) (1946). The opera *Abandan* (by U. S. Meitis and A. Kuliev) (1943) is typical of Soviet patriotic opera, full of Soviet glorification of enthusiasm and self-sacrifice.

At about the same time, Uzbekistani composers created their first works for symphony orchestra, such as *Musykal'nyie kartinki Uzbekistana* (The musical pictures of Uzbekistan; by M. M. Ippolitov-Ivanov) (1931), *Ferghanskii prazdnik* (Ferghana celebration; by V. A. Zolotariov) (1931), and *Lola* (by A. F. Kozlovskii) (1937). Their first experiments in musical drama began with *Gulsara* (by R. M. Glier, T. Jalilov, and T. Sadykov) (1936) and *Farhkad va Shirin* (Farhkad and Shirin; by V. A. Uspenskii, Sh. Shoumarov and G. A. Mushel) (1937). These works were followed by the first Uzbek operas, *Buran* (The Storm; by M. Ashrafi and S. N. Vasilenko) (1939), *Leili va Medjnun* (Leili and Medjnun; by R. M. Glier and T. Sadykov) (1940), and *Velikii kanal* (The great canal; by M. Ashrafi and S. N. Vasilenko) (1941).

Between the 1950s and the 1980s, the second generation of national musicians and composers entered the artistic world in every Central Asian republic, conceiving a new wave of national opera. During this phase, they largely turned to popular Soviet themes, such as civil war, the emancipation of the people, and revolution, although they continued to gain inspiration from their own folklore and traditional local themes.

In the 1990s, the theaters that perform Western classical music in the Central Asian republics faced many problems, including continuously shrinking audiences, the need to attract young talent, and a lack of financial stability. The absence of any tradition of philanthropy and independent endowments made them extremely dependent on state subsidies. In the early 2000s, economic stabilization across the region positively affected development in the artistic world, as both the state and large private and public enterprises began sponsoring the most talented singers and musicians and national philharmonics began touring the Western countries.

DANCE

At present, most classical and folk concerts in Central Asia include bright and technically complex modern folk dances, contemporary Western dances, and ballet. Young people in Almaty, Karaganda, or Tashkent love to spend time at dance clubs, ballet studios, or discothèques, as much as young people in Boston, Philadelphia, or London. However, young Westerners would probably be surprised to learn that modern dance is a very recent phenomenon in Central Asia.

Central Asian folk dance developed under the influence of two major traditions. One had links to ancient shamanic traditions and rituals, some elements of which survived among Turkic tribes well into modern times. The other one was an Islamic interpretation of the performing arts and of the code of public conduct that meticulously regulates sexual segregation in public life and public entertainment. In the Central Asian environment, this often meant that zealous *ulama* and Imams outlawed any dance involving both a man and a woman.

Despite this strong religious influence, dancing was kept alive in premodern Central Asia as the amateur and folk dancing of the ordinary people. At major public events, for example, men danced with their sabers and other weapons, imitating close combat and showing their personal skills and mastery of their weapons. Some folk dances among tribal Kazakhs and Kyrgyzs in various forms emulated scenes from everyday life, such as hunting, racing, and animal imitation, In addition, dervishes sometimes meditated in public, demonstrating their meditation movements to the accompaniment of special musical instruments.

And yet a stigma was attached to professional dancing, especially that performed by women. Annette Meakin, a British traveler and scholar who visited Russian Turkistan in the early twentieth century and observed dancing at a wedding, left a remarkable body of notes:

Outside in the courtyard there would be a row of female musicians seated on mattresses, and dancing-girls performed to the tambourine music.... Round and round they twirled, the center of an admiring crowd, singing as they danced.... All this time the bride sat alone in her inner chamber, never attempting to join the fun. Sart women of good character never dance in public; they consider it undignified.[11]

Indeed, public perception of female dancers often associated dance with immoral behavior, a breaking of social boundaries and norms. It must be remembered that in puritanical Central Asian settled communities of the nineteenth and early twentieth centuries, almost all Muslim women were obliged to fully cover their bodies and faces. But some forms of professional dancing emerged also in the courts of royalty and other rich individuals, who often had female servants (usually bought from outside Central Asia) dance for them.

For the Bolsheviks, the introduction of the art of dance was an aspect of both the Cultural Revolution and the emancipation of women. In the 1920s, in all major cities across the region, dance studios that began accepting both Russian and native people were opened.[12] Furthermore, some studios in the region and in Russia specifically recruited native people to teach dance skills.

Soviet choreographers, scholars, and enthusiasts meticulously studied the Central Asian folk and urban dance traditions throughout the 1920s. As a next step, they experimented with combining traditional Central Asian motifs and dance styles with the Russian and European styles of choreography and composition. A fusion of tempestuous Oriental expression and themes and the strict, systematic approach of the Russian school of dancing gave rise to unique Central Asian dances. They gradually became widely recognizable and popular among ordinary people for their richness, simplicity, and beauty. In Kazakhstan, for example, choreographers rethought old Kazakh traditions and introduced new folk dances such as *Eagle and a Fox, The Dance of Akyns,* and *Akku*.[13]

With the arrival of classical Western music and dance in every village and town, the establishment of professional ballet and dance troupes became the next step. A mass base for ballet was established through hundreds of amateur dance classes, the competitive selection of talents, numerous competitions, and free-board education for the best students at leading dance and ballet schools in Russia. Not surprisingly, the first Central Asian ballets soon followed. Initially, most were based on traditional Central Asian folklore and were written by native or Russian choreographers.

The first Kazakh ballet, for example, was *Kalkan zhene Mamyr* (Kalkan and Mamyr; by V. Velikhanov), whose debut performance took place in 1938. It was followed by *Koktem* (by I. Nadirov), in 1940; *Kambar zhene Nazym* (Kambar and Nazym; by V. Velikanov), in 1950; *Akkanat* (by G. Zhubanov), in 1966; and several others. The first Kyrgyz ballet, *Anar* (V. Fere), was introduced to Kyrgyz audiences in 1940. It was followed by the ballets *Selkinchek* (by V. Vlasov and V. Fere), in 1943 and *Cholpon* (by M. Reikhverger), in 1944. Among Tajikistan's first national ballet performances were *Leila va Medjnun* (Leila and Medjnun; by S. Balasanian) (1947), *Dilvar* (by A. Lenskii) (1954), and *Goluboi kover* (Blue carpet; by V. Volberg) (1958). The first Turkmen ballet, *Aldar Kose* (by K. A. Korchmarev), was staged in 1942. Soon after, additions to the national ballet repertoire included *Devushka moria* (Sea girl; by N. S. Kholfin) (1943), *Akpamyk* (by A. F. Znosko-Borovski and V. Mukhatov) (1945), and *Studenty* (Students; by Kh. Allandurov and I. Iakushenko) (1965). Uzbek choreographers presented the very first Uzbek ballet *Pakhta* (Cotton) in 1933, followed by *Shakhida,* in 1939, *Guliandom,* in 1940, and *Akbiliak,* in 1943.

The government machine then created and maintained a level of superstar status for the highest achievers in the field. Those who gained such status received government awards, medals, apartments, scholarships, and free travel around the USSR. Many studios, orchestras, and theaters were named after them.

The life of Bibisara Beishenaliyeva is an example. Beishenaliyeva was born in Tash Tube, a remote village in Kyrgyzstan, to a family of peasants. She demonstrated her talent at a very early stage and won a government scholarship to study at the Leningrad Choreography Institute, from which she was graduated in 1941. From 1941 to 1949, she was the leading solo dancer at the Kyrgyz State Theater of Opera and Ballet. In 1949, in addition to her ballet career, she began teaching at the Music and Choreography Institute, in Frunze. She performed at the most prestigious theaters in Moscow, Leningrad, and other cities. Beishenaliyeva was considered the premier Kyrgyz ballet dancer, and her achievements and fame brought the Kyrgyz school of ballet into the All-Union and international spotlight. Her performances came to be regarded as classics of Kyrgyz ballet, and the Soviet authorities often held her up as a symbol of the break from Kyrgyzstan's backward feudal past.

In the 1970s and 1980s, the repertoires of the various national ballets included a combination of national, Russian, and Western themes. Several prominent new ballets were introduced in every republic. Local ballet schools were significantly expanded, and ballet groups worked constantly to improve their range. Typical ballets include *Vechnyi ogon'* (Eternal fire) (1985, Kazakhstan), *Tomiris, Skazanie o Rustame* (The tail of Rustam) (1984, Uzbekistan), *Ston tetivy* (The moaning of a bowstring) (1988, Kyrgyzstan), *Poema gor* (The poem of mountains), and *Volshebnyi luk* (Magic bow) (1985, Tajikistan).

Since the 1990s, however, the national ballet groups have experienced a severe downturn of fortunes, as the old Soviet-style model of developing the repertoire and managing finances and performances did not work in a free-market environment. In the early 2000s, national ballets in the Central Asian republics moved in different directions. In Kyrgyzstan and Tajikistan, the ballet currently struggles to survive, while in Kazakhstan and Uzbekistan the repertoire and working conditions have more or less stabilized, with significant support from the state budget and corporate sponsors. A different approach was taken in Turkmenistan, where the government abandoned any kind of support for the national ballet and closed the ballet theater.

THEATER

Central Asian theatrical traditions have their roots in the popular amateur or semiprofessional performances of comics and clowns—*maskharaboz* and *kizikchi* (in the Bukhara and Kokand Khanates) and *ku* and *shanshara* (on the Kazakh steppe). Traditionally, short plays were performed by single or duo performers, though there were very few permanent performing groups. Usually there was no fixed stage, and performers simply entertained audiences with comical scenes from everyday life, parodies, or competitive improvisations between two or more players; sometimes they performed very short moral, religious, or comic plays. Due to religious restrictions, no women actors were allowed, leaving men to perform the female roles.

The idea of establishing theaters met with significant resistance from puritanical sections of society in Central Asia, as traditionalists and religious extremists opposed the new phenomenon on the grounds that the presence and influence of the theater might wreck the traditional moral fabric of society and corrupt the nations' youth, especially the women. However, young, Westernized Central Asians, who attended plays in the Russian theaters in Tashkent, Semipalatinsk, and Orenburgh or in central Russia and other parts of the world, were impressed by the modes and power of theatrical expression and were "seized with a desire" to establish their own native theaters back in Central Asia.[14] The first amateur and semiprofessional groups were established early in the early twentieth century. World War I (1914–1918) and social and political radicalization throughout the Russian Empire encouraged and helped the region's intellectuals and reformists to turn to the theater as a new tool for promoting their ideas. The first professional theaters were opened somewhat later, between the 1910s and 1930s.

The idea of the theater in Central Asia thus began as a quest for new opportunities for artistic expression, entertainment, and the exploration of European cultures. But, in fact, it developed as a very politicized institution. After the Bolshevik revolution, in 1917, the theaters became ideological battlefields between conservatives and reformers, Bolsheviks and their opponents, and their uncompromising confrontations paralleled and reflected the conflicts of the civil war. The depth of these differences is exemplified in the life and work of one of the pioneers of the Central Asian theater, Khamza Khakimzodo Niozii (1889–1929).[15] Even before the revolution, Khamza, who was a writer, poet, and educator, had plans to establish a theater and to train native actors. His dream was realized only in 1918, when he founded the first semiprofessional theater in Ferghana. It began by staging many short plays that propagated the ideas of the Bolshevik revolution, class struggle, and rebellion against social injustice. Khamza's *Boi ila khizmatchi* (The rich [man] and the workers) (1918) and *Ferghona fozhiasi* (The Ferghana tragedy) (1918–1919) became the first modern Uzbek dramas. Khamza led a group of actors to perform many plays as a part of the *Kyzil Shark* (Red Orient) mobile theater. His theatrical work and dramaturgical experiments inspired the opening of many theaters in other cities—Kokand (1919), Andijon (1919), Tashkent (1919), and Khiva (1922). He became a leading advocate of the Soviet regime, Soviet political and social changes, and the emancipation of Central Asian women. Examples of the latter ideal in his work are his plays *Maisaranin ishi* (Maisara's Work) (1926) and *Paranzhi surlaridan bir lavkha eli yallachilar ishi* (A scene from the secrets of the *paranja* or the Yalla people's affair) (1927), which address the challenges in the struggle for emancipation of women in small Uzbek towns. Khamza's political and social activism aroused growing anger among conservative elements of society, and, in 1929, he was killed by a fanatical mob.

Despite the difficulties, the theater established a strong foothold in the Central Asian region. With the creation of the national republics, in 1924, groups of young people were sent to Baku, Moscow, Leningrad, and other centers to study and master theatrical techniques. In the 1920s and 1930s, a large network of small amateur and semiprofessional theaters was established in all urban centers and even in small towns and villages. Theatrical performances, usually by schoolchildren and young enthusiasts, became very popular across the region, especially during public events. As a next step, in the late 1920s and into the 1930s, national theaters were established in all the Central Asian republics. In 1929, the Samarqand Theater was given the status of the State (National) Uzbek Theater (it was moved to Tashkent in 1931). The first Kazakh National Theater was opened in Kyzyl Orda in 1926 (it moved to Alma-Ata in 1928). In 1929, the Tajik State (National) Theater was opened. The first Kyrgyz State Theater was established in 1930 with the reorganization of theatrical groups that had existed since 1926. The first Turkmen Theater, named after Mollanepes, was established in 1929. It was based on a theatrical drama studio that had existed since 1926.

All Central Asian theaters underwent a similar evolution. They began by performing short propaganda plays written by local writers and enthusiasts in local languages and performed before workers, peasants, and soldiers. Gradually, they began working on a more serious repertoire, and native writers began creating plays written specifically for their respective national theaters. Traditional folklore and epics, interpreted as the struggle between good and evil, the emancipation of women, peasants and slaves, and aspects of the civil war and Great Patriotic War (World War II) were among the favorite topics in the national theaters. Mukhtar Auezov's *Enlik-Kebek,* for example, became a classic and one of the most popular plays in the National Kazakh Theater's repertoire. This is a Romeo-and-Juliet-style story about a tragic love between two young Kazakhs—Enlik and Kebek—who are caught up in a vicious intertribal rivalry and are buffeted by the rivals' desire for revenge and their own parents' stubborn attempt to tear apart their children. Enlik and Kebek prefer death to separation and forced marriage to someone else. In the repertoire of the Kyrgyz Theater, Joomart Bokonbayev's *Toktogul* has remained a favorite play for decades. This is a philosophical play about the life of Toktogul Satylganov, the nation's most acclaimed poet and bard. The play reveals the cultural and social roots of Toktogul's philosophy, poetry, and worldview via a series of representative encounters with various people and problems.

In the 1940s and 1950s, the national theaters increasingly began also performing the works of the best classical European and Russian playwrights. Anton Chekhov, William Shakespeare, Nikolai Gogol, Maxim Gorkii, and Alexander Ostrovskii, among others, were particularly popular. It is important to note that the national theaters always maintained their repertoire in the native languages of their republics; they never performed in Russian, even those plays written by Russian writers. For Russian-speaking audiences, Russian drama theaters, such as the Russian Drama Theaters in Frunze, Tashkent, and Almaty, were established and developed in every Central Asian republic. These had their own repertoires, traditions, and performers. They usually performed classic European, Russian, and Soviet plays, exclusively in the Russian language, although periodically they included works devoted to local themes.

But, behind the glossy performances and achievements, there was a different reality: the theater suffered enormously from censorship and political purges under Stalin's tyranny (1922–1953).[16] From the earliest days of Communist rule, the party maintained strict control over the repertoire by institutionalizing the commissioning of plays. As in all other artistic fields, party functionaries had the final say on all issues and demanded that the repertoire be politically correct and fall within the torturous confines of the social realism concept. Many international scholars and musicologists are nonplussed as to how, in the environment of Stalin's mass purges of national intelligentsia, and in an atmosphere of repression and total control, composers and musicians were able to create and perform beautiful pieces and plays for the national folk orchestras.

In the 1960s and 1970s, the national theaters in Central Asia began adding more works on traditional Soviet themes, such as struggles in personal relations and dramas of love or rivalry between people with different values, set against the background of grand historical events—revolution, wars, and postwar reconstruction. For example, the Kazakh drama *Qan men ter* (Blood and sweat), by Ebdizhemil Nurpeisov, tells of the lives of simple Kazakh people in a small fishing village on the Aral Sea and describes the changes and challenges they face from the impact of great social events (such as revolution or war) beyond the control of ordinary people.[17]

Until the 1980s, Central Asian theater was mainly developed in the Russian realist traditions of the nineteenth and early twentieth centuries. The Soviet system promoted the supposed perfection of certain iconic styles, traditions, and expressions and strongly discouraged and even prohibited any innovations or experiments. A very few groups did dare to experiment, but these were usually limited to student or amateur groups at small university- or district-level theaters. Not until the policy of liberalization was enacted in the mid-1980s were there real, positive changes, as direct central control over the repertoire was finally abandoned and theaters gained some flexibility to choose their own programs.

Political independence shook the whole theatrical world. As in many other spheres of the arts, there resulted a mixture of change and continuity in the Central Asian theaters. The most notable change was in the area of freedom of expression and the abandoning of censorship: the Communist Party functionaries no longer imposed ideological restrictions or demanded that quotas be filled regarding the coverage of certain topics. The theaters were finally able to turn to previously banned topics such as the catastrophe of Stalin's mass repressions and difficult epochs in Central Asian history, including stories about colonization, collectivization, and the dark nature of the totalitarian political system. The other change was less anticipated but had long-term consequences: far fewer people could afford to buy tickets, due to plunging living standards and the economic recession.

CONTEMPORARY POP AND ROCK MUSIC

The landscape of contemporary music in Central Asia has been largely shaped by decades of fierce competition between Almaty and Tashkent for the informal title of music capital of the region. For instance, in the 1970s and 1980s, Tashkent attracted many top stars and hosted numerous regional and international music festivals; it therefore held the undisputed leading position in folk, rock, and various experimental forms and hybrids of folk and modern musical forms such as jazz and pop. In the meantime, Almaty was making notable achievements in the areas of country-style music and rock, along with its own experiments in folk-rock and folk-pop. Since 1990, it has outplayed Tashkent by establishing the largest festival of modern pop in Central Asia—*Azia Dauysy* (Voice of Asia).

A vibrant and diverse modern musical culture in both Tashkent and Almaty has been supported by a large multicultural, multilingual, and affluent population. Many groups and individual musicians have moved to these cities from the provinces and smaller towns. Once there, in the time-honored manner of aspiring musicians elsewhere, they try to build their popularity—or simply survive—by performing at small venues such as restaurants, family events, and so on and, if successful, making the move into the professional arena. The younger generations in Central Asia unreservedly choose pop and rock music, so much so that they have penetrated even the Bastille of traditionalism, the *chaikhanas*.

Musicians from all the Central Asian republics at one stage of their career or another performed both in Almaty and Tashkent or were influenced by the trends in these regional cultural capitals. They did well under the state-imposed restrictions and isolations of the iron curtain. But, since the collapse of communism and the fall of all protective walls, they have increasingly been affected by the cultural offensive of globalization. Nevertheless, the local market for contemporary music has preserved a number of aspects that give it a distinctive character. First, it is uniquely diverse, as local youth embrace the latest hits not only from the United States and United Kingdom but also from Russia, Turkey, the Middle East, Iran, and western Europe. In addition, it is multilingual; the music on radios, CD players, and personal recorders is presented in all the region's native languages, plus English, Farsi, Russian, and Turkish. In many urban centers, it is easy to hear songs in all the languages of the region and in the major international languages, although in small towns and cities the native languages of individual republics tend to dominate. Last but not least, local singers and producers often adapt international hits and reproduce melodies in native languages, sometimes to the accompaniment of their national instruments.

The most famous and recognizable pop group of the Soviet era, one with appeal among all the peoples of Central Asia, was *Yalla* (pronounced Yal-lah, which translates as "go-go!"), from Uzbekistan. The group was established in 1970 and long maintained a status similar to that of the Beatles in the United Kingdom and the United States. *Yalla*'s songs, such as *Chaikhana* (Teahouse), *Uch kuduk* (Three wells), *Shakhrisabz,* and *Yallama erim, yalla!,* captured audiences in Tashkent, Almaty, Moscow, Kiev, and many other places across the then-USSR. The group successfully toured in a number of developing countries, such as India and Pakistan. The faces of the group's members—Farukh Zakirov, Abbos Aliev, Javron Tokhtoyev, Alisher Tuliaganov, Rustam Iliasov, and Sarvar Kaziev—could be found on picture calendars in every student dormitory for nearly two decades. Many factors contributed to *Yalla*'s wide popularity, including the group's use of mystic Oriental motifs, its skillful balance of the Uzbek and the Russian languages, the inclusion of traditional local musical instruments in addition to contemporary ones, its mastery of the songwriter's craft, and, not least, its dynamism.

Approximately contemporaneous with *Yalla*, the Kazakh singer Roza Rymbaeva began her career as a pop and folk-pop singer, becoming one of the most recognizable singers in the region. She launched her career as an amateur bilingual performer (singing in both Kazakh and Russian), then, in 1976, joined a semiprofessional group, *Gulder* (Flowers), and, later, *Aray*. Her songs, such as *Lubov nastala, Moy dvorik, Sveti zemlia, Kuda uhodit detstvo, Kua bol, Atameken,* and *Saulem-ai,* fascinated audiences first in Almaty and then across the USSR. She also tried acting, starring in several motion pictures, and won numerous national and international awards. She toured in and outside the USSR, in countries such as Bulgaria, Turkey, and Czechoslovakia.

The group *Kambarkan,* of Kyrgyzstan, is well recognized for its folk songs and dances, performed to the accompaniment of traditional Kyrgyz instruments. It was established in 1988 at the Kyrgyz State Philharmonic. *Kambarkan* became famous in its own country with such songs as *Koichulardyn konuz kuiu, Maipam kuusu, Alym sabak,* and *Kez Togoo.* The group uses exclusively folk musical instruments such as the *komuz, surnai, karnai, sabyzgy,* and *dobulbaz* and experiments with Kyrgyz national folklore motifs. The group not only performs at major public events in the country but also represents Kyrgyzstan at major international and regional music festivals and expos.

Beside officially approved groups that had exclusive access to radio, TV, and concert halls, the Soviet era spawned a whole world of underground music. In the 1970s and 1980s, an old guitar in the hands of any shaggy-haired young male signified a youth protest against Soviet officialdom and the rigid social and cultural bonds imposed on the younger generations. Boys and men with guitars playing country-style music in public parks, or perhaps a band with antiquated instruments striving to produce hard rock in the basement of an official House of Culture or an apartment building had the effect of uniting multiple generations of nonconformists and rebels. Although they were not officially banned, they faced all possible obstacles from the government and Party officials, who viewed them with great suspicion and firmly blocked all roads to television or large performing arenas. Only in the late 1980s and early 1990s did young people gain the freedom to express themselves musically without the need to fit into the Procrustean bed of government-approved ideology.

In the early 2000s, the music market in the Central Asian republics became more or less established, and many new names appeared and became popular in their native countries. Singers and groups began hiring professional managers, songwriters, and producers, and a number of individuals or business groups began investing in young talent and promoting certain hits and albums. However, there developed a sense of fragmentation in the industry, as many groups traveled rarely if at all to neighboring republics.

Kazakhstan represents probably the largest and most diverse music market in the region. Among the popular pop, rock, hip-hop, and other groups worthy of mention are *FM [Famous/Marvelous] Division, Getto Dogs, Gildia, Maranafa, Paradox.kz, Nesolonekhlebavshie,* and *Rakhat-Lukum.*[18] Singers such as Saule Sharipova, Zholbarys Seifullin, Takezhan, Mankurt, and Ksenia have quite large fan bases. A specific characteristic of typical Kazakh rock or pop artists is that they perform well in both Kazakh and Russian. For example, in June 2006, the Internet Music Portal KZMZ voted among top five singles the following songs: Ivan Breusov's *Uhodia uhodi,* Anomalia's *Veter,* FM's *Arabika,* Almas Kishkimbaev's *Mangilik,* and *Getto Dog's Bratishka.*[19]

In Kyrgyzstan, among the popular rock and pop groups of note are *Elsinor,*[20] *Khuligany i Ra, Golfstrim, Brat Fidel, Bloshinnyi Tsirk, 33 Marta,* and *Professor Moriarti* (all rock)[21] and *Insan, Ersai,* and *Eles* (all pop). *Professor Moriarti's* repertoire, for example, includes such popular hits as *Moia dusha, Soldat satany, Brodiaga, Parokhod,* and *Devochka s volosami tsveta ketchupa* and the albums *Genii zloi* (2001) and *Nebesnyi strannik* (2002).[22] Rock clubs in Bishkek such as *Tekila-Bluz, Zhashtyk, Spider, ASK-Magistr,* and *Gagarin* provide venues where Kyrgyz rock fans can regularly come together. One of the features of Kyrgyz rock is that the language divides the music market into two major segments. Rock music, including soft rock, hard rock, and "metal," is represented by groups that use mainly Russian. Folk-pop and folk-rock artists are often Kyrgyz-language singers and groups.

In Tajikistan, such bands as *Avesto, Ajam, Vazir, Farzin, Parem, Zapadnyi kvartal, Dilnoz,* and *Shabnam* have traditionally attracted a large audience of followers. In the early 2000s, several enthusiasts and investors began professional work in Tajik music market, establishing Internet portals for rating songs and albums on radio and investing in individual singers and the most promising start-up music groups. Such singers as Daler Nazarov, Parvina Shukrullaeva, Michgona Khakimova, Jurabek Murodov, Tolib Shahidi, and Bakhodur Negmatov achieved wide recognition within Tajikistan and in neighboring Uzbekistan.[23]

In Turkmenistan, since the 1990s, rock and pop music have developed in relative isolation from the other Central Asian republics, as Turkmen artists developed very close collaborations with Turkey and the Turkish music industry. Among notable pop and folk-pop Turkmen singers are Akmyhammet Hahob, Akyš Sapar, Atabay Caryguly, Cynar Juma, and Laçyn Mämed.[24] Folk-pop and folk-rock dominate the repertoire of Turkmen singers and groups, which perform mainly in the Turkmen language. They must travel to Turkey in order to have access to studios with modern equipment. They regularly record songs not only in Turkmen but also in Turkish. Singers in the country are obliged to have in their repertoire patriotic songs about the country's leader, Turkmenbashy, and about the Fatherland in order to have access to the national mass media stage.

Among the new singers in Uzbekistan should be mentioned Sevara Nazarkhan, Yulduz Usmanova, Muhriddin Kholikov, Ruslan Sharipov, Takhir Sadykov, Rustam Makhmudov, and Nasiba Abdillayeva. There are also a number of bands that, in style and presentation, replicate elements of mass pop culture of the West, spiced up with some local elements. Among these types of groups are *Khuja, Setora, Shahzoda, Faiod,* and *Zindan.*[25] In the early 2000s, folk-rock and folk-pop dominated the TV, radio, and concert repertoires in the country, though hard rock and metal were also well presented and established their own groups of supporters.[26] For example, in June 2006, the Internet music portal http://grand.uz/ voted, as its top "5+1" singles Raikhon's *Aitalmaiman,* Shahzoda's *Kechalar,* Shokhrukh's *Vokea,* Shahrier's *Isming Uragimda,* and Davron Ergashev's *Zhingalak.*[27]

Despite all these achievements, many groups and talented singers continued to have difficulty in the early 2000s. The major problem is that the music markets in their native republics are often small, and it is too difficult to capture international attention from these small bases. The other problem is music piracy. Disrespect for copyright does tangible hurt to legal music sales and thus to the musical groups' incomes. According to some estimates, as much as 70 to 80 percent of music CDs in the local markets consists of pirated products. Contemporary music fanatics in Central Asia do not even need to use complex music swap software, as vast networks of friends and relatives create an unlimited pool of free music. In addition, many groups lack access to modern, professional recording studios and to high-quality professional equipment to develop their own albums.

INDEPENDENCE AND NEW TRENDS

The dynamic Hit-TV (Kazakhstan) probably represents the most important change in the post-Soviet era, as the performing arts were transformed from a collective state-controlled propaganda institution into a complex, independent forum for expression and creativity. The entertainment sector is now fully open to the forces and ideas of globalization, and the newly established market offers a wide range of opportunities to all citizens.

In the 1990s, the dictates of social realism finally disappeared, and artists obtained the freedom to experiment with styles and artistic expression. The whole music and performance industry became driven not ideologically but by the market, as there was no longer a ruling party demanding a specific repertoire in concerts halls or theaters or on television shows, or radio programs.[28] Gone were the Soviet-era quotas on patriotic performances, restrictions on pop and rock music, or requirements for free performances before party functionaries or Soviet labor heroes. No longer did anyone force villagers from mountains or steppe to follow alien traditions or listen to music they did not appreciate.

Artists received opportunities to travel overseas and to establish artistic contacts with their colleagues not only in eastern Europe but all over the world. For example, the most acclaimed contemporary Kazakh violinist, Marat Beisengaliev, decided to move to London, while the Kazakh composer Almas Serkebayev, who has sometimes been called "Kazakhstan's Gershwin," moved to Boston; the Uzbek singer Rustam Iliasov and the talented Tajik composer Alisher Latif-Zade moved to New York.[29] These are but a few of the many who have exercised their freedom to expand their personal and artistic horizons.

One of the most visible changes in pop and rock music has been in the music industry's technological revolution: groups and singers gained access to contemporary technologies, and many of them rushed to replace their trusty but obsolete guitars and other musical instruments with the "coolest axes" and gadgets available on the international market.

Not all the changes, however, have been so positive; some, in fact, have caused considerable difficulties for artistic communities in the Central Asian republics. In one of their first steps after independence, the Central Asian governments ended the Soviet-style subsidies to all theaters, music schools, and children's and students clubs. Those entities had supported musical education and sponsored music programs throughout the region, from the smallest villages in the mountains of Kyrgyzstan and Tajikistan to the towns and cities on the vast steppe and deserts of Kazakhstan and Turkmenistan to the largest metropolitan areas. The advent of the free market ended a half-century-long regime of support for talented children from all social and class backgrounds that had traditionally created a large pool of talent. It was these subsidies that had fostered the development and perfecting of the region's artistic traditions throughout the second half of the twentieth century.

Another outcome of this development was the end of mass musical education at specialized schools and music colleges. Since independence, there have been far fewer people pursuing professional musical education. Such study is simply too expensive for many, because of the skyrocketing cost of tuition, auditions, musical textbooks and notations, and musical instruments. In addition, there are fewer jobs in professional theater and the music field in general, as many theaters, music halls, philharmonics and even folk-instrument orchestras are struggling, forced to significantly downsize their repertoires and freeze further hiring.

Globalization has also affected the national performing arts, as the Central Asian republics have been flooded with Western pop-culture products, from TV and radio soap operas, to pop music in the discos, streets, and concert halls. Local musical, theatrical, and even folk groups have a hard time today competing with these large-scale intruders and are slowly but steadily losing to them their audiences and share of the market. A whole generation of musicians, fed up with the struggle to make ends meet, has simply abandoned the field or emigrated to Russia, western Europe, or the United States.

Additionally, the once-powerful artistic Unions are gone, and with them the many privileges, welfare support, stipends for talented young artists, mentoring traditions, and general assistance that they provided to all their members. Although in the late Soviet era many of those Unions had degenerated into exclusive corporate groups that enforced certain styles, rejected innovations, and were plagued by nepotism and corruption, at least they had also developed comprehensive programs of musical and artistic education, nurtured young talent, and allocated funds to members in need.

The general public and governments have gradually begun to notice these changes, and there have been attempts to reverse the trend. In the early 2000s, some Central Asian governments began in one form or another to support and try to retain their countries' most prominent talents through various stipends and initiatives and to provide avenues to encourage and assist national musical groups, especially folk performers, in their studies and development.

In the very latest trend, as a philanthropic culture gradually takes root in the republics, private enterprise has also begun to spend some money to support young individuals who show potential, to develop and maintain theaters, philharmonics, and music schools, and to sponsor concerts and musical festivals.[30]

In general, the performing arts in Central Asia have managed to preserve their glamour and appeal. It is still de rigueur for the intelligentsia and other educated people to perform a pilgrimage to the theater at least several times every season. And the theaters have become interesting places to be, as some young artists have begun experimenting by abandoning the established traditions, though the experimental theater still faces a lot of difficulties in nurturing its own audience.

NOTES

1. *Yrlak (Zhas Alashtyn muzykalyk kosymshasy),* no. 4 (Mamyr, 2004).

2. In Professor Johanna Spector's classification, the Central Asian musical tradition represents a subculture of Middle Eastern musical culture. See Spector, "Musical Traditions," in Edward Allworth (ed.), *Central Asia: 130 Years of Russian Dominance: A Historical Overview* (Durham and London: Duke University Press, 1994), pp. 436–437.

3. Some experts trace three major musical traditions in modern Central Asia. One is represented by the Kazakhs and Kyrgyzs; another is represented by the Tajiks and Uzbeks; and the third one is represented by the Turkmens. These national musical divisions are further subdivided into narrower musical subcultures. See ibid., pp. 436–440.

4. S. A. Elemanova et al., *Kazakhskaia musykalnaia literatura* [Kazakh musical literature] (Almaty: Oner, 1993), pp. 62–67.

5. For downloadable *dombra* music, see http://worldmusic.nationalgeographic.com/worldmusic/view/page.basic/artist/content.artist/dombra_du_kazakhstan_48177.

6. See http://www.unesco.kz/heritagenet/kz/content/duhov_culture/religia domusulman.htm.

7. There is also a variation of this instrument called the *Afghani rubab.*

8. For observations of the musical culture in nineteenth-century Central Asia, see Earl Danmore, *The Pamirs. Being a Narrative of a Year's Expedition on Horseback and on Foot through Kashmir, Western Tibet, Chinese Tartary, and Russian Central Asia,* 2 vols. (London: John Murray, 1893); A. Vamberi, *Travels to Central Asia: Being the Account of a Journey from Teheran across the Turkoman Desert on the Eastern Shore of the Caspian to Khiva, Bokhara, and Samarkand, Performed in the Year 1863* (London: J. Murray, 1864).

9. There is a heated and ongoing debate among Sovietologists as to whether this atmosphere of public enthusiasm was genuine or was a creation of Soviet propaganda.

10. I use the terms "local," "native," and "traditional" (for instruments and musicians) to describe the development in the region before the state delimitation in Central Asia in 1924. I also use the term "national" to describe the development in the post-1924 period, though it is understood that it took several years before some of the "national" music was developed and certain musical instruments became associated with certain nationalities.

11. Annette Meakin, *In Russian Turkistan: A Garden of Asia and its People* (London: George Allen and Unwin, Ltd., 1915), p. 142.

12. Though dance clubs existed in Central Asia in the 1920s and became popular among the younger generation, most participants were Russians, as the native population looked on this type of entertainment with great suspicion and often prohibited children from going there.

13. For a comparison of the similarities and differences among the modern trends in Turkish traditions, see Ismail Ekmekcioglu et al., *Turk Halk Oyunlari* (Istanbul: Esin Yayinevi, 2001).

14. Meakin, *In Russian Turkistan.* p. 220.

15. Here I use the Uzbek spelling of the name.

16. In fact, many directors, performers, and writers who arrived in Central Asia in the 1930s came there involuntarily, having been exiled for various political offenses.

17. See Ebdizhemil Nurpeisov, *Qan men ter* [Blood and sweat], 3 vols. (Almaty: Zhazushy baspasy, 1976).

18. Several Web sites and radio stations maintain their own hit parades with regular voting for the top 5, top 10, or top 20 singers and groups. For examples, see http://kzmz.region.kz/ top_40 and http://www.hittv.kz.

19. For ratings, see http://kzmz.region.kz/top_40.

20. For information on Elsinor, see the group's Web site, http://www.elsinor. org.

21. All seven groups were nominated as the best groups during the rock festival *Muzyka zhivogo elektrichestva;* see http://www.rock.kg/rasklad/mle2004_1.doc.

22. For the full history of the group and its achievements, see http://www.rock. kg/rock/encyclopedy/pm.php.

23. For examples, see http://music.tajnet.com/; http://tj-rap.ucoz.ru.

24. For news, bios, and some downloadable Turkmen music, see http://turkmen-music.com/ and http://turkmenpop.com.

25. For a review article on modern trends in Uzbek pop, see http://www.sanat. orexca.com/eng/1–04/music.shtml.

26. For news, bios and some downloadable pop and folk-rock Uzbek music, see http://www.show.uz/; http://ino.uzpak.uz/eng/other_eng/music_eng.html, http:// worldmusic.nationalgeographic.com/worldmusic/view/page.basic/country/content. country/uzbekistan_624, and http://www.grand.uz/. Uzbek Hard Rock is covered by: http://www.harddays.net.

27. For ratings, see http://grand.uz/?do=hit&uz.

28. Turkmenistan, however, represents a special case, because the state still fully controls the entertainment industry.

29. For information about Alisher Latif-Zade's artistic achievements, see http://alatif-zade.freenet.uz.

30. In the latest trend, Central Asian republics began hosting competitions similar to *American Idol.* See http://star.uz.

6

Visual Arts

Haly dokamak inne bilen guy gazan yal. Weaving a [good] carpet is [as hard] as digging a well with a needle.

—Turkmen proverb

Among the general public, Central Asian art is probably best known for its carpets, jewelry, and embroidered colorful national dress. Others might argue, however, that miniatures, ceramics, and handcrafted souvenirs are the most recognized Central Asian arts. In a way, such division of opinions reflects a simplified classification of Central Asian visual arts, but it also illustrates the existence of two large segments within the visual arts: one is the art of nomads, the other is the art of settlers. The former traditionally emphasized the practicality of the objects, using simple and straight lines in design and patterns, and they exploited simple if not rough materials produced in their households (wool, leather, animal bones). The latter emphasized rich colors, complex works, and great attention to details and utilized various local and imported materials, including luxurious silk, gold, and fine cotton. These products were combined to create the splendid décor of palaces, great mosques, and affluent country houses.

It is also important to mention that the nomads shared and preserved the ancient Turkic and Mongol traditions and were less exposed to the Persian and Middle Eastern Islamic traditions. Throughout the centuries, some of these Turkic traditions made a significant impact on many aspects of cultural development in the Muslim world far outside the Central Asian region and were absorbed in many parts of Eurasia. Islamic cultural traditions, especially those of the Persian-speaking population, had an enormous influence on the settlers in the fertile oases and cities of the region and also affected those nomadic communities that ultimately decided to move into the cities and towns of Central Asia.[1] Indeed, the Turkic and Persian elements intermingled in such a degree that some scholars were inclined to speak of the "Turkic-Persian" cultural heritage, rather than the Central Asian cultural heritage.[2]

Then, in the early twentieth century, an entirely different cultural universe—Russian, Soviet, and Western—swept through the region, introducing the local population to modern forms of art. Central Asian societies experienced rapid changes that created a very difficult dilemma: how to integrate traditional cultural heritage, which has unique historical, cosmological and metaphysic roots in the preindustrial society, and the modern artistic expressions and value systems of the industrial and postindustrial world? Twenty-first-century scholars and the general public would find many differences in the reaction of the local artistic communities to these changes.[3] Some Central Asians fully embraced the new artistic forms and styles and began trying to work in those styles. Others attempted to experiment, incorporating the best local folk traditions into new forms and styles and taking advantage of the interplay between old and new. A third group learned about the changing world but decided to keep to its traditional ways of making art.

CARPETS

Since ancient times, Central Asian nomads and semi-nomadic tribes have moved around with their animals in search for grazing ground. They perfectly adopted their homes and everyday items to their mobile, spartan, and semimilitary lifestyle. The design, shape, material, and even location of every artifact were carefully thought through and arranged in accordance with centuries of experiments and jealously guarded archaic customs and skills. Practicality was of the utmost importance, and every item was easy to pack, light enough to be carried on horses and camels, and able to survive the severe extremes of the continental weather.

The single most important item of nomadic culture and probably the most famous and distinguished forms of the nomadic art are carpets. Central Asian carpets (also called Turkic or Turkoman nomadic carpets) and woven items are used in many ways. They usually cover the floor of nomadic felt tents (*yurts*), serving as floor mats, on which people sit, sleep, or even eat, as many Central Asians still eat on the floor, especially in rural areas. The carpets also cover walls of houses and especially *yurts,* both for decorative purposes and to provide insulation. Woven items are also made to cover horses (these carpets

Traditional Central Asian carpets. Courtesy of the
author, 2006.

are called *at-khaly* in Turkmen) and camels for weddings *(asmalyk),* and to
frame the interior of the *yurt* entrance *(kaplyk).* There are also various forms
of bags *(chuval, qap* or *mufras, dis torba, bokcha,* and *qazan tutas),* prayer carpets *(namazlyk, aytlyk),* and carpets to cover entrance of the *yurts (engsi).*

In terms of technique, contemporary scholars conventionally divide the
Central Asian carpets into three groups: (1) knotted-pile, (2) flat-woven, and
(3) felt. Knotted-pile carpets are usually made on simple homemade vertical looms, and the wool is two-piled with S-twists and Z-spins. Flat-woven
carpets are made on simple homemade looms, and the horizontal threads of
different colors and length run through vertical threads, forming the design
pattern. Felt carpets are usually made by ramming and rolling unprocessed
raw wool into a firm material, then applying bright color ornament appli-
qué. Most of the Turkic nomadic carpets are rectangular and made of sheep
wool, in rare cases with added silk, cotton, or goat wool. Among important
features of the Central Asian carpets are the wide usage of geometrical figures
(rhombus, hexagon, or rectangle). In the past, many carpets incorporated a
symbolic tribal mark *(tamga)* that every adult could "read," comment on,

and associate with specific tribes, villages, or territory, though at present these marks are often reduced to being simply a part of the carpet's design.

By design, Central Asian Turkic carpets fall into two large categories.[4] One group is often called the Turkmen or Turkoman carpets.[5] The Turkmen handmade carpets have been widely known in Central Asia, the Middle East, and South Asia for many centuries, and therefore they are the best studied. Turkmen carpets with traditional Turkmen patterns can be subdivided into three groups (though some experts subdivide them into five).[6] The first includes Tekin, Akhaltekin, and Pendi carpets. The second includes Yomud and Chovdur carpets. The third comprises Beshir, Ersarin, and Gyzylayk carpets. These groups differ by their pattern and the number of knots per square unit (the higher, the better). In contrast to the Persians, the Turkmen carpet makers use fewer colors (they often prefer monochromatic color schemes with red or burgundy as dominant colors), more geometrical patterns, and minimal flowery ornaments; the carpets are traditionally made in knotted-pile technique.

The second group roughly corresponds to the carpets made in the *Jetisuu*—the part of Central Asia to the east and north of the Syr Darya River.[7] Indeed, the carpets produced among Kyrgyzs and Kazakhs are quite

Felt carpets are especially popular among Kazakhs and Kyrgyzs. Exhibition of felt carpets at the Kyrgyz National Museum of Art. Courtesy of the author, 2006.

Central Asia is also famous for its *suzane* (large embroidered wall-panels). Courtesy of the author, 2006.

different from those made by Turkmens in terms of design and materials (the Kazakhs and Kyrgyzs usually make felt carpets). The tribal carpets made in these traditionally nomadic areas often have large geometrical patterns, fewer details, and a combination of only three major colors—red, black, and white. Kazakhs and Kyrgyzs usually make their carpets of sheep-wool felt that is richly decorated with bright and contrasting color ornaments. For example, Kyrgyz carpets *(ala-kiyiz and shyrdak)* are made by embroidering colorful mosaic applications onto the felt base with contrasting threads. *Ala-kiyizes* are made by ramming and rolling the bright color appliqués into the felt base. Traditionally, carpet makers produced relatively simple appliqués, though skillful masters can create very complex patterns rich in details and colors.

Central Asia is also famous for its *suzane*. *Suzane*—large embroidered wall panels—are usually made of homespun cotton or sometimes silk and are embroidered with bright cotton or silk threads. Each *suzane* center developed its own tradition, with unique compositions: for example, Samarqand is known for its large floral rosettes framed by colorful rings or stylized flowering shrub arranged in checkerboard pattern.[8] In Kyrgyzstan, wall panels called *tush-kiyiz* are made of velvet and are embroidered with colorful national patterns.

JEWELRY AND METALWORK

Central Asian jewelry amazed visitors from the medieval adventurer Marco Polo to modern tourists, and many jewelry experts and designers who visit local museums and bazaars turn into bards singing serenades in praise of the fine metalwork they have seen.[9] On special occasions, women in Central Asia sometimes looked like display models from a small jewelry museum, with their earrings, bracelets, beads, pendants, forehead and chest decorations, silver amulets and talismans, and hair ornaments. They most likely leave at home large old nose rings (which are not fashionable at the moment), little prayer boxes, chatelaines worn at the waist, silver perfume bottles, eyebrow tweezers, and many other things that no man can name without the help of a specialized dictionary. Central Asian men usually limit themselves to two or three, sometimes five or six rings or signet rings (in the past these were a symbol of power and authority) and sometimes they wear heavy metal necklaces.[10] In the past, every wealthy nomad felt obliged to have beautifully made (often of silver) saddle decorations and harness plates and a sword or dagger. Nowadays these works are displayed on walls in some houses both in the cities and villages, since the owner may well have only the modern equivalent of a horse—a car.

In a local tradition, a grandmother customarily gave her granddaughter pieces of her own jewelry, so by the age of marriage a girl would have a full set of beautiful jewelry. When the time would come, this granddaughter would pass her jewelry on to her own grandchildren. Thus, it is not uncommon to find old family treasures that have been in the very same family for five to seven generations. As elsewhere, silver was the favorite and most affordable material for jewelry among ordinary people, and gold was popular among the upper class. In the late twentieth century, however, gold became more popular among all social groups.[11] Precious stones were relatively rare, but Central Asian jewelers used carnelian (some nomads believed that this stone would bring good luck and protect them from diseases), topaz, pearls, rubies, turquoise, and some others.

National museums in Central Asian capitals display remarkably rich collections of jewelry in various styles and forms. These collections reflect the extensive millennium-long cultural exchanges that took place along the Great Silk Road, sometimes called by the jewelers the Nephrite Route, for the long-established trade of jade. The fine tradition of metalwork goes well back to the Scythian era, about the fourth or fifth century B.C. The acclaimed Russian scholar Galina Pugachenkova believes that Central Asian artists produced jewelry and metalwork that represents skills and artistic creativity to rival those found in the Mediterranean and Middle Eastern masterpieces of that era. She distinguishes two major styles that inspired many generations of jewelers. One is what she calls "mythic realism," which prevailed among the settlers and was rooted in the ancient Persian traditions. The other is the "animal style" that was popular among the nomads in the vast Eurasian steppe and that reflected local myths, legends, and beliefs.[12]

The skillful metal and jewelry workers enjoyed great respect among both the settled and the nomadic people.[13] As with other forms of art, jewelry in major settled areas was more sophisticated and fragile and represented the fine artistic and design skills of famous masters. The nomads usually preferred simpler items, though some of the objects excavated by archeologists in parts of Kazakhstan and Uzbekistan display truly distinctive design and forms. In fact, since the 1960s, archeologists have been regularly discovering ancient treasures that represent the so-called animal-style jewelry of the vast Eurasian steppe (e.g., twisted fantastic animals). These findings greatly changed the perceptions of modern scholars about the life of ancient nomads, and many local historians even began rewriting some pages in the history textbooks.

Art experts' and researchers' views about the quality of the artwork and the mastery of ancient metalworkers were revolutionized even further with the finding of the so-called Scythian Golden Warrior in the Issyk burial mount in Kazakhstan, in 1969. Archeologists found the chamber of a young man who was buried in about 400 B.C. and who was ritually dressed and equipped with beautiful and lavish warriors' arms. These arms included golden weaponry— a gilt dagger, a sword, and a whip with a golden handle. The warrior was dressed in a beautiful and elaborate golden armor-tunic, with gold-embroidered trousers and boots. His golden armor consisted of about 4,000 gold plaques. The waist was decorated with an elaborate gold belt. The armor was complete with a stunning conical headdress, about 60 centimeters high (almost two feet), probably made of felt and intricately decorated with gold animal-shaped appliqués, feathers, and arrows. Local scholars believe that the importance of this finding is equal to that attached to the discovery of the gold of Troy or the mummies of Egyptian pharaohs. This discovery will probably require the rewriting of many art history textbooks and a revision of the old view that nomadic society was too simple and unsophisticated to support crafts and industries, especially intricate metalwork and jewelry making.

The Central Asian craft of jewelry underwent a significant change in style, design, and technique between the ninth and the eleventh centuries A.D., as the jewelry masters, heavily influenced by Middle Eastern practices, largely switched from silver to other materials. The changes became even more profound during the Timurid era, in the fifteenth and sixteenth centuries.

Unfortunately, the animal style in jewelry making, so popular in early times, long ago nearly disappeared, leaving few traces in the modern jewelry culture. Contemporary twenty-first-century Central Asian items have no or little connection to that historical period, though, recently, many jewelry masters in the region have attempted to imitate the most unusual examples of ancient and medieval styles in order to meet demands of changing fashion and a growing desire for unique, custom-made items among affluent groups of the society and antique- and treasure-hunting foreign tourists.

NATIONAL DRESS AND EMBROIDERED ARTIFACTS

At present, many Central Asians in both rural and urban areas keep up their old traditions and customs by lavishly decorating their homes. For many centuries, homemade colorful national dress, embroidered velvet floor mats and blankets *(kurpacha),* and many other items were highly valued throughout the region. Very often, in family-owned and family-run handicraft enterprises, skillful masters work with help of their children and grandchildren and, sometimes, great-grandchildren. They provide their extended families

Kyrgyz national dress displayed at the Kyrgyz Historical Museum. Courtesy of the author, 2006.

People often wear traditional headdresses. Courtesy of the author, 2006.

(which can run up to several hundred people if all relatives are counted) with homemade and beautifully embroidered national dress and household items, such as blanket covers, pillowcases, bags, and wall panels. Entrepreneurial masters also sell their products at the local bazaars, amazing foreign tourists with the bright colors and exotic patterns. In fact, even in the modern era, a traditional *yurt* and some private homes can rival an ethnographic museum as they display handicrafts made and arranged according to centuries-old traditions. Many Kazakhs, Kyrgyzs, and Turkmens who moved to urban centers accept urban lifestyle in contemporary apartment buildings with Western interior decoration, furniture, and home appliances. Yet many of them still try to keep one room or at least a corner in the main room in the national style for the most important family events.

The national dress among the Central Asian people has always been very colorful, with various decorating elements that play a functional role.[14] The locals can immediately identify the social, marital, and economic status, age, and even tribal and regional affiliation just by looking at the colors, patterns, types of embroidery, and fabric. The Central Asian region can be described as a land of a thousand tribes and local communities, and there is a multitude of variations in local costume. Yet, some common elements can be observed

Traditional costumes of nomadic Kazakh nobility. Courtesy of the author, 2006.

throughout the region. The traditional woman's costume in most parts of the region consists of a long-sleeved shirt or a long tunic-style dress (usually covering the body to the knees or heels), baggy pants, a headdress, and a scarf or shawl. The costume is finished by a bright or dark cotton-quilted dressing gown. In some areas, especially during the cold time of the year, women put on several layers of shirts, dresses, or overcoats, one on top of another. Until the 1930s, most of the women in settled areas wore a special heavy veil that fully covered their heads, hiding their hair and, often, the face (in accordance with the local conservative interpretation of the Islamic dress code for women that stresses modesty). In the nomadic areas, women interpreted the dress code quite liberally and usually covered their hair (especially married women), but not their faces. Men's costumes also consist of several common elements. This traditionally includes a long-sleeved shirt, baggy trousers, a cotton-quilted robe or buttonless overcoat, called a *chapan* among Kyrgyzs and Uzbeks and a *don* among Turkmen, and tall leather boots or moccasin-style shoes. The hat may be a cylindrical Astrakhan sheepskin hat, worn by the Turkmens; a skullcap *(depe, dupi),* worn by Tajiks and Uzbeks; or a pointy hat (called a *kolpak*) among the Kazakhs, Karakalpaks, and Kyrgyzs. Those who perform the Islamic pilgrimage, the Hajj, and some people in power

Archeologists reconstructed dress of ancient "Scythian Golden Warrior" found in the Issyk burial Mount in Kazakhstan in 1969. Courtesy of the author, 2006.

often wear turbans. According to Central Asian custom, the hats have to be worn all the time, even when men enter a house or public building.

A great variety of national dress in different patterns and colors and types of fabric survived well into the 1950s and 1960s. Then, unfortunately, the practice of making clothing at home began to lose ground, unable to compete with factory-produced goods. The most profound changes in the style of dress happened between the 1960s and the 1980s, as the younger generation opted for European-style clothes and a more liberal dress code. Thus, women began wearing factory-made clothes of bright colors, and the dress became more stylish and less baggy than it is supposed to be, though women sew traditional, local-style dresses for special occasions. For example, it is a must that bride and groom wear traditional clothes for engagement celebrations, weddings, and other family events.

By the 1990s, women in both urban and rural areas have fully abandoned the practice of veiling their faces, though married women continued to cover their hair with a small scarf or shawl, while young unmarried girls often opt for a small, brightly colored skullcap (called *tuppi* or *tokai* in Tajik). In the 1990s and early 2000s, the European style of dress fully conquered fashion among all generations of people in urban areas, though Central Asians usually include at least one element of traditional dress. For example, men may wear a *depe* or *kolpak (qalpoq)* or a belt with Eastern-style buckles, women may choose a national sleeveless jacket, scarf, or belt. In rural areas, there are more people who have preserved many elements of the traditional dress; and the older generation has often simply rejected the European style of dress altogether. They strongly believe that the traditional dress made of natural materials such as wool, cotton, or silk helps them to cope with the extremes of weather much better than modern synthetic fabrics.

CERAMICS

Settlers, unlike nomads, could afford the luxury of having ceramic kitchenware in their homes. Good-quality clay and colors were abundant in the region, and in time the ceramics production grew into large-scale industries producing merchandise for both the domestic and the international market. The early ceramics shops can be traced to ancient times, and some guilds and families ran these businesses for centuries. Central Asian pottery masters produced a wide variety of ceramic wares, from beautifully painted plates and bowls to elegant teapots, amphora, and specialty pots and jars for water, milk, and yogurt. Several cities and towns of Central Asia such as Khiva, Merv, Samarqand, Shash (Tashkent), and Urgench were famous for the quality and design of their crafts.[15] Ceramics were made for people with different tastes and different budgets, from inexpensive unpainted red-body small pottery to expensive fine and hand-painted large masterpieces that still amaze visitors in various museums across the region.

Archaeologists discovered ceramics from different eras at different sites, mainly in the southern areas of Central Asia. Scholars still debate the dating and classification of local ceramics and the extent of foreign influence. Indeed, it is difficult to generalize about Central Asian ceramics because of the variety of local traditions and external influences. Pottery masters came under the influence of different traditions as they benefited from cultural exchanges with Chinese and Persian worlds along the Great Silk Road. In addition, the quality and design of ceramics and the techniques used to make them changed over the time; for example, pre-Islamic ceramics are different from the ceramics of the Islamic era.

The evolution of ceramics production can be best illustrated by an example from Afrasiab (Samarqand). According to Surae Alieva, an Uzbek expert in ceramics, Uzbek archeologists found a large quantity of quality enameled ceramics dating to the eighth century A.D. in the city and its vicinity.[16] She says that these ceramics were ornamented with floral and geometrical motifs and sometimes included pictures of birds, animals, and people. With the establishment of Islam, epigraphic ornaments in Arabic (traditionally in three styles— *Kufi, flowering Kufi,* and Italic Arabic) became popular here, as well as elsewhere in the region. The text usually included a religious blessing *(Baraqa)* or words of wisdom, but masters avoided plain white pottery or depiction of humans, fantastic animals and dragons, and landscapes.[17] In the twelfth and thirteenth centuries, there was another change, as geometrical patterns and ornaments largely replaced the epigraphic writing. After a long interruption caused by the Mongol invasion, another change occurred, and ceramic design began to incorporate stylized vegetative motifs. Experts believe that some of the artifacts from the fourteenth and fifteenth centuries show an increasing Chinese influence, not only in ornamentation but also in technologies. During this era, porcelain could be found in greater quantities in the region because of the proximity to China and the active trade on Great Silk Road, but it was too expensive for ordinary people. From the seventeenth to the nineteenth centuries, artists tended to paint intricate floral motifs, though animal images—symbolic birds, fish, or deer—can also be found. In the nineteenth and twentieth centuries, ceramics production, like many other types of handicraft, faced tough times as local makers were unable to compete with mass factory production.

Today, tourists find that ceramics are again widely available at the Central Asian bazaars. Local masters work mainly for tourists and for art lovers, reproducing patterns and motifs—animal, floral, geometrical, and epigraphic writing—from any era. At the same time, they display their own experiments, expressing their own artistic creativity in various forms.

CALLIGRAPHY AND MINIATURE PAINTING

Calligraphy, or the art of fine handwriting, has had a long tradition in Central Asia. It received a particular boost with the arrival of Islam.[18] There emerged a whole group of people who specialized in the beautiful handwritten and artistic decoration of books,[19] as printing technology was practically unknown in the region until the late nineteenth century. With arrival of the Muslims, the Arabic and Persian languages became the languages of theological discourse, science, and art, and Arabic script replaced all other scripts. The most skillful and famous calligraphers perfected their writing skills by creating beautiful manuscripts with expensive multicolor or gold ornaments for royal libraries *(kitob-khonas),* prestigious Islamic schools *(madrasas),* or private tutors and wealthy families. In the meantime, ordinary calligraphers worked on simpler books for affluent families, smaller *madrasas,* and regular scholars, teachers, and other clients. The Central Asian calligraphers were influenced by Persian masters who had established their own distinguished calligraphy schools in major urban centers, such as Herat, Tabriz, and Meshhed. Unfortunately, not many works of the first centuries of Islam in Central Asia survived, but those that did contain meticulously designed and beautifully embellished pages, each in itself a masterpiece.

Hand-in-hand with calligraphy, another tradition emerged—hand-painted miniatures used to illustrate various creative and theological works and scientific books.[20] Distinctive features of Central Asian miniature paintings include ornamentally posed humans with almond-shaped eyes and characteristic flat faces, deep bright colors, and great attention to the details of animals, landscape, architecture, and people's dress.[21] Unlike European painters of the Renaissance, Central Asian classic painters rarely experimented in portraiture and did not show much interest in reflecting individual psychology. Rather, their paintings remained to some degree an extension of the artistic decoration of books, seamlessly blended with the ornamentation and calligraphy found in the handwritten manuscripts.

Many Islamic theologians categorically opposed the depiction of humans and animals in pictures or painting; they strictly opposed it as a sign of idolatry or worship of earthy subjects. In some areas, these restrictions were followed strictly, and calligraphers and artists complied with the rules by decorating books with fantastic patterns and beautiful lines and by mastering the skill of writing Arabic script in beautiful forms but making no pictures of humans or animals. Others were more flexible in their interpretation of the strict rules and painted wonderful miniatures full of real and fantastic animals or even humans.

The Central Asian miniature tradition had its roots in the Sassanid Iranian traditions (third century to seventh century A.D.), and in the arts of Khorezm (second and third centuries) and Sogd (seventh and eighth centuries). Beautiful samples of painting on papyrus and ceramics have been discovered at many archeological sites in northern Afghanistan and Iran and in southern Tajikistan and Uzbekistan. The ancient painters produced both religious and secular paintings. The former can be found in various temples and shrines (e.g., Kara-Tepe temple). The secular paintings, which reflected the everyday life of the nobility and royal courts, can be found in palaces and castles across the region (e.g., Toprak-Kala Palace).

The works created between the seventh and the ninth centuries A.D. enable scholars to trace both continuity and changes between the Sassanid and the early Islamic traditions in such ancient Central Asian centers as Afrasiab, Penjekent, Varakh'sh, and Adjina-Tepe. The surviving paintings of that era depict hunting scenes, heroic battles, various family, military, and royal court rituals, and official ceremonies.[22] However, from the eighth century forward there was a clear sign that the Islamic influence took its toll, and the Central Asian painting schools began declining.

Yet, by the tenth century, miniature paintings had emerged, probably under the patronage of the royal Fatimid court. Brilliant colors and intricate design characterize the miniatures of this era. The works of the tenth- and eleventh-century masters gave inspiration to many artists in the Islamic world, especially in the Khorasan region. Several schools of miniatures gradually emerged in Herat, Tabriz, and other places, though artistic continuity was disrupted by the devastating Mongol invasion.

The Mongol onslaught in the thirteenth century negatively affected the artistic world in Central Asia. It took many decades before economic and cultural life recovered in the major cities and with it the miniature-painting schools. The establishment of the Timurid Empire played an enormous role in stabilizing the political and economic situation in the southern and western parts of Central Asia. The Timurid era is often described as the Central Asian Renaissance. In the early fifteenth century, a small, but influential school of art supported by Baisunkur-Mirza emerged in Herat, which eventually grew to become the acclaimed Herat miniature school. This school was best represented by Kamaliddin Behzad (1455–1533?), who can be called the Botticelli of the East for his elegant pictures of court life and battles and especially for his pioneering works in Central Asian portraiture.[23]

Another school, the so-called Bukhara school of miniature painting—one of the most celebrated and admired in Central Asia—arose between the early sixteenth and the eighteenth centuries in Bukhara city and its vicinity.[24] It was established under the influence of the Herat school, but very soon its leading painters distinguished themselves with their original creative works. The works of the early Bukhara school can be recognized by their characteristic composition of pictures and their attention to architectural landscape details. Painters of this school, such as Abdullah Bukhari and Mahmud Mozahheb (both of whom worked in the sixteenth century), usually painted complex scenes meticulously depicting groups of people engaged in battles or in religious or political discussions. At the later stage, the miniature artist Mohammad Sarif simplified the compositions but energized them with deeper colors, classic arrangements of landscapes, and depictions of people. All these masters produced remarkable and distinctive pieces of art, decorating such works as *Tales of the Arabian Nights, Shahnama* and various secular and religious books.

The economic decline and political turmoil of the seventeenth and eighteenth centuries in Central Asia contributed to the decline in the artistic community, as well. Very little is known about the miniatures of the eighteenth and early nineteenth centuries, though few masters continued working. During this era, many artists migrated to other regions or abandoned their work, as they lost the patronage of the royal courts or wealthy individuals and printed books from various parts of the Muslim world began entering the Central Asian market.

SCULPTURE

Sculpture in Central Asia has never flourished to the same degree as architecture and carpet making, and most of the known pieces were produced during the pre-Islamic and early Islamic eras. However, what archeologists uncovered and saved represents interesting examples of creative work. Sculptures from Central Asian can be divided into three major groups: sculptures from the ancient states (such as Bactria and Sogdiana) of the third to the first centuries B.C.; Buddhist sculptures of the first to the tenth centuries A.D.; and numerous stone statues (sometimes called *balbals*) made by shamanistic nomadic tribesmen that date to between the second and thirteenth centuries.

A particularly rich heritage was left by the Bactrian, Sogdian, and Persian Empires, and it is best represented in museums and at excavation sites in what are now Tajikistan, Turkmenistan, and Uzbekistan. For example, archeologists, who reconstructed the fortress-palace Toprak-kala (Turkmenistan), built between the fifth and the second centuries B.C., believe that the main halls of the palace were decorated with numerous statues of kings and warriors, though no statue has survived to present. Among the few archeological findings from that era is a head of a local ruler of the second century B.C.; made in the Hellenic style, it was found at the so-called Oxus temple (Tajikistan) and is currently on display in a national museum. Early examples of sculpture were discovered mainly during the excavation of ancient cities in southern parts of Central Asia—what are now northern Afghanistan, Tajikistan, Turkmenistan, and Uzbekistan. Most of them were created during the time of Bactria and Sogdiana. The examples from that era display significant Persian and Hellenic influences.

Another example of sculpture comes from the ruins of numerous Buddhist temples that were discovered practically in every Central Asian republic. Most of them are dated to between the second and ninth centuries A.D. In the mid-twentieth century, archeologists discovered what is now the largest intact clay statue (about 12 meters, or more than 30 feet long) of the sleeping Buddha in the region. This Buddha statue, dated to about the seventh or eight century A.D., was discovered in the ruins of Ajinatepa (in the Kurgonteppa district of Tajikistan).[25] At present, the Buddha is displayed in the national Museum

Central Asian horse rider sculpture on display at the Kyrgyz National Museum of Art. Courtesy of the author, 2006.

of Antiquity in Tajikistan.[26] According to medieval Muslim explorers, some wooden and clay sculptures could have been seen in major cosmopolitan centers, such as Samarqand, even in the tenth century. Unfortunately, many examples of sculpture of that era were destroyed during the turbulent years of the late medieval era and even during the contemporary time.

Numerous nomadic tribes that lived in Central Asia since time immemorial have left a large number of stone statues, usually dated to between the second and thirteenth centuries A.D.; there are very few sculptures that can be attributed to Central Asian artists from between the thirteenth and the seventeenth centuries. In most cases, nomadic masters used long oval stones that distantly resemble a human torso. Usually, the stone statues reproduced only an abstract vision of the main elements of human body—the face, the main body lines, and the hands. Some of those who created them did a wonderful job of depicting human bodies in great details. However, in most cases these statues were quite primitive and basically were no more than shallow lines carved into oval-shaped stones. These statues came in different sizes and shapes. Sometimes they were found alone but sometimes they were found in groups. The consensus is that they were built to perform certain rituals related

V. Dimov *Melody*. Sculpture display at the Kyrgyz
National Museum of Art. Courtesy of the author,
2006.

to shamanistic beliefs, though historians still debate their exact purpose: why
they were made, who really made them, and how they were used.

Islamic theologians perceived that all those sculptures might become
subjects of worship, and they outright banned them. This ban was strictly
followed; during turbulent years of large uprisings or revolts or military campaigns, mobs regularly targeted properties of the minorities, destroying and
looting whatever they could. Even during times of peace, some fanatics felt
obliged to destroy sculptures, frescoes, and decorations in abandoned temples and shrines. The luminaries of Central Asian studies, Owen Lattimore
and Alice Thorner, who witnessed the quick deterioration and disappearance
of the ancient ruins and especially sculptures, wrote, in the mid-twentieth
century:

Easy available ruins had already suffered greatly from the local population who, as
good Moslems, felt found to destroy heathen idols and especially to deface repre-
sentations of human beings. What the European excavators uncovered but did not

remove has largely succumbed to the elements and to the later efforts of Treasure seekers.[27]

Monumental sculpture was reintroduced only during the Soviet era, but in a very different way. Very often these were large and heavy sculptures symbolizing the revolution, the civil war, and the Great Patriotic War or heroes of wars and of postwar reconstructions. Every city and town displayed a statue of Lenin on its main square, in front of which all major parades and public events were held. In addition, many parks and major squares were decorated with sculptures that depicted national folklore and legendary and real heroes of the past or present.

MODERN ART

Painting

Painting is a new cultural phenomenon in Central Asia, as it largely emerged and was established in the twentieth century. One might hypothesize that modern Central Asian painting has its roots in the acclaimed miniature-painting schools, which flourished in the region for centuries, and is a result of the evolution of these old painting schools. The reality is quite contrary to this assumption—the traditions of Central Asian modern painting and classical miniature painting are quite disconnected. Rather, the art of painting in its modern meaning appeared in the region in the words of an art critic as a "transplantation" from one cultural environment to another, namely from the Western world to the Asian.[28]

Despite the fact that for decades Central Asian painting was in the shadow of the Russian artistic traditions and that many early Central Asian artists studied exclusively at Russian schools and institutions,[29] Central Asians developed some elements of their own distinctive style and approaches, contributing to Soviet socialist realism, avant-garde styles, and impressionism in their own ways. Central Asian artists followed the styles and artistic traditions they had learned religiously. Many of their paintings looked like works from other parts of the Soviet Union and often resembled dutiful implementations of the rigid requirements of socialist realism (see also chapter 5). Nonetheless, even the tight regulations imposed by the Artists' Union and Art Academy could not prevent the most gifted artists from expressing themselves and reflecting their true thoughts and inspirations in their works when they were not painting for Soviet officialdom.

The beginning of modern painting in the region probably can be traced into the 1920s, when a large number of young Central Asian enthusiasts were sent to the major artistic centers in Moscow and Leningrad (now Saint Petersburg). The Bolsheviks believed that the introduction of new mass visual forms—painting, political cartoons, photography, and agitation posters—would be a powerful tool for both the introduction of so-called modern culture and for mass propaganda purposes.

After graduating and returning to their homes, the young Central Asian artists founded and joined vibrant artistic communities that began forming in all major urban centers across the region, fueled by an influx of established professionals from all over Russia. Some of them moved to the region in search of "refuge in the East," hoping to avoid being accused by authorities in the "fight against formalism" in art,[30] which was a serious accusation during the time of the political purges. These asylum-seeking artists believed that the remoteness of Central Asia might shelter them from persecution.[31] Other artists came there in an opportunistic search for a comfortable life in a "provincial" environment with a politically correct "tradition of creating ethnographic and geographic pictures" away from political battles.[32] A third group included those artists who had been exiled to the region after facing various accusations in the increasingly tense environment of the political purges, especially in the 1930s.

Groups of incoming artists were assigned to develop "modern national art" and to nurture local talents. Their mentoring and teaching often went beyond the simplistic socialist realism dogmas and teachings about universal socialist values. In the 1920s, for example, P. M. Mazel and A. P. Vladychuk, who arrived in Turkmenistan from Russia, established the first experimental Hit-Movement School of the Orient, in Ashgabat. Very soon, indigenous Turkmen painters began making creative works that became classics of Turkmen painting. Most popular styles and genres of that era can be exemplified by Biashim Nurali's *The Old Way of Life in Turkmenia* and *The New Way of Life in Turkmenia* (Turkmenistan, 1927) and *Cotton Gathering* (Turkmenistan, 1929), S. N. Begliarov's *Turkmen Women* (Turkmenistan, 1929), among others. During same time, in Uzbekistan, a group of Russian painters was busy developing indigenous schools of visual art: P. P. Ben'kov experimented with colors and *plein air* painting; while A. Volkov attempted combining three elements—traditional Russian iconography, Uzbek folk art, and modern Russian cubism. At the same time, indigenous painters such as N. G. Karakhan and U. Tansykbayev incorporated traditional and distinct Uzbek motifs into their works. The Russian painters N. G. Khudov, N. I. Krutilnikov, and V. I. Antoschen-Olenev actively worked in Kazakhstan.

Typical paintings of that era are Biashim Nurali's *Women at a Collective Farm* (Turkmenistan, 1932), which depicts the liberation of Turkmen women; Kh. Allaberdyev's *Bakh'shi Visits Injured Soldier* (Turkmenistan,

1944), which attempts to present a connection between a traditionalist past and the youthful present; and U. Daneshvar's *Sending [Soldiers] to the Red Army* (Turkmenistan, 1943), which illustrates patriotic support for the Red Army and for the war against the Nazis. Also noteworthy are P. Ben'kov's portraits, U. Tansykbayev's landscapes, and V. E. Kaidarov's book illustrations (Uzbekistan), and the works of A. Tashbayev, Kh. and K. Khojikov, and A. Ismailov (Kazakhstan). C. A. Chuikov and V. V. Obraztsov, who lived in Kyrgyzstan in the 1930s, played a key role in establishing Kyrgyz artistic schools. Already in the late 1930s, the Kyrgyz painter Gapar Aitikeev, one of the founders of the indigenous Kyrgyz painting school, presented a series of his works to the public. Typical genres of Kyrgyz artists can be seen in Aitikeev's works such as *The Letter from the [War] Front* (1943), which depicts the anxiety of ordinary people about their loved ones in the war; *On Collective Farm's Yard* (1946); and *On the Outskirts of a Village* (1949), which romanticizes the Soviet *kolkhozes* by depicting a picturesque lifestyle in a small Kyrgyz village. These artistic exchanges not only helped many young native talents to prepare their first personal exhibitions but also sharpened their skills and developed their professionalism.

In this environment, the Artists' Unions played quite a controversial role. On the one hand, they were instrumental in supporting and mentoring the young talents to such a degree that, by the mid-1930s, the indigenous artists presented their first works and established their first galleries. On the other hand, the Unions very quickly degenerated into guard dogs, jealously protecting the principles of socialist realism. Their members displayed extreme hostility toward the rebellious and nonconformists and their experiments in art.

Limitations on artistic freedoms, combined with Stalinist purges among intellectuals, had a very negative impact on the artistic community in the region and in the Soviet Union as a whole. The late 1930s and 1940s probably were the darkest years. The artists had to be very careful in choosing their subject matter, as they were expected to paint on certain prearranged themes. Innovations and experiments were not prized, though the visual artists were relatively free in selecting styles or experimenting with the incorporation of some traditional and national themes, patterns, and ideas into new artistic forms.

The death of Stalin, in 1953, and especially Khrushchev's famous denunciation of Stalin's policies, created an atmosphere of great expectations of liberal reforms in both the political and the artistic fields—the so-called Khrushchev's thaw *(ottepel')*. The 1960s were a time when many artists rebelled against officially approved art norms, the art establishment, and socialist realism and attempted to introduce something fresh and new. The Central Asians took part in search for artistic independence and freedoms, though to much lesser degree than their counterparts in Moscow.

These hopes were crushed by Khrushchev's successors. State-run galleries remained the main and probably the only commissioners of artistic products, and they would accept only paintings created in the spirit of mass social and historic themes and in the patriotic portrait genre (e.g., paintings showing the "builders of communism" in the social realist style). We probably will never know how many interesting works were created by independent-minded artists during this era that were later destroyed for the sake of safety or because there no place to exhibit them. What has remained from this era is represented by works that do not rebel against the existing rules and norms: Ya. Annanurov's *The 1930s* (Turkmenistan, 1962), which portrays a group of Turkmen women in traditional and modern dress, symbolizing social change and the "victory" of the socialist way of life, and D. Bairamov's *First Leaders of the Republic* (Turkmenistan, 1979), which illustrates a typical Soviet belief in the communist present and future. Similar style works were painted by G. Abdurakhmanov, Sh. Umarbekov, and R. Charyev, in Uzbekistan; M. S. Kenbayev, K. T. Telzhanov, S. A. Mambeev, and K. M. Shaykhmetov, in Kazakhstan; S. Ishenov, D. Jumabayev, A. Osmonov, and M. Sydykov, in Kyrgyzstan; and A. Aminjanov, A. Rakhimov, and Kh. Khushvakhtov, in Tajikistan.

The liberalization of the 1980s allowed Central Asian artists to have greater access to the works of modern Western artists, to learn about the latest trends in the international artistic world, and to have a bit more opportunity for traveling overseas and attending various events and exhibitions. Even more important, they could organize independent galleries and showrooms and hold their own independent art exhibitions and art installations. At least partially, they became independent of the strict rules of socialist realism, the watchful eyes of Art Academy officials, and the need for endorsement from the artistic establishment.

Many young individuals and groups began experimenting in surrealism, video art, pop art, and postmodernism. The Kazakh group called *Krasnyi Traktor* (later renamed *Kyzyl Traktor*) is a good example; its members erected installations that "reinstated living contacts with archaic cultural forms and their pre-Islamic past ... shamans, fortunetellers, and dervishes, whose philosophy was often depicted in rituals."[33] The Kazakh artist Shai Zhiya (real name Ziakhan Shaigeldinov) experimented in pop art, setting his installations on the streets of Almaty. His work attracted some attention, and one of them—*The Door to Time*—was bought for the Norton Dodge collection of nonconformist Soviet art (United States).[34] Rustem Khalfin, whom *Impressions* international magazine called "the best known and most influential" among contemporary artists in Kazakhstan,[35] experimented in video art, creating such works as *Love Races* and *Northern Barbarians*. His work *Chinese*

Eroticism, for instance, deals with human sexuality and presents an act of intercourse on horseback.[36]

Recent Trends

The collapse of the Communist system, the advent of independence, and the rise in national consciousness in Central Asia led to a reconceptualization of the national identity, including a rethinking of the past and of present experiences through visual forms. Two powerful trends symbolized these changes in the region in the late 1990s and early 2000s. On the one hand, there was surging interest in various national symbols—national dress, different artifacts, including spiritually empowered jewelry and metalwork, and creative works by native artists. On the other hand, there was an attempt to utilize new opportunities presented by the collapse of the iron curtain and to absorb the new ideas that globalization would bring in.

As a reflection of the growing interest in everything that represents national culture and national symbols in the post-Soviet era, there is a greater attention to national dress. Almost every family feels obliged to have a stylized national costume in its wardrobe. People usually wear them only for the most important occasions, such as large public holidays, family reunions, or family and community events (e.g., weddings, circumcisions). Many people try to have at least one element of the national costume to wear in everyday life. Thus, very often a person who is wearing a classic Western suit might complement the suit with a traditional *kolpak* or *depe (tubeteika)*. While women wearing a classic evening dress to attend a party, reception, or concert might complement it with a bright *depe* for unmarried women or with a scarf or shawl with a national pattern for married one. A small number of women have turned back to the conservative Islamic dress code and wear long, baggy dresses that fully cover the body and scarves that fully cover the hair and neck and, in some cases, the face, too.

Yet, most of the people in both rural and urban areas wear European-style dress in everyday life, with some adjustment for local climate, seasonal weather changes, and lifestyle. The major factor in the dress style, of course, is the level of income, though many people are ready to pay a considerable portion of their income for good-quality, fashionable clothes. Miniskirts, low-cut jeans, and revealing Hollywood-style dresses can be seen in major metropolitan centers but are a rare sight in the provinces. Many urban women opt for modern, casual, Western-style dress that conforms with an increasingly conservative social environment. In rural areas, traditional dress made big return in the 1990s. For example, in Tajikistan and Uzbekistan, many young women wear light silk long dresses and pants that fully cover their bodies, though they choose bright colors and traditional patterns that are suitable for the hot summer months.

Numerous types of talismans have gained wide popularity. It may be a special bracelet, an amulet, or a small locket on a necklace with religious writing, with a piece of a sacred item in it. In fact, since the most difficult years of the transition in the 1990s, talismans and amulets can be found everywhere—above home entrances, on a chain hanging inside a vehicle, or on the desks of government officials and politicians.

Independence and freedom boosted interests in the traditional national arts—carpets, metalwork, ceramics, and calligraphy—both among the middle class and among collectors, but modern art commands significantly less attention outside the few urban centers. In fact, the world of visual arts is rapidly shrinking. With the economic recession there came a shrinking budget for cultural expenditures. During the Soviet era, the state and state-controlled agencies and enterprises were the exclusive buyers of paintings, sculptures, and visual propaganda works. Private collectors were as rare as Russian cars on American streets, and they still are. Since the 1990s, the government and its various agencies have dramatically reduced their commissioning of artworks, while wealthy individuals, private enterprises, and middle-class buyers have not built a critical mass to create a sustainable market for art. In the absence of state support, many artists took their works to the streets and started painting for the mass market and for tourists.

Central Asian artists display their works. Courtesy of the author, 2006.

The economic revival of the 2000s significantly helped the artistic community as it recovered from the double shock of the post-Soviet transition and the aftershock of the Soviet cultural collapse. In this environment, three distinctive trends can be seen in the art market. There is an attempt to incorporate traditional motifs and patterns and to work in pseudotraditional style. There is also an attempt to focus on so-called Western "high culture," with brave experiments in postmodern style and forms. Finally, some artists continue to work in the monumental and pompous Soviet-era style and to preserve Soviet symbolism.

NOTES

1. Richard Frye, *The Heritage of Central Asia. From Antiquity to the Turkish Expansion* (Princeton: Markus Wener, 1996).

2. See, for debates and views on interaction of Turkic and Persian cultures, Robert L. Canfield, ed., *Turko-Persia in Historical Perspective* (Cambridge and New York: Cambridge University Press, 1991); R. W. Ferrier, ed., *The Arts of Persia* (New Haven: Yale University Press, 1989).

3. See, for discussion, Adeeb Khalid, *The Politics of Muslim Cultural Reform: Jadidism in Central Asia* (Comparative Studies on Muslim Societies no. 27) (Berkeley, CA: University of California Press, 1999).

4. There are also other classifications of the Central Asian carpets. See V. N. Basilov, ed., *Nomads of Eurasia* (Seattle, WA: Natural History Museum of Los Angeles County in association with University of Washington Press, 1989); A. A. Bogolyubov, *Carpets of Central Asia* (Ramsdel: Crosby Press, 1973); Louise Mackie and Jon Thomson, eds., *Turkmen Tribal Carpets* (Seattle, WA: University of Washington Press, 1980); Elena Tsareva, *Rugs and Carpets from Central Asia: The Russian Collections* (Harmondsworth, Middlesex, England, and New York: A. Lane/Penguin; Leningrad: Aurora Art Publishers, 1984).

5. They are also sometimes called the Bukhara carpets, reflecting the longstanding monopoly of Bukharian merchants on the export of these carpets.

6. In contemporary Turkmenistan, scholars differentiate five different patterns, according to the number of provinces in the Republic of Turkmenistan. See R. Abazov, *Historical Dictionary of Turkmenistan* (Lanham, MD, Toronto, and Oxford: Scarecrow Press, 2005), p. 34. Some scholars differentiate six different tribal patters. See, for discussion, Bogolyubov, *Carpets of Central Asia*; Mackie and Thomson, *Turkmen Tribal Carpets.*

7. Some scholars classify the second group as Eastern Turkistan carpets. Sometimes these carpets also called "Samarqand" carpets. Here, I do not cover carpets made in Eastern Turkistan, that is, in the Chinese province of Xingjian, since before the colonial era many Kazakh and Kyrgyz tribes maintained strong trade, political, and cultural links to this area. However, 150 years of political isolation in these two regions severed many of the cultural ties between them. I also do not cover carpets made in the traditionally settled areas and especially in the urban centers,

which experienced significant Persian influence and have more complex and flowery patterns in rich colors.

8. See Elmira Gyul, "Samarkand Suzane," *Sanat,* no. 3–4 (2004), http://www.sanat.orexca.com/index.shtml.

9. For detailed discussion and collection of excellent pictures, see T. Abdullayev, A. Fahretdinova, and A. Khakimov, *A Song in Metal. Folk Art of Uzbekistan* (in Uzbek, Russian, and English) (Tashkent: Gafur Guliam, 1984).

10. According to Sh. Tokhtabayeva, Central Asian men often wore rings, necklaces, and other jewelry. See Tokhtabayeva, *Serebriannyi put' kazakhskikh masterov* [The silver way of Kazakh craftsmen] (Almaty: Daik-Press, 2005).

11. See, for a comprehensive overview, Dieter Schletzer and Reinhold Schletzer, *Old Silver Jewelries of the Turkoman: An Essay on Symbols in the Culture of Inner Asian Nomads,* trans. Paul Knight (Berlin: D. Reimer, 1983).

12. G. A. Pugachenkova and L. I. Rempel, *Ocherki iskusstva Srednei Azii* [Essays on the art of Central Asia] (Moscow: Nauka, 1982).

13. O. M. Dalton, *Treasure of the Oxus, with Other Examples of Early Oriental Metal-work* (London: Trustees of the British Museum, 1964).

14. This is a very rough sketch of Central Asian dress, as it is very difficult to cover the enormous variety in the styles, forms, and patterns of traditional dress in the region. The problem is that traditional dress in the Central Asian republics at the beginning of the twenty-first century is quite different from traditional dress at the beginning of the twentieth century; though there are important elements of continuity. Professor Nina Lobacheva, one of the leading Russian experts on Central Asian dress, highlights the difficulties in studying dress styles in the region imposed by rapid cultural and economic changes in the nineteenth and twentieth centuries. She states that Central Asian dress experienced particularly dramatic change at the end of the nineteenth and the beginning of the twentieth centuries because of the arrival of new manufactured materials, the rapidly increasing frequency of contact with Russians, and the appearance of the sewing machine. See N. P. Lobacheva and M. V. Sazanova, *Traditsionaia odezhda narodov Srednei Azii i Kazakhstana* [The traditional dress of the people of Central Asia and Kazakhstan] (Moscow: Nauka, 1989), pp. 5–6.

15. D. A. Khakimov, *Atlas of Central Asian Artistic Crafts and Trades,* vol. 1, *Uzbekistan* (Tashkent: Sharq, 1999), pp. 12–14.

16. http://www.sanat.orexca.com/eng/3–4-04/history_art8.shtml.

17. Esin Atil, *Ceramics from the World of Islam* (Washington, DC: Smithsonian Institution, 1973).

18. For research on impact of discovery of paper, see Jonathan Bloom, *Paper before Print: The History and Impact of Paper in the Islamic World* (New Haven: Yale University Press, 2001).

19. For an overview see Basil Gray, Oleg Akimushkin, et al., *The Arts of the Book in Central Asia, 14th–16th Centuries* (London: Serindia Publications; Paris: UNESCO, 1979).

20. For a history of book illustration, see David Bland, A *History of Book Illustration: The Illuminated Manuscript and the Printed Book,* 2nd ed. (Berkeley: University of California Press, 1969).

21. F. R. Martin, *The Miniature Painting and Painters of Persia, India and Turkey, from the 8th to the 18th Century* (London: B. Quaritch, 1912; repr. London: South Asia Books, 1993.

22. Pugachenkova and Rempel, *Ocherki iskusstva Srednei Azii.*

23. Ebadollah Bahari, *Bihzad, Master of Persian Painting.* Foreword by Annemarie Schimmel (London and New York: I. B. Tauris, 1996).

24. Thomas W. Lentz and Glenn D. Lowry, *Timur and the Princely Vision: Persian Art and Culture in the Fifteenth Century* (Los Angeles: Los Angeles County Museum of Art, 1989).

25. B. A. Elitvinskii and T. I. Zeimal, *Adzhina-Tepa. Arkhitektura. Zhivopis'. Skul'ptura* [Ajinatepa. Architecture. Painting. Sculpture] (Moscow: Iskusstvo, 1971).

26. In fact, the world's largest stone-carved statues of Buddha in Bamian (Afghanistan) could be used as examples of such achievements in sculpture, as the cultural boundaries of the premodern Central Asia were much more fluid than they are today.

27. Owen Lattimore, *Pivot of Asia: Sinkiang and the Inner Asian Frontiers of China and Russia* (Boston: Little, Brown, 1950), p. 224.

28. Vecheslav Titenev, *Anthology of the Art of Kazakhstan: Painting* (Almaty: Zolotaia kniga, 2004), p. 45.

29. Unfortunately, Central Asian painting was for a long time dismissed in the West. The following phrase best represents the ways some works by Central Asian painters were represented by Western scholars: "[the portrait] seems to be an awkward, unprofessional attempt on the part of a new Central Asia artist to conform the Soviet principles of portrait." Edward Allworth, ed., *Central Asia: 130 Years of Russian Dominance. A Historical Overview,* 3rd ed. (Durham and London: Duke University Press, 1994), p. 521.

30. The "fight against formalism" in art is the name of the political campaign against those artists who did not follow the norms of socialist realism. Many artists who faced such accusations ended in exile in Siberia or the Russian Far East.

31. Titenev, *Anthology,* pp. 43, 45.

32. Ibid.

33. Valeria Ibrayeva, "The Fathers and Sons of Kazakhstan's Contemporary Art Movement," *Tamyr,* no. 1 (2005): 107.

34. Ibid., p. 106.

35. *Impressions* (United Kingdom) (April–May 2006): 46.

36. Ibrayeva, "The Fathers and Sons of Kazakhstan's Contemporary Art Movement," p. 108.
Kyrgyz national dress displayed at the Kyrgyz Historical Museum. Courtesy of the author, 2006.

7

Architecture

[Numerous names such as] the Mirror of the World, the Garden of the Soul, the Jewel of Islam, the Pearl of the center of the Universe ... City of famous shadows, reveal Samarqand as witness to the full sweep of Central Asian history.... The city proper claims equity with Rome and Babylon.

—Calum MacLeod and Bradley Mayhew, writers and travelers[1]

Classic Central Asian architecture is traditionally associated with the beautiful blue-dome architectural ensembles of Samarqand and Bukhara. The assemblages of medieval public buildings—mosques, *madrasas* (religious educational institutions), gorgeous minarets, and mausoleums—are among the most recognizable symbols of the region. Fired bricks assembled into beautiful symmetrical patterns strikingly but solidly push ribbed and egg-shaped domes high up to the sky. Many religious buildings are covered with distinctive turquoise tiles (turquoise is the symbolic color of Turkic tribes) that organically connect the earth and the sky in an attempt to convince people throughout the centuries of a simple message: these religious buildings play a spiritually important role by connecting earth and people to the universe and eternity.

The medieval architecture of Bukhara, Khiva, Konergench, Samarqand, Uzgen, and many other places indeed best represents the past architectural achievements of Central Asia. Yet, the architectural heritage of the region is much richer and more intricate. Archeologists have discovered many ruins and put on the map hundreds of ancient and medieval cities and towns that represent the region's rich architectural heritage, and some of these finds date as far back as the sixth to the third century B.C. Unfortunately, many fine examples of this early architecture vanished during numerous wars and conflicts, while development in the twentieth century replaced many aged buildings with modern office and apartment blocks made of standard brick, panel, and concrete. Therefore, the contemporary architectural landscape in Central Asia represents a mixture of very complex indigenous Central Asian design and very strong influence from the Middle East, South Asia, and, to some degree, China; in addition, the mixture includes a combination of the rich heritage of the settled civilizations and the simplicity of the nomadic philosophical approach to developing the landscape.

There are several elements that distinguish Central Asian architecture from that of Russia and West Europe. First, because of the very dry climate and the scarcity of wood in the southern and central areas of the region, clay, sun-dried, and fired bricks became the building material of choice; only in the far north (what is now Kazakhstan) was wood used more widely. Local masters *(ustoz)* perfected unique building and design skills, using a combination of clay and wood frame for fast commercial construction. These types of buildings could survive earthquakes, storms, and, if knocked down, were very easy and inexpensive to rebuild. However, they needed constant maintenance. Second, due to political instability and lawlessness in many parts of the region, people always lived in secluded communities *(mahallia),* which provided defense and economic help for their members. Traditionally, several generations of the same family lived under a single roof in a large family compound. Only the rich and powerful could afford individual housing (cottages, castles). Third, throughout many centuries, the Central Asians invested a lot in the building of religious structures, such as mosques, *madrasas,* and public buildings—*karavan-sarais* (inns), public baths, and palaces—but less into massive European-style stone fortresses.

ANCIENT ARCHITECTURE

Historians and archeologists have accumulated a wealth of information about the architecture of the Greek-Bactrian, Parthian, and Kushan eras, though very little of their architecture has survived to modern times. The ancient builders acquired significant skills in creating fortifications, palaces, residential houses, temples, including Hellenic, Buddhist, and Zoroastrian cult buildings, and public buildings, such as palaces, baths, citadels, and inns. Architects of this era used a combination of several materials: foundations were made of large stone blocks; walls, columns, poles, and arks were made of clay and sun-dried bricks; and ceilings and some pillars were made of large wood logs. Residential houses of wealthy citizens were usually built in a rectangular shape. Small rooms were lined up around large yards with a water reservoir in the middle (Kukhna-kala, Kalay-mir, Shahrinay, and Kei-kabab Sah, all in Tajikistan). The walls were covered with plaster and often were painted or coated with frescoes with religious, mythic, or secular themes. Local historians and archeologists believe that the architecture of the ancient period was largely influenced by Persian and Greek traditions. Examples of the remnants of this era can be found in numerous museums and at excavated archeological sites, which are often open to the public.

The ancient palace and temple in Nisa (Nusai) (southern Turkmenistan) is probably a good example of the Hellenic influences of the third and second centuries B.C.[2] This is a relatively large architectural complex that consists of rectangular buildings, including a temple, a royal chamber, a round-shaped building, and service rooms, and there was a little orchard with small water reservoirs. The temple had a foundation shaped as a perfect square 20 meters by 20 meters (66 feet by 66 feet) with walls that probably reached 7 to 8 meters (21 to 25 feet) in height. There was a large statue and a fireplace on top of the building. The main royal chamber was also built as a square building, 20 by 20 meters (66 by 66 feet), with walls reaching about 7 to 8 meters (23 to 25 feet) in height. Columns divided the interior walls of the royal chamber into several niches, with clay statues in each niche. The buildings in this complex had massive walls 3 to 4 meters thick and made of sun-baked bricks. The columns and some sections of the buildings were built of high-quality fire-baked bricks. The compound was destroyed and abandoned in the ancient era, probably as a result of a war. However, the ruins have survived to the modern era.

Toprak-kala Palace-citadel (Turkmenistan) is one of the largest ancient palace complexes in the territory of Central Asia.[3] It was probably built in about the first century A.D. The compound was built as a palace-citadel on a man-made hill measuring 80 by 80 meters (250 by 250 feet) and rising to about 12 meters in height; it was protected by high brick walls. The complex was divided into several sections. The first group of buildings included a royal chamber with interior walls painted in different colors with floral motifs and decorated with large painted clay statues. The second group included a chamber of warriors and a victory hall decorated with numerous statues of kings and officers with walls painted with various scenes. The third group included living rooms for the king and his family, decorated with paintings, columns, and, probably, small statues. This palace has survived to the present day as a massive ruin on the top of a hill that still captures the imagination because of its size.

Buddhist monasteries in Ajina Tepe (southern Tajikistan), in Fayoz Tepe and Qara Tepe (first to second centuries) (southern Uzbekistan), and in

Ak-Beshim (Kyrgyzstan), as well as some others, provide examples of the distinctive Buddhist architecture of Central Asia. These monasteries consisted of small courts, sanctuaries, encircling passages, and *stupas* (bell-shaped monuments designed as Buddhist shrines). The Buddhist temples were built in many places around the southern belt of what are now the Central Asian republics, as well as in Afghanistan and western China from about the first century A.D. to between the ninth and the eleventh centuries. In general, these temples replicated the Indian models and had a large hall, usually rectangular, with a large statue or symbol of Buddha and a passage around the image for religious processions. Yet, the Buddhist architecture in Central Asia displays the influences of local traditions and building techniques. The temples were usually built of sun-dried bricks, with wooden beams used for the roofing and entrances. The interior walls were frequently beautified with large frescoes depicting various stories from the life of Buddha or various pictures of Buddha. The frescoes were usually painted on the smoothed plaster walls with water-based colors. Unfortunately, no intact Buddhist temples have survived in the region, so it is difficult to discuss specific features of local Buddhist temples and paintings in details.

ISLAMIC ARCHITECTURE

The arrival of Islam changed the architectural landscape of the region tremendously, as Islamic monumental architecture began dominating in both the urban and the rural environments. In fact the religious ensembles became central parts of many cities and towns. The Islamic architecture carried an important message to the people; as George Michell put it, "Islamic building expresses the religious beliefs, social and economic structure, political motivation and visual sensibility of a pervasive unified tradition."[4] The development of the Central Asian architecture is inseparable from the architectural heritage of the Muslim world, though there are many features that put it among the most audacious and unique legacies of Islamic civilization. The local rulers—from the Khorezm-shahs and Sultans of the Seljuk dynasty to Timur and the late Khans of Bukhara and Khiva—ordered the building of magnificent and rich monuments that rose among the sand and oases and captured the imaginations of travelers, who generated legends about the immense richness of this region.

One of the most popular architectural forms in Central Asia was the four-*iwan* courtyard. (An *iwan* is a vaulted hall or space, walled on three sides, with one end entirely open usually in arch form.) It could be found both in religious and secular buildings. Another important architectural element was a large portal *(pishtaq),* usually placed in front of mosques, mausoleums, or *madrasas*. These portals are usually large and tall and are clearly visible to every person who approaches a mosque: they designate the main entrance and signify the main direction where all Muslims have to go and bring their thoughts. The third element is a fired-brick high-rising egg- or helmet-shaped cupola that gives a magnificent and exuberant feeling to the building. Such cupolas are sophisticated pieces of engineering and were built by medieval masters without machines.

Most of the Islamic ensembles consist of three parts: a mosque, a minaret, and a *madrasa*. Mosques were traditionally built in a rectangular shape with an egg-shaped dome on the top. Islamic tradition prohibits painting any earthly pictures, as well as human portraits, or erecting statues along the walls of the mosques, but it does not oppose beautification by other means—the introduction of geometrical patterns, architectural features, or *Kufi* writings of phrases from the Quran. The same rule applies to the interior decoration of Islamic religious buildings. One of the most important structures of every mosque is the *mihrab,* an arch-shaped niche in the wall. The *mihrab* serves two purposes. The first and most important one is that it shows the direction to Kaaba (in Mecca). Second, it serves acoustic purposes, for it permits the voice of the Imam to resonate so that all worshipers can hear it during prayer. Unlike the altar in the Christian world, the *mihrab* has to be kept simple and empty at all times. No pictures or sculptures are allowed. The internal decoration in many mosques included the Muslim rosary, which has 99 beads that derive from the 99 names of Allah, as described in the Quran. Every functioning mosque possesses an ablution fountain with running water that is usually located in the center of the courtyard or close to the entrance of the mosque.

Minarets have always been built next to the mosques as tall, slender, usually cylindrical towers with stairs inside. On top of the minaret is a small room with egg-shaped or pointy domes that have open arch-shaped windows. Unlike the massive bell-towers in the Christian world, the minarets never carry a bell; traditionally, only a *muezzin* calls people to prayer. Therefore, the minarets are tall, light, and gorgeous.

Islamic educational institutions—the *madrasas*—were very often (but not always) built next to the large mosques as modest building complexes with classrooms, offices, and square inner courtyards lined with small, simple lodging cells *(hujra)*. The courtyard was traditionally formed by two- and sometimes three-story buildings of a rectangular shape with an *iwan* in the center of each side. Students and resident scholars lived in cells arranged along the intermediate walls on two or more levels. Students usually studied in summer under the open sky sitting on the floor carpet in small circles spread around the courtyard or in winter in various rooms. The *madrasa* usually operated under the generous sponsorship of rulers, merchants, local communities, and special trust endowments *(waqf)*.

The members of Sufi orders (dervishes) lived in monastic isolation from the earthy world in special monastic-style complexes *(khanaqas)*. These buildings were very modest, had no lavish decorations, and were solely designed to provide year-round accommodation and a spiritual environment for group and individual meditation. The complexes included living rooms, libraries, a kitchen, and halls for group meditations. Unlike Christian monasteries, the *khanaqas* in Central Asia never owned large estates where dervishes were obliged to work. Yet, by the eighteenth and nineteenth centuries, the dervish orders had grown significantly and acquired strong political influence in the courts of the local rulers. This could be seen in the growing numbers of *khanaqas* that were spread around cities and towns across the region.

Mausoleums were built in various sizes but usually strictly followed the classic architectural design of the early Islamic era. Early Islamic tradition prohibited the building of any structure above the graves of believers. This custom was strictly followed until the early ninth century, when the Caliph of the Muslim world ordered the building of a mausoleum and thus set a precedent. Thereafter, Islamic mausoleums usually followed the established traditions and symbolism. The cubic shape of the main buildings of mausoleums has deep symbolic meaning in Islamic culture, as the cube symbolizes the sacred Kaaba in Mecca and the dome symbolizes the sky. These symbols together represent the unity of the universe and are replicated time and time again in numerous mausoleums. Mausoleums were usually designed to immortalize the deeds and achievements of the most powerful rulers or to honor the most respected and popular Sufi leaders or saints (e.g., Haji Ahmad Yasavi Mausoleum). Sometimes rulers or wealthy individuals ordered the building of mausoleums to commemorate their favorite and/or important family members. Traditionally, mausoleums consist of two parts: a tomb chamber *(gurkhana)* and a prayer chamber *(ziaratkhana)*. The interior and exterior decorations of these buildings are usually simple and modest.

Central Asia's Islamic architectural legacy can be subdivided into three periods.

The early period of Islamic architecture is represented by the architecture of the eighth to the twelfth centuries.[5] The architecture of this period can be distinguished by several features. One of them is the introduction of fire-baked bricks on a large scale in the public construction of monumental Islamic buildings. These bricks perfectly matched the needs of builders in this very dry and hot desert climate where a harsh sun shines about 200 days a year. The other feature is the specific type of decorations. During this era, the major external decorations were formed by positioning fire-baked bricks into mathematically perfect geometrical patterns, while specially shaped bricks formed calligraphy writing on the walls of the buildings. Not many monuments of this early period have survived to the present, but several of them are worth mentioning.

The Ismail Samani Mausoleum in Bukhara (Uzbekistan) is the most acclaimed monument of that era. This is one of the very few examples of the early Sasanid era (ninth and tenth centuries A.D.) that has survived to modern time. This is a perfect cube-shaped building, 11 meters (36 feet) on each side, with symmetrically built-in arches on each side. There is a modest egg-shaped dome on the top of the cube and four small domelets on the top corners. This building was made of the traditional material of that era—clay bricks—and therefore its walls are about 2 meters (almost 7 feet) thick. The true majesty and uniqueness of the building comes from its perfect geometric raised-brick decoration in a woven pattern. The design elements are organized in perfect symmetrical lines that in turn form a pattern of shades and contrasts that keeps changing with the movement of the sun and therefore makes the building look different from moment to moment. Some elements of the architecture and architectural decorations suggest symbolic links to the religious beliefs of previous eras, including Zoroastrianism, and thus signify a symbolic transition from past to present and a reinvigoration of past cultures in new forms.

Burana Tower (minaret) in Tokmak (Kyrgyzstan) is a fine example of the architecture of the tenth century from the areas east of the traditional cultural centers of *Maveranahr*. This minaret was built in a classic style on the side of a mosque that did not survive to the present era. This minaret is a round-shaped tower on top of an octagon foundation. At present it is about 24 meters (79 feet) in height, although originally it was probably twice that— about 46–50 meters (145–160 feet). It lacks the bright and colorful glazed tiles that can be seen on some monuments in Samarqand or Bukhara. Yet, it is lovely in its simplicity, as layers of clay bricks are organized in perfect geometrical patterns, especially on the upper section of the structure. This is a monument that outlived the medieval city Balasagun, which existed here between the ninth and the thirteenth centuries A.D.[6] It was destroyed during the numerous wars of the medieval era and was never restored. The harsh climate, earthquakes, and human activities damaged and reclaimed all remains of the city but the minaret.

Sultan Sanjar Mausoleum in Merv (Turkmenistan) is a classic example of the architecture of the mid-twelfth century. The lower part of this building is a cube-shaped structure, 27 meters (89 feet) on each side, with very thick walls (up to 5 meters [15 feet] in some parts). A graceful gallery with numerous columns and arches on top of the cube gives some elegance to the building. The mausoleum is topped with a high-flying dome—up to 36 meters (100 feet)—that sits on an elegant drum. In the past, its windows and doors were decorated with intricate metalwork with traditional geometrical patterns. Its exterior was decorated with beautiful geometrically arranged patterns of raised bricks, and its interior was probably ornamented with frescoes and mosaic. This building was built by a local architect, Muhammad Ibn Aziz, from Sarakh, though some scholars dispute this assertion.[7] This is one of the few structures that outlived Merv, once the largest city in the Muslim world; Merv was destroyed by the Mongols and never returned to its past glories. The building was constructed with the traditional material of that era, such as clay bricks, which survived for centuries in the very dry climate of the deserts. Very few elements of the decoration survived to the present era, though there was a major restoration attempt on the eve of the twenty-first century.

Aisha-Bibi Mausoleum, near Taraz (Kazakhstan), is another classic example of the architecture of the eleventh and twelfth centuries. Like other buildings from that era, the lower part of this mausoleum is a cube-shaped structure measuring 7.2 meters (about 24 feet) on each side, with elegant round columns that are narrower in the middle and wider on the top and on the bottom. It has small *iwans* on each side of the building. One of the unique features of the building is its dome, which is conical in shape and of a yellowish-brownish color. Local experts consider it a pearl of medieval architecture in the territory of modern-day Kazakhstan, as it is the only building from that era whose exterior was completely covered with terracotta tiles with geometrical motifs.

Dakhistan Karavan-Sarai (Turkmenistan) is a classic example of the numerous inns that were built along the Great Silk Road in the medieval era. The complex was built probably in the eleventh century. This rectangular structure, which measures 52 by 56 meters (about 172 by 185 feet), was built as a series of galleries around a central courtyard of 37 by 36 meters (about 122 by 119 feet). The living part of the complex consisted of small living rooms and horse stables that were lined up around the courtyard. High, windowless external walls protected the building. In its early days, it probably had corner towers that could serve as observation decks, a desert lighthouse, and a defense tower to protect against marauders. A single fortified entrance protected the complex from uninvited guests.[8]

The second period of Islamic architecture, the classic Timurid period, is represented by the architecture of the fourteenth and fifteenth centuries. Of course, building technologies and architectural thought were evolving all the time. By the twelfth century, Central Asian workshops began producing intricate carved terracotta with turquoise monochrome glazing on a large industrial scale, and many Central Asian decorators began using them widely, especially during the Timurid era. Timurid architecture can be identified by massive foundations that helped to preserve buildings against frequent earthquakes, marble paved central halls, and high rising crowning domes, usually on a drum. Traditionally, gigantic *Kufi* writing runs around the drums, *pishtaq,* and some other parts of the buildings. During this era, beautifully glazed polychromatic tiles became another widely used element of exterior decoration. Some buildings of this era carry signature ribbed domes—the true innovation of the skillful craftsman of the Timurid era. In addition, the interior upper corners of many buildings are decorated with *muqurnas*—large honeycomb-like vaulting that beautifully covers corners of the halls.

Registan Ensemble in Samarqand (Uzbekistan) is the most acclaimed and most recognizable architectural ensemble in Central Asia, and, in the words of Lord George Curzon, "even in ruin, [it is] the noblest public square in the world."[9] It consists of three *madrasas* that face one another and share a nice stone paved medieval square. To the west is the Ulug Beg *madrasa* that was built between 1417 and 1420 on the order of Khan Ulug Beg, Tamerlane's grandson. This is a large rectangular complex. It consists of a building with a large portal *(pishtaq)* that forms the main entrance, and it is flanked by two elegant minarets 33 meters (100 feet) tall. Four *iwans* in the center of each side are complemented by a small mosque across the courtyard from the *pishtaq* and about 50 cells *(hijras)* lined up in two stories. The building is decorated with shiny green, light- and dark-blue tiles on a brown background. These tiles possess both magnificent geometrical patterns and *Kufi* calligraphy writing. To the east is located the second *madrasa*—Shir Dor. It was built by the order of Yalangtush Bahadur, governor of Samarqand. This *madrasa* is nearly identical to Ulug Beg *madrasa* in façade design and size, although it is slightly shorter in length. It doesn't have a mosque and has fewer classrooms *(daryskhanas).* Shir Dor is decorated with almost the same color tiles and similar patterns, but with a striking element on the *pishtaq*'s arch: two lion figures (Shir Dor means lion) are carefully blended into the geometrical and floral tile patterns with the sun beaming behind their backs. The origin and symbolic meaning of these depictions still remain a mystery; some scholars interpret the suns to represent a pre-Islamic Zoroastrian solar symbolism. To the north is located the third *madrasa*—Tillya Kari. It is significantly larger than the other two *madrasas* and was built later than the others—between 1646 and 1660. This is also a rectangular building with a large blue-tiled dome that replicates the architecture of the Ulug-Beg *madrasa* and is asymmetrically situated on the western side of the complex. Large *pishtaq* are complemented on both sides by a two-level gallery with arched balconies. The architects decided to depart from tradition and built two small towers at the left and right corners of the building. The decoration of this complex resembles its predecessors in color and style and in the use of interlacing geometrical and floral motifs. However, this decoration represents another scandalous departure from strict Islamic tradition: the designer placed two large solar symbols that are blended into the floral motif on the top of the *pishtaq*.

Ahmed Yasavi Mausoleum in Turkistan city (Kazakhstan) is a fine example of early Timurid architecture. It was built between 1394 and 1399 in honor of Ahmad Yasavi (?–1166), a founder of a Sufi order that was named after him. Ahmad Yasavi's fame and the order's influence brought the place of his burial to such prominence that people from all over Central Asia and as far as Kazan, on the Volga River, traveled to visit the tomb. In the eyes of Tamerlane, the mausoleum also symbolized the defeat of the Golden Horde. He ordered that its construction be paid for with reparation funds from the defeated enemy. Historians believe that the architect of the building probably was Abd Al Vahhab Shirazi. This is a 65.5-meter-by-46.5-meter (216-by-153.5 feet) rectangular complex. A massive vaulted *iwan* 37.5 meters (123.7 feet) in height guards large curved wooden doors. The doors open to a large square room that is covered by a huge turquoise onion-shaped dome. The actual tomb is located directly across from the entrance and is covered by

Registan Square in Samarqand, Uzbekistan. Courtesy of the Permanent Mission of the Republic of Uzbekistan to the United Nations, 2006.

a smaller ribbed blue dome. On the left side of the complex are the library, kitchen, and several meditation rooms. On the right side of the building are rooms with a well and several additional meditation rooms. A small mosque is located on the left of the tomb and is covered by a small domelet. The exteriors are decorated by geometric patterns formed with baked bricks. The important part of the interior design is the *muqurnas*—large honeycomb-like vaultings that beautifully cover the corners of the halls.[10]

Bibi Khanum Mosque in Samarqand (Uzbekistan) is a famous congregational mosque *(Masjid-i Jami)* and is popularly known as Old Queen Mosque (Bibi Khanum Masjid), after Tamerlane's favorite wife, Surey Mulk Khanum. It was built between 1398 and 1404 and funded by war reparations from India. At the time it was considered the largest mosque in the Muslim world, with sides measuring 167 by 109 meters (551 by 360 feet). It is also considered to be one of the best examples of Timurid grand architecture. The complex consists of four major structures: a *pishtaq* of 35 meters (110 feet) with a beautiful *iwan* of 19 meters (35 feet) and with two minarets built into the corners of the portal that guards a large courtyard; two nearly identical mosques with blue fluted domes on the sides of the internal marble courtyard; and a main building, a rectangular domed mosque. All four structures were connected by elegant and richly decorated arcades supported by about 400 columns. A huge lectern was located in the center of the courtyard, and in the past it held the greatest treasure of the Islamic world—the handwritten earliest copy of the Quran ordered by the Caliph Uthman, one of the four most respected caliphs in Islamic history. The decoration of the building included carved marbles, terracotta, glazed mosaics, and blue and yellow frescoes. In addition, the entrance and the drums supporting the domes were decorated with Quranic verses in gigantic *Kufi* writing style. A court historian once compared the beautiful decoration of the building with the beauty of the Milky Way. However, from the moment it was built, by slaves and craftsmen who were brought from all corners of the huge Tamerlane Empire, it has been cursed. It began falling apart within a few years after its completion and very soon was lying in ruins. Legend claims that one of Tamerlane's youngest wives was in charge of the construction in his absence, but a slave architect fell in love with her and demanded to place just one innocent kiss to the princess's cheek, after which he promised to complete the work on time. Eager to rush the work, she agreed. Tamerlane learned about the incident and ordered her to climb with him to the highest minaret of the mosque, from which he pushed her to death. By the sixteenth and seventeenth centuries, the building had deteriorated so badly that only birds and animals lived there. It was not until the late twentieth century that the Bibi Khanum was partially restored, thereby bringing back some life and romantic beauty to the complex.

The third period of Islamic architecture is the period between the sixteenth and the nineteenth centuries, and it reflects the state of economic and political decline in the region, as Central Asian once again occupied a peripheral status in the international economy because of the downturn of international trade on the Great Silk Road. There were fewer grand projects, with the limited exception of some in the major cultural and economic centers of Samarqand, Bukhara, Khiva, and some others. The builders opted for smaller public buildings and for cheaper materials, as well as for simpler decorations, and the architects of this era often just followed the classic examples of the previous period. There were very few architectural innovations, and new materials and building technologies from the West began appearing in the region only in the late nineteenth century.

Abdullah Khan Fortress-Mosque in Osh city (Kyrgyzstan) is an example of the architecture of the sixteenth and seventeenth centuries in the Ferghana Valley. It was built as a massive building with walls 2.5 meters (about 7 feet) thick, making it look like a fortress rather than a mosque. Its heavy foundation has a rectangular shape, with a size of 15 by 27 meters (about 50 by 90 feet). A massive *pishtaq* with an *iwan* leads to the main hall with a *mihrab* on the western wall. Two smaller halls are located on the sides of the building and were probably added later. Only the *pishtaq* and the front of the building are decorated. The wooden curved doors represent a masterpiece of local handicrafts. The interior of the mosque is decorated in traditional Central Asian geometrical patters. The absence of the lavish decorations of glazed tiles and the compact size of the mosque reflect the economic difficulties facing the region.

Market (Charsu or Chakarsu) of Hatsellers (Taq-i tilpaq Furushan) in Bukhara (Uzbekistan) was probably built by the 1580s and has survived to the present with numerous changes. This complex is an uneven circle covered by a large central dome, which sits on a drum with large arch-shaped windows and numerous domelets around it. It is made of baked bricks that give it the brownish-yellowish color of a desert. Arched entrances lead to traditional trading areas where numerous traders sold their products. The Oriental charm and beauty of the complex is created by the geometrical patterns of the brickwork and the flawless lines of numerous domelets. This simplified decoration was designed to contrast with the rich variety and color of the goods sold inside the market.

SETTLERS' HOUSING

The mass residential architecture of the sedentary population was adapted to the local climate and traditional lifestyle.[11] Distinctive features of traditional housing in Central Asia included flat roofs and a lack of windows or fancy decorations on the outer walls; but this dull exterior appearance was fully compensated by picturesque decorations inside the houses, including skillfully curved doors and pilaster inside the houses and above the galleries around the courtyard. People used local materials, which were the most widely available. In the valleys and oases, the wooden frames were filled with sun-dried clay bricks covered with plaster. In the mountains and forested areas, people used rocks and wood more widely.

Traditionally, a Central Asian house is organized around an inner courtyard. The high windowless mud-brick outer walls, interrupted only by a single door, completely shelter the house and courtyard, transforming a home into a small fortress. This is the feature that distinguishes mostly Central Asian homes from Russian and European houses. These walls protected the household from thieves and marauders (Ali Baba's band is charming and harmless only in the *Tales of the Arabian Nights*) and provided accommodation for large extended families. Until the mid-twentieth century it was not uncommon for three or four generations of people to live together. It was quite common for animals—sheep, cows, horses—to live under the same roof in a separate section of the house. Very often behind these walls more than one house was built as homes for members of an extended family. These little communities hidden behind high walls and nested together created labyrinths of narrow, unpaved streets in towns and cities. This type of housing, with some regional variations, was quite popular in many settled urban areas, such as Kokand, Khujand, Osh, Bukhara, and Samarqand. These traditional houses can still be found in the old parts of cities and villages *(kishlaqs)* in the southern parts of Central Asia. Both types of materials have been used in the countryside until the present time, and some of the building traditions still have a strong influence on private and small-scale housing projects in small cities and towns.

In the 1920s and 1930s, however, Soviet authorities encouraged the introduction of cottage-style single and multifamily stand-alone houses with light fencing and with small gardens, orchards, or cultivated areas attached. Standardized European-style rectangular stand-alone houses with gable roofs and large windows were widely introduced throughout the region. The local governments made considerable efforts to make sure that the major streets of the cities and towns were wide enough to accommodate more traffic. It became obligatory to plant trees, especially poplar, mulberry, and some fruit trees, along the roads within the towns and between the towns, forming an endless line of woodland.

The beginning of urbanization in the region in the 1950s and 1960s brought a new type of housing—three- and four-story red-brick houses with small apartments, usually with one or two bedrooms. The government initiated large-scale construction of apartment buildings not only in the major urban areas but also in small towns, particularly in the area of new large industrial projects (e.g., Qaragandy in Kazakhstan, Mailusuu in Kyrgyzstan, Navai and Almalyk cities in Uzbekistan).

The 1970s and 1980s added a significant number of apartment buildings constructed of concrete panels—new *mikroraions* in Ashgabat, Dushanbe, Frunze, Tashkent, and other cities. These houses were not well adapted to the hot and dry Central Asian climate and were very uncomfortable during the long summers, as during the Soviet era air conditioners were rare and too expensive for the majority of the population.

Traditionally the Central Asian houses did not contain much furniture. As in some countries of the Middle East, the furniture often consisted of a low table of about 0.5 meters (1.5 feet); people sat on floor mats and cushions or on small stools. In addition, practically every room had trunks of various sizes. Many people kept a small box and bookstand for the sacred book—the Quran. Wealthy families could have small bookshelves or trunks for other books and for paperwork. Piles of mats and blankets were used instead of beds, and people usually slept on the floor during the winter and on a special wooden platform in the courtyard or backyard during the summer time. European-style furniture, including beds, tables and chairs, and sofas, began appearing in some private houses by the mid-nineteenth century, but traditional furniture prevailed well into the mid-twentieth century.

All traditional houses were strictly divided into male and female parts (this tradition is still followed in some places in Tajikistan and Uzbekistan) and common areas, where family members dinned together or received guests. Wealthy families provided separate rooms for every wife and often for every female family member, and access to this area was prohibited for male guests and even for relatives. Entering women's rooms is still considered a very offensive act, especially for outsiders. In the meantime, very poor families shared small houses not only with family members but also with their animals, whose space was often separated from the living quarters only by a thin wall.

NOMADIC HOUSING

Nomads traditionally built very little, as in their philosophical worldview humans should disturb the land as little as possible.[12] Therefore, for centuries, their housing was limited to easily assembled temporary tents *(yurt)* in the springs, summers, and falls, while during the winters people lived in dugouts or simple cottages made of sun-dried bricks or rocks or a combination of both. Thus, very few examples of ancient or medieval architecture can be found in vast areas of Kazakhstan, Kyrgyzstan, and Turkmenistan.

Permanent houses were usually very simple, with small windows and a stove that was used for heating the rooms, cooking food, and drying clothes, but the houses often had no chimney. The smoke from the stove usually escaped through a small high window or a special opening in the ceiling. These houses provided permanent shelter, especially during the cold winters, not only for people but also sometimes for young or weak animals that might otherwise die of cold. Therefore, these houses were not a particularly pleasant place to live for long periods, and people tried to escape to their *yurts* (which were always kept nearby) as soon as the weather permitted and then stayed in them from early spring to late autumn.

A traditional *yurt* in Kyrgyzstan, Kazakhstan, some parts of Turkmenistan and Uzbekistan, and in Mongolia was widely used for dwelling, especially in the *jayloo* (summer camps) and during military expeditions.[13] A Kyrgyz *yurt* is typical.[14] It consists of a light, collapsible wooden lattice frame *(kerege)*, which creates a circular wall and a cone-shaped roof with a smoke ring *(tyundyuk)* on the top. The structure of an assembled *yurt* is covered by felt rugs (traditionally made of sheep fleece). The exterior of the *yurt* is often grey for ordinary dwellers and white for rich tribal leaders, although the color of the exterior may vary or may have some nomadic patterns over the exterior walls.

Kazakh women in front of traditional Kazakh yurt. Courtesy of the author, 2006.

The whole *yurt* can be assembled within a few hours and is light enough to be transported on two or three horses. Traditionally, it was a responsibility of women to assemble the light *yurt* after a day's travel.

The interior of the *yurt* was organized in a circle around the walls. It was usually simple and in many ways similar to the traditional organization of houses in the settled areas. The interior of the *yurt* is divided into a man's part *(er zhak)* and a woman's part *(aial zhak)*, and the center is reserved for a fireplace. The floor is often covered by area rugs and by a *kurpacha* (a traditional Kyrgyz cotton-filled quilt or thin mattress). Wealthy families cover the frame with wall panels and display various signs of wealth and social status on the walls—expensive fur clothes, weapons, skins of prey animals. In the meantime, ordinary people hang the clothes and tools that they use in their everyday life on the walls—horse saddles, bags, and weapons. The place under the wall across the entrance is called *tur* and is the most honorable place in the house. It is traditionally reserved for the most respected family members, *aksakals*, (literally "white bearded" in Turkic, elderly and most respected members of the local communities) or important guests. The family head usually sleeps to the right of the *tur*, and this place is typically separated from the rest of the room by a light screen.

Typical interior decoration of a Central Asian yurt. Courtesy of the author, 2006.

Nomadic housing was quite popular in many parts of what are now Kazakhstan, Kyrgyzstan, Turkmenistan, and Uzbekistan well into the 1930s. The Soviet government implemented a campaign of forceful sedentarization of the pastoral nomads in Central Asia in the late 1920s and early 1930s, forcing people to move into standard houses and apartment buildings. Yet, the *yurts* survived in remote rural areas as a symbol of the local population's link to the past.

MODERN ARCHITECTURE

The architectural landscape in Central Asia fundamentally changed during the twentieth century. During the Russian Imperial era, the new architectural impact was most visible in the cities and towns in the vast Kazakh steppe and in Tashkent and was limited in other parts of Central Asia. The Russian authorities built several new cities on the sites of small villages, including Skobelev (now Ferghana), Krasnovodsk, Pishkek (now Bishkek), and Vernyi (now Almaty). New construction was halted for nearly a decade at the beginning of World War I and the civil war (1918–1922). Since the Russian Imperial era, the dominant feature of Central Asian urban centers has been the coexistence of so-called new city districts, with European-style planning, architecture, and wide streets, and so-called old city districts *(eski shaar)*, with, often, typical Central Asian–style houses, *chaikhanas*, mosques, and twisted, narrow streets. The Soviet authorities believed that the narrow and zigzagging streets of Central Asian cities and towns and the chaos of the bazaars should give way to the Soviet models. The architects and engineers laid out modern landscapes and architectural planning for both new and old cities. In the process, they destroyed many old residential houses and public buildings, especially religious ones—mosques, *madrasas,* and mausoleums. Often, whole districts were bulldozed to make way for new apartment buildings, factories, sports and art centers, and schools. These models were driven by the Soviet concept of industrialization and urbanization and were specially designed for the new mode of transportation that began arriving in the region in mass only in the 1930s—cars.[15] Along with this came an important change—the rise of new urban centers, such as Alma-Ata, Ashgabat, Dushanbe, Frunze (now Bishkek), Tashkent, and many others, while old cultural and political centers—Bukhara, Khiva, Kokand, Samarqand, Uzgen, and others—experienced steep declines. The Soviet city planners tried to compensate for the lack of diversity, color, and architectural fantasy in the newly built urban centers with significant investments in landscaping, planting trees and bushes on a large scale and creating the so-called green-zones of parks and playgrounds.

The Soviet authorities introduced these changes in three stages. The first stage is usually associated with the period from the 1920s to the 1940s, the second with the period from the 1950s to the 1960s, and the third with the years from the 1970s to the 1980s.

The first large-scale investments in the construction sector came between the mid-1920s and the 1940s, as many public and residential buildings were constructed, along with numerous factories and industrial plants. In most cases, their architecture reflected a combination of classicism and Soviet constructivism , sometimes combined with Central Asian traditional ornamentation, which was incorporated into interior and exterior decorative elements. In the 1930s, many government and cultural buildings were built in the neoclassic monumental or Soviet constructivism style, becoming signature ensembles in every capital. Representative examples of that era include the Ashgabat textile factory (architect V. M. Coldish, 1927); the Uzbek Academy of Science Headquarters in Tashkent (architect G. N. Svarichevskii, 1928); Uzbekistan's Government House in Tashkent (architect S. N. Polupanov, 1932); the Kyrgyz Culture Ministry (architect A. P. Zenkov, 1926); and the Abai Theatre in Alma-Ata (architect N. A. Protakov, 1941).

In the 1950s and 1960s, massive, monumental buildings in the neoclassic style, with the obligatory weighty pillars and portals sometimes decorated with curved Soviet or national symbols, appeared in the Central Asian cities. Examples of this include the Turkmen Academy of Science Ensemble (architect L. K. Ratinov, 1952); the Turkmen Council of Ministers (architect V. M. Novosadov, 1952); the elegant Uzbek Navoi Theater in Tashkent (architect A. V. Schusev, 1938–1947); the Kazakh Academy of Science Headquarters in Alma-Ata (architect A. V. Schusev, 1957); the Tajik Aini Theater in Dushanbe (architect D. I. Bililin, 1939–1946); Tajikistan's Government House (architect S. L. Anisimov, 1950); the City Council in Frunze (now Bishkek) (architect P. P. Ivanov, 1956); Kyrgyzstan's Government House (architect G. Nazarian, 1954); the Kyrgyz Polytechnic Institute Building in Frunze (architect E. G. Pisarskii, 1954), the Concert Center *Mir* in Ashgabat (architect F. M. Evseev, 1964); the Dushanbe Hotel (architect G. U. Aizikovich, 1964); and the *chaikhana* Dostuk in Dushanbe (architect G. V. Solominov, 1960).

In the 1970s and 1980s, many industrial centers were significantly enlarged, and numerous three-, five-, and, later, six- and nine-story apartment buildings were built in order to quickly resolve the shortage of dwellings. These buildings created very large residential districts. Most of them built of red bricks or, later, concrete, reinforced concrete, and large panels in a solid but faceless style. Locals often call them *khrushchevki,* after the name of the Soviet leader who promoted the building of mass and cheap accommodation.

Representative examples of this era include the Turkmen Intourist Hotel (architect A. R. Akhmetov, 1967); the architectural ensemble of Tashkent's Central Square (architect E. G. Rozanov, 1970); the building of the Cabinet of Ministers in Tashkent (architect B. S. Menzentsev, 1967); the Hotel Uzbekistan in Tashkent (architect I. A. Merport, 1974); Kazakhstan Hotel in Alma-Ata (architect E. K. Diatlov, 1960); the Central Sport Complex in Alma-Ata (stadium) (architect V. Z. Katsev, 1966); Alma-Ata's central bus station (architect V. A. Babenko, 1967); Kyrgyzstan Hotel in Frunze (architect E. G. Pisarskii, 1971); the Kyrgyz Supreme Court in Frunze (architect V. V. Kurbatov, 1973), and the Kyrgyz Academic Theater in Bishkek (architect F. M. Evseev, 1970).

Throughout the Soviet era, the Central Asian cities and towns always maintained one distinguished institution that did not exist in many parts of Russia—large bazaars. Even at the heights of the collectivization process and the campaigns against "the relics of bourgeois private entrepreneurship" that were vigorously launched throughout the Soviet Union, the bazaars in Central Asia continued to thrive. They always provided viable alternatives to the dreadful shopping experience of the state-controlled superstores and shops. The bazaars were usually built in proximity to the city centers and provided everything—from exotic Asian food to fresh fruits and vegetables and from locally made souvenirs to handicraft items to various consumer goods, including imported items that miraculously found ways to the local market—from American jeans to Indian textiles and Italian shoes.

POSTINDEPENDENCE TRENDS

The Central Asian architectural landscapes have undergone fundamental changes since 1991. The newly independent governments lifted the rigid Soviet-era restrictions and channeled large inflows of private and public investments into the construction sector, including private housing construction. By the early 2000s, all the Central Asian capitals had changed beyond recognition, with new government and private office buildings, new, prestigious hotel skyscrapers that housed such international chains as Hyatt, Marriott, Renaissance, and Sheraton, and newly built national mosques that were given central locations. In addition, hundreds of small and large retail stores and European- and Asian-style restaurants, teahouses, clubs, and service centers have appeared in all major cities and towns. One country—Kazakhstan—even decided, in 1994, to move its capital from the warm but crowded Almaty to the inhospitable but vast open space of the former Tselinograd, on the northern shores of the Ishim River. The capital was named Astana, and within its first decade it received more than $3 billion in investments, mainly for the building of district after district of supermodern private and government office buildings and headquarters for local and international corporations.

There was a major shift in the conceptualization of the symbolic meaning of public architecture. Soviet symbolism, constructivism, and the modest and often colorless practicality and mass usage of cheap materials of that era were abandoned. Post-Soviet architecture began emphasizing national symbols and monumentalism, asserting the independence of the republics and the power and might of the newly independent governments. New construction projects are often very expensive both in their design and in their decorations, as Almaty and Tashkent both plan to bid to host future Olympic Games.[16] Many buildings have been lavishly decorated through the use of the most modern building materials, expensive local and Italian marble, and modern expressionist and traditional folk-inspired sculptures and murals. To ensure that the newly built architectural complexes would highlight the modern nature of the newly independent republics and their adherence to the principles of globalization, the governments invited leading construction and design companies from France, Italy, Turkey, the United States, and other countries to work on new projects.

In Almaty, Astana, and Ashgabat, for example, new large presidential complexes were built in a modern style with large cubic buildings made of concrete and glass and often decorated with expensive imported marble and surrounded by beautiful, *Thousand-and-One-Nights*-style parks, gardens, fountains, flowerbeds, and lawns.[17]

The governments also invested significant funds in the restoration of major architectural monuments both for their symbolism and to foster tourism. Thus, for example, multimillion-dollar restoration projects were completed in such cities as Turkistan (Kazakhstan); Uzgen and Manas (Kyrgyzstan); Bukhara, Khiva, and Samarqand (Uzbekistan); and Kune-Urgench, Merv, and Nisa (Turkmenistan).

Private housing also took off as wealthy individuals raced to the cities' suburbs to build single-family houses and cottages that often were built either like somber fortresses or, in rare cases, like little pseudoclassic-style palaces, both often surrounded by high prison-like walls and metal wire. Most of these new constructions in the suburban areas display an eclecticism that has more to do with wealth and the desire to show off than with traditional or national styles. However, the upper middle class in many provincial areas of the region, especially in Uzbekistan and Tajikistan, has gone back to the traditional architectural style of the early twentieth century. Local builders very often use traditional techniques (frame houses built with sun-dried bricks), with the division of homes into male and female parts, traditional *aivans* (square yard usually in the middle of the property) and Asian decoration.

Yet, the picture is less rosy in smaller cities and towns, especially in remote areas, as the lavish development in the major metropolitan cities has come at the expense of many projects in the provinces. Because of the extremely limited resources available to local governments, they have significantly downsized investments in the public construction and infrastructure sectors. In the meantime, many local industries have been shut down and have never recovered, negatively affecting the local tax and investment bases. In addition, private investments and international aid failed to materialize on a large scale. Thus, these cities and towns have very little new construction, which has been concentrated mainly in the individual housing sector, retail shops, and oriental *chaikhanas* and religious buildings, and while the existing infrastructure, such as roads, canals, parks, schools, and hospitals, decays.

NOTES

1. Calum MacLeod and Bradley Mayhew, *Uzbekistan: The Golden Road to Samarkand* (New York: Odyssey, 1999).

2. For detailed descriptions see Annageldy Esenov, *Istoria arkhitektury Turkmenistana* [The history of architecture of Turkmenistan] (Asghabat: Rukh, 2001), pp. 126–131, 154.

3. Ibid., pp. 149–153, 165–166.

4. George Michell, Ernst J. Grube, et al., eds., *Architecture of the Islamic World: Its History and Social Meaning, with a Complete Survey of Key Monuments* (London: Thames and Hudson, 1978), p. 7.

5. For details, see Galina Pugachenkova and L. I. Rempel, *Ocherki iskusstva Srednei Azii* [Essays on the art of Central Asia] (Moscow: Nauka, 1982).

6. About Balasagun and other cities in the area, see Vasilii Bartold, *Raboty po istoricheskoi geografii* [Works on historical geography] (reprint, Moscow: RAN, 2002).

7. Sarakh is the name of a medieval city located in present-day Turkmenistan.

8. For detailed descriptions see Esenov, *Istoria arkhitektury Turkmenistana,* pp. 412–414, 435; Oktay Aslanapa, *Turkish Art and Architecture* (New York: Praeger, 1971).

9. Cited in MacLeod and Mayhew, *Uzbekistan,* p. 158.

10. For a detailed architectural description of the complex, see Sheila Blair and Jonathan Bloom, *The Art and Architecture of Islam, 1250–1800* (New Haven and London: Yale University Press, 1994), pp. 37–45.

11. In this review I cover housing mainly in the nineteenth and twentieth centuries, as this period has been better studied by local and Russian scholars. I exclude the cities and towns in what is now Kazakhstan that were built as early as the sixteenth and seventeenth centuries, often by Russian settlers on the places of former fortresses, karavan-sarais, and small villages. From the beginning, Russian architectural style and building technology dominated in those areas; thus they are beyond the scope

of this review. For detailed research, see Yakov Vinnikov, *Khoziaistvo i byt sel'skogo naselenia Turkmenskoi SSR* [Household, culture and everyday life of the agricultural population of the Turkmen SSR] (Moscow: Nauka, 1969), pp. 143–177.

12. Renat Tuleov, "Iurta kak fenomen kochevoi kultury" [*Yurt* as a phenomenon of nomadic culture], in *Urban and Nomadic Societies in Central Asia: History and Challenges* (Proceeding of International Conference), ed. Meruert Abuseitova (Almaty: Daik-Press, 2004), pp. 310–317.

13. *Kazakhskaia Iurta* [Kazakh *yurt*]. (Introductory article by B. Kairbekova) (Almaty, 1998).

14. Saul Abramzon, *Kirgizy i ikh etnogeneticheskiie i istoriko-kul'turnyie sviazi* [The Kyrgyzs and their ethnic and genetic and historical-cultural relations] (Frunze: Kyrgyzstan, 1999), pp. 125–134.

15. For a comprehensive review, see Esenov, *Istoria arkhitektury Turkmenistana*.

16. See Ilan Greenberg, "Up, Up and Away: New Towers, and Ambition to Match," *New York Times,* June 21, 2006.

17. For examples of modern architecture in Kazakhstan, see Kazakhstan Investment Promotion Center, *Kazakhstan, 2003. State Directory* (Almaty: Kazakhstan Investment Promotion Center, 2004).

8

Gender, Courtship, and Marriage

My lady, that did change this house of mine Into a heaven when that she dwelt therein From head to foot an angel's grace divine Enwrapped her; pure she was, spotless of sin; Fair as the moon her countenance, and wise; Lord of the kind and tender glance, her eyes With an abounding loveliness did shine.

—Hafiz, medieval poet[1]

The image of the Central Asian woman is hidden behind the veil of Eastern mystery and so is quite difficult to grasp. Rivaling the best Shakespeare love sonnets and devoted to women, there are thousands of beautiful love poems written by Eastern poets, medieval scholars, and even cruel khans and sultans. Alexander the Great ignored all women in conquered Europe and Asia, only to come to Central Asia and fall in love with a local princess, Roxana (Rowshanak). Today, a visitor to the region would be surprised to see, in small and large cities and towns, a great cultural diversity among Central Asian women. Indeed, on the streets of Almaty's "Arbat," Bishkek's central Dubovyi Park, or Tashkent's central square and Chilanzar, young women are not much different from those in Turkey, Italy, or Spain: they wear the latest Western fashions, chat in two or three foreign languages, and walk freely and go out with their friends or colleagues.

But just a few minutes' drive into the narrow streets of suburban areas like Tashkent's *Eski Shakhar,* it is a completely different universe: women wear conservative traditional dress according to strict Islamic norms, and the veil is increasingly prominent, very much as in Afghanistan or Iran. Many rural

Turkmen woman guards her family and her possessions. *Zhivopisnaia Rossia. Otechestvo nashe v ego zemel'nom, istoricheskom, plemennon, ekonomicheskom i bytovom znachenii. Tom 10. Russkaia Sredniaia Azia* [Beautiful Russia: our fatherland in its geographical, historical, tribal, economic and everyday life's meaning. Vol. 10. Russian Central Asia] (Saint Peterburg: Izdanie Tovarishchestva M.O. Volfa, 1885), Vol. 10. p. 19.

Uzbek women know little about the world and probably are not allowed to step outside of their homes without the special permission of their husbands or relatives. In terms of their personalities, some Central Asian women may be forceful and assertive, directing a team of men at their workplace, very much as in the United States—but they may well be absolutely silent and obedient at home. In some places, women freely choose their own educational paths, professional careers, or partners, while in other places marriages lock them at home from the first day of family life. Some of the women might very assertively claim to be true and devoted Muslims; at the same time, they would shock their Middle Eastern counterparts with their full rejection of the veiling of faces and of the dominant position of men in family or public life, as they claim that they share with Western feminists a belief in individual freedoms. In one place, a girl might silently accept her parents' dictates about becoming a second or even third wife or being forced into an unwanted marriage to a senior person for a dowry *(kalym)*. Her friend next door, however, might reject any arranged marriages and prefer to choose her spouse herself. There are cities where a man will not let a woman to talk to him without permission, and there are villages where a local grandma *(apa* in Kyrgyz) rules the local government and the whole village, including all men, with an iron hand.

Indeed, the social status of women in Central Asian society is shaped by myriad invisible social and cultural customs, religious traditions, family experiences, educational achievement, and the history of local developments. Gender, courtship, and marriage are interlinked in every society that endorses strong family values and therefore evince a particularly intricate pattern of development because of the shock waves of the Bolshevik revolution, Soviet social engineering, and, recently, the powerful forces of globalization. Gender relations are very complex and are quickly evolving over time.

POWER OF TRADITIONS

Many Western travelers who visited Central Asia in the nineteenth century and on the eve of the twentieth left romantic stories and memoirs about the mystery of Eastern life and especially of Eastern women, who are "moon-faced, red-cheeked, … [and] appear to perfection [on horseback]."[2] In fact, Europe was so much fascinated with the terra incognita of cultures and customs of Asia that not only European men but also women traveled to the East looking for adventures and to experience the life of the courts and even the harems of the local rulers. They brought back the most exciting poems by Hafiz, Omar Khayyam, and others who romanticized women, passion, and love. Many nineteenth-century European painters, such as Jean-Léon Gérome, John Frederick Lewis, and Pierre-Auguste Renoir, produced depictions of women's lives that revealed, in the words of the acclaimed twentieth-century writer Alev Lytle Croutier, "a mysterious, beautiful, and unbelievably repressive world concealed for so many centuries behind the veil."[3]

The real position of women in Asian society, however, turned out to be very different from those picturesque travel notes and romanticized paintings, and the Western public began discovering these realities very soon. Scholars and politicians of both the left and the right agreed that women in late-nineteenth-century and early-twentieth-century Central Asia lived in the most oppressive, conservative, and unfriendly environment to be found in the territory controlled by the Russian Empire.

There were many scholarly, journalistic, and literary works that portrayed women's social environment in very dark colors. Very often, relatives, parents, or husbands viewed women as their property. Many marriages were arranged, and women usually had no say whatsoever in the choice of a partner. Girls as young as 10 or 11 years old were pushed to become wives or concubines in the harems of wealthy men who might be the age of their grandfathers. As in many Middle Eastern countries, should her husband die, a woman was obliged to marry his younger brother or a relative, even if he was just a little boy or an invalid.[4] Most of the women were secluded and isolated behind the high walls of individual houses or harems and never had an opportunity to get a proper education or job. In fact, a young bride entering a family often came under the full control of the mother-in-law or the oldest wife, who might force her to work for 12 or 14 hours a day on a farm or in the family's carpet, food-processing, or catering business. In some places, girls were married out by their families to the highest bidder—the person who would pay the highest *kalym*—or were not allowed to marry the men they loved just because the fiancé was unable to afford the appropriate dowry. Virginity and "reputation" were so jealously guarded that a woman could be stoned to death just for talking to or having a tête-à-tête meeting with a man other than her father, her male blood relatives, or her husband. Unmarried women were ostracized. A married woman was unable to leave even an abusive or paranoid husband. Dating was absolutely unacceptable, and almost all marriages were arranged by parents or matchmakers.[5]

Some Central Asians, including reformers *(jadids),* were not happy with the Western portrayal of their societies as backward and despotic. They claimed that Westerners and Russians simply did not understand and appreciate their traditions. These traditions were established through centuries of development and experiments as communities and extended families, but not individuals, became the centers of the social fabric and ethics. The communities always provided a kind of social safety net to every member in exchange for compliance with communal norms and an understanding that the community would take precedence over individual interests. It was in the interest of the communities to guard family values and to make sure that every member had a partner through arrangements, but not through competition. Families became the nucleus of economic activities and of the survival of households. Thus, arranged marriages helped to preserve the social structure and social stability. If any member of a community experienced a disaster or an accident, whether caused by nature or by people, the whole community would come together to organize communal work (*hashar* in Uzbek), restoring or repairing damaged properties, orchards, or farms, helping to cultivate land, bringing up orphaned children at communal expense, or finding a partner for a widowed woman. Women always had legal rights both under *adat* and *Shariah* laws, but those rights were granted in the local context. For example, women had the rights to divorce, but they were obliged to prove their case (e.g., husband's abuses or impotence) before local courts, as divorce involved dividing properties and ensuring that the woman had the means to survive after separation. Women had a right to a small part of the inheritance in the case of divorce or death of a spouse, but they still needed a guardian to provide personal security against marauders, robbers, or dishonest people. In the view of the communities, that was especially important, as there were no jobs for women in the public sector and the women could have been in extremely vulnerable positions if they lost their breadwinners or their inheritances. There were many justifications for the existing social order, customs, and traditions. Yet, some local policymakers acknowledged that there were shortcomings in the system, as the courts, government, and economy were exclusively dominated by men.[6]

The situation in the areas populated by the nomads was significantly different, but not much better. Women enjoyed more freedoms in their personal lives as a large part of the everyday economy very much depended on their contribution. Thus, women were not obliged to veil themselves, were not prohibited from communicating with representatives of the opposite sex, could travel, and were never locked behind tall walls, as there were simply no walls at all. Central Asia was the only place in the nineteenth-century Muslim world where queens could rule their communities, as did Kurmanjan-Datkha of the Kyrgyz tribes in the Alai Mountains and Guljamal Khanum of the Turkmen tribes in the Akhal and Merv areas.[7] Yet, even nomad women were often forced to marry leaders or representatives of other tribes in order to seal a peace or a political and military union; sometimes they were taken as a kind of a "trophy" in the horseracing competitions or were simply stolen by bachelors who for some reasons could not get married through legitimate means (this tradition was called "steal a girl," or *kyz ala kachu* in Kyrgyz).[8]

Of course, there were exceptions. People do meet accidentally, fall in love, get married and occasionally elope, thus breaking many communal rules. Also, there were many poor men who were never able to afford more than one wife and in some cases none at all. There were reports about women who achieved significant influence over government affairs by skillfully manipulating their husbands or fathers, or who amassed fortunes by carefully managing large merchant businesses behind the scenes, or who became famous poets and writers. Some women even received good educations, but this was a small minority, about 2 or 3 percent of the total population. These exceptions, however, only confirm the norms that governed how women in Central Asian society were treated up to the beginning of the twentieth century.

GENDER AND SOVIET REFORMS

The Bolsheviks came into power in autumn 1917, and they immediately declared the emancipation of all women in the collapsed Russian Empire.[9] Several women swiftly rose to power in the Bolshevik Party, the Bolshevik-led government, and the Red Army ranks, putting a very public face on the socialist principles of freedom and emancipation of women. Nonetheless, it was one thing to declare the principles and a completely different matter to implement them in this very diverse country. The task was especially difficult in Central Asia. The very idea of breaking customs and traditions that regulated social and family life, including those that governed the status of women, shocked many Central Asian people and drove some of them into the ranks of the anti-Bolshevik resistance. In response, the Bolshevik authorities temporarily relaxed their approach and postponed many changes.

It took about a decade after the revolution and civil war to bring back the reform agenda in the mid-1920s. In the first step, the *Shariah* courts and the practice of *adat* law were banned. All family issues, including marriages and birth registrations, were transferred to the secular civil administration, and the Islamic marriage ceremony *(niqah)* was deprived of legal recognition. The newly introduced civil codes fully endorsed the equality of women. The Soviet authorities also banned forced marriages, dowry *(kalym)*, and polygamy, making them criminal offenses with severe punishments.[10] They also opened education to Muslim women of all ages and not only encouraged but also forced women to take schooling. Thousands of women from all over the Russian Federation were sent to Central Asia to teach and train young local women. The latter were, in turn, sent all over the newly created republics, including the most remote villages and towns, with a single mission—to eliminate illiteracy among all groups of people and especially among the local women.

All of this fighting for the emancipation of female equality culminated in a comprehensive, forceful, and far-reaching campaign—called *hujum*—which was launched in 1927 and lasted for more than a decade.[11] In this campaign, the Bolshevik authorities targeted the single most visible symbol of the past life and traditions—Muslim women's veils *(paranja* in Uzbek). This campaign turned into a large-scale battle between the new authorities, who tried to enforce what they perceived as "modern" and "liberating" practices, on one side, and all the forces of the traditional society, starting with the former and present religious authorities, communal leaders, and many women themselves, on the other side. To understand the complexity of the issue, we have to remember that only one country in the world apart from the USSR had implemented the radical policy of emancipation and unveiling women in the early twentieth century—Turkey, under Kemal Ataturk. In Soviet Central Asia, the battlefield covered most of the cities and towns in the traditionally sedentary areas of Kyrgyzstan, Tajikistan, Turkmenistan, and Uzbekistan. The battle was fiercely fought, and opponents of female emancipation killed thousands of Central Asian women who dared to challenge the centuries-old traditions and to accept the Soviet system. The life of Urkuya Salieva, a simple Kyrgyz woman, is a good example of the ferocity of this battle: young Urkuya and her entire family were stabbed to death for rebelling against the suppressed position of women in the society and for organizing a cooperative.

The intensity of the struggle was fueled by its symbolic meaning. For the Bolsheviks who struggled to establish the Soviet system in the Central Asian republics, it was an attempt to create a powerful army of reformers, as one researcher put it—a "surrogate proletariat."[12] They believed that the Central Asian women would cheer their liberation from "patriarchal oppression" by joining the ranks of the Soviet supporters. Meanwhile, their opponents believed that family traditions and the position of women in this system were the last bastion and the last symbols of the traditional ways of life and resistance to "godless atheistic propaganda" and development. By the late 1930s, the battle was over, as the Soviet authorities claimed their victory over the hearts and minds of Central Asian women, especially the younger generation. They reported mass unveilings, with a few "unfortunate" exceptions when some older women refused to do so. This was wishful thinking, for there were many women, especially in the rural areas, who maintained their strict Islamic dress code well into the 1960s.

These changes in dress code and in public appearance did not make a significant impact on the status of women at the family level. Traditional social roles that highlighted the domination of masculine identity—the man as breadwinner and the woman as mother and housekeeper—remained in place. Many families maintained a high level of control over women's life, demanding that they continue to do all the housework and perform community-oriented duties, such as serving at large family and community events. Women were still restricted in personal movement, educational choice, and individual development. Yet, gradually, social reforms, urbanization, and economic changes began affecting the everyday life of Central Asian women to a greater degree. One of the greatest changes was the creation of greater public space for women and their mass involvement in politics and in social and economic activities.

Women in Public Life

One of the main outcomes of the *hujum* campaign was the increasing and clearly visible and substantial presence of women in public life. The Soviet authorities actively recruited indigenous women into the Communist Party ranks and encouraged them to take up jobs in the public sector, often creating jobs and maintaining job quotas specifically assigned for women. By the mid-twentieth century, working women became the norm.

Paradoxically, even during this campaign and for many years after, no single mass feminist organization appeared in Central Asia. True, the Soviet authorities sponsored several large congresses of "liberated women" and created women's sections *(zhenotdels)* in the Party apparatus and trade unions. These organizations became important tools in the promotion of the equality of women in the public sector; although they never turned into feminist organizations, such as exist in the United States and Europe.

However, Central Asian women were slow to leave the secluded life in their households to join the labor force and the government. In the 1920s and 1930s, they entered female-only environments—all-female schools, all-female groups at farms and factories. Gradually, mixed-gender working environments became quite common, especially during and after World War II. Paradoxically, there emerged new traditions and perceptions about the role of the sexes in society and in the labor force. For example, several professions became regarded as "desirable" for women, and so women became medical nurses, school teachers, textile workers, accountants, office workers, and trade union administrators. Other fields were popularly regarded as "unacceptable," and therefore women did not become drivers, police officers, or army officers. Despite all these limitations, Central Asian women were regularly appointed to top positions, including in the local and provincial administrations and ministerial ranks. They even became directors, senior accountants, and deputies in many enterprises and were elected to the local and national legislature in large numbers.

Schools and institutes of higher learning and, later, universities played a critical role in developing new attitudes among women. One of the most important changes in public perception and traditions during the Soviet era involved the high prestige accorded to education, among both men and women. This was in sharp contrast to the pre-Soviet era, where the education of a girl was widely considered to be an unnecessary luxury. By the 1960s and 1970s, most of the schools (about 90 percent) had become mixed, though there were still some specialized all-boys or all-girls schools or institutes (e.g., the Kyrgyz Women's Pedagogical Institute). The schools and universities introduced to the new generation of women a new culture that included living, studying, and working in a mixed-sex environment and to new forms of activities, such as active sports (volleyball, basketball, and hiking, though women's soccer, boxing, and wrestling were considered "inappropriate") and going out and socializing. Undertaking studies at the postsecondary level at institutions far from home introduced women to the concept of living independent of parents or relatives before marriage. It became quite common for women, having spent four or five years studying for a degree in the large cities, to not want to come back to their home villages or towns. Instead, these women tried to get jobs and settle in urban centers.

In 1924, women in Kazakhstan and Tajikistan received the rights to vote and stand for elections, about 20 years ahead of women in France (1944), Italy (1945), and Mexico (1947).[13] Yet, women were significantly underrepresented in the public sector well into the 1950s. In order to speed up the emancipation of women, the government also introduced "positive discrimination" practices and created an informal system of "quotas." This system assigned a specific percentage of all positions in the Party, public organizations, education, management, government, and legislature of all levels to women (this usually fluctuated between 25 and 35 percent in the 1970s and 1980s).[14] A special system of initiatives and punishments was created in order to force local authorities, governments, and enterprise directors to meet these quotas.

Changing Traditions

As in many other developing countries, the extended family in Central Asia has always been considered a cornerstone of society. Yet, family traditions as well as the role of women have been quite different from country to country and have been very much determined by income levels, professional status, and, most important, by the rural/urban divide (in the early 2000s, between 45 and 60 percent of the population in Central Asia still lived in rural areas, down from 80–90 percent in the 1930s).

Interestingly, the Soviet system, which attempted to introduce new traditions and customs into family life, created a very peculiar "Soviet" concept of family life and ethics. This combined the early-twentieth-century ideals of the Russian conservative urban middle class with some local traditions and customs. Central Asia's local customs and traditions have had a greater influence in the remote areas, even as lifestyles have been more liberal and Westernized in the major metropolitan centers. This development also preserved patterns of social and sexual behavior that were similar to those in many agrarian societies in Europe and the Americas at the time when com-munal ties were still strong.

Among the major changes was the shifting age of first marriage, which con-stantly moved up throughout the twentieth century. The growing importance of education and the ban on teenage marriages significantly contributed to this trend. Yet, even in the 1970s and 1980s, men and women were expected to be married by their early twenties.[15] Marriage signified the beginning of adulthood and full maturity in the eyes of extended family and commu-nity members, and young couples were allowed to move from their parents' homes and establish their own households. The marriages have usually, but not always, symbolized the independence of young people, as they gained a voice in the extended family and the community.

The second important change was the arrival of dual-income families as more and more women picked up jobs in the public sector. By the 1950s and 1960s, it was widely expected that women would work full-time or at least part-time; only wealthy or very conservative families could afford one work-ing partner. This, in turn, reinforced the social position of women both in the family and in the community. Women became more independent in the choice of their education, workplace, and time of marriage, though they were expected to continue doing all the housework, cleaning, household mainte-nance, and childrearing.

These developments provoked the third change—some independence in the choice of a partner. There were significant changes in attitudes toward dating that would have been simply unthinkable in the previous era, because in the past very often the groom and bride saw each other for the first time only at the wedding. However, by the 1960s and 1970s, dating became widely acceptable, though frequent changes in dating partners were strongly condemned and it was still expected that a man would approach a woman first, not the other way around. In many close-knit communities, it was not uncommon for the elders (aksakals) to stop a young dating couple literally in the middle of the street and give them a lecture about family values, express their approval or disproval of this particular coupling, and/or suggest the speeding up of the wedding date.

The next important change was that women and children received signifi-cant legal and social protection in the new environment. It became easier for women to file for divorce or to regulate the number of children in their mar-riages, although having a child outside wedlock was still considered a scandal. Abusive husbands could be restrained by law-enforcement institutions. In the case of divorce, courts usually sided with women, nearly automatically giving children to mothers and obliging men to provide child support to their chil-dren until the age of 18. For the first time in the history of the region, many women entered the legal profession as court judges, lawyers, and prosecutors, thus balancing the male bias in the practice of family law.

Yet, despite all these changes, it was widely expected that couples would marry only once and remain together for the rest of their life. Communities and working collectives could get involved in "ensuring" the continuity of a marriage by publicly discussing the behavior of one or both partners; they could do this by condemning anything that came under the Soviet category of "antisocial behavior," such as adultery, multiple dating, alcoholism, and child neglect, though this practice of public discussion was largely abandoned by the mid-1970s. It was widely expected that only married couples would live together, and unmarried couples who lived together were not common.

One of the manifestations of this conservatism was that there was almost no discussion of sexual issues either in the public or in schools, as it was considered the role of the traditional families to transmit the necessary information to the younger generations. Yet, family planning was introduced, and women could get consultations and help at public medical centers and clinics. Any expression of sexuality in public was disapproved. All foreign and even domestic movies and media were severely censored, and all scenes that even remotely resembled sexual activities were cut out. The distribution and even the possession of pornography was prosecuted, and sexual offenders, if convicted, could spend the rest of their lives in Siberian prisons. It was not surprising when a woman representing the Soviet Union in a televised dialogue with an American audience proudly declared: "There is no sex [in the Soviet Union]." In this environment, even buying a condom became an adventure to such an extent that a whole line of jokes *(anekdots)* emerged about the funny situations that occurred when people tried to buy the "item" but shied away from saying its actual name. Not surprisingly, many teenagers and young people genuinely believed that babies were bought in the bazaars. But, jokes apart, inadequate sexual education often led to unwanted pregnancies, and consequently to abortions, the level of which was quite high by Western standards, as well as the spread of sexually transmitted diseases and other related problems.

Dating, Matchmaking, and Weddings

The modern changes and urbanization that had intensified since the mid-twentieth century left imprints on national traditions related to the pre-marriage experience by creating new customs, but myriad other social customs, norms, values and even superstitions still exist.

Traditionally, when young people reached the age for marriage and expressed a desire to establish a family of their own, all close and distant relatives were put on alert. Family and community members, friends, classmates, and colleagues were given the task of finding an appropriate spouse. They regularly organized various events and often set up "accidental" meetings between prospective partners. Professional matchmakers and fortunetellers were regularly called for help. In the rural areas of Tajikistan and Uzbekistan, there was a whole class of professional matchmakers who not only arranged marriages for whole villages or towns but also organized and worked on developing positive images for their clients. In addition, there were matchmakers who arranged marriages for close-knit groups—celebrities, the political elite, wealthy merchants, and exclusive ethnic or religious communities.

Of course, as in many Western countries, young people could meet each other at various events—at the cinemas, theaters, teahouse, public parks. or sport events—and to take the initiative into their own hands. The main difference was that they were obliged to introduce each other to their prospective in-laws, and the parents' approval was a must if they decided to date seriously. The marriage was considered an important achievement for the parents of the bride and groom, as it often sealed a union or partnership not only between two families but also between kinship clans and "ensured" the continuity of two honorable and respected lineages. It was expected that young people would obey the parents' decision, especially in rural areas. Many factors affected the individual experience. By the 1970s and 1980s, communal and ethnic ties influenced the choice of a partner to a lesser degree, though interethnic marriages remained relatively rare. Usually they did not exceed 12–18 percent of total marriages and were more common between locals, for example, Uzbeks and Tajiks, Kazakhs and Kyrgyzs, and less frequent between the locals and "newcomers"—for example, Russians, Germans, and Koreans.

Young people dated each other anywhere between 6 and 18 months or even longer. It was strongly encouraged that there be no sexual relations between dating partners before marriage, as parents on both sides still jealously required the bride's chastity. This rule was strictly followed in small villages and towns but was more flexible in the large cities. Of course, young people found ways around the rules, still "innocently" claiming, like their famous counterpart in the United States, "I did not have sex with this woman [man]." Nonetheless, expressions of affection or sexuality, such as passionate kissing in public, have remained relatively rare.

Yet, the search for potential partners for a young person could be a short one, as parents or relatives might arrange the marriage, choosing the partner they considered most appropriate for their child. Their power to influence their offspring's marriage was very strong, as it relied not only on customs and traditions but also on economic and social initiatives—after all, they usually paid for the wedding and honeymoon and raised funds to help the young

Central Asian wedding. Courtesy of the author, 2006.

couple buy their first home and also household items. The position of the parents was especially important, as the family of the bridegroom was expected to pay the family of the bride a large dowry *(kalym)* in the form of money or gifts. The size of the *kalym* could vary from symbolic gifts to very substantial sums of money (sometimes up to three to five years' average salary).

The wedding was always a grandiose event that had many symbolic meanings. As a norm and in order to highlight Islamic identity and values, most of the families invited Islamic clerics to perform the Islamic marriage ceremony *(niqakh)*. Only after that would young couples happily go to the Soviet registry office (ZAGS) and have their customary photos taken in front of various Soviet monuments and memorials. The bride and groom were introduced to all each other's relatives and friends and to community members. By organizing large weddings, the clans or extended families showed their strength and their mutual solidarity. Weddings also created excellent opportunities for social networking through the invitations extended to local community leaders and to eminent community members who had achieved prominence somewhere else—at the district, province, or national level. Young families were introduced to members of social and political patronage networks who could be useful for them later in the search for jobs or business opportunities or time of need. In return, all invited guests brought gifts and, in a recent trend, cash that could create a financial foundation for beginning a family life.

Family Life

As in many other countries of Central Asia and the Middle East, all Central Asian men and women of adult age are expected to establish a family, and an extended family is a cornerstone unit in the Central Asian society. This concept has changed little in the twenty-first century. Yet, the Central Asian republics are listed among the countries with moderate marriage rates in the world, with Uzbekistan at 16th place with 7.9 marriages per 1,000 population, followed by Tajikistan, with 6.8; Kazakhstan, with 6.2; Kyrgyzstan, with 6.0; and Turkmenistan, with 5.9. By comparison, this rate is 10.7 for the United Kingdom; 8.6 for the United States; and 8.0 for Turkey.[16] People keep strong personal relations not only with their parents and grandparents but also with all their close and distant relatives, as they rely on them for help and support. It is considered a social obligation to know the names of all close and distant relatives, including all cousins and nephews, sometimes more than 100 people in total, as well as their birthdays and their most important anniversaries. Among the first questions people ask each other when they meet are questions about the health and wellbeing of family members and other relatives. In the past, most young families remained within their birth communities and rarely moved away to different cities or towns. Traditionally, families attend most important celebrations, such as weddings, the birth of new children, and circumcisions and help their relatives and community in the upbringing of their children.

It is quite common for several generations of close relatives to live together in the same place and sometimes in the same housing complex. For example, very often a traditional household consists of an adult married couple, their parents, and their children. No wonder that some Central Asian republics are ranked among top 50 countries in the world with the biggest households. For example, Uzbekistan is in 13th place, with an average of 5.9 people per dwelling; Kyrgyzstan is in 45th place, with 5.2 people per dwelling, and Kazakhstan and Turkmenistan share 48th place, with 5.1 people per dwelling. For comparison, the numbers are 2.1 in Sweden; 2.3 people in the United Kingdom; 2.8 in the United States, and 3.0 in Japan.[17] In the past, it was customary for married sons to move into their parents' households, though at present this tradition is slowly disappearing. After marriage, young people are obliged to ask for their parents' permission to move out of their parents' houses and to build or to buy a house of their own. Still, very often, young families stay at their parents' home if they lack the financial means to move out, as there has been a significant shortage of cheap and affordable accommodations in all major urban areas and a shortage of land in major oases. These traditional families maintain and transmit cultural, social, and religious norms and traditions. The impact of this is twofold. On the one hand, this makes families an extremely effective survival unit, where people get personal, financial, and moral support in these time of social and economic turmoil. They can also acquire skills or get training and jobs through family connections. On the other hand, these families impose very strict gender-age hierarchies and conformity, and very often they reject social, political, and cultural innovations and resist many outside ideas or changes.

It has been considered a sign of happiness in a family to have many children. Rural families with 6, 7, and even 10 children were quite common. Until the 1930s, wealthy members of society practiced polygamy and had several wives, as Islamic law (*Shariah*) allows up to four wives; this practice was banned by the Soviet government and later by the governments of the independent Central Asian states. Nevertheless, a small percentage of men continued practicing polygamy, especially in rural areas.

In order to keep the parents of big families in the workforce, the Soviet authorities created huge welfare, health-care, and childcare networks that covered all towns and cities in the region by the 1970s and 1980s. Between 31 and 52 percent of children attended childcare centers, and almost 100 percent of school-age kids were enrolled in schools.[18] This educational system began to erode the very essence of patriarchal families—parent-children relations.

Urbanization, which arrived in Central Asia in the 1950s and 1960s, also significantly changed the lifestyle of the people. The most important change was that the urban families began having considerably fewer kids. In addition, it became a part of urban tradition for young people to buy or to rent a property and to move away from their parents' home immediately after marriage, as most of the urban houses and apartments could not accommodate large families.

RECENT TRENDS

Central Asian societies have undergone substantial changes in all aspects of gender and family life since 1991. However, different republics in the Central Asian region have been moving in different directions. International comparison might give some clues. For example, according to the United Nations Development Program's Gender-related Development Index (2005),[19] industrialized and rapidly growing Kazakhstan was in 61st place, behind Thailand, Venezuela, and Ukraine, but ahead of the Philippines and China. In the meantime, largely agricultural Kyrgyzstan and Uzbekistan were listed in 85th and 86th place, respectively, behind such countries as Iran, Algeria, Vietnam, and Syria but ahead of Indonesia and Nicaragua.[20] Yet, it is very difficult to obtain a grasp of the depth and direction of the changes.

By the early 2000s, the state guarantees of lifelong employment, social and health-care benefits, and pensions, enjoyed by the previous generation, was no more, and young people had to adapt to new realities. As a result, there was a significant drop in the fertility rate.[21] Although between 40 to 60 percent of the population still lives in rural areas, the crisis in traditionally labor-intensive agriculture and the attractions of the urban lifestyle lured increasingly large numbers of people to the major metropolitan centers, which nearly doubled in size between 1991 and 2006. There have emerged huge differences between urban and rural communities, between republics, and between generations. As a result, the Central Asian societies have become fragmented as never before.

The most visible transformation can be observed in the major metropolitan centers and can be compared to the social and sexual revolution in the United States and Europe in the 1950s and 1960s. A flood of advertising began bombarding the young generation, promoting the consumer culture, consumer-driven behavior, and very liberal sexual attitudes. For the first time, colorful and erotic contests like "Miss Kazakhstan" and "Miss Kyrgyzstan" were held and were widely televised throughout the republics. Young contestants began marching on the stage in swimsuits, drawing excitement from the young generation and outrage and condemnations from the most conservatives and religious groups in the society. Yet, young urbanites are less bound in their personal relations and receive much better sex education than their parents. With a contraceptive use rate between 62 and 66 percent, Central Asia is on par with Italy, Mexico, and Portugal, though far behind the United States and the United Kingdom.[22]

The removal of state censorship and state control also led to a flood of movies and various visual materials of dubious qualities. Pornography in various forms became widely available, often without any restrictions or regulations. The Internet has been packed with erotic and suggestive pictures of young half-naked and fully naked local girls. By the 2000s, a sex-service industry had emerged in all Central Asia, although prostitution and brothels have remained illegal across the region. At the same time, alcoholism and drug abuse are on the rise.

The arrival of international corporations and the establishment of homegrown private enterprises have led to the creation of small numbers of highly paid jobs for young men and women. In addition, small groups of highly successful businesspeople and children of the local political elite have (by local standards) an enormous amount of money in their hands. Their high-profile celebrity-like lifestyles and entertainment and spending habits have created a model that many young urban girls and boys would like to follow or at least to copy at any cost. In fact, this has led to the emergence of a small group of the so-called New Generation (so-called New Kazakhs, New Kyrgyz, and so on) who have very liberal attitudes and who spend time in expensive restaurants, casinos, and resorts, spending their parents' or their own money and bathing in scandals and rumors that have filled the Internet and local tabloids. The Central Asian society reacts to such a show of wealth and inequality with special pain because of the nearly century-old egalitarian and prudish traditions ingrained during the Soviet era.

At the same time, the middle class, especially professional women, struggles to maintain decent living standards. Paradoxically, the market pressure has energized many women, as many of their men could not adapt to the transition or were consumed by alcoholism or depression or the stresses of the new ways of life.[23] For instance, in 2003, there were more self-employed women (42 percent) than men (36.8 percent) in Kazakhstan.[24] Many female professionals try to stay close to one another and share similar values and face similar difficulties with the transition. They still remain largely products of the Soviet system: well-educated, accustomed to the opportunities and social guaranties of the Soviet-era welfare system and opposed to both the most conservative premodern traditions of their ancestors and the excesses of the so-called New Generation. They still speak Russian well and manage to master one or two foreign languages. Many of these women have been very active in the NGO sector, but not because of their radical feminist inclinations. The picture is much more complex than that and includes factors such as what Professor Andrea Berg, a scholar on gender issues in Central Asia, has called the "gendered division of political participation," where women dominate the NGO sphere but are significantly underrepresented in formal politics.[25] A significant injection of aid money and international advocacy helped women to assert their place in the nongovernment sector. Though throughout the 1990s they lost their representation in government institutions, they still keep trying to maintain their public space. For example, in 2004, women occupied 10.4, 16, and 16.4 percent of the seats in the national parliaments in Kazakhstan, Turkmenistan, and Uzbekistan, respectively, on par with their representation in

France (13.9) and Greece (14.0) but far ahead of Turkey (4.4), Egypt (4.3), and Japan (9.3).[26]

The weakening of state institutions has been hard for the working class, especially women. Although many privileges and guarantees of women's rights and freedoms are written clearly into the new constitutions and laws, state institutions are increasingly unable to enforce those laws and rules. Thus, working-class women are among first to lose their jobs, to be abused, to be the subject of harassment or unwanted advances, or to face discrimination in pay.[27]

One of the indicators of the weakening role of women in public life can be seen in the labor market, though there are winners and losers. There is a very small group of highly successful business women, like Dariga Nazarbayeva and Roza Rymbayeva, who run very successful businesses and maintain high public profiles. Some women have managed to quickly adapt to the new realities of the market-oriented economy by undergoing training or retraining programs and finding new opportunities in a quickly changing environment. Others struggle to get used to the collapse of the world they lived in, and they flounder because their jobs disappeared and, with them, the old social welfare, health-care, and education systems. Large groups of families plunged to a life below the poverty line, especially women with large families, and so they struggle to survive.

In response to these changes, there have emerged extremely conservative groups, especially in the most remote cities and towns and on the outskirts of major urban centers. These groups strongly advocate a return to the traditional way of life, including strict and very conservative interpretations of Islamic traditions, polygamy, and seclusion of women. This has created a deep divide and mistrust between conservative and liberal groups in society. A large chunk of the rural population perceives the large cities as corrupt bastions of decadent Western culture and Western lifestyles. Many people in rural Central Asia see life in major urban centers as too liberal, too alien, and in conflict with the genuine national cultures. They express disgust at the lifestyles of the New Generation, and they try to isolate their children from the negative elements of the West and urban culture. In this environment, women are often required to return to traditional roles—to get into early and forced marriages, to stay at home, to be obedient wives, and to behave and dress strictly according to conservative rules.[28] By and large, in these areas, the male-dominated culture, with its traditionalist roles, values, and behavior patterns, is returning. This culture yet again reinforces the concept of women as housewives, with a limited role in public life, and the absolute domination of family values.

NOTES

1. *Poems of the Divan of Hafiz,* trans. Gertrude Bell (London: William Heinemass, 1897), p. 94.

2. Frederick Burnaby, *A Ride to Khiva. Travels and Adventures in Central Asia* (1876; reprint, Oxford and New York: Oxford University Press, 2002) , p. 178.

3. Alev Lytle Croutier, *Harem: The World behind the Veil* (New York: Abbeville Press, 1989), p. 13.

4. Burnaby, *A Ride to Khiva,* pp. 357–358.

5. Many travelers left notes about these customs. See Burnaby, *A Ride to Khiva,* pp. 179–180.

6. For some recent writings about position of women in Islamic society, see Archna Chaturvedi, ed., *Encyclopedia of Muslim Women,* vols. 1 and 2 (New Delhi: Commonwealth, 2003).

7. For a concise biography of Kurmanjan-Datkha, see Rafis Abazov, *Historical Dictionary of Kyrgyzstan* (Lanham, MD, and Oxford: Scarecrow Press, 2004), p. 169.

8. This tradition also exists in some areas of Kazakhstan, Karakalpakistan, and Turkmenistan. See Saul Abramzon, *Kirgizy i ikh etnogeneticheskie i istoriko-kulturnie sviazi* [The Kyrgyz and their ethnic and genetic and historical-cultural relations] (Frunze: Kyrgyzstan, 1999), p. 245.

9. For the Soviet interpretation of the changes, see Aminova, R. Kh., *The October Revolution and Women's Liberation in Uzbekistan,* trans. by B.M. Meerovich (Moscow: Nauka Pub. House, Central Dept. of Oriental Literature, 1977), pp. 4–34.

10. For comprehensive overview of the legal changes, see Ibid., pp. 36–60.

11. Comprehensive research on this campaign can be found in Douglas Northrop, *Veiled Empire: Gender and Power in Stalinist Central Asia* (Ithaca: Cornell University Press, 2003).

12. The phrase was first coined by Gregory Massel. See Gregory Massel. *The Surrogate Proletariat: Moslem Women and Revolutionary Strategies in Soviet Central Asia, 1919–1929* (Princeton: Princeton University Press, 1974).

13. United Nations Development Program (UNDP), *Human Development Report 2005: International Cooperation at a Crossroad* (New York: United Nations Development Program, 2005), pp. 316–318.

14. For example, in the national parliament of Uzbekistan, in 1985, 183 out of 510 parliament members were women, or about 36 percent of the total. The figures are taken from Asian Development Bank, *Women in the Republic of Uzbekistan,* (Manila: Asian Development Bank, Programs Dept. East and Office of Environment and Social Development, 2001), p. 13.

15. For example, in Kazakhstan, the figure was 21.4 in the 1970s; it rose to 24.6 in 1989. For comparison, it was 28.4 in 1991 in the United Kingdom and 28.7 in 1995 in the United States. See United Nations, *World Marriage Patterns* (New York: United Nations, 2001), http://www.un.org/esa/population/publications/worldmarriage/worldmarriagepatterns2000.pdf [accessed on July 18, 2006].

16. *The Economist Pocket World in Figures* (London: The Economist, 2002), p. 82.

17. Ibid., pp. 84–85.

18. *Narodnoie Khoziaistvo SSSR v 1989* [National economy of the USSR in 1989] (Moscow: FiS, 1990), p. 189.

19. UNDP's Gender-related Development Index includes such indicators as women's life expectancy at birth, the literacy rate, the proportion of female students at the primary-, secondary-, and tertiary-level schools, and estimated earned income.

20. UNDP, *Human Development Report 2005: International Cooperation at a Crossroad*, pp. 299–301.

21. For example, it fell from 6.83 in 1970–1975 to 3.81 in 2000–2005 in Tajikistan and from 3.5 in 1970–1975 to 1.95 in 2000–2005 in Kazakhstan. For comparison, during the same period of time, the fertility rate fell from 6.6 in 1970–1975 to 4.27 in 2000–2005 in Pakistan, while in the United States it remained roughly unchanged at 2.02 in 1970–1975 and 2.04 in 2000–2005. United Nations, *World Population Prospectus,* 2004 revision, http://esa.un.org/unpp/ [accessed on July 10, 2006).

22. UNDP, *Human Development Report 2005: International Cooperation at a Crossroad,* pp. 236–238.

23. In fact, the economists Kathryn Anderson and Richard Pomfret claim that "on the whole women have fared no worse, probably better, than men" and that this trend is confirmed in the "Asian and Islamic setting of the Kyrgyz Republic": Kathryn Anderson and Richard Pomfret, *Consequences of Creating a Market Economy. Evidence from Household Survey in Central Asia* (Cheltenham, UK, and Northampton, MA: Edward Elgar, 2003), p. 128.

24. UNDP, *Gender Equality and the Status of Women in Kazakhstan* (Almaty: United Nations Development Program, 2005), p. 7.

25. Andrea Berg, "The Worlds Apart: The Lack of Integration between Women's Informal Networks and Non-governmental Organizations in Uzbekistan," in *Post-Soviet Women Encountering Transition: Nations Building, Economic Survival and Civic Activism,* ed. Kathleen Kuehnast and Carol Nechemias (Baltimore and London: The Johns Hopkins University Press, 2004), pp. 11, 195–214.

26. UNDP, *Human Development Report 2005: International Cooperation at a Crossroad,* pp. 303–305.

27. According to the statistical data on Kyrgyzstan, women receive almost 40 percent less pay than men for comparable work. Quoted in *Zhenshchiny Kyrgyzstana v perekhodnoi ekonomike. Monitoring* [Women of Kyrgyzstan in the transitional economy. Monitoring] (Bishkek, 2003), p. 27.

28. For example, according to the statistical data, 50.9 percent of violence against women in Kyrgyzstan was in the form of forced marriages. *Zhenshchiny Kyrgyzstana v perekhodnoi ekonomike,* p. 107. According to the UNDP report, the Kazakhstan legislature even lacks a definition of "sexual harassment." UNDP,. *Gender Equality and the Status of Women in Kazakhstan,* p. 47.

9

Festivals, Fun, and Leisure

> In the Orient there is no life without *chaikhana* [teahouse].
> —Popular Central Asian song

Central Asians take fun and leisure very seriously. Even if there is an economic or political crisis in the country or in the region, or an important business deal in the works, people still go on vacation, to the beaches of the Ysyk Kol Lake or somewhere else. In summer 2006, President Kurbanbek Bakiyev of Kyrgyzstan was even forced to bar government officials from taking vacations during holiday season because the government offices were so deserted that the whole government stopped functioning.[1] People love celebrating holidays and organize nearly every family, community, and national event on a grand level.[2] This has been especially true since 1991, as people and their governments use every opportunity to revive old traditions, customs, and festivals that highlight national pride and historical roots. The national governments' efforts have been largely directed to the deconstruction of the Soviet legacy in building Soviet ways of life.[3] The governments have also attempted to build entertainment industries around the "genuine" national cultures and customs.[4] As in many other areas, the Soviet authorities tried to establish a Soviet way of organizing and managing events and everyday life by introducing new, ideologically charged Soviet symbols, but they failed to develop the entertainment, tourism, and recreational sectors of the economy.

In the postindependence era, Central Asian holidays and leisure activities emerged as a complex mixture of Islamic traditions, national festivals, and modern, often state-sponsored secular events. The national traditions,

Young people in national costumes lining up for a parade. Courtesy of the author, 2006.

public festivals, and holidays are different from country to country, though there are many similarities across the region. Several factors determine how the Central Asians celebrate these events. The most important factor is whether one lives in the country or in the city. Rural populations are more devoted to the celebration of agriculturally linked Islamic and traditional local festivals. City dwellers often celebrate both Islamic and secular festivals, and they maintain lifestyles quite similar to those of people in urban Russia, Turkey, or western China. Because the city dwellers earn much higher incomes, they adhere to modern values and have much greater access to modern means of communication, such as television, radio, and the Internet.

Another factor is what generation a person belongs to. There are many norms and expectations that regulate and prescribe certain behavior according to the age and gender of a person. Central Asians usually tend to follow those norms. Thus, younger people often feel more comfortable with the cosmopolitan and dynamic international mass culture. Meanwhile, it is widely expected that mature people will act according to their age and so they are more devoted to national traditions and social duties, especially family responsibilities; a 50-year old man is expected to attend a concert of national instruments but definitely not a rock festival.

The third factor that determines lifestyle is social status. Many social groups use festivals and leisure activities to come together and strengthen personal, business, communal, and even tribal relations. As the maintenance of social status is an important part of the everyday life, many people feel obliged to reaffirm their place by participating in the activities of certain social circles and by showing generosity, hospitality, and prosperity through the sponsorship of large family and community events.

Central Asians highly value their close-knit communities and the sense of belonging that they provide. Therefore, they tend to celebrate many festivals and holidays with their extended families and neighbors. They are ready to undertake long travel several times a year or even come from overseas, and by doing so they demonstrate a level of devotion like that associated with the American celebration of Thanksgiving. It is customary on the day of a festival for many people go out in their best national costumes or wear at least one element of their national dress, even if they wear formal Western dress or business suits most of the time. Western visitors would be surprised to see all kinds of performances on the streets of both small and big cities, from ram

Central Asian horse riders preparing for a parade on the streets of Almaty. Courtesy of the author, 2006.

and rooster fighting to traditional musical virtuoso performances, horse races, and wrestling competitions.

The mix of old traditions and modern Western influences adds a specific flavor to many events. Some leisure activities resemble old religious and national traditions, and so a casual Western visitor might find himself or herself taken back many hundreds of years in time. Other traditions, like sports games, especially soccer, volleyball, and wrestling; attending the theater or cinema; or eating out, might closely remind the visitor of events in New York, Manchester, or Istanbul.

ISLAMIC FESTIVALS

Until the modern era, the Central Asians celebrated all Islamic festivals. During the Soviet era, however, the celebration of those festivals in public was outlawed, and people were allowed to celebrate only in private, within the community or family.[5] In fact, people were encouraged to celebrate secular holidays only. Since 1991, the Islamic holidays have made a strong come-back and have become official public holidays on the national calendar. The Islamic festivals are celebrated according to the lunar calendar that consists of 12 months, each between 29 and 30 days. The lunar year is 10 or 11 days shorter than the Gregorian calendar year used in most Western countries. Therefore, all events and festivals in the lunar calendar move forward 10 or 11 days every year.

Ramadan

Ramadan is the ninth month in the Islamic calendar. During Ramadan, all devoted Muslims are obliged to fast from sunrise to sunset. This fasting is one of the five pillars of Islam, and it is considered to be an important duty for every Muslim.

According to Islamic teachings, it was during Ramadan that Prophet Muhammad began receiving messages from God. Fasting during Ramadan reminds people of the difficulties that poor people suffer, teaches self-discipline, and helps people to cleanse themselves of selfishness and to become closer to the teachings of God. It is expected that all Muslims will refrain from all wrongdoing, harming of others, and fighting during this month. They should also not eat or drink during the daytime. However, Islamic doctrine allows for some exceptions. For example, pregnant or nursing women, travelers, and certain other categories of people are allowed to abstain from fasting during Ramadan. However, they are required to make up the number of missing days later in the year.

In some areas in Central Asia during Ramadan, food stores, restaurants, cafeterias, and *chaikhanas* are closed during the daytime and open only late in the day. However, the rules are not as strict as in other Muslim countries, particularly those in the Middle East. Many shops and food stores remain open, as there are communities of non-Muslims and there are some secular people who do not fast. Still, businesses and public work slow down during this time.

People break their fast after sunset. It is always done in a grand way, as many family members, friends, colleagues, or neighbors come together to share a prayer and then food. Children use this opportunity to visit other houses, and they receive small gifts from adults, usually sweets. Rich or simply successful people are strongly encouraged to invite poor members of the communities to their homes to share food after sunset or to give away the food. All mosques are also obliged to offer food to all visitors without discrimination by race, social status, or ethnic origin; these meals are usually sponsored by local communities.

Uraza Bairam (called *Eid Al-Fitr* in Arabic)

This is one of the biggest holidays in the Islamic calendar. It signifies the end of the fasting month, Ramadan. Muslims also celebrate this event together and use this opportunity to visit one another, as it is strongly encouraged that doors be open to all members of the community and that people visit one another without special invitation. Traditionally, wealthy members of the communities are expected to organize big feasts and invite all their relatives and all neighbors to share in their fortune and success. The celebration usually continues for the whole day, sometimes until midnight.

Kurban Bairam (called *Eid Al-Adha* in Arabic)

People celebrate *Eid Al-Adha* in the twelfth month of the lunar calendar in the *zul-hajj* month, when Muslims commemorate the end of *Hajj*, the pilgrimage to the holy city of Mecca. Like all other Islamic festivals, this holiday moves forward by several days every year.

This event has a deep meaning in Muslim culture, as it is connected to the story from the Quran about Ibrahim's (Abraham's) readiness to sacrifice his son Ismail (Isaac) in the name of God. At the last moment, the angel replaced Ismail with a sacrificial animal. The holiday begins with a prayer at a congregational mosque. Then, devoted Muslims sacrifice a domestic animal (but never poultry); in the case of the Central Asian republics, it is usually a sheep or goat. Two-thirds of the meat should be given to the poor, orphans, or the disabled.

Traditionally, families buy a whole lamb for this festival and organize a big feast for the family and close friends. People are also encouraged to make donations to various charities or to poor members of their communities. In general, this is an opportunity to remember all members of the family, to visit graves of relatives and to give away food to the poor.

NAWRUZ

Nawruz (also *nooruz*) is a traditional spring festival and marks the beginning of the New Year. It has been celebrated by Central Asians since ancient, pre-Islamic times. Some scholars link it to the mythical king Jamshid, and in Iran some people believe that it marks the day when the Qa'im defeated the Antichrist. The religious and philosophical meaning of the festival is long forgotten, and for most Central Asian it is the largest and most inspiring festival of the year, something like carnival for Brazilians. It is also a festival of youth, as many strict rules and norms are relaxed for duration of the holiday. *Nawruz* starts on the first day of spring according to the ancient Iranian solar calendar (by convention usually fixed on March 21 or 22), and people often call it the Spring Festival. *Nawruz* was not celebrated during the Soviet era, but it was reestablished after 1991 as a national holiday of spring in all the Central Asian republics. Although it is formally a one-day event, people celebrate it for two or three days and sometimes for up to seven days.

This is one of the most loved festivals, and people celebrate it in splendid ways. Local communities and local governments set up performances of various music and dance groups in the major public parks or central squares of towns and cities. Merchants set up outdoor food stores and large bazaars, and families visit one another or attend major community events. This is also an opportunity for everyone to watch local artists perform or to take part in such performances on the streets of their cities.

There are several important attributes of *Nawruz*. People believe that a cheerful *Nawruz* sets up a good mood and good luck for the whole year. It is also important to have the house spotlessly clean at least few days before the festival. It is the time of the year to buy new clothes or to sew new dresses; some people spend considerable time and money to get ready.

Swings are installed for young people on the major squares and parks in every city and town. Usually, during these days, young people of the opposite sex can socialize without being accused of breaking any social customs or taboos. Often, young boys invite girls whom they like or to whom they are attracted but to whom they are usually not allowed to talk to swing with them. In the evening, people make small campfires on the streets or outskirts of their villages, and young unmarried males have to show their bravery and cleanse themselves

During *Nawruz* (Festival of Spring) all ethnic groups come together to celebrate. The representatives of the Tatar-Bashkir community in Bishkek display their national food. Courtesy of the author, 2006.

of their past sins by jumping over the fire. Sometimes, very brave unmarried girls also venture to jump over the fire in order to encourage reluctant boys.

One of the important parts of the celebration is visiting parents and relatives and having the holiday meal together. According to ancient Iranian tradition, there should be seven objects and seven-course meals on the table, although nowadays few people know anything about the meaning of the tradition and just ignore it. People also cook special food for the festival. For example, in Kazakhstan families cook the ritual dish called *Nawruz Kozhe,* which, according to ancient tradition, must be prepared from seven ingredients. At present, on the day of *Nawruz,* the streets of all major cities and towns are full of entrepreneurial old ladies who sell their freshly made *kozhe* to everyone.

During recent years, it has become customary in many parts of Kazakhstan, Kyrgyzstan, and Turkmenistan to erect *yurts* (woolen nomadic tents) on the main squares and in the parks. These *yurts* often serve as improvised cafeterias or shops. Ram and rooster fighting and horse-racing contests have also become increasingly important. In addition, some wealthy individuals and local communities sponsor local competitions of wrestlers *(palvans)* in national wrestling *(kuresh)*. Many young people try their luck, since, besides glory and the smile of the ladies, they might win a hefty prize—a sheep, a cow, a bull, or even a horse—or its modern equivalent, a car.

OTHER PUBLIC HOLIDAYS

For many decades, the Communist government used most of the public festivals to organize public displays of support for official policies. Many festivals were organized on a grand scale, with military, sport, and public parades.[6] As was said earlier, the Communist-led government tightly regulated and controlled all public events. It was also forbidden to hold any officially unsanctioned rallies or demonstrations or to display antigovernment signs.

Since independence, people have been free to choose whether they will celebrate secular or religious holidays or both. It is not uncommon to see families that cheerfully celebrate various religious holidays regardless of their religious affiliation—*Nawruz, Eid Al-Fitr,* Christmas, New Year, and other holidays—while other families do not celebrate any at all. The governments of the Central Asian republics have retained some public holidays from the Soviet past, like New Year's Day (on January 1), Victory Day (on May 9), and First School-Bell Day (on September 1). They have also introduced some new ones, such as Independence Day (varies from country to country) and reintroduced some old ones. In addition, there are several informally celebrated days, like Men's Day (February 23, formerly Soviet Army Day) and Women's Day (March 8, formerly International Women's Day). The government of Turkmenistan went further and renamed all months and days of the week and introduced some exotic public holidays, like Flag Day, and holidays marking the birthday of the President of Turkmenistan and day of the election of the first president of Turkmenistan.[7] Local communities also celebrate their own events and festivals.

Independence Day is celebrated in the most splendid way,[8] usually with large parades in the best Soviet tradition and with a lot of public speeches, anniversary concerts, and fireworks. For several days, all major streets in all cities and towns across every republic are decorated with national flags and national symbols.

The most-loved holiday is New Year's Eve. Many people across the region buy and decorate New Year's trees—traditionally fir trees. During the week before the New Year, people take their children to special New Year's concerts, circuses, theater and ballet performances (usually the famous *Nutcracker*), and public, school, and, in a recent trend, privately organized masquerades. At these events, children receive their New Year's presents and goodies. Unlike in many European countries and the Americas, children and parents find their presents under the New Year's tree on January 1, not on Christmas (therefore they are called New Year's presents). On December 31, people make a lot of phone calls, visit friends, and do their final shopping and cooking. In the evening, they are found around their festive dinner tables with close family members, often glued to the television, which broadcasts New Year's shows, concerts, interviews, and direct programming from various cities and towns across the nation. After the clock strikes midnight, many people go into the streets with a bottle of champagne, screaming, "Good-bye to the Old Year" and "Hooray for the New Year." There is a widespread belief among young people that a kiss after the stroke of midnight will keep couples happy together for the year to come.

Many urbanites celebrate with great enthusiasm Men's Day (February 23) and Women's Day (March 8). The political context of these events is long forgotten or ignored. People just enjoy these holidays, very much like Americans enjoy Father's and Mother's Days. These are days when children make little presents for their dads and moms. In the workplace, the women usually organize a little festive table on February 23 and give little presents to all the men in their workplace, and, of course, after office hours, to their husbands or loved ones. Meanwhile, on March 8 all men are obliged to behave as gentlemen, to organize a table, and to present a lot of flowers—probably more than during the rest of the year—to their fellow students, coworkers, or colleagues. Sometimes the parties spark little romantic affairs, as the Central Asian workplace environment is not as severely restrictive as that in the United States, although, in a recent trend, "romantic banquets" are banned in some foreign-run companies. On March 8, all men are obliged to be at home with wives, sisters or mothers as early as possible, and often they are required to cook a festive meal.

In recent years, Valentine's Day has gained wide recognition in Central Asia among the young generation. On this day, the young send SMS (Short Message Service) and Internet pictures on cell phones to each other. It is considered really cool among teens to get reservations for their beloved partners in a Western-style adult café or restaurant and to manage to get a margarita (which is not really allowed until the age of 18). Fueled by large marketing and advertising campaigns run by large consumer-goods companies and retail outlets, this holiday has been gaining increasing appeal across generations.

Victory Day is commemorated on May 9 and was established after World War II to honor people who lost their lives in the war against the Nazis. Today this is a day of remembrance not only of those who perished in the what the Soviets called the Great Patriotic War but also of those who died in all other conflicts. This is a day when many Central Asians visit their grandparents and take them to official commemorations, parades, and other public events. In the evenings, they usually organize large dinners at home or at restaurants and invite several generations to come together and pay their respects to the veterans. In recent years, it has become quite common for large corporations and companies to sponsor special events for veterans, such as concerts and receptions.

FAMILY AND COMMUNITY CELEBRATIONS

People in Central Asia usually build their leisure and entertainment activities around family and community *(mahallia)* life. Within the Central Asian republics, one finds a range of local traditions, cultures, climates, available facilities, and living standards, and, therefore, people in different places have different choices and preferences. In general, in rural areas, most of the large and small events are organized around the four seasons of the year, as people celebrate the beginning of spring, the end of harvest, and so on. Meanwhile, in the large urban areas, people enjoy leisure and entertainment similar to those found in most urban areas around the globe, such as popular sports, attending the theater, eating out, and participating in national parades. Yet, both in small villages and in large cities, people go out with their large families, as many celebrations are built around family events.

All Central Asians have a strong sense of family values, and they take advantage of every possibility to meet close and distant relatives and to bring relatives together. There is even an informal rule that all family members should take turns in organizing feasts at their homes during a year, so a large extended family visits each of its members' homes at least once or twice a year. People believe that this way they keep strong links between the family members and cherish each other in times of success and provide all necessary support to each other in times of need.

Tois

Family celebrations—*tois*—are important events in the personal lives of all people of all ages in the region. People usually celebrate all such events, including marriages, the birth of a first child and a first grandchild, boys' circumcisions, and the building of a new home.

The *tois* are usually quite large. It is not uncommon to get 100 or 200 or even 300 or 400 people—if neighbors and friends are counted—for a single event that might last anywhere from just one evening to two or three days. People usually invite all close and distant relatives, neighbors, colleagues, and friends. To Westerners, it might seem quite unusual to invite a stranger or foreigner to a family event, but that is not the case in Central Asia. All people who happen to be in the neighborhood are invited to join. Even former rivals come to the *tois,* as these occasions provide an excellent opportunity for reconciliation.

The celebrations are organized in a grand manner, with music, dance, and plenty of food and drinks. In a recent trend, some wealthy members of communities have begun reviving old pre-Soviet-era traditions of sponsoring national music and songs competitions or local sports events (e.g., wrestling, horse racing). Such events need to be planned well in advance, and many people are involved in the organizational process. It is also expected that the guests contribute to meeting the financial burden imposed by such events by offering small sums of money nicely packed into an envelope or by various other means, including providing furniture, transportation, or food for the event or just by servicing and cleaning during and after the event.

The *tois* are more than simple family celebrations. They are also an opportunity to learn about developments and achievements in the personal lives of friends and colleagues and are excellent networking occasions. These celebrations are also regularly used by young people to meet potential partners and by their parents for matchmaking. For young artists and musicians, the *tois* are excellent places to demonstrate their talents and to gain mass recognition.

Gap

In traditional settled communities, people organize themselves into informal interest groups. These groups are called *gaps* (translated as "talk" or "discussion"). A *gap* (pronounced *giap*) is a group of friends or neighbors who get together for entertainment or to discuss art or political or nonpolitical issues or to provide mutual support through consultancy or other means or just to gossip. Usually, there are two types of *gaps*—those organized according to professional interest (e.g., music, sport, hunting) and those that are community-based (usually people from the same neighborhood, village, or town). The *gap* traditionally consists of people of the same sex: female *gaps* and male *gaps* would never mix. Even an extremely jealous and conservative husband is obliged to allow his wife to attend a *gap*.

The *gaps* resemble social clubs to some degree. For example, women come together in *gaps* to cook and to discuss their life plans, education, and prospective partners and to share their experiences on how to deal with difficult situations. Married women discuss family issues, the upbringing of children, or family budget planning. In the meantime, men come together in kinds of all-boys parties to discuss essential issues related to their neighborhood life, community development, and businesses. Other groups discuss literature, poetry, and politics and seek mutual help from their members in gaining recognition or voicing their own opinions. Like social clubs in Western countries, most of the *gaps* are quite exclusive, and membership is usually for life, unless a member is excluded for misbehavior or other wrongdoing or moves away to other city or country.

Bazaars

Many places in Central Asia are famous for their specialized bazaars. They may be animal bazaars, handicrafts bazaars, carpet bazaars, food bazaars, or consumer-goods bazaars where people can find all kinds of goods in one place, from locally made silk shirts and teapots to imported electronics and toys for children.

People go to bazaars, for example, to buy fresh and dry fruits and meat, exotic spices and herbal teas, mare's fermented milk (*kumys*), camel's fermented milk (*shubat*), and many other things, though these products are also available at convenient shops. The bazaars often offer the freshest products at affordable prices for those who can bargain well. Bargaining is a ritual on its own, as it requires skills, knowledge of market traditions, and also a fine understanding of human psychology. In some occasions, the deals might be done quietly over a cup of green tea. On other occasions, the negotiation might be a temperamental event, with lots of emotion, including dramatic performances and arguments, depending on the size of the deal and the regional background of buyer and seller. Many people love bazaars for these colorful and emotional conversations and bargaining, and they cannot even imagine dealing in different ways. A short story illustrates the point. A local anecdote goes that one day a foreigner came to a local bazaar in a village and wanted to buy a melon. He asked, "How much is it?" An *aksakal* (a community elder) answered, "Five hundred *som* [the local currency]!" The foreigner liked the melon and began counting his money. To his surprise, the *aksakal* said to him, "I am not selling this melon to you! You did not bargain, you did not talk to me, you spoiled my day! Go away!"

For people in Central Asia, the bazaars are more than places to shop. They are places to socialize, meet friends and colleagues, gossip, show off wealth and success, or search for help or partnership in small businesses. Very often, whole families dress up in their best clothes and go to a bazaar in the morning and come back in the evening, combining shopping, socializing, eating out, and business negotiations in one event.

Chaikhana

A *chaikhana* is a traditional teahouse. *Chaikhanas* are very popular in the country and can be found in practically every town and city, though they are

Turkmen women selling carpets in a bazaar in
Ashgabat. Courtesy of the author, 2004.

less common in Kazakhstan and Turkmenistan. In *chaikhanas,* people usually
sit on a special elevated platform or around a low table. The *chaikhanas* nor-
mally serve traditional drinks, like tea, and traditional food, like *pilov, samsa,
manty, mastova, shashlyk* (grilled meat), and *shorpo* (soup). It is not uncommon to see people order vodka, which they sometimes playfully call "white
tea" *(ak chai).*

Again, in Central Asian culture, the *chaikhana* is not only a place to eat
and drink. It is an important institution for social networking and socialization. It is also a kind of a social club where some tables are reserved for those
who come together regularly. Over a cup of tea, people discuss community
needs and development at the local level, as well as their major political,
social, and economic activities. Community leaders, especially in rural areas,
regularly gather in teahouses to learn the opinions of the *aksakals* (respected
elderly members of their communities), to settle minor disputes, or to organize local charity events *(khashar).* The *chaikhana* is a place where local public opinion can be formed or influenced, family and personal reputations
can be established or ruined, and new businesses can be accepted or rejected.

Chaikhana (Central Asian tea-house) offers a great variety of exotic food. Courtesy of the author, 2006.

By and large, this is a central place where many community activities take place.

Meals

People in Central Asia, like people in neighboring South Asia or in the Middle East, love to indulge themselves with great varieties of food. National Central Asian cuisine was enriched by influences from many other regions, especially from the Indian subcontinent, the Middle East, and the Eurasian steppe.[9] Within the region, there are many variations in everyday food and in the food prepared for major feasts, as the cuisine in Kyrgyzstan, for example, is quite different from that in Tajikistan or Turkmenistan. Horse meat is popular in Kazakhstan, Kyrgyzstan, and some parts of Uzbekistan, and lamb and beef, homemade noodles, bread, and baked pies are popular all over the region. The local population does not eat pork, as it is not permitted by Islamic tradition.

Central Asians also have a very strong sense of hospitality. It is traditional to invite a guest or even a stranger who has entered a house to share food with the host family. It is quite normal to spend several hours at a lunch and especially at a dinner, as people can discuss family affairs, current events, or even business deals over the dinner or lunch. Hosts usually offer several courses and in large quantities. They are quite offended if their guests do not eat or eat only a little.

The traditional meal often starts with a cup of green tea or homemade bread called *non (nan)*. This is followed by soup. Usually, it is a thick meat soup with vegetables *(shorpo)* or with homemade noodles *(lagman)*. After the soup, there is the main dish. Very often it is *pilov (polov)*, made of spiced meat, rice, and thinly cut carrots. There are hundreds variations of *pilov*, and some claim that every city and town has at least one variation. People add herbs, apricots, raisins, garlic, nuts, quinces, or many other ingredients to *pilov*, making it really delicious. In many parts of Kazakhstan and Kyrgyzstan, the main dish is *besh-barmak* (translated as "five fingers"); this is freshly cooked lamb (very often a whole lamb, including the lamb-head) with homemade noodles. The most honored guests often get whole lamb-head and are obliged to eat at least one piece out of it—tongue, ear, or eye—depending on the local interpretation of the meaning of these gesture. If you have enough space in your stomach after the main meal—and even if you do not—you are offered *manty* with *shsahlyk*, a variation of nicely grilled kebab. The meal usually ends with fresh fruits—apples, pears, sweet honeydew melons, watermelons, grapes, or fresh or dried apricots. In addition, the guests are always served plenty of tea, especially during the hot times of year. Traditionally, the Central Asians do not drink carbonated drinks or fruit juices, though in recent years the younger generation has increasingly switched to these drinks. The single most important and most popular drink is tea. People often prefer green tea, as they strongly believe that green tea is the best drink to overcome thirst and dehydration. Black, herbal, and fruity teas are also popular in some areas.

Storytelling

Storytelling is one of the important parts of everyday life, especially among the older generation. It takes different forms in the region. At family events, *aksakals*—elderly people—tell stories about their adventures, misadventures, travels, and battles or talk about legendary and imaginary heroes of the past. In an informal and captivating way, they derive moral and personal lessons for their young offspring and pass family traditions on to them.

In *chaikhanas,* storytelling is a part of the entertainment, as there is always a skillful storyteller who remembers hundreds of stories about the life and adventures of one of the favorite comic personalities, Afandi (Hoja Nasreddin), or about local heroes or colorful personalities of the past and present. In Kyrgyzstan, for example, there even exists a special class of storytellers; the best of them become local celebrities and the best of the best are remembered for many generations for their fine jokes, stories, and fables. These people, called *tamasha,* have an endless series of stories covering all parts of human activities and can go nonstop from sunrise to sunset.

Sometimes friends and colleagues come together to listen to and discuss history, literature, and poetry or historical Islamic characters. They can invite local musicians, singers, or poets to present their creative works or to sing about their favorite legends—very much like Meet the Author events in the West, but in a much more informal setting. It is quite common for famous or respected poets or writers to be invited to such parties, where they tell a parable, followed by their poetry or prose story.

SPORTS

Traditionally, sport have always been part of all major celebrations. Local strongmen—*palvans*—showed their strength by wrestling and lifting rocks; local farmers showed their best horses in horse racing; local weapon makers showed the quality of their swords and other weapons and their skills in swordplay. Rich people organized outdoor events, such as hunting for wild animals, or hunting with birds of prey. In fact, the vast steppe and mountains of Central Asia were so well known for hunting with falcons and eagles that for centuries sultans and khans from distant lands invited experienced bird trainers and bought Central Asian hunting birds. In the medieval era, Central Asia was also known as a hunting ground for tigers, deer, gazelles, brown bear, mountain goats *(arkhars),* and mountain sheep (there is a famous Marco Polo sheep, *Ovis Poli*), snow leopards, and other animals, but by the eighteenth and nineteenth centuries, many of those animals had been hunted to extinction.

Rich landlords, local tribal leaders, and local communities regularly sponsored horse racing, wrestling, heavy weightlifting, and other competitions. Most successful sportsmen *(palvans)* were well respected and participated in numerous events, bringing glory to their native cities or towns. Many Western travelers have been fascinated by the exotic and ancient version of polo that has survived in popularity among the Kazakhs, Karakalpacks, and Kyrgyzs. In the Central Asian version of the game—called *ulak* (or *kupkari* among the Uzbek)—players ride on horseback and use the carcass of a goat or a calf instead of a ball and carry this carcass to the special finish line.[10] These traditional sports are still quite popular and can be seen during large celebrations, such as *Nawruz*.

Mass Western-style sports were introduced to Central Asia during the Soviet era through the thousands of sport clubs that were established in every corner of the region, even in the most remote and inaccessible villages. Within a decade, modern sports made strong inroads into the everyday lives of people. For example, by 1927, Kyrgyzstan had already held its first national competitions in modern sports. The Soviet bottom-up approach succeeded in creating a large pool of sportsmen at the school, university, and enterprise levels, because most of sports clubs were free for kids. Many children and teenagers were also involved in various sport competitions at the local level. The best sportsmen, regardless of their social, family, or ethnic background, would get a pass to allow them to compete at the next level, and if they were good enough, they could go all the way to the most prestigious international events. Every champion in a major sport activity was surrounded by a cult-like following. Champions received state grants, travel opportunities, access to the best sport facilities, and opportunities to rub shoulders with the national elite—the most prominent politicians, celebrities, and journalists. In addition, every international trophy and medal was immediately widely publicized in order to boost national pride. For many people, semiprofessional sport was a ticket from dusty village streets to national and international glory and fame. Televised transmissions of the Summer and Winter Olympic games and international competitions in such sports as soccer, ice hockey, gymnastics, and figure skating are still among the most popular television programs in the region.

It became a part of the modern Central Asia national culture to send children of school and university age to different sport clubs. Among the popular types of sport are fencing, wrestling, and archery. In fact, in the past, sportsmen and sportswomen from the region have won Olympic medals in fencing, archery, gymnastics, and other sports.[11]

Soccer became the single most popular sport in the country, especially after the 1970s, when a local team from Uzbekistan—*Pakhtakor*—successfully beat many established Soviet teams and became one of the most powerful teams at the All-Union level. At present, there are thousands of soccer fields in every republic, and there are probably hundreds of registered and unregistered soccer clubs. Men of all ages usually play soccer during weekends on soccer fields in practically every city and town. Teenage boys often play soccer after school on school fields, while adults come together a few times a month to play in intercommunity or intertown formal and informal tournaments, usually at the community soccer fields. Women's soccer, however, is not popular in the country, and there are no professional women soccer teams. Since 1991, soccer teams have regularly played in the Central Asian regional tournaments and participated in several international tournaments within the Commonwealth of Independent States and the Asian Soccer Confederation. To the great dismay of Central Asian women, every fourth year all Central Asian men become unmovable for about two weeks—the time of the World Cup tournament. Large and small crowds of men gather at the home of the friend with the largest television set, drink beer, eat special dried fish, and watch matches with great emotion, very much like British, Spanish, or Mexican fans.

Wrestling, boxing, and the martial arts are probably next in popularity after soccer. Events in these fields regularly attract large crowds and always have steady groups of followers, and several Central Asian sportsmen have achieved a lot in these fields. As in many other countries, pictures of favorite champions hang on the bedroom walls of many teenage boys and girls.

In 1992, at the Barcelona Olympic Games, the Central Asian sportsmen competed as a part of the United Soviet Team for the last time. Since 1992, all Central Asian republics have established their own national Olympic committees and have begun competing independently. Mass sport still helps to create large pools of local talent who are ambitious enough to challenge the major players in international competitions. For example, at the Athens Olympic Games in 2004, Kazakhstan won one gold (in welterweight), four silver, and three bronze medals, while taking 40th place overall. Uzbekistan won five medals, including two gold (both in wrestling), one silver (also in wrestling), and two bronze (both in boxing), taking 34th place overall—ahead of such countries as Argentina, Chile, and Denmark. The Central Asian teams were even more successful at the Asian Games. For example, at the Fourteenth Asian Games in Pusan, South Korea, in 2002, Kazakhstan won 76 medals (including 20 gold), taking overall fourth place behind China, Japan, and South Korea; Uzbekistan won 51 medals (including 15 gold); Kyrgyzstan won 12 medals (including 1 gold); Turkmenistan won 4 (including 1 gold); and Tajikistan won 6 medals.

Basketball, volleyball, and baseball are among the mass sport activities played at nearly every school, and there are numerous school and college competitions at every level. Surprisingly, college sports (or interuniversity sport activities) have very little popularity among the mass public and have never found their way to national television as in the United States. Yet, these competitions attract large groups of spectators, usually young people. However, their organizers have never been able to build national professional leagues.

Since independence, mass sport, like many other state-sponsored activities, has suffered greatly. Fewer financial resources have been available for supporting and promoting sport events and activities, and sport activities have been increasingly commercialized. The number of sports clubs has drastically decreased, especially those in rural areas and small towns, though sport enthusiasts still try to reach the most talented children.

Tennis received a particular boost in the region when it garnered personal attention from two local leaders—Islam Karimov and Nursultan Nazarbayev. Mr. Karimov even established an International Tournament of the President of Uzbekistan with a prize pool of about $500,000. New clubs were established in all major provincial centers, and the younger generation embraced this sport as a status symbol associated with being a successful businessperson. Several players from Central Asia were even briefly ranked among the top 100 tennis players in the World. There have been numerous attempts to introduce American football, baseball, golf, and bowling, though they have not received wide recognition so far.

Only in the early 2000s have private sponsorship and sport entrepreneurship begun to be established in the Central Asian republics; in addition, the national governments have to provide greater support to their national sport teams. At the Athens Olympic Games, in 2004, the national team from Uzbekistan took 34th place overall and the team from Kazakhstan took 40th place overall. In preparation for the Beijing Olympic Games (2008) the governments of Central Asian republics and private sponsors sharply increased financing of their national Olympic teams to increase chances of winning more medals and thus boosting the national pride.

RECENT DEVELOPMENTS

Since independence, there has been a significant change in public attitudes toward the celebration of various festivals and public holidays. State officials do not force people to participate in various public events, nor they oblige the public to show solidarity with government policies (with the exception of Turkmenistan, where it is still compulsory). The rigid control over cultural developments that was typical of the Soviet era has nearly disappeared, although the Soviet legacy can be still seen across the region in various forms. During the first years after independence, the Central Asian governments attempted to continue the Soviet practice of providing state funding for all events, from the local to the national level. Gradually, this idea was abandoned, and at present local communities and governments, private individuals, and sponsors have to provide support on many occasions. The sole exception is Turkmenistan, where the government continues to control all aspects of life and provides funding for all major events.

This development has led to the decentralization of festivals and leisure activities.[12] Local rural communities and governments tend to sponsor indigenous sport events and music and storytelling competitions—events that appeal most to their communities and to ordinary people. In the meantime, in urban centers, festivals are increasingly business- and profit-oriented; they provide opportunities to organize large bazaars, promote trade, and thus increase revenues and strengthen local businesses. For decades, Central Asia was protected from foreign influences and from the powerful forces of mass culture and consumerism by the iron curtain. This helped to preserve many indigenous traditions and ways of life. Many remote areas in the region still remained untouched by modern civilization. However, this has been rapidly changing since the beginning of the twenty-first century. In a new trend, all Central Asian governments are making attempts to increase mass tourism and to attract wealthy foreign tourists. In fact, many events and artistic works around the most popular tourist destinations are increasingly tailored to mass tourists.

At the individual level, people now are free to choose their sports or leisure activities depending on their financial situation, though in many places leisure and sport play an important role in maintaining social status. Thus, midlevel businesspeople have enthusiastically embraced such activities as billiards and bowling, and, to a certain degree, tennis. Most successful businessmen have begun experimenting with golf, though good golf clubs are still rare and expensive. Several local and foreign companies invested in building skiing facilities and lifts in close proximity to Almaty, Bishkek, and Tashkent, but skiing remains a favored sport only for very small groups of urbanites and expatriates.

All social strata enthusiastically embraced Russian (steam) and Finish (dry) saunas. These became especially popular as the Soviet-era shortages disappeared and hundreds of private saunas—small and large—popped up in all major cities across the Central Asian region (with the exception of Turkmenistan). Saunas became a favorite place to meet on weekends, to celebrate business deals, or just to escape when the weather outside was miserable. The popularity of saunas grew hand-in-hand with the popularity of beer, as the dreadful Soviet-era draft beers were replaced by a huge variety of western European, American, Chinese, and Russian beers. The cultural perception of the sauna in the region is very different from its perception in the United Sates. If, for Americans, using a sauna is largely an individual experience for health benefits—to lose weight or to relax after the gym—for Central Asian men it is an extremely important socializing event. Close friends, colleagues, and business associates regularly organize small and large group tours to their favorite saunas to chat, gossip, discuss business deals, and consume gallons of beer or tea. These sauna meetings have become a kind of exclusive social or business club, and "membership" requires recommendations and trust.

Casinos have become the upscale entertainment destination of choice for middle-class and wealthy people. The local regulation of the casino business is quite lax, and numerous casinos have opened in practically all urban centers, thereby creating a small space for the Western experience. On the downside, casinos have been attracting the criminal world, causing numerous personal and family dramas and tragedies, very much as in many Western countries. In spring 2006, the government of Kazakhstan announced that it would establish a Las Vegas of Central Asia on the shore of the Kapchagai Lake, and it requested all casinos in Almaty to move their activities to the new location.[13] The authorities believe that in this way they will be able to better monitor casino activities and to curb the negative effects that the casinos have in large metropolitan centers.

Meanwhile, the younger generation, especially teenagers, has embraced cultural globalization and turned to all kinds of pursuits that are popular among youth on the streets of Los Angeles, London, and Tokyo. Computer games and computer cafés have emerged in every town and city, becoming a magnet for local geeks. Rollerblades and skateboards also are quite popular. In

Mountain resort on the outskirts of Almaty. Courtesy of the author, 2006.

another development, rock discothèques and rock cafés have popped up in all major urban centers, immediately attracting large crowds of fans.

Another new trend is the rise of mass tourism. During the Soviet era, a popular joke explained the difference among American, French, and Russian tourism in the following way: Americans usually travel overseas on airplanes, the French usually use their cars, and the Soviets—they only travel overseas on ... tanks. The bitter truth in this joke is that there were many restrictions that prevented many ordinary people from traveling overseas. With independence, most of the restrictions were lifted, and tourism underwent a remarkable evolution. In the early 1990s, a lot of people began traveling overseas, mainly for shopping tours, as ordinary people tried to get goods that were not available in local shops. In fact, the so-called *chelnoki*—shuttle traders—filled the local retail markets with all kinds of consumer products that were unavailable or were in short supply during the Soviet era. There even emerged a whole class of businesspeople (usually women) who got their first lessons in capitalism and in small business and who supported their families during those difficult years through these activities. They traveled overseas exclusively to buy certain types of consumer goods on a small scale and then sold them at home markets for profit. By the early 2000s, however, the situation had changed somewhat with the emergence of the middle class and a wealthy business class. These people began traveling exclusively for leisure to the most popular tourist destinations. Such countries as Thailand, Turkey, India, Italy, and United Arab Emirates emerged among the favorite places.

By and large, people have been abandoning the Soviet concept of festivals, leisure, and sport for the masses, and they have begun organizing events for themselves according to their individual tastes, social status, and income.

NOTES

1. *Tsentr extremal'noi zhurnalistiki* (The Center for Extreme Journalism), http://www.cjes.ru/lenta/view_news.php?id=687&year=2006&lang=eng.

2. This chapter is largely based on my personal experience and on studies in the Central Asian republics. I learned great deal about current cultural trends thanks to the generous help of friends and colleagues.

3. For scholarly assessment of the Soviet experiment, see Jukka Gronow, *Caviar with Champagne: Common Luxury and the Ideals of the Good Life in Stalin's Russia (Leisure, Consumption and Culture)* (Oxford and New York: Berg, 2004).

4. See, for scholarly discussion of the Soviet symbols and the ideologization of everyday life and holidays, Richard Stites, *Revolutionary Dreams: Utopian Vision and Experimental Life in the Russian Revolution* (New York: Oxford University Press, 1989).

5. Sergei Poliakov, *Everyday Islam: Religion and Tradition in Rural Central Asia* (New York: M. E. Sharpe, 1992).

6. For a general overview of the Soviet society and everyday life, see Michael Rywkin, *Soviet Society Today* (New York: M. E. Sharpe, 1989).

7. See Rafis Abazov, *Historical Dictionary of Turkmenistan* (Lanham, MD, and London: Scarecrow Press, 2005), pp. 113–114.

8. Independence Day is celebrated on different days in different Central Asian republics. In Kazakhstan, for example, it is celebrated on December 16, in Kyrgyzstan on August 31, and in Tajikistan on September 9.

9. For discussion of food traditions, see Glenn Mack, and Asele Surina, *Food Culture in Russia and Central Asia* (Westport, CT: Greenwood Press, 2005).

10. In the early 2000s, the Central Asian republics, along with China, Pakistan, and Turkey, even set up an international federation in this sport. For *Buzkashi* in Afghanistan, see Hafizullah Emadi, *Cultures and Customs of Afghanistan* (Westport, CT: Greenwood Press, 2005), pp. 160–161.

11. For detailed information about participation in the Olympic movement, see national Web sites. For example, the site of the National Olympic Committee of Uzbekistan is http://www.olympic.uz/en/.

12. For various local festivals, see Helene Henderson, ed., *Holidays, Festivals, and Celebrations of the World Dictionary: Detailing Nearly 2,500 Observances from All 50 States and More Than 100 Nations: A Compendious Reference Guide to Popular, Ethnic, Religious, National, and Ancient Holidays* (Detroit: Omnigraphics, 2005).

13. http://news.bbc.co.uk/2/hi/asia-pacific/4869274.stm.

Glossary

Adat. Customary law in traditional Central Asian society, guided by authoritative members of communities. It is based on a tribal code of conduct and on centuries of experience in resolving conflicts among individuals, communities, and tribes.

***Ail* (also *aul*).** Village, rural settlement, especially in the mountains: a kind of tribal and extended family unit, as people who live in *ails* often (but not necessarily) represent members of the same tribal unit or community.

Aitysh. The art of improvised epic, often accompanied by the traditional musical instruments.

***Aksakal* (also *aqsaqal*).** "White bearded" in Turkic. A respected elderly member of a local community or the oldest member of an extended family; head of a craftsman shop or a craftsman order in Central Asia; administrator in a *mahallia* (a local neighborhood community) or in a town or village.

Akyn. A popular bard, who sings and improvises traditional folk songs or epics; this makes him different from the *zhyrshy* (entertainment singer); a respected member of the community to whom people traditionally turn for political advice, foretelling, or entertainment.

Aqsaqal. See *Aksakal.*

***Ashkana* (also *Oshkhona*).** A traditional café, restaurant or teahouse, which serves national dishes such as *pilav* and *besh-barmak*.

Aul. See *Ail.*

Baba. Father, grandfather, or ancestor; polite reference to the respected oldest member of an extended family; saint, or patron, e.g., Zengibaba, saint of cattle; Musababa, saint of sheep.

Bai. Rich person; sometimes used together with a person's name to show respect (i.e., Serik-bai); the term refers to rich and influential political leaders among Central Asians in pre-Soviet society.

Bek (also beg). The title used to refer to the tribal leader in Turkic society; the title used in the medieval era to refer to the tribal and local administration leader in the khan's (king's) service; sometimes used with the name of a male person to highlight his honorary position in society (Kadyr-bek), equivalent to "master" or "sir."

Chaikhana (chai-kha-na). A traditional teahouse in Central Asia.

Dastan. An epic created both in verse and in prose that presents a historic, heroic, or romantic story.

Glasnost. The policy of openness and freedom of speech that was launched by Mikhail Gorbachev, leader of the Soviet Union from 1985 to 1991.

Hajj. The pilgrimage to Mecca, required of all Muslims who are able to go.

Hijab. A headscarf worn by Muslim women; the term also refers to a veil-dressing that covers woman's hair, arms, and feet.

Hoja (also Khoja). A title for people or groups of people who claim descent from Prophet Muhammad through his daughter, Fatima, and her husband, Ali, or from companions of Prophet Muhammad who arrived in Central Asia with the first wave of Arabs in the seventh century A.D.

Hujum. A veil that covered the faces of Muslim women in Central Asia, worn in public until the middle of the 1920s.

Ishan. An esteemed religious person; a Sufi teacher or authority.

Ismailis. An Islamic sect with close links to the Shia teaching of Islam.

Iwan. A vaulted hall or space, walled on three sides, with one end entirely open, usually in arch form.

Jadid. A member of reformist movement in Central Asia in the late nineteenth and early twentieth centuries.

Jigit (also Yigit). A young man, horse rider, or warrior; in present-day Central Asia, the term is often used to refer to a brave and energetic young man.

Kalym. A dowry in a form or money or gifts that is expected to be paid by the family of the bridegroom to the family of bride.

Karavan-sarai. A traditional guesthouse or inn in the cities and towns along major routes and mountains passes.

Khan. The traditional title of a chief of a tribe or a confederation of tribes; the title of a ruler (king) of a state or a principality during the medieval era; sometimes the term is used as an equivalent of "lord" or "your highness," usually after the first name.

Khoja. See *Hoja.*

Kishlak (also *qishloq*). Village, rural settlement, especially in the settled areas, where people form close-knit communities.

Kolkhoz (plural in Russian *kolkhozy*). This stands for the Russian acronym "*kollektivnoie khoziastvo,*" or collective farm.

Koran. See *Quran.*

Kui. A short musical composition traditionally performed on the national instruments, such as the *dombra* or the *kobuz.*

Kumis. See Kymyz.

Kurban Bairam (also called *Eid Al-Adha* in Arabic). The Islamic festival celebrated in remembrance of Ibrahim's near-sacrifice of his son Ismail and God's sparing of Ismail's life in recognition of Ibrahim's faith.

Kymyz (also *kumis*). The national drink among Kazakhs, Karakalpaks, and Kyrgyzs, prepared from mare's fermented milk. Traditionally, the milk is poured into a special leather bag for fermentation and is then stirred with a special wooden stick to turn the milk into *kymyz.*

Madrasa. An Islamic school, which provides postprimary religious education; a theological seminary and law school, which provides Islamic religious education and is usually attached to a mosque: a building where the boarding students of Islamic seminaries stay.

Mahallia (ma-ha-lia). A neighborhood community in Kyrgyzstan, Tajikistan, or Uzbekistan.

Mihrab. An arch-shaped niche in the wall that shows the direction to Kaaba (in Mecca).

Magtab. See *Mekteb.*

Majlis. Council, parliament, or legislative and representative assembly.

Mekteb (also *magtab*). A school in prerevolutionary Central Asia; a term that refers to primary and secondary schools in contemporary Central Asia.

Mualim. A teacher or educator.

Muezzin. A person who calls Muslims for obligatory prayers five times a day.

Mufti.   The highest Islamic legal authority and the official leader of the Muslim communities in the Central Asian republics. A *mufti* overviews the activities of the Islamic clergy in the republic, the work of the mosques, *madrasas,* and Islamic universities. He has the authority to proclaim a *fatwa,* a binding opinion on religious or public issues.

Mullah.   An Islamic scholar or clergyman who leads Muslims in their daily prayers and who oversees the work of mosques and *madrasas.*

Murid.   A student at Islamic school or follower of an individual Islamic teacher.

Namaz.   Prayer.

Nawruz (**nav-ruuz**).   A spring festival in the Central Asian Republics and some countries in the Middle East.

Oblast.   Province; an administrative unit in Kazakhstan or Kyrgyzstan.

Oshkhona. See *Ashkana.*

Qishloq. See; *Kishlak.*

Quran (**also** *Koran*).   The holy book of Islam. Muslims believe that it was revealed by Allah to Prophet Muhammad.

Raion.   District or county; an administrative unit in Kazakhstan or Kyrgyzstan.

Ramadan (**ra-mah-dhan**).   The ninth month in the Islamic calendar, a time of fasting and atonement for sins.

Shariah (**also** *Sharia, Shariat*).   The Islamic law practiced in Muslim societies. It is based on four fundamentals: the Quran, the message revealed by Allah to Prophet Muhammad; the Hadith (Sunna), the recorded story of the life and deeds of Prophet Muhammad; the Ijma, the universal decisions agreed to by Islamic scholars; and the Qiya, or legal precedent. The *Shariah* imposes a strict regulation of public and private aspects of life according to divine revelation.

Shazhere (**also** *Sajare, Shejere*).   A genealogical tree of a family, which every male Central Asian must know by heart.

Sufi (**also known as** *tasawwuf*).   A follower of a mystical movement in Islam, which emphasizes the development of a personal spirituality and an internal comprehension of divinity.

Uraza Bairam (**also called** *Eid Al-Fitr* **in Arabic**).   The Islamic festival celebrated to end the month-long fast of Ramadan.

Ustoz (**also** *ustaz, ustad,* **or** *usta*).   A master, teacher, or highly qualified expert in his field; the head of a craftsman shop or a craftsman order in

Central Asia; a term used in present-day Kyrgyzstan to refer to an expert, lecturer, or head of a working group.

Yigit. See Jigit.

Yurt (also *yurta* or *boz-ui* in **Kyrgyz**). A traditional felt tent in Kyrgyzstan, Kazakhstan, and Mongolia, which is used for dwelling, especially in the summer and during military expeditions.

Welayat. Province; an administrative unit in Tajikistan, Turkmenistan, and Uzbekistan.

Zoroastrians. Followers of an ancient religion, founded by Zoroaster, that originated in Central Asia.

Selected Bibliography

INTERNET SOURCES

Central Asia, news and other information about: http://enews.ferghana.ru/main.php.

Central Asian languages (e.g., texts, dictionaries): http://www.franklang.ru/.

Central Intelligence Agency World Factbook (select countries from the list): http://www.cia.gov/cia/publications/factbook/geos/ti.html.

Columbia University, Central Asia: http://www.columbia.edu/cu/sipa/REGIONAL/ECE/CACR.

Energy Information Administration, country analysis briefs of Eastern Europe and Former Soviet Union: http://www.eia.doe.gov/emeu/cabs/cabsfsu.html.

Eurasia, news: http://www.eurasianet.org/.

Gateway Kyrgyzstan: http://eng.gateway.kg/.

Gateway Uzbekistan: http://www.gateway.uz/.

International Crisis Group: http://www.crisisweb.org/.

Kazakh cinema: http://kino.kz.

Kazakh National News Agency: http://www.khabar.kz/eng/.

Kazakhstan, UN: http://www.un.kz/.

Kyrgyz National News Agency: http://www.kabar.kg.

Kyrgyzstan, Parliament of: http://www.kenesh.gov.kg/.

Kyrgyzstan, UN: http://www.un.org.kg.

Soros Foundation Kyrgyzstan: http://www.soros.kg/.

Soviet and post-Soviet cinema: http://kinoexpert.ru/.

Tajikistan, culture and art: http://www.naison.tj/.

Tajikistan, news: http://tajikistan.tajnet.com/index.cgi.

Tajikistan, news and other information about: http://www.pamirs.org/history.htm.

The Times of Central Asia: http://www.times.kg.

Turkmenistan, news: http://www.turkmenistan.gov.tm/index_eng.html.

UNESCO focus on Central Asia: http://www.unesco.org/webworld/focus_central_asia/.

UNESCO publications on Central Asia: http://www.unesco.org/culture/asia/.

U.S. Department of States International Information Programs: http://usinfo.state.gov/sa/.

U.S. Embassies and Diplomatic Missions: http://usinfo.state.gov/usinfo/US_Embassies.html.

Uzbek cinema: http://kino.uz.

Uzbek National News Agency: http://www.uza.uz/.

World News Connection (formerly FBIS): http://wnc.fedworld.gov/.

ANNUAL REPORTS AND YEARBOOKS

"*Kazakhstan.*" "*Kyrgyzstan.*" "*Tajikistan.*" "*Turkmenistan.*" "*Uzbekistan.*" *Human Development Report.* United Nations Development Program (UNDP) (annually from 1995).

"*Kazakhstan.*" "*Kyrgyzstan.*" "*Tajikistan.*" "*Turkmenistan.*" "*Uzbekistan.*": *Recent Economic Development.* Washington, DC: International Monetary Fund, 1995, 1996, 1997, 1998.

"*Kazakhstan.*" "*Kyrgyzstan.*" "*Tajikistan.*" "*Turkmenistan.*" "*Uzbekistan.*" In *Nations in Transit.* Washington, DC: Freedom House (annually).

"*Kazakhstan.*" "*Kyrgyzstan.*" "*Tajikistan.*" "*Turkmenistan.*" "*Uzbekistan.*" *Freedom in the World: The Annual Survey of Political Rights and Civil Liberties.* Piscataway, NJ: Transaction (annually from 1992).

"*Kazakhstan.*" "*Kyrgyzstan.*" "*Tajikistan.*" "*Turkmenistan.*" "*Uzbekistan.*" London: Economist Intelligence Unit (quarterly, from 1992).

"*Kazakhstan.*" "*Kyrgyzstan.*" "*Tajikistan.*" "*Turkmenistan.*" "*Uzbekistan.*" In *Europa World Yearbook.* London: Europa Publications (annually).

United Nations Development Program, *Human Development under Transition: Europe and CIS.* United Nations Development Program (1998).

BIBLIOGRAPHIES

Encyclopedias and Reference Books

Akiner, Shirin. *Islamic People of the Soviet Union.* London: Kegan Paul International, 1983.

Azim, Nanji. *The Muslim Almanac: A Reference Work on the History, Faith, Culture, and Peoples of Islam.* Detroit: Gale Research, 1996.

Curtis, Glen, ed. *Kazakhstan, Kyrgyzstan, Tajikistan, Turkmenistan, and Uzbekistan: Country Studies* (Area Handbook Series). Washington, DC: Federal Research Division, Library of Congress, 1997.

Gocgun, Onder, ed. *Turk Dunyasi Edebiyat Tarihi* [The history of the literature of the Turkic world]. 6 Vols. Maltepe, Ankara: Ataturk Kultur Merkezi Baskanlıgi, 2001–2004.

Kadyrov, Shokhrat. *Rossiisko-Turkmenskii istoricheskii slovar'* [Russian-Turkmen historical dictionary]. 2 vols. Bergen, Norway: Bodoni Hus, 2001.

Katz, Zev, ed. *Handbook of Major Soviet Nationalities.* New York: Free Press, 1975.

Kazakhskaia Sovetskaia Sotsialisticheskaia Respublika. Entsiklopedia [Kazakh Soviet Socialist Republic. Encyclopedia]. Almaty: Glavnaia Redaktsia Kazakhskoi Sovetskoi Entsiklopedii, 1982.

Kirgizskaia Sovetskaia Sotsialisticheskaia Respublika. Entsiklopedia [Kyrgyz Soviet Socialist Republic. Encyclopedia]. Frunze: Glavnaia Redaktsia Kirgizskoi Sovetskoi Entsiklopedii, 1984.

Levinson, David, and Karen Christensen, eds. *Encyclopedia of Modern Asia.* 6 vols. New York: Charles Scribner's Sons, 2002.

Motyl, Alexander J., ed. *Encyclopedia of Nationalism: Leaders, Movements and Concepts.* Vol. 2. San Francisco: Academic Press, 2001.

Olson, James S., et al. "Turkmen." *An Ethnohistorical Dictionary of the Russian and Soviet Empires.* Westport, CT: Greenwood Press, 1994: 646–657.

Pope, Arthur Upham, and Phyllis Ackerman, eds. *A Survey of Persian Art from Pre-Historic Times to the Present.* 16 vols. London and New York: Oxford University Press, 1938– .

Reuel, Hanks. *Central Asia: A Global Studies Handbook.* Santa Barbara, CA: ABC-CLIO, 2005.

Rhyne, George N., ed. *The Supplement to the Modern Encyclopedia of Russian, Soviet, and Eurasian History.* Gulf Breeze, FL: Academic International Press, 1995–2003.

Rubin, Don, et al. *World Encyclopedia of Contemporary Theatre: Asia/Pacific.* Routledge, 2001.

Tural, Sadik. Türk Dünyasi Edebiyatçilari Ansiklopedisi [The Encyclopedia of Turkic World Literature]. 5 Vols. Ankara: Atatürk Kültür Merkezi Başkanligi Yayinlari, 2002-2004.

Turkmen Sovet Entsyklopediasy [Turkmen Soviet encyclopedia]. Ashgabat: Glavnaia Redaktsia Turkmenskoi Sovetskoi Entsiklopedii, 1974–1989.

Turkmenskaia Sovetskaia Sotsialisticheskaia Respublika. Entsiklopedia [Turkmen Soviet Socialist Republic. Encyclopedia]. Ashgabat: Glavnaia Redaktsia Turkmenskoi Sovetskoi Entsiklopedii, 1984.

Readers and Collections of Documents

Brzezinski, Zbignev, and Paige Sullivan, eds. *Russia and the Commonwealth of Independent States: Documents, Data and Analysis.* New York: M. E. Sharpe, 1997.

Clarke, Kenneth, and Mary Clarke, eds. *A Folklore Reader.* New York: A. S. Barnes, 1965.

Elcin, Sukru, et al., eds. *Turk Dunyasi Edebiyat Metinleri Antolojisi* [The anthology of the literature of the Turkic world]. 5 Vols. Maltepe, Ankara: Ataturk Kultur Merkezi Baskanliggi, 2001–2004.

Foreign Policy of Neutral Turkmenistan: Speeches, Statements and Interviews by President of Turkmenistan Saparmurat Turkmenbashy. Ashgabat: Ministry of Foreign Affairs of Turkmenistan, 1997.

Gettleman, Marvin E., and Stuart Schaar, eds. *The Middle East and Islamic World Reader.* New York: Grove Press, 2003.

Hebert, Raymond J., and Nicholas Poppe. *Kirghiz Manual.* Bloomington: Indiana University, 1963.

Hu, Chen-hua, and Guy Imart. *A Kirghiz Reader.* Bloomington: Indiana University, Research Institute for Inner Asian Studies, 1989.

Lewis, Bernard. *Music of a Distant Drum: Classical Arabic, Persian, Turkish, and Hebrew Poems.* Princeton: Princeton University Press, 2001.

Olcott, Martha B., ed. *The Soviet Multinational State: Readings and Documents.* Armonk, NY: M. E. Sharpe, 1990.

Paksoy, H. B., ed. *Central Asia Reader: The Rediscovery of History.* Armonk, NY: M. E. Sharpe, 1994.

The Permanent Neutrality of Turkmenistan: Collection of Political and Legal Documents. Ashgabat: Ministry of Foreign Affairs of Turkmenistan, 1998.

Revolutsionnoe dvizhenie v Turkmenistane v 1905–1917 gg. Sbornik arkhivnykh doku-mentov [The revolutionary movement in Turkmenistan in 1905–1917. Collection of archival documents]. Ashgabat: [s.n.], 1970.

Russia and Eurasia Documents Annual (Formerly *USSR Documents Annual*). Vol. 2. *Central Eurasian States.* Gulf Breeze, FL: Academic International Press. Semi-annual publication, from 1992.

Sahni, Kalpana. *Crucifying the Orient: The Colonization of the Caucasus and Central Asia.* Oslo, Norway: Institute for Comparative Research in Human Culture, 1997.

Travel and Descriptions

Bailey, F. M. *Mission to Tashkent.* London: Folio Society, 1999. First published in 1946 by Jonathan Cape.

Baker, Valentine. *Clouds in the East: Travels and Adventures on the Perso-Turkoman Frontier.* London, Chatto and Windus, 1870.

Burnaby, Frederick. *A Ride to Khiva. Travels and Adventures in Central Asia.* 1876. Reprint, Oxford: Oxford University Press, 2002.

Clarke, Maj. F.C.H. *Statistics and Geography of Russian Turkestan.* London: [s.n.], 1879.

Conolly, A. *Journey to North of India, Overland from England, through Russia, Persia and Afghanistan.* 2 vols. London, R. Bentley, 1834. Reprint, New Delhi: Asian Educational Services, 2001.

Curtis, William Eleroy. *Turkestan: The Heart of Asia.* New York: Hodder and Stoughton, George H. Doran company, [1911].

Curzon, George. *Russia in Central Asia in 1889 and the Anglo-Russian Question.* London: Longmans, 1889.

Danmore, Earl. *The Pamirs. Being a Narrative of a Year's Expedition on Horseback and on Foot through Kashmir, Western Tibet, Chinese Tartary, and Russian Central Asia.* 2 vols. London: John Murray, 1893.

Eichwald, E. *Reise auf dem Caspischen Meere und in den Caucasus unternommen in den Jahren 1825–1826.* Stuttgart: [s.n.] 1834–1838.

Fleming, Peter. *Travels in Tartary: One's Company and News from Tartary*. London: Jonathan Cape, 1948.

Fraser, J. B. *Narrative of a Journey into Khorasān, in theYears 1821 and 1822*. London: Longman, Hurst, Rees, Orme, Brown, and Green, 1825.

Huntington, E. *The Pulse of Central Asia: A Journey in Central Asia Illustrating the Geographic Basis of History*. Boston: Houghton-Miffin, 1907.

Ibn Batuta. *The Travels of Ibn Baṭṭūta, A.D. 1325-1354*. Translated by H.A.R. Gibb. Millwood, NY: Kraus Reprint, 1986.

Komroff, Manuel. *Contemporaries of Marco Polo*. New York: Boni & Liveright, 1928.

Meakin, Annette. *In Russian Turkistan*. London: George Allen, 1903.

Murav'ev, N. N. *Puteshestvie v Turkmeniiu i Khivu v 1819–1820 godakh, gvardeiskogo general' nogo shtaba kapitana Nikolaia Murav'eva, posslannogo v sii strany dlia peregovorov* [Travel to Turkmenistan and Khiva in 1819–1820 of Guards' General Staff Captain Nikolai Murav'ev, who was sent to these countries for negotiations]. Moscow: [s.n.], 1822.

Pahlen, Count Konstantin. *Mission to Turkestan*. Reprint, London: Oxford University Press, 1964.

Parks, George B., ed. *The Book of Ser Marco Polo, the Venetian*. New York: Macmillan, 1927.

Polo, Marco. *The Travels of Marco Polo*. Translated by Ronald Latham. New York: Abaris Books, 1982.

Rockhill, W. *The Journey of William Rubruck*. London: [s.n.], 1900.

Vamberi, A. *Ocherki o Srednei Azii* [Essays on Central Asia]. Moscow: [s.n.], 1868.

———. *Sketches of Central Asia: Additional Chapters on My Travels, Adventures, and on the Ethnology of Central Asia*. London: W. A. Allen, 1868.

———. *Travels to Central Asia; Being the Account of a Journey from Teheran across the Turkoman Desert on the Eastern Shore of the Caspian to Khiva, Bokhara, and Samarkand, Performed in the Year 1863*. 1864. Reprint, Lahore: Vanguard Books, 1996.

Whitfield, Susan. *Life along the Silk Road*. Berkeley: University of California Press, 1999.

Introduction

Abazov, Rafis. *Historical Dictionary of Kyrgyzstan*. Lanham, MD, and Oxford: Scarecrow Press, 2004.

Adshead, Samuel. *Central Asia in World History*. London: Macmillan, 1993.

Allen, Terry. *Timurid Herat*. Weisbaden, Germany: Reichert, 1983.

Allworth, Edward, ed. *Central Asia: 130 Years of Russian Dominance. A Historical Overview*. 3rd ed. Durham and London: Duke University Press, 1994.

Bacon, Elizabeth. *Central Asians under Russian Rule: A Study in Culture Change*. Ithaca: Cornell University Press, 1966.

Christian, David. *A History of Russia, Central Asia and Mongolia*. Vol. 1. *Inner Eurasia from Prehistory to the Mongol Empire*. Oxford and Malden, MA: Blackwell, 1998.

Gafurov, Bobozhan. *Central Asia: Pre-Historic to Modern Time.* Introduction by Devendra Kaushik. Delhi, India: Shirpa Publications, 2005.

Grant, Bruce. *In the Soviet House of Culture: A Century of Perestroikas.* Princeton: Princeton University Press, 1995.

Gryaznov, Mikhail. *The Ancient Civilization of South Siberia.* London: Barrie and Rockliff, 1969.

Khalid, Adeeb. *The Politics of Muslim Cultural Reform: Jadidism in Central Asia.* Comparative Studies on Muslim Societies No. 27. Berkeley: University of California Press, 1998.

Lattimore, Owen. *Pivot of Asia: Sinkiang and the Inner Asian Frontiers of China and Russia.* Boston: Little, Brown, 1950.

Lazzerini, Edward, and Daniel Brower, eds. *Russia's Orient: Imperial Borderlands and People, 1700–1917.* Bloomington: Indiana University Press, 1997.

Newby, L. J. *The Empire and the Khanate. A Political History of Qing Relations with Khoqand c. 1760–1860.* Leiden and Boston: Brill, 2005.

Olcott, Martha. *The Kazakhs.* 2nd ed. Stanford: Hoover Institution Press, 1995.

Park, Alexander. *Bolshevism in Turkestan, 1917–1927.* New York: Columbia University Press, 1957.

Poliakov, Sergei. *Everyday Islam: Religion and Tradition in Rural Central Asia.* Armonk, NY: M. E. Sharpe, 1992.

Roy, Olivier. *The New Central Asia: Creation of Nations.* New York: New York University Press, 2000.

Ro'I, Yaacov, ed. *Muslim Eurasia: Conflicting Legacies.* London: Frank Cass, 1995.

Rakhman, A. *India's Interaction with China, Central and West Asia.* Project of History of Indian Science, Philosophy, and Culture, vol. 3, part 2. New York and Oxford: Oxford University Press, 2002.

Sadyqov, T. S., et al. eds., *Cultural Legacy of Kazakhstan: Discoveries, Problems, Prospects.* Materials of International Science Conference, October 19, 2005. Almaty: KazNPU, 2005.

Saray, Mehmet. *The Russian, British, Chinese and Ottoman Rivalry in Turkestan.* Ankara: Turk Tarikh Kurumu, 2003.

Shnirelman, Victor. *Who Gets the Past? Competition for Ancestors among Non-Russian Intellectuals in Russia.* Washington, DC: Woodrow Wilson Center Press, 1996.

Suny, Ronald Grigor. *The Revenge of the Past: Nationalism, Revolution, and the Collapse of the Soviet Union.* Stanford: Stanford University Press, 1993.

Thought and Religion

Akbarzadeh, Shahram. *Uzbekistan and the United States: Authoritarianism, Islamism and Washington's New Security Agenda.* New York: Zed Books, 2005.

———. "Political Islam in Kyrgyzstan and Turkmenistan." *Central Asian Survey* 20, no. 4 (2001).

Akiner, Shirin. "Islam, the State and Ethnicity in Central Asia in Historical Perspective." *Religion, State and Society* 24, no. 2/3 (1996).

Arberry, Arthur John. *Sufism, an Account of the Mystics of Islam.* London: Allen and Unwin, 1963.

Ayatollah Jafar Sobhani and Reza Shah Kazemi. *Doctrines of Shi'i Islam: A Compendium of Imami Beliefs and Practices.* New York: I. B. Tauris, 2001.

Baldick, Julian. *Animal and Shaman: Ancient Religions of Central Asia.* New York: New York University Press, 2000.

Balzer, Marjorie Mandelstam, ed. *Shamanism: Soviet Studies on Traditional Religion in Siberia and Central Asia.* New York and London: M. E. Sharpe, 1990.

Bennigsen, Alexandre, and S. Enders Wimbush. *Mystics and Commissars: Sufism in the Soviet Union.* Berkeley: University of California Press, 1985.

Bennigsen, Alexandre, et al. *Soviet Strategy and Islam.* New York: St. Martin's Press, 1989.

Boyce, Mary. *Textual Sources for the Study of Zoroastrianism.* Chicago: University of Chicago Press, 1984.

Daftary, Farhad. *The Isma'ilis: Their History and Doctrines.* Cambridge, UK: Cambridge University Press, 1990.

DeWeese, Devin. *Islamization and Native Religion in the Golden Horde: Baba Tükles and Conversion to Islam in Historical and Epic Tradition.* University Park, PA: Pennsylvania State University Press, 1994.

Foltz, Richard. *Religions of the Silk Road: Overland Trade and Cultural Exchange from Antiquity to the Fifteenth Century.* New York and London: Palgrave Macmillan, 2000.

Gross, Jo-Ann, ed. *Muslims in Central Asia: Expressions of Identity and Change.* Durham, NC: Duke University Press, 1992.

Hall, Manly. *Twelve World Teachers: A Summary of Their Lives and Teachings.* Los Angeles: Philosophical Research Society, 1996.

Heissig, Walther. *The Religions in Mongolia.* Translated by Geoffrey Samuel. Berkley and Los Angeles: California University Press, 1980.

Keller, Shoshana. *To Moscow, Not Mecca: The Soviet Campaign against Islam in Central Asia, 1917–1941.* Westport, CT: Praeger, 2001.

Khalid, Adeeb. *The Politics of Muslim Cultural Reform: Jadidism in Central Asia.* Berkeley: University of California Press, 1998.

Kondybai, Serikbol. *Kazakhskaia mifologia. Kratkii slovar'* [Kazakh mythology. A concise dictionary]. Almaty: Nurly Alem, 2005.

Lewis, David C. *After Atheism: Religion and Ethnicity in Russia and Central Asia.* New York: Palgrave Macmillan, 2000.

Myer, Will. *Islam and Colonialism: Western Perspectives on Soviet Asia.* London: RoutledgeCurzon, 2002.

Naumkin, Vitaly, *Radical Islam in Central Asia: Between Pen and Rifle.* Lanham, MD: Rowman and Littlefield, 2004.

Orynbekov, M. S. *Genezis religioznosti v Kazakhstane* [Genesis of religiosity in Kazakhstan]. Almaty: Daik-Press, 2005.

Poliakov, Sergei. *Everyday Islam: Religion and Tradition in Rural Central Asia.* Armonk, NY: M. E. Sharpe, 1992.

The Meaning of the Holy Qur'an. Translation and commentary by Abdullah Yusuf Ali. 7th ed. Beltsville, MD: Amana Publications, 1995

Thomas, Nicolas, and Caroline Humphrey, eds. *Shamanism, History, and the State.* Ann Arbor: University of Michigan Press, 1996.

Folklore and Literature

Akiner, Shirin. *Cultural Change and Continuity in Central Asia.* Monographs from the African Studies Centre, Leiden. London: Kegan Paul, 1991.

Chadwick, Nora, and Victor Zhimunsky. *Oral Epics of Central Asia.* London: Cambridge University Press, 1969.

Clayton, Sally Pomme, and Sophie Herxheimer. *Tales Told in Tents: Stories from Central Asia.* London: Frances Lincoln, 2005.

Dankoff, Robert [with James Kelly]. *Mahmud al-Kashgari, Compendium of the Turkic Dialects (Diwan Lugat at-Turk).* Edited and translated with Introduction and Indices. 3 parts. Cambridge, MA: [s.n.], 1982, 1984, 1985.

Davidson, Olga. *Poet and Hero in the Persian Book of Kings.* Ithaca: Cornell University Press, 1994.

Durdyeva, A. *"Gorogly" eposynda fantastika. Fantastika v epose "Ger-ogly"* [Fantasy in the epos "Ger-oglu"]. Ashgabat: Ylym, 1981.

Ferdowsi, Abu Al-Qasim. *The Tragedy of Sohrab and Roustam: From the Persian National Epic, the Shahname of Abul-Qasem Ferdowsi.* Translated by Jerome W. Clinton. Seattle: University of Washington Press, 1987.

———. *The Epic of the Kings: Shahnama, the National Epic of Persia by Ferdowsi.* Translated by Reuben Levy, revised by Amin Banani. London: Routledge and Kegan Paul, 1967.

Garryev, Seiit. *Turkmen eposy, dessanlary ve Gundogar khalklarynyng epiki doredijiligi* [Turkmen epos, *dastans,* and epic works of the people of the Orient]. Ashgabat: Ylym, 1982.

Kalafat, Yaşar. *Türk Dünyası Karşılaştırmalı Türkmen Halk İnançları: Afganistan, Ozbekistan, Türkmenistan, Nahcıvan-Azerbaycan, Kafkasya, Iran, Irak, Anadolu, Makedonya.* Çankaya, Ankara: Avrasya Stratejik Araştırmalar Merkezi Yayınları, 2000.

Kedrina. Z., and S. Kasymov. *Istoria uzbekskoi sovetskoi literatury* [The history of Uzbek Soviet literature]. Moscow: Nauka, 1967.

Khayyam, Omar. *A New Version Based upon Recent Discoveries.* Edited by Arthur J. Arberry. New Haven, CT: Yale University Press, 1952.

Lewis, Geoffrey. *The Book of Dede Korkut.* Reprint, New York: Penguin Classics, 1974.

Makhtumkuli. *Izbrannoie, perevod s turkmenskogo* [Selected works translated from Turkmen]. Ashgabat, [s.n.], 1960.

Mamazhonov S. *Urta osië va qozoghiston khalqlari adabiëtidagi roman zhanrini tipologik urganish* [Study on typology of novel genres in the literature of Central Asian and Kazakhstan people]. Toshkent: Uzbekiston SSR "Fan" nashriëti, 1991.

Manas. Vols. 1 and 2. Moscow and Bishkek: Door, 1995.

Reichl, Karl. *Singing the Past: Turkic and Medieval Heroic Poetry (Myth and Poetics).* Ithaca and London: Cornell University Press, 2000.

————. *Turkic Epic Poetry: Traditions, Forms, Poetic Structure*. New York and London: Garland, 1992.

Shoolbraid, G.M.H. *The Oral Epic of Siberia and Central Asia (Uralic and Altaic Studies)*. London: Curzon Press, 1997.

Smirnova, N. S. *Istoria kazakhskoi literatury* [The history of Kazakh literature]. 3 vols. Alma-Ata: Nauka, 1968–1970.

Zhirmunskii, V. *Tiurkskii geroicheskii epos* [Turkic heroic epic]. Leningrad: Nauka, 1974.

————, and Kh. Zaripov. *Uzbekskii narodnyi geroicheskii epos* [Uzbek people heroic epic]. Moscow: OGIZ, 1947.

Media and Cinema

Androunas, Elena. *Soviet Media in Transition: Structural and Economic Alternatives*. Westport, CT: Praeger, 1993.

Beumers, Birgit. *Pop Culture Russia!: Media, Arts, and Lifestyle*. Santa Barbara, CA: ABC-CLIO, 2005.

Eaton, Katherine Bliss. *Daily Life in the Soviet Union*. Westport, CT: Greenwood Press, 2004.

Faraday, George. *Revolt of Filmmakers. The Struggle for Artistic Autonomy and the Fall of the Soviet Film Industry.* Philadelphia: University of Pennsylvania Press, 2000.

Freedom House. *Freedom of the Press: A Global Survey of Media Independence*. New York: Freedom House, 2005.

Gillespie, David. *Russian Cinema*. Harlow, NY: Longman, 2002.

Hachten, William, and James F. Scotton. *The World News Prism: Global Media in an Era of Terrorism*. 6th ed. Ames: Iowa State Press, 2002.

Hopkins, Mark. *Mass Media in the Soviet Union*. New York: Pegasus, 1970.

Karatnycky, Adrian, Alexander Motyl, and Amanda Schnetzer. *Nations in Transit 2002*. New York: Freedom House, 2002.

Kenez, Peter. *Cinema and Soviet Society: From the Revolution to the Death of Stalin (KINO—The Russian Cinema)*. New York: I. B. Tauris, 2001.

Leyda, Jey. *Kino: A History of the Russian and Soviet Film*. Princeton: Princeton University Press, 1983.

Nowell-Smith, Geoffrey, ed. *The Oxford History of World Cinema*. Oxford and New York: Oxford University Press, 1996.

Parkinson, David. *The History of Film. (World of Art Series)*. New York: Thames and Hudson, 1996.

Price, Monroe, ed. *Media Reform: Democratizing the Media, Democratizing the State*. Routledge Research in Cultural and Media Studies. London: Routledge, 2001.

Radvanyi, Jean, and Jean-Loup Passek, eds. *Le cinéma d'Asie Centrale sovietique*. Paris: Centre Georges Pompidou, 1991.

Ruffin, Holt, and Daniel Waugh, eds. *Civil Society in Central Asia*. Seattle and London: University of Washington Press, 1999.

Sabahi, Farian, and Daniel Warner, eds. *The OSCE and the Multiple Challenges of Transition: The Caucasus and Central Asia.* London: Ashgate, 2004.

Sosnovskaia, A. G., et al. *Khudozhniki teatra i kino* [Theater and cinema artists]. In Russian and English. Tashkent: Izd. Gafura Guliama, 1982.

Wilson, Andrew, ed. *Virtual Politics: Faking Democracy in the Post-Soviet World.* New Haven: Yale University Press, 2005.

Woll, Josephine. *Real Images: Soviet Cinemas and the Thaw (KINO—The Russian Cinema).* London and New York: I. B.Tauris, 2000.

Performing Arts

Akhmedova, Margarita Enverovna. *Turkmenskaia fortepiannaia muzyka* [Turkmen piano music]. Ashgabat: Ylym, 1991.

Blackwell, Carole. *Tradition and Society in Turkmenistan: Gender, Oral Culture and Song.* London: Taylor and Francis, 2001.

Dadasheva, Olga Islamovna. *Kamerno-instrumental'naia muzyka kompozitorov Turkmenistana* [Chamber-instrumental music of Turkmenistan composers]. Ashgabat: Ylym, 1993.

Eastep, Wayne. *The Soul of Kazakhstan.* Photographs by Wayne Eastep, text by Alma Kunanbay, edited by Gareth L. Steen. New York: Eastern Press, 2001.

Ekmekcioglu, Ismail, et al. *Turk Halk Oyunlari.* Istanbul: Esin Yayinevi, 2001.

Elemanova, S. A. *Kazakhskaia muzykal'naia literatura* [Kazakh music literature]. Alma-Ata: Ener, 1993.

Kaufmann, Walter. *Musical Notations of the Orient: Notational Systems of Continental East, South and Central Asia.* Bloomington: Indiana University Press, 1988.

Khalid, Adeeb. *The Politics of Muslim Cultural Reform: Jadidism in Central Asia.* Comparative Studies on Muslim Societies No. 27. Berkeley: University of California Press, 1999.

Larionov, V., and Allaiar Churiev. *Khazirki zaman turkmen kompozitorlary: medeniet universitetlerine komek* [Modern Turkmen composers]. Ashgabat: Turkmenistan, 1990.

Levin, Theodore. *The Hundred Thousand Fools of God. Musical Travel in Central Asia.* Bloomington: Indiana University Press, 1996.

Mamiliyev, A. *Melodies of the Turkmen Land.* Translated by O. M. Merebov. Ashgabat: Turkmenistan Pub. House, 1970.

"The Middle East." In Danielson, V., ed. *Garland Encyclopedia of World Music,* vol. 6. London and New York: Garland, 2001.

Music of Central Asia, Uzbekistan. Music CD. Tokyo: Seven Seas, 1991.

Musiques du Kirghizstan [Music of Kyrgyzstan]. Sound recording. Paris: Distribution Adès, 1995.

Rough Guide to Music of Central Asia. Audio CD. Rough Guides World Music CDs, 2005.

Saifiddinov, Sh., et al. *Kompozitory Tadzhikistana: spravochnik* [The composers of Tajikistan: a guide]. Dushanbe: Adib, 1987.

Sipos, János. *Kazakh Folksongs: From the Two Ends of the Steppe.* Contributions by Dávid Somfai Kara and Éva Csáki. Translated by Judit Pokaly. Budapest: Akadémiai Kiadó, 2001. (With CD-ROM).

Slobin, Mark. *Music of Central Asia and of the Volga-Ural Peoples.* Teaching Aids for the Study of Inner Asia. Bloomington: Indiana University, Asian Studies Research Institute, 1977.

———. *Kirgiz Instrumental Music.* New York: Society for Asian Music, 1969.

Solomonova, T. E., ed. *Uzbek muzikasi tarikhi* [The history of Uzbek music]. Tashkent: "Uqituvchi", 1981.

Spector, Johanna. "Musical Traditions and Innovations." In *Central Asia: 130 years of Russian Dominance, A Historical Overview,* edited by Edward Allworth. Durham and London: Duke University Press, 1994.

Songs from the Steppes of Central Asia: The Collected Poems of Makhtumkuli: 18th-Century Poet-hero of Turkmenistan [set in verse by Brian Aldiss from translations by Youssef Azemoun]. Caversham, Reading, UK: Society of Friends of *Makhtumkuli,* 1995.

Visual Arts

Atil, Esin. *Ceramics from the World of Islam.* Washington, DC: Smithsonian Institution, 1973.

Azarpay, Guitty, et al. *Sogdian Painting: The Pictorial Epic in Oriental Art.* Berkeley: University of California Press, 1981.

Bahari, Ebadollah. *Bihzad, Master of Persian Painting.* Foreword by Annemarie Schimmel. London and New York: I. B. Tauris, 1996.

Bland, David. A *History of Book Illustration: The Illuminated Manuscript and the Printed Book.* 2nd ed. Berkeley: University of California Press, 1969.

Bloom, Jonathan. *Paper before Print: The History and Impact of Paper in the Islamic World.* New Haven, CT: Yale University Press, 2001.

Bogolyubov, A. A. *Carpets of Central Asia.* Basingstoke, UK: Crosby Press, 1973.

Canfield, Robert L., ed. *Turko-Persia in Historical Perspective.* Cambridge and New York: Cambridge University Press, 1991.

Chuvin, Pierre, Gilles Béguin, et al. *Les arts de l'Asie Centrale.* Paris: Citadelles and Mazenod, 1999.

Dalton, O. M. *Treasure of the Oxus, with Other Examples of Early Oriental Metalwork.* London: Trustees of the British Museum, 1964.

Dekorativnoe iskusstvo Kazakhstana 20 stoletia [Decorative arts of Kazakhstan: 20th century]. In English and Russian. Astana-Almaty: [s.l.], 2002.

Elitvinskii, B. A. and T. I. Zeimal. *Adzhina-Tepa. Arkhitektura. Zhivopis'. Skul'ptura.* [Ajinatepa. Architecture. Painting. Sculpture]. Moscow: Iskusstvo, 1971.

Ferrier, R. W., ed. *The Arts of Persia.* New Haven, CT: Yale University Press, 1989.

Golombek, Lisa, and Maria Subtelny, eds. *Timurid Art and Culture: Iran and Central Asia in the 15th Century.* Muqarnas Supplement. Leiden and New York: Brill Academic Publications, 1992.

Gray, Basil, et al. *The Arts of the Book in Central Asia, 14th–16th Centuries.* London: Serindia Publications; Paris: UNESCO, 1979.

Grube, Ernst J. *The Classic Style in Islamic Painting: The Early School of Herat and Its Impact on Islamic Painting of the Later Fifteenth, Sixteenth, and Seventeenth Centuries; Some Examples in American Collection.* Venice, Italy: Edizioni Oriens, 1968.

————, et al. *Architecture of the Islamic World: Its History and Social Meaning, with a Complete Survey of Key Monuments.* London: Thames and Hudson, 1995.

Harvey, Janet. *Traditional Textiles of Central Asia.* London: Thames and Hudson, 1997.

Hillenbrand, Robert. *Islamic Art and Architecture.* London: Thames and Hudson, 1999.

Kalter, Johannes, and Margareta Pavaloi. *Uzbekistan: Heirs to the Silk Road.* London: Thames and Hudson, 2003.

Kate, FitzGibbon, and Andrew Hale. *Ikat: Splendid Silks of Central Asia.* London: Laurence King, in association with Alan Marcuson, 1999.

Khakimov, D. A. *Atlas of Central Asian Artistic Crafts and Trades.* Vol. 1. *Uzbekistan.* Tashkent: Sharq, 1999.

Lentz, Thomas W., and Glenn D. Lowry. *Timur and the Princely Vision: Persian Art and Culture in the Fifteenth Century.* Los Angeles: Los Angeles County Museum of Art, 1989.

Lobacheva, N. P., and M. V. Sazanova. *Traditsionnaia odezhda narodov Srednei Azii i Kazakhstana* [The traditional dress of the people of Central Asia and Kazakhstan]. Moscow: Nauka, 1989.

Mackie, Louise, and Jon Thomson, eds. *Turkmen Tribal Carpets.* Seattle: University of Washington Press, 1980.

Martin, F. R. *The Miniature Painting and Painters of Persia, India and Turkey, from the 8th to the 18th Century.* 1912. Reprint, South Asia Books, 1993.

Pugachenkova, G. A., and L. I. Rempel. *Ocherki iskusstva Srednei Azii* [Essays on the art of Central Asia]. Moscow: Nauka, 1982.

Rice, Tamara. *Ancient Arts of Central Asia.* London: Thames and Hudson, 1965.

Rozwakowski, Andrzej. *Symbols through Time: Interpreting the Rock Art of Central Asia.* Oxford, UK: David Brown Book Company, 2004.

Rowland, Benjamin. *The Art of Central Asia (Art of the World).* New York: Crown, 1974.

Schletzer, Dieter, and Reinhold Schletzer. *Old Silver Jewelry of the Turkoman: An Essay on Symbols in the Culture of Inner Asian Nomads.* Translated by Paul Knight. Berlin: D. Reimer, 1983.

Summer, Christina, and Guy Petherbridge. *Bright Flowers: Textiles and Ceramics of Central Asia.* Lund Humphries, 2004.

Summer, Christina, et al. *Beyond the Silk Road: Arts of Central Asia.* Sydney, Australia: Museum of Applied Arts and Sciences, 2000.

Tapper, Richard, and K. McLachlan. *Technology, Tradition and Survival: Aspects of Material Culture in the Middle East and Central Asia.* London and Portland, OR: Frank Cass, 2003.

Titenev, Vecheslav. *Anthology of the Art of Kazakhstan: Painting.* Almaty: Zolotaia kniga, 2004.

Tsareva, Elena. *Rugs and Carpets from Central Asia: The Russian Collections.* Harmondsworth, Middlesex, England, and New York: A. Lane/Penguin; Leningrad: Aurora Art, 1984.

Watt, James C. Y., et al. *When Silk Was Gold: Central Asian and Chinese Textiles.* New York: Metropolitan Museum of Art, 1997.

Architecture

Abuseitova, Meruert, ed. *Urban and Nomadic Societies in Central Asia: History and Challenges.* Proceeding of International Conference. Almaty: Daik-Press, 2004.

Baimagambetov, Sultan. *Arkhitektura i stroitel'stvo Kazakhstana* [Architecture and construction in Kazakhstan]. Almaty: Zolotaia kniga, 2004.

Blair, Sheila, and Jonathan Bloom. *The Art and Architecture of Islam, 1250–1800.* New Haven, CT: Yale University Press, 1994.

Chuvin, Pierre and Gerard Degeorge. *Samarkand, Bukhara, Khiva.* Paris: Flammarion, 2003.

Esenov, Annageldy. *Istoria architektury Turkmenistana* [The history of the architecture of Turkmenistan]. Ashgabat: Rukh, 2001.

Golombek, Lisa, et al. *The Timurid Architecture of Iran and Turan.* Princeton: Princeton University Press, 1988.

Grube, Ernst J., et al. *Architecture of the Islamic World: Its History and Social Meaning, with a Complete Survey of Key Monuments.* Edited by George Michael. New York, NY: Thames and Hudson, 1984. First published in London in 1978.

Hallet, Stanley Ira, and Rafi Samizay. *Traditional Architecture of Afghanistan.* New York: Garland, 1980.

Hattstein, Markus, and Peter Delius, eds. *Islam: Art and Architecture.* New York: Konemann, 2001.

Hillenbrand, Robert. *Islamic Art and Architecture.* World of Art Series. London: Thames and Hudson, 1999.

Knobloch, Edgar. *Monuments of Central Asia: A Guide to the Archaeology, Art and Architecture of Turkestan.* London, New York: I. B.Tauris, 2001.

———. *Beyond the Oxus: Archaeology, Art and Architecture of Central Asia.* London and Totowa, NJ: Rowman and Littlefield, 1972.

Gender, Courtship, and Marriage

Acar, Feride, and Ayse Gunez-Ayata, eds. *Gender and Identity Construction: Women of Central Asia, the Caucasus and Turkey.* Leiden and Boston: Brill, 1999.

Anderson, Kathryn, and Richard Pomfret. *Consequences of Creating a Market Economy. Evidence from Household Survey in Central Asia.* Cheltenham, UK, and Northampton, MA: Edward Elgar, 2003.

Asian Development Bank. *Women in the Republic of Uzbekistan.* Manila: Asian Development Bank, 2001.

Barker, Adele Marie, ed. *Consuming Russia: Popular Culture, Sex, and Society since Gorbachev.* Durham, NC: Duke University Press, 1999.

Bauer, Armin, et al. *A Generation at Risk: Children in the Central Asian Republics of Kazakhstan and Kyrgyzstan.* Foreword by S. Nishimoto. Manila: Asian Development Bank, 1998.

Bauer, Armin, David Green, and Nina Boschmann. *Women and Gender Relations in Kazakhstan: The Social Cost.* Manila: Asian Development Bank, 1998.

Bauer, Armin, David Green, and Kathleen Kuehnast. *Women and Gender Relations: The Kyrgyz Republic in Transition.* Manila: Asian Development Bank, 1998.

Buckley, Mary, ed. *Post-Soviet Women: From the Baltic to Central Asia.* Cambridge and New York: Cambridge University Press, 1997.

Caner, Ergun Mehmet. *Voices behind the Veil: The World of Islam through the Eyes of Women.* Grand Rapids, MI: Kregel Publications, 2004.

———. *Unveiling Islam: An Insider's Look at Muslim Life and Beliefs.* Grand Rapids, MI: Kregel Publications, 2002.

Croutier, Alev Lytle. *Harem: The World behind the Veil.* Reprint, New York: Abbeville Press, 1989.

Doi, Mary Masayo. *Gesture, Gender, Nation: Dance and Social Change in Uzbekistan.* Westport, CT: Bergin and Garvey, 2001.

Einhorn, Barbara. *Cinderella Goes to Market: Citizenship, Gender, and Women's Movements in East Central Europe.* London: Verso, 1993.

Goody, Jack. *The Oriental, the Ancient, and the Primitive: Systems of Marriage and the Family in the Pre-Industrial Societies of Eurasia.* Cambridge and New York: Cambridge University Press, 1990.

Falkingham, Jane. *Women and Gender Relations in Tajikistan.* Manila: Asian Development Bank, 2000.

Harris, Colette. *Muslim Youth: Tensions and Transitions in Tajikistan.* Westview Case Studies in Anthropology. Boulder, CO: Westview Press, 2006.

———. *Control and Subversion: Gender Relations in Tajikistan.* Anthropology Culture and Society Series. Sterling, VA: Pluto Press, 2004.

Hambly, Gavin. *Women in the Medieval Islamic World: Power, Patronage, and Piety.* New York: St. Martin's Press, 1998.

Kuehnast, Kathleen R., and Carol Nechemias, eds. *Post-Soviet Women Encountering Transition: Nation Building, Economic Survival, and Civic Activism.* Washington, DC: Woodrow Wilson Center Press, 2004.

Kisliakov, Nikolai. *Ocherki po istorii sem'i i braka u narodov Srednei Azii i Kazakhstana* [Essays on the history of family and marriage in Central Asia and Kazakhstan]. Leningrad: Nauka, 1969.

Massel, Gregory. *The Surrogate Proletariat: Moslem Women and Revolutionary Strategies in Soviet Central Asia, 1919–1929.* Princeton: Princeton University Press, 1974.

Northrop, Douglas. *Veiled Empire: Gender and Power in Stalinist Central Asia.* Ithaca: Cornell University Press, 2003.

Svanberg, Ingvar, ed. *Contemporary Kazaks: Cultural and Social Perspectives.* New York: St. Martin's Press, 1999.

Zhenshchiny Kyrgyzstana v perekhodnoi ekonomike. Monitoring [Women of Kyrgyzstan in the transitional economy. Monitoring]. Bishkek: [s.n.], 2003

Festivals and Fun

Babu, Suresh, and Alisher Tashmatov, eds. *Food Policy in Central Asia: Setting the Research Priorities.* Washington, DC: International Food Policy Research Organization, 2000.

Batmnglij, Najmieh. *Silk Road Cooking. A Vegetarian Journey.* Washington, DC: Mage, 2002.

Buell, Paul, Eugene Anderson, and Charles Perry. *A Soup for the Qan: Chinese Dietary Medicine of the Mongol Era as Seen in Hu Szu-Hui's Yin-shan cheng-yao: Introduction, Translation, Commentary and Chinese text.* London: Kegan Paul, 2000.

Dabars, Zita, and Lilia Vokhmina. *The Russian Way: Aspects of Behavior, Attitudes, and Customs of the Russians.* Chicago: McGraw-Hill, 2002.

Foster, Dean. *The Global Etiquette Guide to Asia.* New York and Toronto: Wiley, 2000.

Glants, Musya, and Joyce Stetson Toomre, eds. *Food in Russian History and Culture.* Indiana-Michigan Series in Russian and East European Studies. Bloomington: Indiana University Press, 1997.

Gronow, Jukka. *Caviar with Champagne: Common Luxury and the Ideals of the Good Life in Stalin's Russia (Leisure, Consumption and Culture).* Oxford and New York: Berg, 2004.

Henderson, Helene, ed. *Holidays, Festivals, and Celebrations of the World Dictionary: Detailing nearly 2,500 Observances from All 50 States and More Than 100 Nations: A Compendious Reference Guide to Popular, Ethnic, Religious, National, and Ancient Holidays.* 3rd ed. Detroit: Omnigraphics, 2005.

Mack, Glenn. "Central Asia." In *Encyclopedia of Food and Culture,* ed. Solomon H. Katz. New York: Charles Scribner's Sons, 2002.

Mack, Glenn, and Asele Surina. *Food Culture in Russia and Central Asia.* Westport, CT, and London: Greenwood Press, 2005.

Macleod, Calum, and Bradley Mayhew. *Uzbekistan: The Golden Road to Samarkand.* New York and Leicester, UK: Odyssey, 2004.

Malleson, George Bruce. *Herat. The Granary and Garden of Central Asia.* London, W.H. Allen, 1880. Reprint. New York: Elibron Classics, 2005.

Pandya-Lorch, R., and M. Rosengrant. "Prospects for Global Food Security: A Central Asian Context." *Food Policy* 25, no. 6 (2000): 637–646.

Poliakov, Sergei. *Everyday Islam: Religion and Tradition in Rural Central Asia.* New York: M. E. Sharpe, 1992.

Stites, Richard. *Revolutionary Dreams: Utopian Vision and Experimental Life in the Russian Revolution.* New York: Oxford University Press, 1989.

Svanberg, Ingvar, ed. *Contemporary Kazakhs: Cultural and Social Perspectives.* New York: St. Martin's Press, 1999.

Türk Dünyasında Nevruz Dördüncü Uluslararası Bilgi Şöleni: 21–23 Mart 2001, Sivas/hazırlayan, Şebnem Ercebeci. [Nawruz in the Turkic World. Fourth Information/Knowledge Festival, March 21–23, 2001], Ankara: Atatürk Kültür Merkezi, 2001.

Yasa, Azize Aktas. Türk Kültüründe Nevruz Uluslararası Bilgi Şöleni (Sempozyumu) bildirileri: *15–16 Mart 2002* [Communiqué of the International Information Festival of the Nawruz in Turkic World, March 15–16, 2002]. Ankara: Atatürk Kültür, 2002.

Index

About the Author

RAFIS ABAZOV is Adjunct Assistant Professor, School of International and Public Affairs/Harriman Institute, Columbia University. He has written four books, including the *Historical Dictionary of Kyrgyzstan* and *Historical Dictionary of Turkmenistan.*

Recent Titles in
Culture and Customs of Asia